THE
PRICE
OF
FORTUNE

THE
PRICE
OF
FORTUNE

The
untold story
of being
James Packer

A BIOGRAPHY

DAMON
KITNEY

HarperCollinsPublishers

HarperCollins_Publishers_

First published in Australia in 2018
by HarperCollins_Publishers_ Australia Pty Limited
ABN 36 009 913 517
harpercollins.com.au

HarperCollins_Publishers_
Level 13, 201 Elizabeth Street, Sydney NSW 2000, Australia
Unit D1, 63 Apollo Drive, Rosedale, Auckland 0632, New Zealand
A 53, Sector 57, Noida, UP, India
1 London Bridge Street, London, SE1 9GF, United Kingdom
Bay Adelaide Centre, East Tower, 22 Adelaide Street West, 41st floor, Toronto,
  Ontario M5H 4E3, Canada
195 Broadway, New York NY 10007, USA

National Library of Australia Cataloguing-in-Publication data:

978 1 4607 5669 0 (hardback)
978 1 4607 1055 5 (ebook)

Jacket design by Darren Holt, HarperCollins Design Studio
Front cover image: Steve Christo–Corbis/Getty Images
Back cover image: Peter Morris/Fairfax Syndication
Author photo: _The Australian_
Picture section design by HarperCollins Design Studio
Typeset in Bembo Std by Kirby Jones
Printed and bound in Australia by McPherson's Printing Group
The papers used by HarperCollins in the manufacture of this book are a natural,
recyclable product made from wood grown in sustainable plantation forests.
The fibre source and manufacturing processes meet recognised international
environmental standards, and carry certification.

For my beautiful family,
near, far and above

CONTENTS

PROLOGUE   1

INTRODUCTION *I am Icarus*   5

ONE *In the Name of the Father*   26

TWO *The One.Tel Curse*   44

THREE *The Pen is Mightier than the Sword*   64

FOUR *Changing Channels*   87

FIVE *Wheel of Fortune*   107

SIX *The Gambler*   123

SEVEN *No Sacred Cows*   139

EIGHT *Crowning Glory*   158

NINE *The Brotherhood*   178

TEN *Dancing with the Stars*   197

ELEVEN *The Israeli Affair*   218

TWELVE *Blood Battle*   238

THIRTEEN *Rocked to the Core*   259

FOURTEEN *A Hero No More*   280

FIFTEEN *Crown of Thorns*   306

SIXTEEN *Above and Beyond*   326

SEVENTEEN *Everglow*   341

EIGHTEEN *The Corridors of Power*   361

CONCLUSION *The Pursuit of Happiness*   377

ACKNOWLEDGMENTS   395

PROLOGUE

I FIRST MET JAMES Packer in the second half of 2002, more than a year after the collapse of One.Tel. Then Publishing and Broadcasting (PBL) chief executive Peter Yates introduced us over lunch in Kerry Packer's famed fifth-floor dining room at the company's Park Street offices.

I remember James being extremely courteous and respectful, although you always sensed a short fuse lurking beneath. When you struck a match — for instance, by raising the subject of my employer at the time, Fairfax — he was not short of a vocal opinion or an expletive.

Back then I was the companies editor and media writer at *The Australian Financial Review*. Over the coming years, we lunched — just the two of us and always totally off the record — a few times a year in the PBL dining room. I would meet James outside his third-floor office and we would take the lift to the fifth. On one occasion when his father was in the building, James turned to me as we got in the lift and whispered, 'If Dad gets in the lift, you are not a fucking journalist, okay?!'

That never happened. It is one of the regrets of my life that Kerry Packer passed away before I had the chance to meet him. Meeting James's father – one of the nation's most colourful, combative, controversial and larger-than-life figures – would have helped me better understand his son.

As the years went by, James and I would occasionally catch up over coffee in the chairman's office deep in the bowels of Melbourne's Crown Casino complex. He kindly sent my wife and me flowers on the birth of our two daughters, in 2004 and 2006.

But during the Global Financial Crisis (GFC) in 2009, I – like many – became persona non grata in his world when I wrote several articles in *The Australian Financial Review* that he didn't appreciate. I received several angry emails. When I reached out to catch up on one occasion, he snarled back: 'Why would I bother?'

The turning point came in September 2010 when I travelled to Macau for the premiere of Franco Dragone's water-based stage production, *The House of Dancing Water*, at the City of Dreams casino. When we bumped into each other at the gala reception for the event, there was only small talk, but it broke the ice. By then I was working for *The Australian* newspaper and had seemingly earned myself a chance at redemption.

We have maintained a cordial, professional relationship since, even during his bid to win approval for Crown Sydney, when his campaign was unashamedly conducted through the pages of *The Australian Financial Review* and *The Daily Telegraph*, at the expense of *The Australian*.

During 2016, as his life went off the rails, I regularly proposed to him on email that we catch up. I did the same in 2017. His replies were always courteous, but we never did.

Then in September 2017, by chance, my patience was rewarded. I was in the back of an Uber on the way to San

Francisco airport when an email from James lobbed into my inbox. He wanted to meet for an on-the-record interview, to tell his story – good and bad – of the past two years.

A few weeks later I travelled to his Ellerstina polo ranch outside Buenos Aires in Argentina, where we did the interview that later appeared in *The Weekend Australian Magazine*. He was nervous and it was hard work. But it proved to be cathartic – with every word I could see the load lifting from his shoulders, even if it was only temporarily.

On the morning I left Ellerstina, I asked him if he would ever cooperate in sharing his extraordinary personal story for a book. He politely declined the offer, but left me with one glimmer of hope in his final sentence to me as I left: 'If I ever do a book, Damon, I give you my word it will be with you,' he said.

After the magazine article appeared I was approached by a publisher to write James's biography. They asked if he would assist. I told them his response in Argentina, but they urged me to try again. When I did, to my surprise and gratitude, he agreed.

James never wanted this book to happen. But once he had resolved in his mind that he was assisting with it, he threw himself into the project. We did countless hours of face-to-face interviews on three continents and even at sea – our final meeting was on his new superyacht in France. We exchanged hundreds of emails and texts, and spoke on the phone.

James told me on several occasions how much the project was taking out of him, physically and emotionally. The manifestation of that became shockingly apparent and publicly revealed on 20 March 2018 when he resigned from the Crown board, citing mental health reasons.

For two and a half weeks he didn't reply to any of my messages as he was treated at the Pavilion clinic in Boston.

When he finally responded on 9 April at 10.20pm Melbourne time, he was back at peaceful Ellerstina, and he honourably recommitted to the project, vowing to continue to be as transparent and honest with me as possible.

At the outset James said he did not want to read the manuscript, nor know the title of this book. He kept his word right throughout the production process.

What I have tried to do is tell the human story of being James Packer: the son of one of the toughest and most famous fathers of them all, the brother of Gretel, the lover of celebrities, the husband of Jodhi and Erica, and the father of Indigo, Jackson and Emmanuelle. And the businessman who almost lost it all yet managed to survive – but at a cost, reflected in his addictions, broken marriages, lost friendships and his eventual admission that, despite his vast wealth and fortune, he needed help.

Some describe the Packer family as the closest thing to royalty in Australia. As the most powerful and public heir to the family fortune, James Packer has worn his title with honour. But it has also been a heavy burden to carry.

The Price of Fortune is my attempt to shed some light on how James Packer has borne the gifts of his privilege and the weight of his responsibilities, and to unravel what makes him tick. Ultimately, I hope this book will show more of the complex private man behind the public persona.

———

'Uneasy lies the head that wears a crown.'
– William Shakespeare, *King Henry the Fourth, Part Two*

I am Icarus

THE SKY IN LOS Angeles was still jet black when James Packer stumbled out of bed on the cool autumn morning of 28 October 2016. He'd barely slept a wink in a fortnight, and the previous night had been no exception. Holed up in the guest house of the vast estate that is home to movie legend Warren Beatty, perched atop the storied Mulholland Drive in the Hollywood Hills, Packer looked every bit a nervous wreck. For weeks, the favoured dawn panacea for the chain-smoking billionaire had been a few of his favourite menthol cigarettes and a shot or two of straight vodka, before he'd drained the bottle and more by dusk.

Today there was no need for even a shot glass. His plane was due for take-off at 6am, so his chauffeur was waiting. Packer grabbed his favourite vodka and, for the first time in his life, sculled straight from the bottle. Half of it was gone in less than a minute. As he drifted in and out of consciousness, his car hurtled down Mulholland Drive and onto the 405 freeway. Its destination was Van Nuys airport, known as the 'airport to the stars' for the extravagant collection of private jets that adorns its aprons. With Packer were his best friend and old schoolmate Ben Tilley and his legal eagle Guy Jalland.

By 6am, as the first rays of light glimmered on the tarmac, Packer was comatose on the couch of a chartered Bombardier Global Express. (His regular jet was in for maintenance.) He was bound for the sanctuary of his salubrious polo ranch 'Ellerstina' – named after his family's NSW polo property, 'Ellerston' – twelve hours' flying time away in Argentina. When he finally regained consciousness, he thought he'd been in the air for five minutes. In reality, it was five hours.

Ten months out from celebrating his fiftieth birthday, Packer was coming apart at the seams. Born into great wealth and given all the advantages money could buy by a powerful father, he'd become a friend, confidant, partner and lover to a who's who of A-list celebrities, political leaders and powerful business figures. Yet one of Australia's most recognisable and scrutinised corporate giants was staggering under the weight of being the heir to the multibillion-dollar fortune that his legendary father had built and handed down to him.

Beyond a circle of his closest friends and confidants, few appreciated the depth of the personal crisis into which he had sunk. To the cynics, he was the sort of person for whom there was unlikely to be much sympathy had his private traumas been public knowledge. Yet, among those who inhabited his private world, there was deep and growing consternation about what was happening to the man they called 'JP', the real, troubled and tormented James Packer, now barely conscious at 40,000 feet above Mexico. In the rarefied atmosphere of

Packer's high-flying life, where he counted among his inner circle names that ordinary people knew only as those of untouchable celebrities, Warren Beatty had grown to become one of his closest friends.

*

PACKER FIRST MET BEATTY in 2014 through Packer's ritzy Hollywood film production company known as RatPac, which he had formed with film producer Brett Ratner in 2012. Beatty, who has been dubbed the 'Prince of Hollywood', 'the Pro' and 'Boss' – and is the only person in Tinseltown to have been twice nominated for an Oscar for acting, directing, writing and producing in the same film – introduced Packer to a bunch of big names in America. They included the late John McCain, the US senator who lost to Barack Obama in the 2008 American presidential election.

Packer and Beatty soon bonded over politics. Beatty has been one of the – if not *the* – most famous of the so-called Hollywood Democrats for at least the last fifty years. He personally knew President John F Kennedy and all the Democrat presidents that followed. But Beatty also knows how to play both sides of politics. On the Republican side, in addition to John McCain, he counted former Republican president Ronald Reagan as a friend.

Beatty had given Packer free rein over his guest house, part of the sprawling Los Angeles compound the movie star calls home with his wife, four-time Oscar-nominated actress Annette Bening, and two of their four children. The 6.7-acre estate features three residences, including a V-shaped Mediterranean-style mansion where Beatty and Bening reside, which has its own swimming pool, gym and tennis court, and a grand piano in its vast living room. On a clear day the views from the back lawn and pool extend over Bel-Air all the way to the Pacific Ocean.

Beatty's guest house, which has its own separate entrance from Mulholland Drive, gave Packer a Los Angeles base to host his three children, who had moved to America with their mother, Erica, following their split in mid 2013. The three-bedroom weatherboard home, which Packer refurbished when he took up a three-year lease in October 2014, has its own pool and spa, and boasts stunning views over the San Bernardino Valley. Packer even converted the adjoining garage into bedrooms for his kids.

While he and Beatty first met doing business, their relationship has become so much more. 'Warren is a very kind man who is living a huge life. He was generous enough to let me live in his guest house for almost three years,' Packer now says. 'This is said with zero disrespect [to my father]. Mum met and absolutely adored Warren. And Dad and Warren would have loved each other. I ended up calling Warren "Dad".'

*

IN 2014, WHEN RATPAC helped bankroll Beatty's first screen-acting role in fifteen years, for the romantic comedy-drama *Rules Don't Apply*, it financed the film in a joint venture with New Regency Productions, owned by Israeli businessman and Hollywood film producer Arnon Milchan. In presenting the 2014 Israel Film Festival Vision Award to Milchan, Beatty called the producer of Oscar-winning films *12 Years a Slave* and *Birdman* 'a Medici of movies'. The connection between Milchan and the Packer family dated back to the 1990s, when Kerry Packer acquired a stake in New Regency.

Milchan was the one who first introduced James Packer to Israel, when he took him there for a week-long visit in mid

2013. They dined with then President Shimon Peres and Prime Minister Benjamin Netanyahu. Packer became intoxicated by the country and its politics. For a time in 2016 and 2017 Israel became his official place of residence, after he bought a house adjacent to Netanyahu's private home in a wealthy gated community in the beachside town of Caesarea. Packer became so close to the Netanyahu family that he sat with the official party when Netanyahu spoke to the US Congress and UN General Assembly in 2015. But it was a connection that soon became toxic.

By early October 2016, as his 88-metre-long luxury cruiser known as the *Arctic P* drifted off the coast of Israel for the first and only time, the Australian was deeply embroiled in a corruption scandal involving the Israeli PM and Milchan. It was being alleged that Netanyahu had accepted lavish gifts from both Packer and Milchan. The police eventually claimed that Netanyahu's family received from both around US$280,000 worth of free champagne, cigars, food, accommodation and even tickets to a Mariah Carey concert. Packer was under mounting pressure to testify about his actions to the Israeli authorities in the saga that became known as Case 1000. Israeli media was speculating that he could be charged.

But there were also other things on Packer's mind at the time.

*

ON 11 OCTOBER PACKER had been met on board the *Arctic P* by Robert Rankin, who was both the chairman of his casino company, Crown Resorts, and the boss of his private company, Consolidated Press Holdings (CPH), Crown's biggest shareholder. At Rankin's side that day was Michael (Mike) Johnston, the financial controller of CPH. With the rocky

Israeli coastline as a backdrop, they presented Packer with more details of a radical plan to split Crown's local and offshore businesses, which had been approved by the Crown board and announced to the sharemarket in mid June.

The deal was the brainchild of Rankin, a former investment banker, who believed the split would boost the value on the sharemarket of Crown's Australian businesses. Packer had stepped off the Crown board in December 2015, after resigning as chairman four months earlier to pursue his Hollywood dreams, so Rankin was squarely in strategic control of the casino group. Packer recalls: 'Rob and Mike presented me with this straw man, if that's the right word, which showed Crown separated into Crown International and Crown Domestic. Off the back of that, what it showed was dividends to CPH increasing by 10–15 per cent a year. And I just didn't believe the numbers. This was August. We were two months into the fiscal year and we were missing budgets every day. And then I got these forecasts. The numbers they were presenting were, in my view, optimistic.'

Rankin and Johnson knew their boss was unimpressed. When they finished their presentations and quietly headed downstairs on the *Arctic P*, Packer stayed on the top deck, slumped in his chair. He stared blankly at the documents for another ten minutes and then turned to Guy Jalland. 'I don't know if I started crying, but I thought to myself, "I don't want to have $1.4 billion of debt any more. Why am I doing this?"' he recalls.

In addition to Crown's woes, CPH was swimming in debt after Packer had negotiated a $1.25 billion framework to split the family fortune with his sister, Gretel, which was signed at the end of 2015. And CPH's costs were, seemingly, out of control. 'Subconsciously, I had lost confidence in Rob [Rankin],' Packer now says, reflecting back on that time.

But worse was to come. A few hours later, Packer jumped aboard his private jet bound for Los Angeles, leaving Israel for the last time. He received an urgent text message from Rankin to call as soon as possible. When he was finally back on the ground in Los Angeles and able to speak to Rankin, his lieutenant had some horrific news: nineteen of Crown's staff – including Crown's head of international VIP business, Jason O'Connor – were being held at two detention centres in Shanghai for allegedly committing gambling crimes in mainland China. The Crown share price immediately fell 20 per cent.

Rocked by the biggest scandal ever to hit his company, Packer was lost for words and paralysed with fear when he returned to Beatty's guest house on the evening of 13 October 2016. Rankin, a veteran of working in China, was so worried about his conversations being monitored by the Chinese authorities that he sent Packer and Jalland a package in LA containing two small antique-looking mobile phones for them to speak to him more securely. Packer's Asian gaming partner Lawrence Ho recalls of Rankin's rationale: 'There was plenty of radio silence. With the whole team, we were communicating cryptically. They were concerned that their communications might have been being monitored.' For all Packer had talked up Australia's relationship with China and the opportunity provided by its burgeoning middle class, the arrests were the ultimate slap in the face – and the last thing he needed after a horror 2016.

*

WARREN BEATTY, A DEEPLY private man nominated for fourteen Academy Awards, doesn't do media interviews. Sixteen biographies have been written about the 81-year-old and he never spoke to any of the authors — nor, he claims, has he read any of them. Yet, with Packer's assistance, he has agreed to talk to me on a cool and cloudy late-spring morning at his Los Angeles mansion.

From the road it is a blink-and-you-miss-it address at the end of a sharp corner on Mulholland Drive. After walking through a nondescript wrought-iron gate, you make your way up a long concrete driveway, past a Porsche, Mustang and a Mercedes convertible parked at the base of the entrance stairs. On either side ageing pine trees tower over perfectly manicured lawns, which at the top of the hill are adorned by small rose gardens draped over a balustrade that overlooks a full-sized tennis court also furnished with two basketball hoops. Beatty's affable, thirty-something bearded assistant greets me at the door and shows me to the library, complete with its collection of *Encyclopaedia Britannica* and *World Books*. In the centre of the room sits a 1980s-style Sony big box television.

When Beatty finally arrives, dressed in a cream spray jacket, dark jeans, black sneakers and white socks, he apologises for the TV, which he says is never used. He plonks himself down in his favourite chair, with a box of pencils, yellow notepad and chunky landline phone at the ready on its left arm. He nibbles on cashews and drinks green tea as we cautiously start our conversation. Beatty warns me that on the rare occasions he does speak to media, he makes a boring interviewee. But after some initial guarded responses about how he got to know Packer, he starts to open up about his friend.

'He has been both graced and victimised — and I would say more graced — by the inheritance,' Beatty says. 'He is a very good father. He has a very good relationship with the mother of his children. I met James's mother; I liked her. I thought she was fun. I'll tell you what an important factor is — and I think you should emphasise it — this little thing called humility.

I think he has genuine humility. If humility is genuine, you can learn faster.'

Beatty never knew Kerry Packer but he wishes he had. 'I have never questioned James about his father — that is so deep. I would not want to in some superficial way invade that territory. But of the people I know that knew Kerry Packer, I don't know that the father had the capability of self-analysis that I think I see in James,' he says.

In October 2016 Beatty was a central figure in a remarkable fortnight in James Packer's life. It started on the afternoon of 14 October, when he paid his friend a visit at his guest house. Packer says of his state after learning of Crown's China arrests, 'I didn't know what to do when I got back to LA, so I was just drinking. There have been stages of my life when I drink way too much. I was drinking straight vodka then. Straight tequila later. Warren rang me the day after we arrived and I didn't really want to see anyone. But Warren said, "I am going to come over and say hello." So I am waiting at the guest house and it is the afternoon and Warren comes in, sits down and we start speaking. He said, "I think you need to see someone. A psychiatrist. And you need to check the medicines you are on."' Packer had been put on powerful medication earlier in the year in Israel, which now had made it difficult for him to function.

Beatty, who doesn't smoke or drink and is in remarkable condition for a man in his early eighties, knew plenty of people in Hollywood who had been helped by psychiatry. He made a few phone calls. 'I am one of those people in Hollywood who still believes in certain things that Sigmund Freud [the founder of psychoanalysis] and other compatriots in the field of psychotherapy and psychoanalysis espoused,' says Beatty. 'I believe it is very valuable. I feel that so much can be accomplished by that, making ourselves happier by not resorting to the prescription drugs that are sold on every television show that we see.'

Beatty compares psychoanalysis to a form of exercise, but for the mind. 'Going into psychotherapy in the '50s or the '60s in New York or Los Angeles, I would compare it to going to the gym. Now we have put that aside and said, "Let's take a pill – now I feel much happier." There is great value in not going to the pharmaceutical solution,' he says. 'I have suggested to many people, "You might like to try some psychotherapy. That doesn't mean you have to stay in it."'

Within two hours of Beatty's talk with Packer, they were in a suburban psychologist's office in the San Bernardino Valley. The star of hit films such as *Shampoo*, *Dick Tracy* and *Bugsy* had taken it upon himself to drive his sick friend – who had more than sixty times his wealth – to the clinic. Beatty looks slightly taken aback when I ask him why he undertook such an act of generosity. He responds with just four words. 'He is a friend,' he almost whispers, slowly, before repeating himself. 'He is a friend.'

*

A SINGLE SENTENCE WAS on Packer's mind as he sat frozen in the seat of Beatty's luxury Lexus as it hurtled down Mulholland Drive. When he arrived at the psychiatrist's office, it was the only one emanating from his lips. 'I am going broke,' he told Beatty's doctor of choice.

Each day, Mike Johnston was emailing his boss his usual five-page report on CPH, which shows in minute detail how Packer's wealth has changed over the past twenty-four hours. It records the value of his shares in Crown and his private equity investments, such as his stake in the Bondi Icebergs restaurant and bar in Sydney (which was recently sold), the

Ellerston Capital funds management operation now run by his former lieutenant Ashok Jacob and the Square Peg venture capital business co-founded by his good friend Paul Bassat and others. It also tallies up the value of Packer's 'shareholder assets', such as his two Sydney properties (his Bondi apartment was sold in early August 2018), his homes in Israel and Aspen, his apartments in Switzerland and Dubai (the latter is on the market), and his Argentinian polo ranch. And, of course, his two private jets. Most importantly, it also details his net debt position – his cash minus borrowings and provisions. And on that day in LA, the report was flashing red.

'The daily reports I was getting from Mike Johnston showed my net worth was $3.5 billion, but I was convinced it was going to zero,' Packer says. Revenues at Crown Resorts were falling off a cliff. After spending billions of dollars to upgrade its Melbourne and Perth properties, the company had missed its annual budget by more than $100 million. In mathematical terms, Packer reckoned it meant the business was worth $3 billion less than he had hoped. And now the China arrests had trashed the company's reputation on the global stage.

But as Packer sat before him, Beatty's doctor had more on his mind than money. He asked Packer how much he had been drinking. The answer from his patient was blunt: 'A lot.' The doctor quickly responded with another question: 'How much is a lot?'

'I probably said a bottle of vodka a day, but I think it was more than that,' Packer recalls. 'I was still relatively lean at that point. So vodka was my alcohol when I was leaner.' The doctor urged Packer to cut back on his alcohol intake, and he reluctantly pledged to have no more than five vodka nips a day.

The doctor also took Packer off the powerful drugs that had been prescribed for him eight months earlier in Israel and put him on another form of prescription medication to help his mood. As Packer left, they shook hands on an agreement that he would return to see him every day for the next month. When Packer walked out of the psychiatrist's office that evening, Beatty was still in the waiting room. He drove his friend back up into the Santa Monica Mountains to his guest house.

But Packer's vodka pledge lasted only two days. On 17 October, after receiving more bad news about the Crown crisis unfolding in China, he sat in a chair at Beatty's guest house and polished off a bottle of vodka, before cancelling his psychiatric appointment. He repeated the ritual the next day. On the third day, as he was three-quarters through another bottle, his staff stepped in. Jalland, Tilley and Packer's then adviser in Los Angeles – former Scientology spokesman Tommy Davis – as well as the staff at Beatty's guest house, were fed up. They pleaded with their boss to return to the psychiatrist and offered to go with him for what is known in psychiatry as an 'intervention', where urgent actions are performed to bring about a change in people suffering from substance abuse or other psychiatric issues.

Packer reluctantly agreed. But as Crown's share price continued to fall, a single thought remained front and centre of Packer's mind: he was going broke. Surrounded by his closest friends in the psychiatrist's office, Packer felt too embarrassed to admit he felt he was going to lose everything. Instead, he simply listened as the psychiatrist asked pointedly: 'Are you trying to kill yourself?'

The shock tactics had no effect. The next day Packer again drank himself into oblivion. It prompted his staff, led by his devoted butler at Beatty's guest house, Nat, to try another tack. This time they succeeded in getting Packer to visit Ronald Reagan UCLA Medical Center in Westwood. There Tommy Davis introduced his boss to a new doctor, a non-psychiatric specialist, who took a series of blood tests. It brought back bad memories of six months earlier in Los Angeles, when Packer had agreed to similar tests and the results had been shocking. They had revealed for the first time the extent of the damage he was doing to his liver. 'I stopped drinking for a couple of months after those tests and when I went to Israel it was easier for me not to drink, because of the way my house was staffed and the fact there was no alcohol in it,' he recalls.

But this latest round of tests in LA would be surprisingly different. 'I can't believe this,' the doctor told Packer. 'You are perfect everywhere!' Packer was elated and immediately called Arnon Milchan, who was also in Hollywood, to extoll the success of his vodka diet. Milchan called for a celebration, which Ben Tilley was asked to organise. But Tilley was in no mood to party. The man known by gossip columnists as 'the billionaire's babysitter' had had enough, and he point-blank refused.

Tilley had always been one to speak his mind. For years he had travelled the world with James's father, Kerry Packer, to play poker and golf. Sometimes he'd had to stand his ground in the face of Packer Senior's volcanic temper. This time he did the same with his son. A fierce row ensued, but Tilley not only lost the fight, he lost his job, with Packer sacking him on the spot.

Packer then turned on his loyal assistant Ian Morris, who had served him for a decade and a half after starting as a deckhand on the *Arctic P*. He too was fired with immediate effect. An angry Morris packed his bags and headed to the Beverly Hills Hotel, where he booked a one-way airfare back to Sydney. It took six months of Packer's pleading for Morris to return to his job. Packer now says he couldn't do without him. 'Ian Morris is fantastic to me. He never ceases to amaze me with his wit and wisdom, and he is selfless in his service,' he says. 'He comes from humble origins in Sri Lanka and has seen a lot of the world. He loves Israel with a passion and is incredibly knowledgeable about the Jewish faith. We are friends first and foremost.'

Tilley had assured Morris that day that he wouldn't be far behind him as he headed upstairs and packed up his own belongings. But before he left, he decided to confront a steaming Packer one last time. 'Well, son, I'm all packed, I'm leaving and I won't darken your door again,' Tilley said, standing in the doorway, bag in hand. (James and Tilley regularly address each other as 'son', a figure of speech favoured by the late Kerry Packer.) But the boss was now having second thoughts. He asked Tilley to wait. After twenty minutes of soul-searching, the two were tearing into a bottle of tequila together, best friends again.

Tilley hoped Packer's mea culpa might herald a return to sanity. But he was wrong. 'Then I really started drinking,' Packer recalls. He had taken the positive blood test results as a licence to kick things up a notch.

*

ON THE MORNING OF 28 October 2016 in Australia, the gossip magazine owned by Packer's good friend and fellow billionaire Kerry Stokes dropped the biggest bomb of all. With a front-page exclusive, *Woman's Day* broke the news that Packer had abruptly ended his engagement to pop singer Mariah Carey, blaming her new reality-TV show *Mariah's World* and her extravagant spending. If Packer thought his problems with Crown, China and Israel were bad, the break-up with Carey was off the Richter scale. Once the US celebrity websites got the story, it became a feeding frenzy.

Despite months of tortuous negotiations, Packer and Carey had never formally settled on a prenuptial agreement. So after the break-up, the advisers for both sides had begun quietly working on a suitable settlement. After one confidential meeting, a sum of US$5 million was put on the table and was close to being agreed. But the afternoon the *Woman's Day* article was read by those in LA, Carey's camp reportedly jacked up their demands to US$50 million. Carey and her fiery then manager, Stella Bulochnikov, took the article – which they assumed had been planted by Packer's side – as a declaration of war, even though Packer and his advisers argued otherwise, which they still do to this day. 'I had absolutely nothing to do with the story,' Packer now declares.

In Beatty's guest house on Mulholland Drive, Packer felt trapped on top of Hollywood. There was no garden to walk in, just a small balcony and a long concrete driveway that led to the front entrance of the guest house. There was no escape. Jalland and Tilley were deeply worried that things had suddenly become far too intense in Los Angeles. They quickly agreed that only the billionaire's secluded Argentinian polo ranch could provide solace. With Packer's plane in maintenance, Tilley quickly found a replacement that would take his boss to safety. The next morning Packer bade farewell to Warren Beatty, his staunch friend during the most difficult period of his life.

'By the time the Israel so-called Case 1000 had become public, the China arrests and Crown's sale of Macau had occurred and the break-up with Mariah had happened, I had become toxic. The phone stopped ringing and people were out when I called them. There were, of course, a few exceptions. Every month or so Warren would ring. And apart from my kids, he was the only person I travelled to LA to see,' Packer says.

They still keep in touch and have lunch together every few months at the Beverly Hills Hotel's famed Polo Lounge, a favourite with generations of Hollywood stars. They sit at the table Beatty has called his own for more than twenty years. 'Warren has continued to be a friend, even when it was less fashionable to be my friend,' Packer says. 'And for that I am truly grateful.'

When presented with Packer's compliment, Beatty struggles for a few moments to find the words to respond before muttering, softly: 'Well, that's, that's, um, that is very nice to hear.'

Beatty has four adult children with Annette Bening whom he jokingly refers to as 'four small Eastern European countries that I negotiate with and I send ambassadors to'. But he eschews the parental label to describe his relationship with Packer. 'That would not come to mind, a father figure,' he says, slowly. 'I would say a friend.'

*

WITH ITS LONELY TREE-LINED lanes, locked gates and armed security guards, Ellerstina, an hour's drive out of Buenos Aires, is one of the few places in the world where Packer genuinely feels safe. When he arrived, he plonked himself on his favourite cream couch, which looks over the lush polo field he calls the 'Field of Dreams'. To the left of the TV in a grand floor-to-ceiling bookcase is a photo of his late father with the ranch's founder, Argentine polo legend Gonzalo Pieres Senior. Alongside are photos of Packer's children – Indigo, Jackson and Emmanuelle – including one with their mother. And in the corner of the room stands a stunning model of the $2.2 billion Crown Sydney casino hotel, due to open in 2021.

For days, Packer barely moved from a line between his bedroom and the couch, often simply staring at the giant television screen hanging on the wall. And for a time he kept drinking: morning, noon and night. His staff at the ranch, led by his deeply loyal house manager Valeria, knew their boss was in a bad way. Through the fog of alcohol, cigarette smoke and prescription medication, Packer tried to take stock of the horrors of the previous weeks and months. 'We arrived in Argentina just in time,' he now says. 'My Israel experience and my LA experience were over, and they had been the two places I had spent the most time for the last three years.'

Again he sought psychiatric help in Argentina and was prescribed new drugs that he says were 'very bad for weight gain. When I went to Argentina I weighed around 100 kilograms and blew out to 130 kilograms,' he says, noting the medicine also 'changed his tastebuds'.

But the refuge of Argentina provided Packer, Jalland and his advisers with vital time and space. Each morning he and Jalland would methodically work through the issues before them. This process would prove to be a turning point. Whether it was responding to the demands of Carey's advisers and the press reports that exploded after the break-up, or dealing with the problems of Crown in China and the debts of CPH, Packer eventually pulled back his drinking and started to focus on how to turn his business and his life around. As one observer familiar with the period puts it: 'For weeks it simply became a question of survival for them and getting through each day.'

Several times each day Jalland and Tilley sought respite from the onslaught by walking laps of the Field of Dreams, sometimes deep into the twilight of the late spring evenings, while their boss remained firmly rooted to the couch inside. 'I thought the pressure James was under was just massive,' Jalland now recalls. 'It was coming from every direction. It was very personal. And every day I was just moved by his ability to deal with it and get through it. It makes me emotional now. We had to sit there every day and just deal with it.'

Crown's then executive deputy chairman, John Alexander, also visited Ellerstina in the weeks after Packer's arrival, where they discussed making him chairman.

'I got a call to go over three to four days before I went. We started conversations on the phone. After I arrived I spent two days there. I spent a lot of time walking around the Field of Dreams with Guy,' Alexander says. 'James was not in great shape because he had the whole weight of the world on his shoulders. We talked about changes to how we were going to run the place, the priorities and what was needed. They were then discussed with the board and the board signed off on them.'

By January 2017 Alexander had taken two jobs in one at Crown, replacing both chairman Robert Rankin and chief executive Rowen Craigie.

In December 2016 the Crown board had also voted to abandon its plan to split the company in two, instead selling down more of its casinos investment in Macau worth over $1.6 billion. It was a decision supported by Packer and CPH. By the time Crown sold the rest of its Macau stake in May 2017, it had made six times its original investment. And it effectively saved Crown's staff in China, putting them on a path to release two months later. Yet the subsequent recovery in the Macau gaming market and the increase in the Melco Crown share price in the eighteen-month period after the sale enraged Packer.

*

THE HORRORS OF 2016 had left Packer, for the third time in his life, suffering a nervous breakdown. Those who know him well and saw the private pain of his two previous mental crises say this latest iteration was by far his worst. It led him in March

2018 to acknowledge to the world for the first time that he was battling mental health issues, as he resigned from the Crown board for the second time in the space of two and a half years.

The news came as a shock to many, but not to Warren Beatty. 'I don't pry, but I think he's in a process of self-analysis that we certainly don't see in certain public figures – who I won't name – who are carrying infinitely greater responsibilities. This process is continual. I think we all need to continue to be re-examining,' he says. 'I think it is very open for him to come out publicly that he is attempting to evaluate the health of what he is going through or doing.'

Long-time Packer family adviser and former Labor senator Graham Richardson says it was clear to those close to the family that Packer had been wrestling with his demons periodically for almost two decades. 'We all knew James was suffering from depression. On and off over the years he certainly has. I was not surprised to hear in March [2018] that things were grim,' he says. 'James can't go anywhere or do anything without photographers. That has really got to him over time. It has been the same for thirty years. That must get pretty annoying. We've all got a different make-up. Some court it. Some tolerate it. James has never courted it or liked it. He has always hated it. That is a genuine thing, not a creation.'

Packer's first breakdown occurred after the infamous 2001 collapse of One.Tel, when his father was still alive and the Packers lost hundreds of millions of dollars on the mobile phone company that was also backed by Rupert Murdoch's News Corporation. In the wake of the disaster, James Packer was unrelentingly punished for a year by his father before Kerry Packer realised what damage he was doing to his son. It followed a troubled childhood where Kerry had ruled his household and at times terrified his son, as his own father once had him. While James and Kerry reconciled before Kerry passed away in late 2005, the One.Tel episode also cost James his first marriage, to swimsuit model Jodhi Meares.

'His father was often unhappy but not necessarily depressed,' Richardson says when I ask if he thought Kerry Packer also suffered from the same ailments as his son. 'Kerry carried with him great anger that he would explode with regularly. For Kerry that was enough of a release for whatever tension he held within. James does the same thing but it is obviously not enough. I don't think James has had the release that his father had.'

Packer's second breakdown had come after Crown was saddled with debt when it paid too much for a laundry list of casino investments in America just before the GFC hit.

Four years later, the stresses of a Sydney casino bid and the distractions that came with his move into Hollywood film producing cost him his second marriage, to Erica Packer. After they divorced, Packer followed Erica and his children when they moved to Los Angeles. With that move he gained some necessary distance from the town of his birth.

The Sydney casino success pushed Packer into a world that he now acknowledges was 'wild, really wild'. When Crown Sydney was approved in late 2013, Packer's Hollywood RatPac film production company was in full swing and he was rubbing shoulders with Hollywood A-listers Martin Scorsese, Robert De Niro, Leonardo DiCaprio and Brad Pitt. With his marriage to Erica over, he was also single again. By late 2013 there were media reports linking him to supermodel Miranda Kerr, and those reports continued through 2014. Then in 2015 his romance with Mariah Carey blossomed.

At the same time, the stunning success of his bid for a Sydney casino licence saw him bombarded with casino opportunities in places across the world, as far afield as Cyprus, Rome and Sri Lanka. He was also opening others with his Macau partner, Lawrence Ho, in the Philippines and Macau.

Suddenly, Packer was building a global brand and a global company. Publicly, he appeared to be revelling in it. But privately, he was falling apart. Being on a plane sometimes twenty-four hours a day, seven days a week, coupled with a life of celebrities, parties and heavy drinking, was taking its toll. 'I was flying way too much. Between Israel, to LA, back to Australia at the start, then to New York. The kids were in LA the whole time. I was living in LA but I was flying back and forth everywhere,' he now says. By the end of 2016 it all became too much.

While he lost hundreds of millions of dollars on the One.Tel disaster and billions during the GFC, this time around, Packer acknowledges that he has lost something far more important than money. 'I haven't actually had a company threatening financial loss this time. I lost $100 million on RatPac, but that was basically it, and I made $100 million in the US at the same time on other investments. Macau is so heartbreaking because I lost my reputation, and serious people treat me differently, both because of the charges that were levied against our staff in China and because we sold out of Macau,' he says. 'This time I have lost my reputation globally. I am not sure how easy it is to get it back a fourth time. I am really not sure.'

He turns to Greek mythology in an attempt to explain the most exciting yet tumultuous period of his fifty years on earth. 'With RatPac and Hollywood, Mariah, Israel, China, all of those things, I was like Icarus,' he says, referring to the fable of the man who crashed to earth when the sun's heat melted his wings of feathers and wax. 'I flew too close to the sun.'

ONE

In the Name of the Father

IT IS ONE OF the most poignant memories of James Douglas Packer's childhood. When he was just fourteen, his father purchased an American-made, fully automated pitching machine designed to fire baseballs at speeds of up to 190 kilometres per hour. In the Packer family compound, on the high side of Victoria Road in Sydney's exclusive Bellevue Hill, the machine was firing not baseballs but cherry-red six-stitcher cricket balls. They were hurled at young James – armed with only a matchstick bat and paper-thin pads – across an old helipad that had been transformed into a net-encircled, curated 22-yard stretch of turf, often juiced up by the morning dew.

At the controls for each session was former England Test cricketer Barry Knight – a visitor to the Packer compound each Saturday morning for private coaching sessions with James – or a cricketing legend such as Tony Greig, Clive Lloyd or Ian Chappell. Kerry Packer himself at times sent down a few at his only son at top pace from the fearsome machine. He relished taking the controls and cranking it up to full speed when Knight and the others had wound it back to safer levels.

'I used to get hit on the left side of the right leg directly opposite my thigh, trying to play a back defence to a lightning bolt at 95 miles an hour. I wasn't allowed to stay down,' James now says of the experience. 'There were no runs to be scored from the attempted shot, just survival. It might have been Tony Greig or Ian Chappell or Dad bowling the bowling machine. It was not fun. I would get bruises the size of a watermelon.' Barry Knight told the ABC's *Four Corners* in 1999 that the sessions 'knocked James around a little bit' but that 'he knew he had to be tough. It was as simple as that.'

It is unclear whether his extraordinary training regime improved his game, but nevertheless James went on to open the batting for his school's First XI at the age of seventeen. He was later selected for the Combined Associated Schools XI, an honour that even surpassed the cricketing achievements of his sports-mad father. But he rarely scored runs when Kerry was watching. He sums up his short sporting career in a single sentence: 'I never amounted to much as a cricketer.'

*

To MANY, THE IMAGE of a young James sinking to the ground in pain in his own backyard while facing an onslaught cheered on by his father might sum up his relationship with the man he called Dad. But there are conflicting views among those who saw the relationship at close range. Some believe Kerry was tough but fair towards James, while others claim he brutalised his son in a way that left deep psychological scars.

One who observed the relationship more closely than most, Sydney broadcaster Alan Jones, has a foot in both camps. Jones says James always felt that his father thought he was 'unworthy': 'That he wasn't up to it. They were always arguing about nothing. He'd always find a reason to find fault. You know if James said black, he'd say white.'

For decades Jones was a close friend of Kerry Packer's and has remained the same with his son. James notably gave one of his rare public speeches in 2010 when he addressed a gala party celebrating Jones's twenty-five years in the media. Now Jones for the first time publicly recounts a story that he will never forget. 'There was a famous showdown years ago when the father rang me and asked could I come in [to Park Street in Sydney, where Kerry Packer had his Australian headquarters]. And I went into his office, and as I went in, James – who would have been twenty-three at the time – walked out crying. Clearly, he'd been crying a lot,' he says slowly. 'I went in and said to the father, "What's going on?"

'And Kerry was raving a bit, and he said to me: "What do I do? What do I do?"'

Pained by what he had just witnessed and knowing he could get away with more than most with Kerry, Jones decided to respond facetiously. 'I said, "Nothing has happened. Well, that's not quite right. You just lost your son. But that probably doesn't matter …"'

Kerry, leaning back on his chair with his feet characteristically perched on his desk, instantly returned them to the floor, sat bolt upright and barked at Jones: 'It fucking matters, what are you talking about?'

Jones took a deep breath and delivered a reply that was anything but facetious. It was a call for mercy for the broken young man. 'The kid has walked past me – he's shot. You've destroyed him,' Jones said, before urging the man he called 'the father' to call his son back and apologise. 'To his credit he called him in and in my presence said, "Sorry, son." He got up from the table and hugged him.'

Crown chairman John Alexander remembers another occasion, eighteen months before Kerry Packer passed away, when he received a phone call from James he will never forget. It was the first and only time James ever quit the family business.

'He was in tears and said he was leaving. He told me "I can't cope with Dad any more." He wanted to leave the building and the company,' Alexander recalls.

'Within ten minutes of James leaving the building, I got a phone call from Kerry and he called me to his office. He sat there and said to me, "Who are you going to back, son? Me or James?' He threw down a blank piece of paper and said, "Tell me how much you want to back me."

'I said, "It is not a question of me backing you or him, Kerry. It is going to be very bad for both of you and the company if you don't put this back together." He then said, "I can run this company from the grave, son!", before adding, "He left me, I didn't leave him!"'

Alexander – who was perceived at the time to be closer to Kerry than James and had lunched with the family patriarch every Tuesday for the last two years of his life, sometimes for three hours or more – then assured Kerry he would attempt to retrieve the situation with his distraught son.

'I called James and said, "It would be really good if you come back in tomorrow and apologise to your father." And he did.' Alexander adds, 'That morning I got a phone call from Kerry's office. They asked me to come down. And they were both there hugging each other.'

*

KERRY PACKER HAD ENDURED his own torment at the hands of his father, the legendary Sir Frank Packer, a former heavyweight boxer who mounted two unsuccessful challenges for the America's Cup and ruled his publishing empire with an iron fist. He regularly called his son, who suffered from dyslexia, 'boofhead' and beat him with a polo whip.

When Kerry was sent to live with an aunt at Bowral in the NSW Southern Highlands following the submarine attacks on Sydney Harbour during World War II, he contracted polio and pneumatic fever. He spent nine months in hospital before moving to Canberra for two years to recover. Broadcaster Phillip Adams, a Kerry confidant in the 1970s and '80s who once wrote a book on Kerry that he never published, says the polio became a part of Kerry's insecurity.

'He always thought of himself as hideously ugly. He called himself the elephant man. He always insisted cartoonists were drawing a palsied cheek on one side of his face, even if they were not and knew nothing of it. That was all he could see,' Adams says.

Peter Yates, whom James installed as chief executive of the family company Publishing and Broadcasting Ltd (PBL) in 2001, bought a five-bedroom house the same year in Kambala Road, Bellevue Hill, just a stone's throw from the Packer family compound. The Packer family provided an interest-free loan of almost $6 million for Yates to purchase the property. Speaking for the first time in detail about his experience as part of the Packers' inner sanctum, Yates recalls, 'One day Kerry called me and said, "Come on over for a drink." So I went over there and he was sitting in the study watching TV. And he just started talking about his childhood.

'Then he showed me the bar. And he said to me, "You know every morning by 10am I had to be back here to make a martini drink for Frank. And if it wasn't absolutely perfect the glass would be thrown at me. I would just be either verbally or physically abused."' As he was speaking, Yates says, Kerry – a noted non-drinker – started rehearsing what had been his daily routine for many years, shaking up one of the cocktails. 'Kerry then said to me, "I had to do this every single day and make it perfect, and my day started with this fear and trepidation and angst about whether or not I would make this martini perfect. That was 10am each and every morning."'

A long-serving adviser to the Packer family, Peter Barron, adds that Kerry stopped drinking 'because he saw what his father was like when he was drinking'. Kerry had reportedly been a heavy drinker until his late teens, once telling TV personality Don Lane that his father had made a deal with him that if he got off the drink until his twenty-first birthday, he would give him a sports car. Kerry was also lucky enough to walk away from a fatal car accident near Goulburn in September 1956, after which he resolved to give up drinking for good. He remained a teetotaller till his death, preferring Coca-Cola to the martinis his father used to call his 'mullets'.

Kerry said many times that the happiest day of his life was when his father died.

*

JAMES WAS BORN TO Kerry and Ros Packer on 8 September 1967, a younger sibling for his sister, Gretel. He was born under the Virgo star sign which, intriguingly, to some astrologers suggests a life pursuit to 'do the right thing' but also a penchant for enjoying the material side of life, especially owning possessions. When James was only seven, Frank Packer passed away and Kerry inherited the $100 million family estate, which included the Nine Television Network and the Australian Consolidated Press (ACP) magazine business.

James attended the exclusive Tudor House School in Moss Vale and then the Anglican school Cranbrook in Bellevue Hill.

While he passed his higher school certificate at Cranbrook, he did not go to university because – as he told Ray Martin on *A Current Affair* in 1997 – he 'didn't have the marks', and 'because Dad always said to me that when I finished school he wanted me to go out and do a job which made me understand how lucky I was'.

In one of her only public interviews, Gretel told *The Australian Women's Weekly* in February 2006 that, as a child, she never thought her life was unusual. 'Some people might be surprised to hear it, but we had a very normal childhood. We were a close family. We went to school, had to do our homework, the dogs slept on the beds and we played with our father in the swimming pool,' she said. 'As I grew older, I realised what an incredible gift Dad was. He may not have been tame and he was rarely predictable, but he was out of the ordinary – unique. He was one of the funniest people I have ever known. He had an extraordinary dry wit and great comic timing. I feel blessed to have had him as my father.'

Kerry was dead against both his children going to university, once justifying his position on James with the quote: 'Why would he want to go there? To learn how to smoke marijuana?' Instead, James knew from about the age of fourteen that when he left school he would be following the Packer tradition of working as a jackaroo on his father's Newcastle Waters cattle station in the remote Barkly Tableland region of the Northern Territory. Peter Barron recalls; 'Kerry wanted both Gretel and James to see that the real world wasn't like their life. It wasn't a crazy hardening-up exercise. It was to see other people outside the eastern suburbs/Cranbrook circle. I think it did a good thing for James.'

When Kerry purchased the Newcastle Waters cattle station in 1983 from his best mate, cattle baron Ken Warriner, he built a magnificent homestead to replace the historic stone building that had been on the site for almost a century. Designed by architect Espie Dods, it took two years to build and wasn't complete until two giant satellite dishes were installed, giving the Nine Network owner direct, advertising-free feeds of his own channel and the Seven and Ten networks, far away in Sydney. The airstrip at the small town of Elliott, 10 kilometres away from the homestead, was even upgraded so it could take the Packer family Learjet.

But when James arrived at Newcastle Waters in February 1986, two months after leaving school, he could only dream of watching Sydney television or flying over the countryside in a private plane. He was sent to a stock camp 120 kilometres away from the homestead, where the work was hard in temperatures that regularly nudged — or topped — 40 degrees for almost six months of the year. 'Kerry used to ring Ken Warriner and check on James. And Kerry told me it was great to hear from Ken that he was not behaving like the boss's son,' Peter Barron recalls. 'James never whinged about it. He got in and did all the things that other jackaroos would do and became mates with them.'

While James told Peter FitzSimons in *The Sydney Morning Herald* in 1994 that he did not enjoy his time at Newcastle Waters, he did praise his father for giving him the experience. Whenever James and the other stockmen returned to the Newcastle Waters homestead after weeks in the field, they would always stop by the pub at Elliott for a well-earned drink or three. But he now reveals that he was affected by this experience in more ways than just the alcohol. 'I went to the pub in Elliott several times, which was largely frequented by Aboriginal people. It was a real eye-opener to see those people in the outback, living like that,' James recalls.

'There was also a small Aboriginal community that I visited just outside the Newcastle Waters homestead area.

I was surprised at how they lived. It gave me an appreciation of the alcohol problems in those communities and the hard life that they led.' Referring to the work his casino company Crown Resorts now does with its award-winning Indigenous employment program in Melbourne and Perth, he adds: 'I saw the disadvantage, and in a small way we have done our best at Crown to do our bit to help.'

*

WHEN JAMES RETURNED TO Sydney from the Northern Territory in 1987, he initially joined Channel Nine as a researcher on the early-morning *Today* show, before switching to ACP's *The Bulletin* and *The Australian Woman's Weekly*, where he sold advertising. In 1988 he moved to the United Kingdom to work for investment bank Rothschild, where he met Damian Aspinall, son of billionaire English businessman John Aspinall, who was good friends with Kerry Packer. The two sons also became good friends. 'There is a lot of similarity between James and Kerry. Kerry going to London to play polo, hanging around with James Goldsmith, John Aspinall and others as he once did is remarkably similar to James going to Hollywood,' says Peter Barron. 'The wealth never made his father or James a member of the establishment. They remained who they were.'

In a rare interview in 2000, Damian Aspinall declared that 'Jamie is my best friend. [He's] the only son of [Australia's band of rich kids] that I am close to. I have met so many sons like that and they are useless.' In 1999, Aspinall was best man at James's wedding in Sydney to Jodhi Meares. Ironically, Aspinall's partner at that time was Erica Baxter, who would go on to marry James in the French Riviera in June 2007, five years after James and Meares split. To this day, Crown Resorts still holds a half-share of the Aspers Group – named for Damian's late father's nickname – which operates four regional casinos in the United Kingdom. In 2011, Crown also purchased the prestigious Aspinall's Club in London, developed through a joint venture between Crown and Damien Aspinall, and subsequently rebranded it Crown London Aspinall's.

James returned from London to Australia in mid 1990 and was at Warwick Farm in Sydney on the day his father suffered a heart attack that left him clinically dead for seven minutes. It is now folklore that Kerry Packer was revived by a passing ambulance, one of the few equipped with a portable defibrillator, and a year later donated $2.5 million to help equip the state's 888 ambulances with the devices. Kerry famously told reporters at a press conference afterwards: 'I've been to the other side and let me tell you, son, there's fucking nothing there … there's no one waiting there for you, there's no one to judge you, so you can do what you bloody well like.'

In 1991, after his dice with death, Kerry pulled back from the day-to-day running of the family businesses and hired an American executive and turnaround specialist, Al 'Chainsaw' Dunlap, as CEO of the family's private company, CPH. James had met Dunlap during his time in the UK, when the American was working for another billionaire businessman, James Goldsmith. James has described Dunlap to friends as a 'seriously complex person' and 'unemotional'. Dunlap once said his dictum in business was simple: 'You are not in a business to be liked. If you want a friend, get a dog.' With Kerry focused elsewhere and often overseas, the American slashed and burned his way through the bloated Packer empire, selling and closing businesses and sacking staff. But Phillip Adams says Dunlap had another important job: 'To turn Jamie Packer into James.'

'Growing up, James was the sweetest little boy, like a little puppy, desperate for affection. When he started in business

Jamie was soft, gentle and decent. A charming kid. But James had to be a toughie. It was a fairly dramatic change. He was thrust into a world, a set, of problems that wasn't his first choice,' Adams says.

'I never knew Dunlap but I saw what he did to the boy. I bumped into James on two occasions (after he had been working for a while with Dunlap); one was on a Qantas flight. Both conversations were terribly sad. What I heard was a pseudo Kerry, not the soft, gentle character I knew. It was someone who had been worked over and turned into someone he wasn't.'

Dunlap told *Australian Story* in 2014 that he initially found James to be a 'very nice young man' who was 'interested in polo and beautiful women but he wasn't tough like Kerry. But when he learned what had to be done, I felt that he toughened up and I felt that he was a very quick learner. He did not want to disappoint his father and I thought that was a great motivating factor in his life,' he said. Dunlap saw that willingness to learn come through in another conversation he had with James. 'I remember Jamie came in the office one day and he said, "You know, Al, this just isn't worth it." I said, "What's wrong, Jamie?" He said, "Well, you chewed me out all day this week, my dad chews me out when I get home, it isn't worth it." And I said, "Well, Jamie, your dad's the richest man in this country, you're going to inherit billions of dollars." And he looked at me and said, "You're right, what do you want me to do?" And I always thought that was kind of funny.'

Former Victorian premier Jeff Kennett, a long-time Packer family friend, describes James's education at Newcastle Waters and then under larger-than-life figures such as Dunlap as 'real time, real experience, under some very capable, experienced mentors. The result of that is that he is, without doubt, one of the smartest "figure" guys I have ever met. He got a real, earthy, financial education. It was hard, it was tough. When I look back to what the majority of fathers would want for their sons – a good academic education – I think this one was far more profound,' he says.

By early 1993 Dunlap was gone from the Packer empire. He was later barred from serving as an officer of US public companies in the wake of a massive accounting scandal at Sunbeam Products in America, a company he ran for two years and that went bankrupt a few years later.

Dunlap was followed at CPH by another fast-talking American, Brian Powers, previously of US investment bank Hellman & Friedman. Powers served as CPH chief executive for five years, overseeing a big debt-reduction strategy at the group. When Powers arrived, CPH had over $2 billion of debt. By the time he left in 1998, CPH was virtually debt-free and its only assets were its pastoral properties, the Perisher ski resort and its stake in PBL – the owner of Channel Nine, ACP and film production company New Regency. Its net worth was over $2.5 billion. Powers had developed a close bond with Kerry Packer, who did not want him to leave the company. His relationship with James was more distant, but during Powers' tenure James became a PBL executive for the first time. James later told friends later that Powers did a better job than he gave him credit for at the time.

Powers' exit was not without controversy. Within hours of leaving CPH he had joined the board of Fairfax, of which the Packers then owned a 14.9 per cent stake through an entity called the FXF Trust. Powers started running the FXF Trust and subsequently became chairman of Fairfax, sparking an inquiry by the Australian Broadcasting Authority on whether the Packer family or Powers had breached the Broadcasting Services Act when Powers resigned his positions at CPH and PBL and was financially assisted by Kerry Packer to join the

Fairfax board. The Act prohibited the owner of a TV station from controlling a newspaper in the same city, either directly or through an 'associate'. Both were exonerated.

While Powers' move to Fairfax was a loss for the Packers, they would get something unexpected in return. Before he had joined the Fairfax board, Powers had taken the editor of the Fairfax-owned *Sydney Morning Herald* newspaper, John Alexander, on the *Arctic P* for a weekend in Fiji. When the trip was subsequently reported in the press, Fairfax chief executive Bob Muscat promptly fired Alexander. Following Powers' departure, thirty-year-old James had taken over as chairman of the publicly listed PBL. And he took the chance to pounce on Alexander. 'I hired John Alexander without Dad even meeting him,' James now recalls. 'I rang him up and asked to meet. I offered him the job of running the specialty publishing business of ACP, including *The Bulletin*. He said yes. He and Dad eventually met and Dad liked him immediately and a lot. The specialist magazine titles started doing better. A bit down the track, the ACP CEO Colin Morrison resigned and Dad and I agreed John should become ACP's CEO. ACP started doing much better, and growing and growing.'

While James made the move to hire Alexander, he always knew who was in charge at PBL, remarking in one public statement: 'I'm the boss except when Kerry wants to be the boss.'

Powers went back to America in 2000, where he rejoined Hellman & Friedman as chief executive. James says, 'His record at Hellman & Friedman speaks for itself. It is better than anyone else's in America, and that means the world.' But before Powers returned to America, he was involved in one of the more inglorious moments in the Packer family's corporate history, one that still haunts James to this day.

*

IN MARCH 1999, OUT of left field, CPH launched a $600 million takeover bid for cinema operator Hoyts. The Hoyts board was then chaired by one of Kerry Packer's key advisers, lawyer and investment banker David Gonski, and Powers himself was a director. PBL had been a significant shareholder in rival cinema operator Village Roadshow before cashing out for a handsome profit in 1996, but this was the Packer family's biggest play into the sector. The Hoyts board initially knocked back CPH's $2.03 per share offer, but despite Kerry Packer's concerns about the deal, PBL pushed on. With the urging of Gonski and Powers, eventually PBL – championed by James – won the day when it sweetened the bid price.

The Packers soon realised they had bitten off more than they could chew. Hoyts began to sell off cinemas in Poland, the UK, Germany and Mexico. It then sold its American operations to Regal Entertainment Group for $340 million to concentrate on its Australasian business. 'They paid too much for it [in 1999] and they've been trying to get their money back ever since,' one analyst told Australian Associated Press after the American deal was announced in early 2003.

In December 2005 PBL and West Australian Newspapers (WAN) purchased the company from CPH. Less than two years later, PBL and WAN sold each of their 50 per cent shares in the company to private equity firm Pacific Equity Partners in a deal that valued the company at $440 million. 'Hoyts was a genuine cash-flow business with some problems and has proven it is good over time,' says another analyst who has followed the fortunes of the business.

Hoyts was also an operating business with real cash flows. So it allowed its owner, CPH, to borrow long-term money from the US debt markets. Until that point CPH had been purely regarded as an investment company, which couldn't access debt in those markets.

Looking back, James now reveals for the first time that he considers the Hoyts deal one of the business disasters of his life. He says the deal impaired the CPH balance sheet for six years. 'CPH was debt-free before we bought Hoyts,' he says. 'The reality is CPH's debt, which went up when we bought Hoyts, never came down from that point going forward, even after we sold Hoyts. We were cash-flow negative every year for more than fifteen years.'

Another constant drag on the CPH balance sheet that remained firmly out of the public eye were the huge sums Kerry Packer lost on currency trading and gambling – up to $150 million every year. One year he apparently lost $102 million in five minutes betting on the US dollar–Japanese yen trade. In 1993 alone he reportedly lost $500 million on currency trading. As a former editor of the Packer-owned *Bulletin*, Trevor Sykes, told Michael Stahl for his book *Kerry Packer: Tall tales and true stories*: '[Kerry's] real gambling was on foreign exchange. Some nights he came close to betting the farm on the US dollar against the deutschmark. James was quite petrified by it ... I heard one or two numbers on it and they were so large, it took my breath away.'

But while foreign-exchange trading was a business hobby for Kerry Packer, playing golf and gambling were just for fun. In 1992, with champion golfer Greg Norman by his side, Packer won the AT&T pro-am golf tournament at Pebble Beach, California, the biggest pro-am in the world. In the words of those who saw his performance that day, 'He played unbelievably well.' Kerry also punted millions at the blackjack, poker and baccarat tables of the world's top casinos. He once famously proposed to a Texas millionaire at a Las Vegas casino who was boasting about his wealth, 'Toss you for it.'

James remarked on his father's famed gambling habits in the eulogy he gave at Kerry's memorial service at the Sydney

Opera House in February 2006. 'In many ways he was acting out the fantasies of millions of Australian punters,' he said. 'They were not the only ones awestruck by the size of the bets. So were we!'

In the speech, despite their at times troubled relationship, James spoke of his father in glowing terms. 'My father used to think the word "legend" was tossed around far too often. I want to say today that in the opinion of his family, my father was a legend. My most precious memories are, of course, not about the legend, but about my dad,' he said. 'I have a million small memories that will sustain me through my life … Dad was my mentor and my teacher but, above all, he was my father, and that was my greatest fortune.' Village Roadshow co-chief executive Graham Burke, who was there that day and remains a close friend of James's after enjoying a close friendship with his father, now describes the speech as 'twelve out of ten': 'James gave an amazing, moving speech that day. Afterwards a close circle of us went back to the family home in Bellevue Hill and toasted his father, the great man.'

Peter Barron describes as 'rubbish' the common view that Kerry and James were never happy with each other from the day they started working together at PBL. 'Kerry's view was that if you are going to work in the place, you work in the place. If you get yelled at, you get yelled at. The fact you are his son doesn't come into it. He lets off steam by yelling at people. There were times James found that hard,' he recalls. 'If I had to say what was Kerry's number-one thought about James, it was pride. It didn't stop him yelling at him. And it always influenced him in that he felt he had to train James. He probably felt that more than he should have. But that wasn't because he felt James was inferior.'

'He told me once that he thought James would do a whole lot better than [Kerry] had. He admired his capacity to look beyond the horizon and to look forward, which Kerry was not so good at. He said to me, not once but several times, that [James] was one of the most numerically smart people he had to know. He knew James's capacity to deal with numbers was better than his own.'

Former long-serving Channel Nine boss David Leckie says he saw Kerry's relationship with his son evolve as James became more involved with the family business. 'At first he was very much just the son. Then he became very involved in the business. Kerry really respected that. Yes, he was very tough on James, but was probably reasonably fair,' he says. 'I think Kerry was challenged by James's adaption and understanding of technology and how the world was moving on. James understood the value of the mobile phone as soon as it came out.'

In his speech at his father's memorial service, James also mentioned the darkest days of his father's life flowing from the infamous Costigan Royal Commission, established by the Fraser government in 1980 to investigate criminal activities, including violence, associated with the infamous Painters and Dockers Union. In the process of its investigations, the commission began examining so-called 'bottom of the harbour' tax evasion schemes. Kerry Packer was drawn into the affair in 1984 when extracts of the commission's draft report were leaked to the media alleging that a rich businessman code-named 'the Goanna' was involved in tax evasion and organised crime, including drug trafficking. Kerry subsequently outed himself as the Goanna and vehemently denied the allegations. With the assistance of his legal counsel Malcolm Turnbull, Kerry successfully turned the heat back on the commission, and three years later the allegations were formally dismissed by then federal attorney-general Lionel Bowen.

Turnbull told *Australian Story* in April 2014 how his star client, in his darkest moments during those three years, thought about taking his own life. 'He was becoming increasingly concerned that he could never get out of this thicket of injustice into which he had been flung and that it could result in his company, his family, losing the television licence,' Turnbull said. 'So Kerry was thinking, "Is my family better off without me?", "Am I better off checking out?"'

In his memorial speech, James remarked how his father 'never forgave Mr Costigan'. 'He never could and nor could we,' he said. 'It made [my father] a less trusting person, and I think it had an impact upon his health.' Now reflecting upon that time, he reiterates that his father was 'permanently bruised' by the affair. 'That was an experience that scarred him deeply and scarred him forever. It wasn't so much tall poppy [syndrome], rather that an innocent man can be convicted,' he says. 'I am not always the person who said Kerry was right and wonderful. But on Costigan he was innocent, and the things they were saying about him were pretty horrific.' He reveals that his father would even ask him if he had been teased at school about the affair. 'He spoke to me about it enough for me to know it was incredibly painful for him,' James says.

Publisher Richard Walsh, who worked for Kerry Packer for twenty years, has previously commented that his former boss felt the mud 'never quite came off him' after Costigan, despite being exonerated, while Phillip Adams has remarked how the Costigan affair made Kerry Packer feel 'like poison' to those around him.

But history was to repeat itself. A decade and a half later, his son would be made to look the same to the public eye after the spectacular collapse of a fledgling telecommunications group he backed with Lachlan Murdoch named One.Tel.

TWO

The One.Tel Curse

O n Saturday 2 June 2001, an intimate gathering took place away from prying eyes, deep in the bowels of Melbourne's Crown Casino. Never in the storied history of the Packer family had the company's business executives gathered together for a day – let alone a whole weekend – to actually talk to one another. Kerry Packer, especially, had never been one for executive 'love-ins'. Yet on this weekend, all the senior people from PBL's divisions – names like David Leckie, John Alexander, Daniel Petre and David Gyngell – had flown to Melbourne for the company's inaugural two-day conference.

The Packer empire had always been a top-down organisation. Kerry and his father before him were old-fashioned 'my way or the highway' tycoons: dominating figures barking orders, making the big decisions, demanding that their executives do as they were told. But times were changing. James Packer had begun to step into his father's shoes. He had been made chairman of PBL three years earlier and given the freedom to make his own decisions.

In March 2001, in a move straight out of his father's ruthless playbook, he had defied the wishes of the investment community and sacked the company's well-respected chief executive, Nick Falloon. The swiftness of Falloon's sacking by the heir to the Packer fortune showed the apple had not fallen far from the tree. But James's decision to replace Falloon – a trained accountant – with investment banker Peter Yates showed he was of a different generation in a business world that was rapidly changing. James wanted PBL to become more aggressive and thought Falloon was stifling that ambition, especially through his resistance to the company putting more money into the fledgling phone company One.Tel. But Yates also came from the Macquarie Bank culture, where conferences designed to bring together the company's divisions and executives were commonplace. His was a mantra of structure and process. The seeds had been sown for a cultural revolution inside PBL, which led to the inaugural Crown weekend conference.

Yet five days before he was due to co-convene the forum with Yates, James Packer's world was suddenly turned upside down. On 28 May 2001, One.Tel went broke.

The following weekend James had to stand in front of his entire executive team and talk about PBL. He felt like a laughing stock. Years earlier he had been introduced over lunch by One.Tel CEO Jodee Rich to one of the most important executives in the audience that day, Daniel Petre. In the months after that meeting, Packer told friends that Petre saw – more than anyone else he had known – how the internet was going to change the world. Petre went on to found online companies ecorp and Ninemsn for the Packers, helping them make hundreds of millions of dollars from the internet. But over the course of that weekend at Crown in mid 2001, Petre decided he'd had enough of being second-guessed by an avowed internet sceptic like Kerry Packer. He discreetly approached his chairman and resigned.

James was completely broken. He had been worth a cool $200 million when One.Tel shares surged to be worth $13.55 in December 1998, hailed as a self-made man who had escaped from the imposing shadow of his father at the age of only thirty-one. In a subsequent court hearing following the collapse of One.Tel, its founder, Jodee Rich, claimed James once told him, 'Jodee, I love you. You have bought me my independence.' As James rode the One.Tel wave, he overcapitalised his luxury three-level apartment in the Sydney beachside suburb of Bondi, living well beyond his means. When One.Tel crashed he was left with a $20 million bank overdraft, which was covered by his father. Suddenly he was worth nothing. His newly earned freedom from his father was gone.

*

KERRY'S RESPONSE TO THE One.Tel fiasco was certainly a case of the father giving the son a lesson in Packer-style corporate leadership. Kerry took care of James's personal debts resulting from the collapse. But he made his son pay dearly for the public humiliation of PBL booking a writedown of $327 million on its One.Tel investment. PBL's partner in One.Tel, News Corporation, took a $400 million hit from the collapse. But its founder, Rupert Murdoch, made sure his son, Lachlan – who had sat with James Packer on One.Tel's board – wore almost none of the public flack that followed the collapse. By contrast, Kerry Packer's brutal treatment of his son in the eighteen months following the One.Tel collapse has been extensively documented in numerous books about the disaster.

For a start, Kerry resumed running PBL in a much more public and authoritarian way. In the months after the collapse,

Kerry told a bunch of PBL investors invited to lunch at Channel Nine's Willoughby headquarters in Sydney that One.Tel had been a 'fuck-up'. Then federal treasurer Peter Costello reveals he got 'particularly close' to James after the collapse and saw the profound impact the father's return to PBL was having upon the son. When Costello was in Sydney, he would often drop by James's Bondi apartment. 'For him that was a very difficult period. A lot of people who he thought were friends turned out not to be friends. I can remember a number of conversations where we talked about what had happened. Kerry stepping back into the business was extremely hard for him,' Costello says.

Yet former Packer family adviser Peter Barron claims Kerry Packer only ever had one conversation with his son about One.Tel. He says Kerry even once privately acknowledged that he had lost millions of dollars more during his corporate career. 'He told me, "Don't tell James, but I have made bigger mistakes than that in my lifetime,"' Barron recalls. 'He was irritated James wanted to do One.Tel his way. But he was also of the view, not very openly, that James might have been more right than wrong. When Frank Packer was in television, it drained their resources. At one stage Frank borrowed money off his secretary to survive. But it was about the future. Kerry could see the point of being in a business like One.Tel where you had to look forward over the horizon. So he was half reluctant to shut it down. But he just couldn't get his head around it. He always felt if they pushed on, it could have been a good business for them, but he just couldn't bring himself to put more money in.'

Peter Yates also offers a unique perspective on the strained relationship between father and son in the wake of the disaster. 'I'll never forget one of the most emotional interactions between Kerry and James was the morning of the decision to put One.Tel into receivership. We'd had David Gonski come in [to Park Street] and give us his views on what James and Kerry needed to do,' Yates recalls. 'The only thing [Kerry] was concerned about was James. Kerry actually started crying, as did James, because they were just so concerned for one another. I'd been [at PBL] for six or seven weeks, and I'd just seen headbutting and an unmanageable relationship, and then there was a sudden moment where all that was washed away. It was this constant competition, but there is a moment where the competition ends and a reality of consequence suddenly unfolds.'

Gonski – who, despite repeated reassurance-seeking glares from Kerry across the table, hardly said anything in the meetings that day and instead kept his own counsel until the conclusion – agrees with Yates's assessment of the emotions on display. 'It was one of the first times I saw absolute recognition by father and son of their strong feelings for each other,' he now says.

But with One.Tel's demise, suddenly Yates had lost his most important ally. PBL insiders were pushing hard for James to be replaced as the company's chairman. His father was torn between an innate concern for his son and his enjoyment of being back as number one in the company. He had never believed in what James called the digital revolution. 'I remember Kerry once taking me with James and Lachlan through the One.Tel experience at their offices in Sydney,' remembers former Victorian premier Jeff Kennett. 'When we had finished, Kerry sat down next to a window, out of earshot of the rest, and said to me: "Son, this will never work."'

Yet after the One.Tel collapse, Yates stood firm against the push to oust James as PBL chairman. 'I always believed that if James had resigned as chairman he wouldn't come back, because there was no simple path to get him back. I fought as hard as I could against that,' Yates says. 'I was adamant that

James didn't lose his title, even though he was out. Because if he would have actually been formally removed, he would never come back.'

And James was certainly out. He initially disappeared for nearly two months, much of it in Europe on a holiday with his new wife, Jodhi Meares. After a short reappearance in Sydney, looking overweight, James then fled with his wife to America, encouraged by the actor Tom Cruise, who had befriended him during the filming of the hit movie *Mission: Impossible II* in Sydney. In America Cruise introduced James and Jodhi to Scientology, and they buried themselves in copies of the book *Dianetics*, the philosophical manifesto of American pulp science-fiction writer L Ron Hubbard, the father of the religion. According to its official website, Scientology is a 'religion that offers a precise path leading to a complete and certain understanding of one's true spiritual nature and one's relationship to self, family, groups, Mankind, all life forms, the material universe, the spiritual universe and the Supreme Being'. Some friends have said it 'saved James'.

Jodhi now agrees with them. 'There are some really insightful ways to view life and handle life and that is really what Scientology is ... particularly if you are going through a difficult time,' she says. 'I had not heard of Scientology before [Cruise introduced her to it]. I wasn't christened. I had a very liberal, free-thinking mother who didn't christen us on purpose. She believed it was our right to pursue our own belief system. It was interesting to me to go and look at Scientology. There was some really interesting stuff there and there were some really great people. It was really quite helpful. I really had a strong need to understand things deeply at a theological level.'

She rejects claims that in the wake of her marriage break-up, the group's doctrines fuelled her insecurities and made it harder to get over James. 'No, I don't think that is right. It was separate things,' she says. So is she still a devotee? 'No. I don't think that organised religion is my thing. James has never said he regrets it — we talk about it sometimes. But I don't think that sort of organised religion is for him either.'

James told Pamela Williams and me in an interview for *The Australian Financial Review Magazine* in 2006 that Scientology had helped give him a better outlook on life. Jeff Kennett remembers visiting a Scientologist facility with James outside Melbourne where he was struck by James's devotion to the religion. 'I saw a time when he was under the weather, early on, and he and I went up to the hills. We got a helicopter and went up to see the Scientologists, to try to help them to help other people. James wanted to try to get them more funding,' Kennett recalls.

James got so close to Scientology devotee Tom Cruise that he scored an extras part on a horse in the charge at the end of the actor's movie *The Last Samurai*. James now says Cruise was 'as good a friend as a person could hope to have' during that period. 'We spent from December 26 to January 3 together every year from 2001/2002 till 2006/2007 at his house at Telluride [a ski resort in Colorado],' he says. 'Most importantly, in 2002 he put me back together. He came to Dad's funeral, came to my wedding to Erica, and Erica and I went to his wedding with Katie. It's his choice that we aren't friends any more.'

Contradicting comments that have been made by others, James says his father was very supportive of his relationship with Scientology in 2001–02. 'I don't want to say my father was a huge proponent of Scientology for the sake of it. My dad saw how damaged I was [by the One.Tel collapse]. It took my father longer than perhaps it should have to see that,' James says. 'But after he realised I was seriously floundering, then I went away for a couple of months in 2002 to America to do

Scientology courses. I spent a significant amount of time with Tom Cruise and he was incredibly kind and generous to me. And he would actually ring my father and manage my father. The biggest movie star in the world – people take their calls – Tom would ring up Dad and say, "James is a good person and he's getting better." So when I came back from America, Dad saw that I was a lot better. He accepted that if Scientology was helping me, he wasn't going to say anything. He was grateful to it for what he saw it was doing to me.'

James says it took his father a year to realise he was depressed and emotionally exhausted – or, as he puts it, 'in a bad way' after the One.Tel collapse. Friends even feared he was in danger of taking his own life. Jeff Kennett recalls, 'I know when One.Tel collapsed, I ran into James down at the Capital Golf Course [in Melbourne]. He was on his own. He was absolutely desolate. He said to me, "I feel like a general without an army." Those words have stuck with me. He got into an awful spot then. He was absolutely suicidal at times.'

To rub salt into the wounds, in August 2002 Kerry sold PBL's share in the online-retailing platform eBay for $120 million without consulting his son. It angered James. Since then eBay has gone on to be worth billions.

So I ask James why it took his father so long to realise his predicament. He lights a cigarette and takes a long pause before answering slowly. '[The late former Nine Network CEO] Sam Chisholm had a great line about my father – that Kerry is a great bunch of guys. The reality is Dad could have noticed sooner. But when he did notice, he was more forgiving than I had the right to hope for or expect.'

Peter Barron puts it another way. 'Kerry was never of the view that he was too hard or unreasonable on James. But there were times when he did not understand the impact of his actions on his son.'

*

JAMES RETURNED TO SYDNEY from America for good on 1 October 2002. By then his marriage to Jodhi Meares was well and truly over. James agrees it took Jodhi more than a year to summon up the courage to walk away. 'That's true – in a way we stayed friends all the way through it,' he says. 'I was catatonic, that's how I was. I don't blame Jodhi at all for leaving me. She has behaved incredibly well every day since then. She has been an incredibly valued friend to me every day since then.'

Jodhi now says she and James 'always wanted to see one another happy. When we decided that we needed to go our separate ways, it was amicable. When we were separating we had dinner every week. It was deeply painful because we loved each other – we still do – but it was the right thing to do at the time,' she says. 'I wish I had the insight to be more helpful to James but I just didn't. I just really didn't understand what was going on.'

James's return to Sydney also provided both a challenge and opportunity for Peter Yates, who had for the first time in PBL's history engaged external advisers to help write a strategy document for the company. In 2003 Yates also succeeded in convening a second 'love-in' of PBL executives, this time at the Packer family's 25,000-hectare Ellerston property near Scone, north of Sydney.

Ellerston had been a Packer family icon since 1972 when Sir Frank Packer bought 40,500 hectares of land in the area. That was later pared back before his death to around 9000 hectares. After Sir Frank's passing, Kerry bought several adjoining properties to rebuild the family's landholdings and, after he sold the Nine Network to Alan Bond for $1.05 billion in 1987, embarked on a spending spree to turn Ellerston into a luxury retreat. He added several small homesteads to the main thirteen-bedroom house as well as a pub, restaurant, general store, cinema, swimming pool, a school for the children of the 100 or so staff and, later, a Greg Norman–designed golf course and a go-kart track.

Yates recalls, 'And so James arrived back in Australia. The idea was that he would come back at the first Ellerston conference, receive the budgets and all of the CEOs as the returning chairman, and away we would go.' But he saw warning signs in the demeanour of James when he showed up to Ellerston the night before the conference. Then, during the countdown to proceedings kicking off on the Saturday morning, there was a last-minute hitch.

Years earlier Kerry had purchased six spindly ultralight aircraft that were based at Ellerston. Few guests or staff were qualified to fly them, but James was. 'James was late, and in fact we were waiting for him. And the reason he was late was that he decided to go and fly his light plane, this absolutely bizarre bloody thing,' Yates recalls. 'And we're all sitting around at the conference. I told everyone to be on time. And James was not there because he was flying around in his ultralight. And I'm thinking to myself, "James, what are you doing? Here is your moment!"' But Yates soon realised the reasoning behind the apparent madness. 'When he turned up I realised that he was actually just frightened, trying to get his head together. Working out that if he went in there, he was going to now have to take on the responsibility of running the place properly. There was no going back from the moment,' Yates says.

History now records that James did indeed front the meeting and return as PBL chairman, not just in body, but also in spirit. With the pressure valve released that afternoon at Ellerston, he joined fellow PBL executives in several rounds of golf. There were also helicopter rides, darts games and wine tasting. Kerry even took to the go-kart track. Garry Linnell, editor of the Packer-owned *Bulletin* in 2002–06, recalled in Michael Stahl's book *Kerry Packer: Tall tales and true stories* how his boss had done a fifty-something-second lap time: 'Kerry walked over and I said, "So, what sort of time should I be expecting to do per lap?" And he said in his characteristic politically incorrect style, "Anything over sixty seconds, son, and you should be wearing a skirt."' And in the early hours of Saturday morning, despite his ailing health, Kerry was still cracking jokes around the dart board.

James was also supported in his recovery by other friends at the time, including global private equity doyen Guy Hands. Hands had lunched with Kerry Packer on several occasions during the late 1990s when he was looking at setting up his investment group Terra Firma. Through that association he got to know Kerry's son. 'James became a friend. We just got to know each other. We have known each other since,' Hands says. 'I saw him through that period. It was a very tough time for him. I thought he handled it as well as anyone could be expected to. People always underestimate the pressure that comes with having a very successful, strong parent. With One.Tel, he took responsibility, he tried to be as positive through it as he could. It wasn't easy. He didn't get a lot of support. I felt very sorry for him during the period. I'm sure I told him a number of times, "Don't let the bastards get you down." But all you can really do for someone going through something like that is just be a sounding board for them.'

Another who tried to help James was Hollywood movie producer Arnon Milchan, who was a good friend of Kerry's. 'In 2002 I was finding life difficult. Dad was understandably running the company. I would sit in my office all day long and sometimes find it hard to do anything,' James now reveals. 'Whenever I went to LA after we invested in New Regency,

Arnon would take me out. He loved having fun. He'd always bring along a movie star or a famous director. He would always make me feel very welcome. We had gotten to know each other, by that time, well. He made sure he kept in touch. We would talk on the phone and catch up. He was obviously aware of One.Tel.

'So when we were speaking one day in late 2003, Arnon said to me, "Come and live in LA." I said to him, "What would I do?" He said, "Come and be president of New Regency." He said he would pay me US$1.5 million and that he would smooth it over with Dad. I believed it was real – other things Arnon said he would do, he did. His actions were almost always as good as his words. I decided not to accept his kind offer. It would have been the wrong thing all round. But I was very grateful. Then I was grateful for the way he introduced me to Israel and tried to help me in Hollywood.'

*

FORMER FOXTEL CHIEF EXECUTIVE Kim Williams, who knew Kerry Packer and has long enjoyed a good relationship with his son, describes Kerry as an 'extremely hard man' who 'wanted his pound of flesh from James because of the One.Tel outcome'. Williams says, 'He seemed never to be reconciled with that. He would always look for points of weakness in James and then move to exploit them.'

Kerry was never a fan of pay television. In stark contrast to his son, he hated it, only accepting it in his dying days. Williams recalls, 'I remember when I went to the first lunch I had with Kerry, [PBL director] Ashok [Jacob] and James. James came in and made a reference – jokingly – to whether he should sit in the corner or at the table. Kerry replied with words to the effect of, "Don't be a smart arse, sit down." But the tension in the room was palpable. Then when I had sessions with Kerry about the Foxtel business when James was in the room, these sessions went for hours and James would just quietly leave the room after some time.'

James agrees: 'It wasn't easy, those years with Dad. He did not believe in the internet and he did not believe in China.' But in hindsight, James says he has grown to appreciate how smart his father really was. 'I didn't used to think Dad was brighter than I am, but I have come to the conclusion that he must have been,' he says.

Packer family adviser and former Labor senator Graham Richardson says there was always some strain in the relationship between father and son, but stresses that they were never estranged. 'Kerry gave James some unnecessary bollockings in front of other people. I saw it happen two or three times. It wasn't pleasant. But his father was a volatile character.' Richardson adds that he only once saw James really abused by his father. 'He was very upset. Otherwise James knew it was just part of the territory. They are different people. The thing that links them is they are both very clever. James has an extraordinary mind.'

Outsiders, newcomers to PBL and attendees of the company's annual general meetings were always surprised to see James unselfconsciously kiss his father, especially in public at the annual general meetings. But Richardson disputes assertions Kerry Packer was 'abusive' towards his son, as does James himself. 'My old man could be very tough and very unreasonable. He also had moments of incredible generosity. And he did all he could for me and gave me all the chances he could give me. My father was terrifying when he wanted to be. Terrifying. He terrified me to a point where I was physically affected. But he never hit me,' James says, before quickly correcting himself. 'Actually he did once, when I

1000 per cent deserved it. He used a belt and whacked me over the bum three times. He went close to hitting me a few times. And that was terrifying,' he adds, taking another puff of a cigarette. 'I don't know how much, if at all, I was damaged by those instances. But be under no misunderstanding, he was a wonderful caring father who deserved the status of living legend that he was accorded.'

I ask James whether he thinks the way he was treated by his father had any impact later in life, particularly in the tough times. 'That is an interesting question,' he replies before a pause and another puff of a cigarette. 'I think it's a complicated answer. I'm trying to give you an honest answer.' There is another long pause before he replies: 'I think possibly. I don't think definitely, but I think possibly. I think in One.Tel I put myself under a lot of pressure and I just overloaded. I think I had almost an obligation to show how much it was hurting me before I was going to be accepted back into the fold. I think that in other areas it was definitely more of an impact. My father lived an incredibly big life. I saw a lot of things as a result of being his son. And in terms of my relationships, Gretes [as he calls his sister, Gretel] and I had a very rough time settling Dad's will. But that's behind us and we both love each other and are moving forward.'

James doesn't quite say it, but it has been said many times that Kerry led a very 'Roman' life. There was much about Packer's lifestyle that ordinary people would have found quite shocking: his bad temper, his language, his extravagant gambling and his extramarital relationships. James certainly grew up in a world utterly removed from what might be considered 'normal' for the times. James had to accept things about his father that must have been confusing as one of his children.

Shortly after Kerry's death Kate McClymont revealed in *The Sydney Morning Herald* that he had bequeathed more than $10 million to his mistress Julie Trethowan, who was twenty years his junior. Melbourne-born Trethowan, who ran Kerry's Hyde Park fitness club at the base of his 54 Park Street headquarters in Sydney, was also left a home in the city's northern beachside suburb of Whale Beach. She still lists her address as the famed Sydney harbourside Toft Monks building in Elizabeth Bay – one of the city's most prestigious addresses – where the Packers once owned four apartments. Alan Jones remembers attending a number of awkward dinners with Kerry at Toft Monks. '[Kerry] was there and Julie was there, and I'd be there. I would go thinking I was just having dinner with Kerry and Julie,' Jones recalls. But James would also often turn up. 'I always felt uncomfortable that James was there. He wanted to please his father.'

Jones says James, to his credit, still maintains a friendship with Trethowan. She has visited him in Aspen and was there as recently as early September 2018, when Crown's executive team paid Packer a visit for a day of meetings. 'The one thing that he admires about Julie is that since Kerry's death, she's unheard of. She never has made a false move, ever, in any way that might prejudice Kerry, Ros or James,' he says. 'James always had a problem with Julie, because of that awkward environment there at Toft Monks. But since his father's death, Julie has shown herself to have a bit of class and has won a lot of respect from a lot of people. James actually incorporates her into his world. This is his way of saying, "Well, you could have poured shit all over us and you've said nothing,"' Jones says.

Other family friends claim Trethowan even encouraged Kerry to return home to Bellevue Hill from Toft Monks for his final days, which won her 'brownie points' with the family. 'And to be fair to Kerry,' one says, 'he never ever asked James to pick a side.'

In his book *Who Killed Channel 9?* Gerald Stone claimed Kerry also fell madly in love with Ita Buttrose when the pair worked closely on the launch of women's magazine *Cleo*. The book subtly claims that Kerry and his wife, Ros, experienced the occasional 'difficult patch' through their forty-year 'European style' marriage and that Ros tolerated his 'outside adventures, provided they were discreet'. Alan Jones says Ros Packer was 'very sensible and mature about all of that'.

Friends have often wondered if James has struggled in his own relationships with women because of the things he saw and experienced growing up. 'I think all of that affected James very much. I don't think there's any doubt about that,' Jones says. 'I think that it's not just that. In many ways it was a fairly brutal childhood. Obviously, there is a tendency with people with wealth to indulge people. We'll have the best cricket coach and we'll have the best ... That's not love. That's not affection, that's not hugging, that's not caring, that's not doing the simple things together. And [James] never had that. So, in a way he most probably had a very distorted view of affection and its rewards. If you stand back and look at it. And so, he would think he was in love but may not have been. And only when he had absolutely, pardon the expression, completely fucked up, did he realise that it was love and he's missed it.'

*

VILLAGE ROADSHOW CO-CHIEF EXECUTIVE Graham Burke says James Packer sat at his father's elbow and soaked up all of this wisdom by example. 'I can remember meetings in Kerry's office where he would regale me for hours and James, at probably twenty, sat there quietly listening,' Burke says. He describes James, whom he has known for thirty years, as 'a unique and remarkable human being like his father. He has intellect that is extraordinary for its speed, and its ability to recall is almost a phenomenon. He becomes single-minded and full of purpose when he is on a mission. Of all the young executives I have met, he is up there as a world-class CEO. However, James's highest quality is his loyalty. He is loyal to a fault to his friends and always with extraordinary generosity of spirit.'

Burke says James is a combination of both his father and mother. 'He has Ros's grace and Kerry's dynamite,' he says. But James thinks he is more like one than the other. 'I think I might be more like my mum. Gretes is probably more like Dad. Mum has a real resilience to her. She has much more resilience than I do,' he says. 'My mother has made a real life for herself since my father's passing, and for that she gets another enormous credit.' He says his relationship his mother is 'very good. She is a very loving mother. Very supportive. Mum is simply wonderful. She loves me and she loves Gretes.'

But Ros Packer still worries about her son, to whom she and others refer simply as 'JP'. In recent years she has been a regular visitor to Aspen and to the villa her son rents at the One & Only resort at the Mexican seaside mecca of Cabo San Lucas. When James went public in March 2018 about his mental health battles, his mother flew to America the next morning and spent a fortnight visiting him at a clinic in Boston. Graham Richardson says, 'She is a great lady. She is pretty special. She does worry about James. I think over the past year or two she has witnessed the estrangement of the two children. She loves James. She is a good mum.'

There is one memory of his father from his last month on earth that James will cherish forever. In early December 2005, James was on the stand in a courtroom for his cross-examination by the liquidator of One.Tel. He was in the witness box for twelve days. 'My father had gone to Argentina because he didn't want to put any more pressure on me. It was three weeks before he died but none of us realised how sick he was. I thought he had at least two years or more in him,' James recalls.

'Jodee Rich's legal strategy was to try and prove that Dad stopped me from putting more money into One.Tel when I had wanted to. I was asked this question on the stand: "Mr Packer, didn't you say to Mr Rich that you wished your father was dead?" I weakly replied, "No." It was front-page news: "James Packer denies wishing his father would die." Dad read all the clippings in Argentina. I didn't hear from him for a few days. I feared the worst. About five days later Dad rang me when I got off the stand. He said, "Son, the lawyers tell me you did great." He never mentioned [the headline]. He died two weeks later.'

When the end for Kerry was drawing near, Alan Jones received a call from his son. 'I remember James ringing and saying, "I think Dad's going to die. You better come." I was down at the farm,' he says of his property at Fitzroy Falls in the NSW Southern Highlands. 'When I got there, God, Kerry was funny. I walked into [Royal Prince Alfred Hospital]. He was only five days from death or something. I was on my own. I said, "How are you feeling?"

'"How the fuck do you think I feel?" he replied. "How many people do I employ when I can't get a fucking pie!" Ros then walked through the door. I said to her, "He wants a pie."

'She looked at me and said to him, "Well, darling, you know that you're not supposed to eat pies." But we ended up getting him one. You know, all he wanted was a pie!'

Kerry was also advised by his doctors in his final months to drink red wine for his heart. It is now folklore among his close friends that he ordered some fine Bordeaux wine to be delivered to his hospital bedside and for the first time in more than four decades, drank some.

When Kerry died on Boxing Day 2005, James was just two years older than his father had been when he inherited Sir Frank Packer's empire. In an emotional interview on Channel Seven's *Sunday Night* program in 2013, James spoke of the 'beautiful call' he received from his father in the days before his death. During the hour-long conversation, Kerry told his son he should carve his own path in life. 'Twenty-four hours later, his doctor rang me and said, "Get on a plane, he's only got twenty-four hours to live,"' James told *Sunday Night*, breaking into tears as he recounted the conversation. 'I got home and held his hand and he passed.'

The sunny afternoon James spent at Ellerston in late 2005 will be forever etched in his mind. With his mother and sister by his side, the 38-year-old looked on in silence as his father was buried, his grave nestled in a stand of elm trees next to one of his beloved polo fields. It is now adorned by a 9-metre-high bronze sculpture of a Greek horse's head, inscribed with the words: 'I will look beyond for a distant land.'

Since Kerry's death, James has sold most of his father's so-called collectibles, including interests in cattle stations, ski resorts, cosmetics companies, even the family's legendary Park Street building in Sydney, all in the name of reducing debt.

James told Christine Lacy and me for *The Weekend Australian* in late 2015, in an interview to mark the tenth anniversary of his father's passing, that being a father to three children had given him 'an appreciation of what Dad was trying to achieve and why sometimes he was so hard – he just wanted the best for us'. Kerry summed it up in one of his only wide-ranging media interviews, with broadcaster Terry Lane in 1978. 'I want them to know only one thing, really – that I adore them. I'd do anything for them and they know that. They know they're loved. They're excited and happy to see me as I am to see them. That doesn't mean I don't put them over my knee – I do, but I hope fairly and never in anger,' he said. 'It's a belief that when you've done something wrong you've got to pay a price. Then we talk about it after it happens and say, "It's paid now, but let's learn the lesson and not do it again."'

David Gonski says he doesn't subscribe to the view that James is the way he is today because of his father. 'We are a composite of our genetics, our circumstances, our education, etcetera. James has inherited from his father an incredibly quick mind. He also got a lot of the caring side from his mother. He is able to deal with people in an incredibly caring way and he got that from Ros,' he says. 'I think Kerry did give James business experiences when he was young that he would not have got if he was making his way in normal life and in business. He taught James a lot of the way he thinks in business.'

But Peter Yates says James will forever struggle to escape his father's shadow, that growing up with wealth and benchmarking his achievements against those of his father will always shape his identity. Money will be his ultimate scorecard on life. 'If you arrive on the planet with wealth, you have to build an identity, and the patriarch or the matriarch who owns the wealth really struggles to allow the child to build their own identity, regardless of how much you love them, pat them on the back or encourage them. At the end of the day, building your own identity is really really hard,' Yates says. 'How can you not be impacted if your father is one of the wealthiest men in the country or one of the most powerful men in the country? You are always impacted by the environment in which you are born. You just can't deny it.'

THREE

The Pen is Mightier than the Sword

JAMES PACKER AND LACHLAN Murdoch were born on the same day of the year, 8 September, four years apart. Raised in the shadows of their famous fathers, they both spent time as jackaroos – Packer, the older of the two, in the Northern Territory and Murdoch at Boonoke, then one of his family's stations in New South Wales. They grew up watching the battles between their families that traced back to a famous brawl in 1960 when Sir Frank Packer was trying to take over the Anglican Press printing plant, one of the most strategically important in Sydney.

Sir Frank wanted to use Anglican to take on Rupert Murdoch's Cumberland Newspaper Group. But Anglican's owner, Francis James, refused to sell. Sir Frank would not take no for an answer and sent his burly sons, Kerry and Clyde, with a gang of thugs in a late-night raid on Anglican to forcibly take control of the premises, which they duly did. When Rupert Murdoch found out, he sent in his own midnight mercenaries to wrest it back, leaving Kerry – an amateur boxer – with black eyes and a badly swollen face. Clyde was hit in his backside with a dart. 'Knight's son in city brawl', *The Daily Mirror*'s front-page headline screamed the next morning, carrying a colourful picture of Clyde in battle.

It set the scene for decades of power struggles between the Packer and Murdoch families for control of Australia's newspaper, magazine and television industries. The rivalry even became the subject of an Australian mini-series, aptly titled *Power Games: The Packer-Murdoch Story*, which screened on the Nine Network in 2013. But when they were both in their twenties, James and Lachlan decided to put aside the tribalism of their shared history and make their own together.

Ironically, their friendship was forged in a battle to the death between their fathers for control of the winter football code known in New South Wales and Queensland as the 'working man's sport', rugby league. It was a battle for broadcasting rights that would define the evolution of pay television in Australia. Galaxy, the nation's first pay-TV provider, launched its broadcasting on Australia Day 1995. The same year a joint venture between News Limited, the local subsidiary of the Murdochs' News Corporation, and the then government-owned Telstra launched a pay-TV operation known as Foxtel. In Australia, News wanted to replicate its strategy of using exclusive sport to open up pay-TV markets, as it had done with soccer in the UK and the NFL in America. But the stumbling block was an existing seven-year $80-million rights agreement between the Australian Rugby League and the Packers' Nine Network. Nine claimed the deal covered both the free and pay-TV rights to broadcast rugby league, and it on-sold the pay rights to Optus Vision, the then fledgling pay-TV service of Telstra's telco rival Optus.

In response to being locked out of rugby league, on 1 April 1995 the Murdoch-backed Super League made its infamous raid on the cream of the nation's playing talent, triggering the most tumultuous period in the game's history. James Packer, who had just become chief executive of PBL when the war broke out, was at its epicentre. The Brisbane, Canberra, Cronulla, Canterbury, Penrith, North Queensland, Auckland and Perth clubs all quickly defected to Murdoch's rebel league, which was broadcast on Foxtel. Balmain, Gold Coast, Illawarra, Manly, Newcastle, Norths, Parramatta, South Queensland, Souths, St George, Sydney City and Wests stayed loyal to the Packer-backed Australian Rugby League, which was broadcast on Optus Vision. While News Limited had gained a head start in signing players, the PBL counterattack, run by James Packer, then Nine Network boss David Leckie, and celebrated former coaches and players Bob Fulton and Phil Gould, had surprising success. 'The legendary league coach Jack Gibson was renowned for saying, "Done well, played good." And I reckon James did it in spades,' Leckie now says of James's role in the counterattack.

The battle for signatures left a relatively even match between the Super League and ARL teams when they took the field for rival competitions in 1997. ARL chairman Ken Arthurson was under enormous pressure to fold and reach a resolution with News and Super League, but he pushed back because of the relationship he had with Kerry Packer – he was both a friend and a colleague. 'One of the things they agreed among themselves was that they were in it together and forever,' James Packer now recalls.

While James was CEO of PBL at the time, his father remained active in the business and Brian Powers was still chairman of the company. But James and Peter Barron soon realised that the emotion of the battle with Murdoch was overriding Kerry's sanity. 'What became apparent to Peter Barron – a close friend of Dad's and a valued adviser – and me was that we were never going to beat News. It had become very personal. Rupert had said that he was going to win and that he would win. Rupert had even made some unflattering remarks about my father, which cut close to the bone for Dad,' James says. 'Dad knew my view and, in one of my rare acts of bravery towards my father, one day I went into his office and said, "Do you want the good news or the bad news? The good news is News is losing $4 for every $1 we are losing. The bad news is we go broke first." And that was not well received.'

Peter Barron recalls that Powers and the PBL management were convinced that the Packer camp would win. 'Brian was the guy that Kerry talked to every day about the business. They were all for the war. But James couldn't see the point. Kerry wasn't interested in telling Powers and management "No". So James had to have a substantial argument with management on it,' he says.

James then made the calculated decision to begin reaching out to Lachlan, which helped neutralise the ego battle between the PBL and News management teams. 'To a significant extent it is where Lachlan and I became friends,' James says.

Indeed Lachlan says a friendship actually grew out of their enmity. 'We both fought each other and then we worked together. It showed each other the strengths we have when we are enemies and then highlighted our ability to cooperate. The Packers – Kerry and James – have worked out pretty quickly historically if they can bully people and treat them as their enemy or whether they should work with people. We showed through Super League we can be formidable enemies.'

They started catching up for casual lunches and soon came to a meeting of minds that a peace had to be brokered. Barron recalls, 'Lachlan and James couldn't see the sense to the war. They could talk, and they talked long before a peace deal was signed. What they agreed about was both sides were discounting the value of the product and neither of them was getting anywhere.'

From that point the media scions played a significant and historic role in bringing their fathers and companies back from a state of war. After just one season of parallel competitions, the two sides agreed to come together in December 1997 under the National Rugby League (NRL) partnership. But the ARL and its loyalists believed James and his father had sold them out to News and Foxtel, and it was years before James could watch a rugby league game again. It took more than a decade and a half, until October 2014, for James to agree to buy an interest in the South Sydney Rabbitohs league team from entrepreneur Peter Holmes à Court. James now co-owns the team with his good friend actor Russell Crowe. 'I never really went to a league game after we resolved Super League. Phil Gould didn't speak to me for two years. [Former ARL CEO John] Quayle, Arthurson and Dad never really spoke again. Bob Fulton has never spoken to me again,' James says.

As part of the Super League truce, Nine agreed to broadcast the NRL games on free-to-air TV and Foxtel acquired the pay-TV rights. News Limited agreed to split its shareholding in Foxtel in two, giving PBL an option to buy a 25 per cent share in the company, with Telstra retaining the remaining 50 per cent. PBL was also given a similar option over half of News's holding in the Fox Sports group of pay-TV sports channels. Despite resistance from Kerry Packer, the PBL board agreed to exercise both options in October 1998. 'The resolution enabled us to come in to Foxtel. If Super League had not been resolved, Foxtel would never have been a chance of happening,' James says.

Along with the purchase of Crown Melbourne at a similar time, PBL's Foxtel investment provided James with an important win in the battle of wills with his father. Kerry had a strong emotional attachment to free-to-air television and to the Nine Network in particular. He seriously believed until his dying days that Australians would never actually pay to watch TV. But James now says that with then PBL chief executive Nick Falloon's help, the Foxtel deal got done. 'Foxtel was a deal that Nick and I negotiated and got done from the PBL side, and Nick was fundamental in getting it through the PBL board,' he says. 'Dad at the start didn't believe in Foxtel. But he let Nick and me do it.' Telstra, the Packers and the Murdochs endured almost a decade of heavy losses before Foxtel started making money in late 2005, just before Kerry Packer's death.

Falloon and James Packer later famously fell out over the former's opposition to PBL's investment with News Limited in One.Tel, the first deal James and Lachlan genuinely did together. Falloon declined to be interviewed for this book, but those familiar with his thinking at the time say he always believed that had One.Tel been managed properly, it could have been a good business. He also thought buying into the fledgling telco would be a good investment for a private company, not the publicly listed PBL. 'Nick never thought it was a case of him being right and James being wrong, it was more complex than that,' one observer says.

But James now reflects on the time in more black-and-white terms, in the process offering Falloon an olive branch that has been coming for more than a decade and a half. 'Looking back, I wish I had not fallen out with Nick Falloon,' he declares. 'We worked together constructively on Foxtel, and he was right about One.Tel and I was wrong.'

*

JAMES PACKER WAS TO have more fights with his father over PBL's investment in the new world of pay television. But

Kerry also knew for a long time before he died that free-to-air television was not going to be a licence to print money in the future. Peter Barron says, 'TV made most of its money out of movies and American programs. Long before the internet, Kerry realised that pay TV would make that virtually impossible in the future. That was one of the reasons he was anxious to keep sport [to drive pay-TV subscriptions as it had done for Rupert Murdoch].'

Former Foxtel chief executive Kim Williams says Kerry never made any secret of his lack of enthusiasm for the emerging pay-TV business. 'I remember the first time we gave a presentation to Kerry on the digital product. He was apoplectic with rage about being able to fast-forward programs and bypass advertisements. It was something to be seen and remembered forever,' Williams recalls. 'But he reluctantly acknowledged it was going to be a growth business.'

James Packer, born into a different time from his father, soon developed a keen interest in Foxtel. Williams, who was hand-picked by Rupert and Lachlan Murdoch to take over as CEO of Foxtel in December 2001, recalls James always maintained a close engagement with Foxtel's directions and plans. 'We would talk regularly on the phone and have meetings from time to time,' Williams says. In fact, he claims there was 'no person involved with Foxtel who had such a sophisticated understanding of the numbers, the moving parts and the drivers of outcomes in the business than James. He has astonishing commercial instinct and is the most numerate person I have ever met.'

James had an undistinguished academic record and developed his aptitude for numbers on the job in the Packer family businesses. His passion for Foxtel came to the fore in January 2008 when, almost seven years after the collapse of One.Tel, he reunited with Lachlan to make an audacious

$3.3-billion bid to privatise Consolidated Media Holdings (CMH), which housed the Packers' investments in Foxtel and Fox Sports, removing it from the boards of the Australian Stock Exchange (ASX).

CMH was formed in November 2007 when PBL split in two. Its gaming assets went into a company called Crown, while its media assets were held in CMH. The name PBL would become a relic of history.

The CMH privatisation was the first big deal for Lachlan's new private investment company Illyria, a name that comes from a pre-Christian confederation of tribes that controlled an area around modern-day Albania, as well as the name used as the setting of Shakespeare's *Twelfth Night*. Illyria was formed after Lachlan's shock decision to quit his New York–based executive duties at News Corporation in July 2005, after a falling-out with then Fox News supremo Roger Ailes. Lachlan recruited Siobhan McKenna, an old friend and former McKinsey & Company consultant, to be his second-in-command at Illyria.

In addition to its interests in Foxtel and Fox Sports, CMH also had a one-quarter stake in PBL Media, which controlled both the Nine Television Network and magazine publisher ACP. Advertising industry legend Harold Mitchell at the time described the Packer–Murdoch CMH privatisation as 'a very clever' one to take advantage of the sharemarket's low valuation of 'some valuable assets'. They were backed in the deal by the San Francisco–based buy-out firm SPO Partners. 'I agreed to go fifty-fifty,' James now says of the deal.

By March 2008, the global credit crunch had hit and SPO Partners told Lachlan it wanted to pull out of the CMH privatisation deal. At the same time, Crown's US casino investments had gone awry and James was also having cold feet. 'All of a sudden the GFC is happening around me, and I said to Lachlan I wanted to be 25 per cent, not 50. What became apparent, which I had not thought of before, was that I was not sure I could afford to buy any more CMH shares,' he now says. 'And I thought, if this deal happens, I am not going to have liquidity. It is going to be locked up in an Illyria vehicle. [Lachlan] had made it quite clear in his words and actions that if we did the deal, he expected to run it.'

For a year James had been a buyer of CMH, but suddenly – without warning – he became a seller, going from contributing money to taking it off the table. 'That was hard. James should have been more direct with Lachlan about wanting to pull it,' says one corporate adviser familiar with the negotiations at the time. Lachlan found another partner in the form of US private equity group Providence Equity Partners. But when it, too, pulled out in early April, the deal collapsed. It proved to be a blessing in disguise. By October, as the GFC took hold, CMH's market value had fallen to $1.5 billion, $1.8 billion less than Lachlan and James had been prepared to pay for it.

'We were so lucky it fell over,' James now says. But he also acknowledges the difficulty it caused for his relationship with Lachlan. After the disaster of One.Tel, it rekindled bad memories. 'For me it was embarrassing because sometimes I thought the Murdochs felt [that] when you dealt with the Packers they always tried to change the goalposts,' he says.

But Lachlan agrees that they both dodged a bullet. 'Arguably we are better off as friends than as business partners. But in a funny way the privatisation of CMH was more out of our control. That was a good deal not to do in retrospect. I wouldn't put that in as a big failure between us.'

Lachlan quickly moved on from the deal, as Illyria made an eclectic range of investments, including stakes in Indian Premier League cricket team the Rajasthan Royals, online retailer Quickflix and even a toy maker, the listed company Funtastic. In November 2009 Illyria agreed with the Daily

Mail Group in London to buy half of DMG Radio Australia, which owns the Nova and Classic Rock radio networks, for $53 million. Lachlan became chairman of the company. He later bought the other half for a reported $100 million, and it has since proved to be Illyria's most profitable investment.

But James would eventually end up taking the biggest cheque out of Foxtel, in a deal that proved a master stroke of timing. In 2012 the Murdochs agreed to pay around $2 billion to buy CMH. The Packers' private company CPH held 50 per cent of CMH, while another 25 per cent was owned by Kerry Stokes (who controlled the Seven Network) and the rest by retail investors. Seven also made a bid for CMH but was blocked by the competition regulator. James could see that digital platforms – the internet, smartphones and tablets – were challenging pay TV's revenue growth. At the time he also needed cash to support his ambitions to build a casino in his home town of Sydney. 'Foxtel was a very good deal for CPH. PBL's entry cost was around $300 million. And CMH was sold for around $2 billion, and we had half of it when it was sold,' James says. Since the CMH sale to News, Foxtel's revenue and subscriber numbers have been falling, hit by the rise of internet-streaming services like Netflix and of piracy.

It was another deal that, on the face of it, surely tested the Packer–Murdoch relationship. 'I had so much gratitude for the way [Lachlan] treated me after One.Tel that I regarded myself in his debt. I kept on trying to help him generally and actually ended up hurting him,' James says. 'The things I put to Lachlan, none of them ended up being good.'

But Lachlan says News has always viewed its CMH purchase as a long-term play. 'From an investor and financials perspective, his sale was good timing. But from a media perspective, how you build those assets together with News Corporation, I think time will tell. I am very optimistic. News having real control of the merged Foxtel–Fox Sports entity will make a difference,' he says of the 2017 merger of the two companies. 'We are in media, we are not going to do anything else. For us it is about building these assets over a long period.'

*

IN EARLY OCTOBER 2010 an intriguing email landed in the inboxes of a few select fund managers with significant holdings in the listed Ten television network. Marked as confidential, the ten-page attachment to the email was headed 'Ten Network Holdings: Strategic Considerations' and had been assembled by James Packer's favourite adviser at investment bank UBS, Matthew Grounds. It detailed a blueprint to abandon the network's strategy based on sport and news and make better use of the new digital channels that local free-to-air television networks had been allowed to broadcast from 2009.

In its heyday when it focused on a young demographic, Ten had made more money than the other two commercial networks combined. James Packer and Lachlan Murdoch wanted to take Ten back to its glory days. The select investors, including Perpetual's star stock picker John Sevior – who had always been close to the Packer family – were then asked if they would be prepared to sell some of their shares to Packer's CPH. They jumped at the opportunity. On the afternoon of 19 October 2010, CPH made a lightning sharemarket raid on Ten. The next day it revealed James Packer had become the network's largest shareholder overnight, paying $280 million to buy a 17.9 per cent stake.

Two years had passed since the failure of the CMH privatisation, and One.Tel was almost a decade-old memory. James thought Ten provided a chance for him and Lachlan to prove the truth of the old adage 'third time lucky'. For emotional reasons Lachlan had long coveted the network, which had once been owned by his father, and finally he had his chance to buy into it. James quickly agreed with Lachlan to split his stake fifty-fifty and they both joined the Ten board.

The next six months proved to be an extraordinary period in Ten's history, which was superbly documented in James Chessell's award-winning feature in *The Australian Financial Review*, 'Ten Ways to Kill a TV Network'. Without warning, mining magnate and Australia's richest person Gina Rinehart suddenly emerged with a 10 per cent stake in the network. Rinehart bought her interest in Ten – and another in Fairfax around the same time – in an attempt to gain greater exposure for her political views, especially pushing governments to slash taxes.

In the Ten boardroom James quickly took aim at his old adversary from PBL, then Ten executive chairman Nick Falloon, who he claimed was one of the architects of the network's flawed strategy. By early November Falloon had resigned. Alarmed at the network's cost blowouts and lack of a clear strategy, James then turned his guns on Falloon's replacement, Grant Blackley.

Blackley, who had run Ten's TV business under Falloon for five years, believed the network's traditional focus on a younger demographic was getting riskier as new media fragmented its audience, but James didn't agree. The billionaire was also reportedly angered that Ten had let its rivals steal good talent like the high-rating comedy duo Hamish & Andy, who were poached by Nine. By late February 2011 Blackley was gone and Lachlan had taken over as acting CEO.

Next came the decision that would prove a turning point in the history of the network. Lachlan had only been Ten's interim CEO for a week when he decided to poach Seven's rising star, then its chief sales and digital officer, James

Warburton. Warburton had approached Ten as part of its search process for a new CEO, frustrated at remaining number two to David Leckie at Seven. He would start at Ten in July. It was a declaration of war on Seven's owner and chairman, Kerry Stokes.

On the morning of 2 March 2011, after Warburton's appointment was announced to the ASX, a furious Stokes rang Lachlan, reportedly declaring he would 'fucking kill' Ten. He did the same to James, vowing to 'kill' him. But Stokes had missed a secondary – but bombshell – one-sentence announcement from Ten that morning, revealing James had resigned from the Ten board, effective immediately. After warring for many years over the failure of Seven's pay-TV ambitions, James and Stokes had finally made peace fourteen months earlier, and James had no appetite for allowing his Ten play to reopen old wounds.

After reading the release, Stokes was quickly back on the phone to James. His voice was far more conciliatory. 'James, you've resigned?' Stokes asked almost rhetorically.

James replied: 'Yes, Kerry, I have.'

There was a pause before Stokes almost whispered in response: 'Everything is going to be okay, James.'

That day Stokes, who was in Perth, invited the then boss of Crown Perth, Barry Felstead, to lunch. It was a symbolic act of thanks.

'It wasn't Warburton,' Stokes now says of his fury at the time, which prompted Seven to launch legal action to stop Warburton starting at Ten until October 2012. The judge in the case eventually ruled he could start in January that year. 'It was the fact we had agreed some stuff, and I had people who had given me undertakings and they broke them. James felt the same way and that is why he resigned. I was grateful for the fact he did that.'

But news of James's shock resignation came as a complete surprise to Lachlan Murdoch. He felt blindsided and, as one observer puts it, 'thrown under the bus' with Stokes by his good friend. On the evening of Warburton's appointment, Lachlan made a rare visit to James's Bondi apartment in Sydney, where they sat drinking together until the early hours of the morning. James was deeply apologetic. But his actions robbed his friend of a vital ally on the Ten board, and in future negotiations with advertisers. While James retained his 9 per cent investment in Ten, his departure from the board proved to be a turning point in his strategic and emotional backing for the company. 'It meant that the company didn't have James's support for the turnaround. Lachlan was left carrying the baby,' says one observer from the time.

Lachlan himself says of the time: 'Ten was tough and I was disappointed when James got off the board. We were going to do that together. But I understood his reasons and I take responsibility for a lot of what happened there. You have to go into difficult turnarounds with your eyes wide open. Ten is not something I blame James for.'

One of James's last public displays of support for Ten came in February 2014, when he, Lachlan and Brett Ratner attended the opening ceremony of the winter Olympic Games in the Russian city of Sochi. Lachlan, who was then Ten chairman, was hosting a week of hospitality for the network's key advertising clients. On the Sunday evening of 9 February, Lachlan and James hosted a party for Ten's contingent, including then CEO Hamish McLennan, chief sales officer Louise Barrett and the network's executive general manager in Melbourne, Russel Howcroft. The party was at Packer's penthouse suite on level 6 of the luxurious Solis Hotel, located on a sunny mountain slope surrounded by the picturesque Caucasus Mountains. It was better known during the Games as 'the Network Ten party suite'. While Lachlan jetted out of Sochi several hours into the event, James ensured the vodka flowed freely until the early hours of the morning for the guests, who included Gina Rinehart's daughter Ginia.

James agreed to put more money into Ten three more times after he left the board: twice in 2012 when the network raised money from its investors, and again in June 2015 when Ten launched a $150-million capital raising that saw Foxtel emerge with a 15 per cent stake in the company.

But in January 2017, after James's rush of asset sales during 2016 to reduce the debt of CPH and Crown, Lachlan met with his then clearly unwell friend. 'Lachlan came to see me at my house in Aspen and I was in a bad way. We talked about Ten,' James recalls. He asked Lachlan, '"Do you mind if I am out? Can I sell my shares?" He said yes and that he was sorry about Ten,' he adds. They then started talking about their investment record together. James says he told Lachlan, 'Ten was my fault and I really owe you for all the trouble I have caused you.' He says Lachlan simply responded: 'You don't owe me. You never did.'

Lachlan says he found James that day 'in a super dark place'. He explains: 'I had heard he was in a bad place. I happened to be in town, I went to see him. He was worried about going broke and thinking through radical changes to his portfolio ... I told him we all go through these challenges in life and what defines us is our actions and how we react in difficult times. I said this was a defining moment for him. I told him he would look back on this time with strength in the future. I was trying to rev him up a bit.

'We did talk about Ten. There had been points in Ten where he had offered to take me out and make me whole. But he didn't owe me anything and, yes, I said that to him. We were partners, so I didn't want to owe him anything either.'

Bankers at UBS started looking for buyers for CPH's Ten stake but made little headway. In mid January CPH formally told the Ten board that it wanted no part in any new deal to refinance the network. James, Lachlan and billionaire Bruce Gordon were shareholders and guarantors of a $200 million loan facility with the Commonwealth Bank for Ten that was due for repayment in December 2017. CBA had said it was willing to renew the loan and increase it to $250 million, but to do so it needed guarantees from the three shareholders. With Packer out, it was the beginning of the end.

On 14 June 2017, Ten collapsed under the weight of its debts after Lachlan Murdoch and Gordon refused to extend the CBA's credit facility, hoping to buy the company on the cheap out of administration. It was eventually purchased by American media giant CBS, the network's largest creditor. Its successful bid meant Packer and Murdoch lost their entire investments.

Kerry Stokes now says he told James when he was first contemplating investing in Ten that it 'would not be easy. He thought putting Ten and News together would be successful. I said to him at the time that may be your biggest problem,' Stokes says. 'Ten was moulded and run and put together as a particular model. And the model worked. Then the model was showing signs it needed to evolve. When they got control, their efforts to evolve it were far too rapid. Ten wasn't ready in its culture for it to be changed like that. That was the biggest issue.'

Lachlan describes Ten as 'a much more difficult turnaround than we expected'. He says, 'The thing that hasn't been told about Ten was the shape it was in when we bought in. The business was at the beginning of a steep decline and I don't think the market appreciated that. There were a few things like buying the NRL rights that could have turned it around …

Would we have done it again? I think yes, but we would have made a few decisions differently.'

James is reluctant to say more about his Ten experience, but he does acknowledge for the first time that the investment was a mistake. 'At Channel Ten, I should never have bought in,' he says, before adding that their Ten experience showed that he and Lachlan have a 'complex relationship. I feel the reason Lachlan still likes me – and I'm sure Lachlan has been through some periods of introspection and reflection the past couple of years – is because he believes I have always had honest intentions. The outcome of some of the business deals that I've proposed has been far from good. But I believe Lachlan thinks my intentions were always honourable.'

Despite the failure of their deals together, which has seen their relationship 'cool' over the past eighteen months, Lachlan agrees with the sentiments. 'We went into everything with honourable intentions. One of James's best attributes, which is also a weakness, is his generosity. Unfortunately, some people take advantage of that. James is a fantastic businessman. His financial acumen is really incredible,' he says.

He says he would be open to them being business partners again. 'Absolutely, if an opportunity came along to work together again, and if it made sense to do it, we would certainly consider it,' he says.

*

Lachlan Murdoch is no stranger to the region known as the winter playground of the American jet set. He attended high school in Aspen, Colorado, graduating from the town's exclusive Country Day School. In September 2017, he and wife Sarah decided to buy their own mansion in Aspen, just up the road from Packer in West Buttermilk. The Murdochs purchased their 45-acre equestrian ranch known as the Mopani Estate for a reported US$29 million, a bargain compared to the original listing price of US$44 million. The 13,491-square-foot home on the site has six bedrooms, six full-size and two half-size bathrooms – including one with a million-dollar view – and tall floor-to-ceiling windows engineered from skyscraper glass.

The Packer and Murdoch families are yet to host each other at their respective homes, but James says he hopes to do so in the future and is effusive about Lachlan – so much so, his critics might say it borders on cringeworthy. 'Lachlan is one of the best people I know, full stop, he really is. Sarah and Lachlan have been unbelievable friends to Erica, especially since she moved to LA. For that I am so, so grateful,' he says. The words make you wonder if Packer feels bad or even embarrassed about what has happened between them.

Though born in London, schooled in America and still boasting a strong American accent, Lachlan is often described as the most Australian of his siblings, the three children from his father's 32-year marriage to journalist Anna Torv. Boasting a tattooed forearm, he is the only one who maintains a connection to Australia and regularly welcomes people in conversation with the nation's trademark 'G'day, mate'. This association is one of the reasons that – despite their troubles in business – Lachlan says he still feels an affinity with James and his family. Because of Lachlan's ongoing connection with Australia as the chairman of News Corporation, he certainly feels a continuation of the historic, intergenerational relationship between the Packer and Murdoch families.

But friends of both say James and Lachlan have drifted apart in recent years, living in different worlds as the former pursued his ambitions in Hollywood and started dating Mariah Carey. While James has often done business deals with people he has called friends, most of Lachlan's friends tend not to be business people at all, and rarely people he works with. Those who know him well say it takes a long time for Lachlan to become true friends with someone. He sets a high bar.

Asked if he and James have moved in different worlds somewhat since the latter moved overseas at the end of 2013, Lachlan replies: 'By definition, yes. But I am an introvert by nature so I don't like the spotlight. We have a very different business to what James has.'

Lachlan also seems more cautious about his personal relationships than James, who seems to easily become besotted with charismatic people and leaves himself exposed to being hurt. In the second half of 2015, when they moved to Los Angeles, the Murdochs purchased a secluded estate in the Brentwood area. Yet Lachlan kept his distance from his friend's high-flying Hollywood world. 'We have been around Hollywood for a long time. Hollywood knows how to suck money out of newcomers,' he says. 'I don't want to judge James at all, but the Hollywood seduction is something that is hard for people to resist. I am lucky because I have been around that for a long time and you can see it at work.'

Lachlan's penchant for privacy and his focus on his wife and children has certainly influenced the make-up of his business and social networks. His friends say he'd rather have a quiet family dinner at home than go out to a fancy restaurant in London, Hong Kong or New York.

In 2012 journalist Pamela Williams secured James's and Lachlan's assistance to write an award-winning book titled *Killing Fairfax*, which chronicled the downfall of the Fairfax media empire under attack from online classified sites Seek, Carsales and REA Group. The first two were backed by James, the third by Lachlan. All three coveted Fairfax's traditional 'rivers of gold' classified advertising markets – in employment, motor vehicles and property. Lachlan says he agreed to do the project with James to document how they both saw the opportunity provided by the internet to challenge the business models of traditional media. 'For me and for us to tell that story about the inception of our investment and participation on REA was an important thing,' he says.

James reckons it was probably the best thing he and Lachlan ever did together. 'In 2012 no one was talking about REA Group and it was worth a lot of money. People were obviously talking about Channel Ten, which I put Lachlan in. *Killing Fairfax* gave him some clear air because it was the first time anyone had told the REA story – what a great deal Lachlan had done. It has become one of the best deals in Australian media history. Since then Nova has also come good,' he says. 'For a period of time Lachlan was underrated. One of my best decisions was to not underrate him.'

In a cryptic reference to the burdens they both carry as the sons of two of the giants of Australian business, James says: 'I know how hard it is to try and fill big shoes. One day Lachlan is going to have to fill some of the biggest shoes in the world. I think Lachlan will do better than people expect.'

*

IF THERE HAS BEEN one constant in Packer's life, it has been his incessant desire to keep News Corporation and the Murdochs onside: in editorials, in business and in friendships. Some friends say he has obsessed about it, often to his detriment. 'James is too hard on himself with the Murdochs,' says one. 'In his eyes, he has become poor and weak [in comparison to the Murdochs], even when that is not true. But that is his mindset.'

James famously fell out with long-serving News Limited supremo John Hartigan in 2006 after a front-page headline in *The Daily Telegraph* on 30 June at the height of the turmoil engulfing Channel Nine following the death of Kerry Packer. The previous week James had travelled to the UK to play polo at Cowdray Park in West Sussex, while his CEO John Alexander had attended the Wimbledon tennis championships. 'He's just sacked 100 staff, his network is a mess, and he's in England for tennis and polo – HOME, JAMES,' the headline roared.

The Channel Nine CEO at the time, Eddie McGuire, remembers how painful the period was for James. 'When they turned in that first year and News Limited really went after him, that was brutal. And it was unfair,' McGuire says. 'I have no doubt at all that there were a few people who thought, "Right, we're going to square up for everything that Kerry has done to us by beating up James."'

Conspiracy theorists at the time also figured it was the result of James's ill-judged decision not to attend a gala lunch days earlier at Sydney's Machiavelli restaurant staged by ACP's flagship magazine, the now defunct *Bulletin*. At this glitzy function the magazine feted Rupert Murdoch as the most influential Australian of all time. Rupert turned up in person but James was nowhere to be seen. He now claims he was never told that Rupert would be attending the lunch before he organised to visit the UK but acknowledges his trip was a mistake. 'That was clearly the wrong decision on my behalf and was disrespectful,' he says.

James was also angered in 2014 when News Limited agreed to pay more than $200,000 for exclusive photos of his Sydney street brawl with his long-time friend and former Nine CEO David Gyngell. 'My experience in dealing with News in Australia has been on two sides – an editorial side [what is printed in the Murdoch media] and a business side [the financial dealings between the two empires]. On the business side with

News, traditional media was a big part of our business. I always tried to separate editorial from business in my relationship with News,' James says. 'I hope people at News would agree that I have complained less than most [about the way the Murdoch media has carried stories about him]. That is not to say I have never complained. I was really hurting when the Gyngell fight stuff came out.'

James says he has only had, at most, a dozen serious conversations with Rupert Murdoch in his whole life. But, again, in characteristically self-deprecating fashion, he says: 'Rupert has been kinder to me than I deserve. After One.Tel went broke, Lachlan invited me to his birthday party in New York, he was turning thirty,' James recalls. It was 8 September 2001, and James celebrated his thirty-fourth birthday the same day. 'I was in a seriously bad way. It was three days before 9/11. Lachlan gave a speech and said, "I would like to give a special mention to my good friend James Packer." I went up to Rupert and apologised [for One.Tel]. He said, "It's okay, James, as long as you learned your lesson."'

A year later James travelled to Los Angeles with Tom Cruise. One evening Lachlan invited him and Cruise for dinner at Rupert's Beverly Hills mansion. 'Rupert couldn't have been nicer to me and I appreciated it very, very much,' James says.

When rumours were running rife in 2009 that James was going broke during the GFC after his disastrous, ill-timed splurge on US casinos, News also had the opportunity to hurt him financially by cutting off the dividend from Foxtel to his CMH. They didn't. 'News were as a good a partner as you could hope for all the time I was in Foxtel. They behaved impeccably as managing partners,' James says.

Curiously, he acknowledges that News, with the power of its tabloid and broadsheet mastheads and its corporate financial muscle, has always scared him. 'Yes, very much so,' he replies when I put the proposition to him, before adding: 'In a business sense they could have hurt me. But they could also help me. And in my life, News has helped me far more than they have hurt me.'

Lachlan says 'scared' is the wrong adjective to use to describe James's relationship with News. 'I haven't seen fear. He is definitely conscious of our influence. So he has been careful with us, he pays a lot of respect to our editors and our journalists,' he says. 'I see it more as the fact he respects News.'

FOUR

Changing Channels

THE SWISS ALPINE RESORT of Davos, near the border with Austria, was abuzz in late January 2000 as it played host to the world's corporate, political and intellectual elite. The occasion was the thirtieth anniversary of the World Economic Forum, an international talkfest where 2500 top business leaders, political leaders, economists, celebrities and journalists gathered to discuss the most pressing issues facing the world. The star attraction was Bill Clinton, the first sitting US president to appear at Davos, alongside British prime minister Tony Blair, US secretary of state Madeleine Albright and Microsoft founder Bill Gates. Australia had its own contingent, headlined by James Packer, Lachlan Murdoch, billionaire cardboard-box king Richard Pratt and Telstra chief Ziggy Switkowski.

Yet as the crowd gathered beneath the snow-covered peaks, Packer and Switkowski had more on their minds than just exchanging business cards and skiing.

A fortnight earlier, on 10 January, the largest deal in American-corporate history had been struck when the high-flying king of the dial-up internet world, America Online (AOL), merged with incumbent media giant Time Warner in a deal valued at a stunning US$350 billion. It was a classic, transformative 'convergence' play, giving Time Warner tens of millions of new subscribers and AOL access to its partner's lucrative cable network and suite of content.

The deal had caught the eye of both Packer and the new Telstra chairman Bob Mansfield, the one-time Australian CEO of burger chain McDonald's, who had become the founding CEO of local telecommunications group Optus in 1992. Mansfield had a long history with the Packer family. When he began his Telstra role on 1 January 2000, one of his first suggestions to CEO Ziggy Switkowski was to meet with Packer in Davos. When they finally got together, away from the assembled delegates and media, Packer talked up the opportunities to put Telstra together with PBL, giving the telco access to its crown jewels: the Nine Television Network and the real stars of its portfolio, ecorp and One.Tel. The former had emerged as the nation's best online play under the direction of Daniel Petre, to be valued at more than $6 billion. The latter, James Packer's fledgling telco alliance with his good friend Lachlan Murdoch, was also flying at the time.

The meeting went well. 'Project Patrick', as it became known, was born, but its problems became apparent early. How could a government-owned corporation own a casino company, given PBL's gaming interests? And what would Telstra want with PBL's magazine business, ACP? But the biggest obstacle became price. Inflated by the value of its stakes in ecorp and One.Tel, PBL was trading at $13.50 a share and the Packers wanted Telstra to pay a hefty premium. In fact, James Packer now reveals his father had a single number in his head: $18. Despite the repeated protests of his son, Kerry refused to budge from the price. And the Telstra board refused to countenance it. James was shattered. 'The deal would have made a huge difference for CPH positively,' he now says in his first public comments on the plan.

Under the deal, PBL would sell all its assets to Telstra, then buy back Crown. 'We were buying back Crown [which only had its Melbourne property at the time] at $2 billion and it is worth $6 billion today. And we were selling all those media assets, as well as One.Tel and ecorp,' James says. 'It was on the back of the AOL–Time Warner deal that people briefly thought would change the world. I wanted to do it, Dad didn't. He was wrong and I was right on that one.' But James acknowledges in hindsight that 'the board of Telstra made the right decision. We could have got it done at a lower price. Dad wouldn't budge. I understand that. In 2000 I can understand someone thinking that the internet was unproven,' he says.

The proposed deal was important for defining an early critical difference in business between father and son. At the age of thirty-two, James had already shown that he was an unemotional businessman, prepared to trade any asset for a price. He was utterly calculating in his attitude to Nine, regardless of the huge part it had played in his father's life and the enormous political clout it had given the Packer family in Australia. By contrast, his father was a businessman who wanted to be more. Like his nemesis Rupert Murdoch, he wanted to wield power, especially political power. He saw his media assets as both a means of making money and a way to influence the affairs of the nation.

The failure of Project Patrick ensured that PBL would be saddled with its impending One.Tel disaster and all the financial, physical and mental consequences that carried for James, but it also failed to rid James of the asset his father coveted above all else – one that soon became a problem child that would haunt James for the rest of the decade.

*

DAVID LECKIE'S HARD-DRINKING, HEAVY-SWEARING ways were the stuff of television industry legend. He had successfully headed the Nine Network since 1990, and a decade later was widely acknowledged to be one of Australia's most successful TV executives. But in 1999 he led Nine to a decision that two years later would cost him his job: joining the OzTAM consortium, a cooperative with rivals Seven and Ten to oversee television ratings. It quickly became a rod for its own back.

Nine had always won easily under the longstanding ACNielsen ratings system. But in the new regime, which measured a younger demographic of viewers, it quickly fell to second in the weekly ratings behind Seven. Nine threatened legal action over the figures, and Leckie even got the rival networks to agree to an independent audit of the new system, which ensured Nine remained the number-one network for another two years. But the damage was done. After Leckie's departure it would lose the mantle to Seven and never get it back.

PBL chief executive Peter Yates, who by January 2002 had been in the job for nine months, had also quickly determined that simply winning the ratings would no longer cut it for Nine. 'We had [management consultant firm] Egon Zehnder do a complete review of all of the executive roles and responsibilities, which identified that Channel Nine was just a PR and organisational basket case,' Yates recalls. 'It was obvious from the numbers there was no growth. So we had a view that the business was ex-growth.'

Unsurprisingly, Yates and Leckie clashed. 'He had no feel whatsoever for the entertainment business,' Leckie now says.

Despite Nine's success in the ratings, Kerry Packer — against the wishes of his son — had long been baying for Leckie's blood. Advertising baron Harold Mitchell remembers defending Leckie to Kerry because 'he was one of the nation's outstanding executives. He understood the television viewer. He, like Kerry, was one of them. But that's why they clashed,' Mitchell says.

Leckie himself says Kerry could never get around to firing him because Nine was doing so well. 'When you are a winner, it is hard to get rid of the winner. I knew the moment I dropped from being the winner, I would walk out the door. Life is based on winning; if you don't win, forget it.' Leckie describes Kerry Packer as 'extraordinarily tough. I would challenge anybody to go through what I went through. But since his passing, I have more respect for his point of view, looking back, than I did at the time. I took probably too much of the pressure. I went head-on against Kerry to keep my people steaming along and being number one,' he says.

He recalls James often telling him when his father was 'pissed off about something. Our relationship was good fun. I did rely on James to get a barometer on how things were going with Kerry,' Leckie says. He says despite the traditional perceptions, James did display an affection for television. 'I think he watched a lot of television. I always got phone calls about why didn't we do this and that,' he says.

But in early 2002, with James weakened by the loss of his authority inside PBL following the One.Tel disaster, and with the OzTAM debacle as ammunition, Kerry had the perfect excuse to strike against Leckie. Yates was ordered to deliver the death blow, calling in Leckie in early January from Sydney's Palm Beach where he was on holidays. James was in the room for a time. John Alexander, then the chief executive of ACP, was promoted to a key role as head of a new entity called PBL Media, overseeing both Nine and ACP Magazines. Leckie was replaced as head of Nine by the knockabout Melbourne-based Ian Johnson, the former CEO of Crown Casino.

Executives who were at Nine at the time believe Leckie's sacking was an important inflection point for the company. Four years of turmoil followed. 'They should never have let him go. For me, that was the turning point. What better were they going to do? Ian Johnson didn't want to do the job, he was forced into it,' one says upon reflection.

It didn't take Leckie long to find another job – at Nine's arch rival Seven. Leckie quickly took Seven to the top of the ratings charts and poached a host of Nine stars including Ian Ross, Molly Meldrum, Daryl Somers, Jamie Durie, Mark Ferguson, Mike Munro, Mike Willesee and Kerri-Anne Kennerley.

While Leckie left PBL on good terms with James Packer, their relationship was never the same. It later became toxic. In early 2006, Packer's then girlfriend Erica Baxter signed a multiple-album recording contract with SonyBMG Music Australia. Leckie says that when he was asked by Packer to express a professional opinion on her music, he said that he did not think it was 'commercial', which upset Erica greatly. Packer says it left her 'in tears'.

'I'm no expert in music and I never intended to upset Erica, but that was my view at the time,' Leckie now says. 'She's a great lady.'

Then, during the depths of the GFC, Seven ran a series of unflattering stories on its *Today Tonight* current affairs program about Packer's personal and business dealings in Macau. Packer was apoplectic. 'At one point in my life I liked David enormously and thought we were great friends. I argued with my father for years and years about David's competency. I was CEO and then chairman of PBL at that point,' Packer says. 'Dad was desperate to fire David for years before he ended up firing him. When he was running Channel Nine, Nine was winning by the most ever, but Dad still ended up firing him. Then he took Seven to number one. Impossible. What an achievement. Then he got fired from Seven. David ran two networks, took them to or kept them at number one, and managed to get fired by Dad and then Stokes.'

Leckie politely takes issue with Packer's use of the word 'fired' when it comes to his departure from Seven. 'I fired myself because I had totally run out of steam, and that is the truth,' he says. But it was the *Today Tonight* campaign that led to a bitter falling-out between the former friends. 'We have had three fallings out, all from him to me. It is sad,' Leckie says, adding that he misses Packer's friendship.

The biggest confrontation came on 8 October 2009 during a party for TV industry legend Sam Chisholm's seventieth birthday at the Guillaume at Bennelong restaurant at the Sydney Opera House. Leckie approached Packer at the party with a big friendly smile only to be greeted with an expletive-ridden tirade. News of the sensational clash made headlines across the country. Leckie says, '[Packer] was furious. He was standing at the top of the stairs waiting for me to come in. As soon as I walked up the stairs with [Seven's legal head] Bruce McWilliam I thought, "Oh no, here we go."' Leckie says he never felt physically threatened that day, but was 'really pissed off because James did it so publicly. I think if he had rang me and talked to me about it, I could have sat down with the journalist concerned and walked our way through it. But I also looked at the stories and I didn't think they were bad,' he says.

Asked about the Leckie encounter at Guillaume, Packer makes no apologies for being angry but says it was one of several occasions in his life where he blew his cool. He explains: 'Leckie says "James Packer" and raises his arms as if he's my friend. So I just snapped,' he says. 'Yes, I regret it.' The two came together again during a function on an AFL Grand Final day. It was the last time they saw each other. Leckie says,

'[James] walked passed me and said, "We should catch up." But he never called, so I never bothered calling.'

The Leckie blow-up wasn't the first time Packer had lost his temper in public over media matters. At the Nine Network's 2001 program launch party in Sydney, he openly delivered another expletive-ridden diatribe against *The Sunday Telegraph*'s gossip columnist, Ros Reines, for one of her column items.

In March 2006 at the Opening Ceremony of the Melbourne Commonwealth Games, Ron Walker, chairman of Fairfax and of the Games Organising Committee, was waiting with then British prime minister Tony Blair to greet the Queen when Packer aggressively approached him and put him in a headlock. Packer was angry Fairfax had pulled out of a deal to buy ACP's magazine group in New Zealand and roared at Walker that his father would not have been treated the same way.

Six years later, in November 2012, during the prime minister's Christmas drinks at Kirribilli House in Sydney, former Fairfax chief executive Fred Hilmer was making polite conversation with Packer and his then wife Erica when he said something that set Packer off.

Pamela Williams reported in her book *Killing Fairfax* that Hilmer had joked to Packer that he had 'got out at the right time' from Fairfax before its classifieds business was mortally wounded by the internet.

'Don't come up and try to be my friend,' Packer reportedly said. 'The damage had already been done by the time you got out, Fred. Fuck off.'

Asked to comment more generally about his big mood swings, in explaining them Packer doesn't seek to justify bad behaviour. Rather, in his self-analysis he seeks to offer some explanation for sometimes blowing his stack. While Packer's default demeanour is to be kind and cheerful – he can also be extraordinarily charming – you sense there's a short fuse lurking underneath, especially when he feels unreasonably crossed. 'When I think someone has fucked me over, I get really upset. Whether I'm right all the time about whether someone did that or didn't is up for interpretation,' he says, looking me straight in the eye. 'People I've fallen out with in my life, they would all think it was my fault. They'd think it was precipitated by actions and events on my behalf that were bad and were unreasonable. I look back at those instances and I think they fucked me over.'

So it is that black and white? I ask.

'No,' he replies, before a pause followed by a wry smile. 'It's grey, but it's grey falling on my side. I think it relates to mood swings and things I say to people when I'm angry. When people hit me or I feel I've been wronged, I punch back … I think I go ruder and perhaps more personal than others do.'

Former Victorian premier Jeff Kennett says he has seen the changes in Packer's moods, as has the Seven Network's Kerry Stokes and countless others. But Stokes describes Packer's temper as 'a bad thing' and not 'naturally who he is'. 'We all have some degree of darkness. Without doubt, James has that. When he is mentally on his game, he doesn't have those moments. He is a builder, not a destroyer; he likes building stuff,' Stokes says. 'People prone to be physically; aggressive tend to want to pull things down.'

Guy Hands, the founder of UK private equity firm Terra Firma and a long-term friend of Packer's, says James takes things very personally. 'A lot of people see the bluster. The bluster is really a mask for what is going on inside. He is a very generous and trusting human being. He is constantly looking for that relationship that will give him the support he really needs,' Hands says.

Warren Beatty says Packer is well aware of his ups and downs, and is trying to manage them better. 'We all have, I would call it, mood swings. When someone is in denial of mood swings, that is a problem. I don't think he's in denial of that at all,' he says.

Packer's ex-wife Jodhi Meares says his temper is nothing like that of his father. 'He has never had a bad temper with me in the twenty years we have known each other,' she says, before quickly adding: 'But walk a mile in James's shoes. There are days when you would not know who to trust. And plenty of people have done the wrong thing by him. I don't think James feels getting angry with people is the right way to resolve things, but he is a human being. He has emotions. You see James coming. With his level of honesty, he is going to tell you how he feels. James is a deeply emotional, kind, caring person. It is much easier to be a narcissist in business and there are plenty of them. James isn't one.'

Critics have long pointed to the hypocrisy of the Packer family in being so sensitive to media intrusion and criticism while for years they made millions of dollars from gossip magazines such as *The Australian Women's Weekly* and *Woman's Day*, and Nine's weeknight tabloid news program, *A Current Affair*. But Packer reckons he gets more than his fair share. 'There is no one in town who has copped as much bad press as I have copped,' he bristles. 'I see all these other people I know with thin skin – they have one article written about them and they freak out. I get two a week and I'm expected to just sit back and cop it. And how often have you seen me complain to a publication or media outlet? I wouldn't say I have a thin skin, but I would say my skin isn't thick enough.'

*

JAMES PACKER HAS NEVER been one to put nostalgia ahead of good business sense. He showed that in spades when he returned to his duties as PBL chairman in 2003 in his post-One.Tel resurrection. It heralded a brave new era for the Nine Network. For the first time in two decades, Nine was run from PBL headquarters in Park Street, Sydney, rather than from Nine's base in Willoughby. James implored Peter Yates and John Alexander to dismantle the culture that had been the network's hallmark for decades – pampered stars, budget blowouts, executive largesse and minimal accountability. Even the legendary Nine bar at its Willoughby bunker in Sydney became but a memory, replaced by a nondescript office, while the six-figure salaries of many former stars were slashed.

The changes again put him on a collision course with his father. Kerry was prepared to let Nine cop a few flesh wounds, but the muscle and bone remained sacrosanct. Into this arena was thrust David Gyngell, James Packer's best mate and son of Australian television pioneer Bruce Gyngell, when he took on the role of Nine CEO in June 2004. It followed the sacking of Peter Yates as PBL CEO, who was replaced by John Alexander. In an unusual move, Kerry at the time took on the newly created position of PBL deputy chairman, a signal to investors that he was still playing a major role in the company.

In September that year Kerry also brought back the 64-year-old Sam Chisholm as a director of PBL. The wily Chisholm had been the boss of Nine for fifteen years before moving to British Sky Broadcasting in 1990. His return was too much for Gyngell, who was gone six months later, famously slamming the door of Kerry Packer's Park Street office after handing in his resignation, blaming the multiple levels of management between PBL and Nine. His decision reportedly left Kerry in tears.

In an act of desperation, Kerry appointed Chisholm executive director of PBL's television interests and asked him to assume the day-to-day running of Nine. It set up an internal power struggle between Chisholm and Alexander, as the latter pushed for greater accountability to PBL's Park Street management, including more consultation on key decisions. James struggled to intervene. One former Nine executive says, 'Sam never wanted to be there. His style was to pit people against each other. It was the old philosophy of Channel Nine. When Sam was around, James was hands off. He knew Sam was problematic but he wouldn't do anything about it. He didn't have a solution.' Another Nine executive based at Willoughby says the staff often talked about 'making sure Park Street was aware of what was happening. Everyone felt helpless. And it was very destructive. The company wasn't moving forward, it was moving backward.'

Gerald Stone claimed in his book *Who Killed Channel 9?* that many of Kerry Packer's moves in his final years were motivated by concerns his son and Alexander would destroy Nine. Stone linked much of Nine's ratings slide to the conflicting agendas of father and son, and was scathing of Alexander who, he claimed, never grasped the subtleties of television. Alexander will not comment on the time. But with Kerry Packer's health problems becoming well publicised, James was looking to the future. Half a decade after the failure of Project Patrick, Nine was a shadow of its former self. And the private equity kings of the corporate world would soon spy an opportunity.

*

HE'S KNOWN BY THE moniker 'Eddie Everywhere'. In 2002, Eddie McGuire was just that on the Nine Television Network, hosting a range of hit programs such as the AFL *Footy Show*, *Friday Night AFL*, *Who Wants to Be a Millionaire?* and – in early August that year – the inaugural National IQ Test. The last of these, which McGuire hosted with Catriona Rowntree, was the most watched Australian television show for 2002.

Almost sixteen years later, sitting in his Melbourne office at the end of a short alley off South Yarra's shopping precinct – furnished with a bunch of flat-screen televisions and paraphernalia from his beloved Collingwood Football Club – McGuire recalls a big contract negotiation at the end of 2002, off the back of the IQ Test ratings bonanza, where he hit it off with James Packer. A year earlier, McGuire says he struck the same chord with Kerry Packer after Nine bought the rights to broadcast the AFL for the first time. McGuire's presidency of Collingwood and being a match-day commentator carried obvious conflicts of interest. But both James and Kerry still came to Melbourne to discuss what role McGuire could play in Nine's coverage. They ended up spending the entire afternoon together. 'We built up a good relationship, then that relationship turned to the business of television. Sales components on the shows I was doing, interaction between Crown, football and my radio shows. We had a good friendship, a working relationship and one of trust,' McGuire says.

When he dined with James and an ailing Kerry in Sydney in November 2005, less than two months before Kerry's death, the idea of McGuire becoming Nine CEO was formally discussed for the first time. 'James was looking for a certain [type of] CEO at that time and I was probably looking for a change up in my career as well … so we decided to have a go at it,' McGuire remembers. 'There's no doubt in my mind that I was a good photo-fit candidate for what they needed at that stage.'

The deal to make McGuire Nine's fifth chief executive in as many years was sealed aboard James Packer's private jet en route from Sydney to New Zealand on 1 February 2006. Also on board were John Alexander and PBL director Chris Anderson.

'James and John Alexander and Chris Anderson realised at that stage that there was no fat left in the business, because most of the machinery was held together by elastic bands. Kerry was never big on capital expenditure at the television station,' McGuire says. 'There were old ways of doing television and we all sort of knew that there was going to be a new way forward. Did we exactly know what it was? No. But we knew that there was a revolution coming up. So we set ourselves up.'

The decision to hire McGuire was a massive gamble for James Packer. It was his first major executive appointment following his father's death. 'Sam Chisholm had decided to resign after Dad's passing. So Channel Nine needed a new CEO. I knew David Leckie was doing a great job at Channel Seven. And I was sure that he was going to be very hard to beat. My conclusion was that an accountant-like CEO of Channel Nine had no chance against David. It had to be a more creative-type of CEO,' Packer now says. 'Eddie had been putting himself forward in late 2005 to my father and me as the right CEO for Channel Nine. Dad was far from disinterested. I looked around the room and couldn't see anyone else.'

But the appointment did not go down well inside or outside the company. Insiders immediately questioned McGuire's knowledge of the business of television, especially for someone being paid over $4 million a year as CEO. One former Nine executive recalls, 'It was an appointment that was symptomatic of the time. There wasn't anybody to run it. Nine was as its lowest ebb. Eddie was a Melbourne person, but had to run a company out of Sydney. I remember one day it took until midday for him to ask me what numbers *A Current Affair* did the previous night. Eddie wasn't steeped in the business of television. For all you can say against Sam Chisholm, that was not something he would do.' Chisholm would have been on the phone at the crack of dawn.

Packer also reveals — slightly in jest — that he put two conditions on McGuire's appointment. Neither became reality. 'The first condition was he wouldn't appear on air any more as the CEO of Nine. The second was he would resign as the chairman of Collingwood at the end of the year,' Packer says. 'Eddie and I agreed he could give an interview to [*A Current Affair* host] Tracy Grimshaw on his appointment as CEO of Nine. The next week was the Tasmanian miners disaster. Eddie said to me he was the only one who could do the interview. So Eddie did the interview for Nine as CEO of Nine.'

Packer immediately knew he had a big problem — he wouldn't be able to keep his new CEO off the air. He now also notes with a wry smile and with affection for his friend's football fetish: 'Eddie is still chairman of Collingwood.'

McGuire did do some good things, like play a central role in reinvigorating the network's drama department, which led to the commissioning of shows like *Sea Patrol*, *Underbelly* and *Canal Road*. But critics say he also promoted people who lacked TV industry experience to senior positions and encouraged a 'blokey' workplace culture, which led to the infamous 'boning' incident with star Jessica Rowe. Former Nine News director Mark Llewellyn famously claimed McGuire had said: 'What are we gonna do about Jessica? When should we bone her? I reckon it should be next week,' when discussing whether to remove her as the host of *Today* in 2006. McGuire later told *GQ* magazine he'd used the word 'burn' instead of 'bone'. Rowe has since described it as 'a terrible time in my life', alleging that what McGuire put her through was 'horrific'.

With morale described by insiders at the time as having hit rock bottom, amid a hotbed of leaks and backbiting, things were about to take a dramatic turn for Nine and McGuire.

*

WHEN PACKER PAID AN unexpected visit to Eddie and Carla McGuire's rented Sydney home one evening as winter descended in mid 2006, he politely asked for a drink, sat down in the living room and cut to the chase. 'I've dropped you right in the shit,' Packer told McGuire bluntly. The business was about to be sold from under him. 'We've got two offers on the go at the moment for four and a half billion dollars to buy Channel Nine and the magazines. I've dragged you out of Melbourne, I've taken you away from your career … All the things that we discussed about what we were going to do together, they're gone. Because we're going to have to get the place ready to go to sale.'

McGuire hesitated before asking his boss if he had heard him right. 'Four and a half billion dollars, you said?'

Packer nodded.

McGuire replied instantly: '"Mate, as CEO of your business, I'd take the skin off their hand grabbing that cheque." So I said, "Let's go to town." But I also said, "Look, when it's all said and done, just don't forget me." He gave me a big hug and said, "Thanks. I can't believe the way you have taken it."'

Packer's decision to put a 'For Sale' sign on Nine and ACP ended any hope McGuire had of rebuilding the network's shattered morale or boosting its ailing production schedule. But his critics would say it gave him the ultimate get-out-of-jail-free card. The sale in October 2006 of a half-share in Nine, ACP and PBL's investments in internet portal Ninemsn and online auto classifieds site Carsales through a fifty-fifty joint venture with private equity buyer CVC Asia Pacific is now part of Australian corporate folklore. It pitted the two heavyweights of Australian investment banking, Macquarie and UBS, against each other in a six-week auction process to win the deal.

'Make no mistake, the decision to exit traditional media [Channel Nine and magazines] was James's idea. We just came up with the financial structure,' says Packer's adviser on the deal, UBS Australasia boss Matthew Grounds. 'The decision to fix the selling price and have a race to the post with four bidders didn't come out of any corporate finance textbook; again this was James's idea. Not your traditional corporate approach but it certainly worked!'

Despite the close relationship that existed between Packer and Macquarie CEO Nicholas Moore, the PBL board opted to take UBS's advice in the transaction over Macquarie's. In her book *Killing Fairfax*, Pamela Williams quoted Packer as criticising Macquarie for failing to give him good advice on the deal. 'I just don't trust Macquarie. I believe they solve for themselves, not their clients,' he told Williams. 'I regret what I said about Nick Moore in *Killing Fairfax*,' Packer now says. 'He has built an amazing international business. It is an incredible success. I tried and failed in terms of building an international business. He has something incredible that has been successful in some of the most competitive parts of the world.'

The price tag on the PBL Media deal was a stunning $4.54 billion, delivering PBL around $4 billion in cash and capital. Only six weeks after his thirty-ninth birthday, Packer had bettered the deal done by his father at age forty-nine when he sold the Nine Network to Alan Bond in 1987 for $1.05 billion. Carsales chairman Walter Pisciotta, who sold half of his business to CVC as part of the deal, says, 'James took over a family fortune in a crumbling industry. He recognised it, he exited at the top. He put together a unique deal. No one else has done that.' Carsales would later float on the ASX and become one of the top growth stocks on the market.

The PBL Media deal inevitably reignited speculation that Packer may finally deliver on one of his father's unfulfilled ambitions: buying Fairfax. The reality turned out to be anything but. Later that month he told the PBL annual general meeting that the company had 'minimal interest' in Fairfax. To him newspapers were, literally, yesterday's news. Asked now if he has any regrets about never owning Fairfax, his reply is instant. 'None,' he snaps proudly. '[Former Fairfax CEO] Greg Hywood is a decent man and is doing a good job at Fairfax,' he says. Hywood has visited Packer in recent years in Aspen. 'It is a different world we are living in today where Google has a $1-trillion market cap. I grew up with my father talking about Fairfax and the rivers of gold. They clearly went away.'

In late July 2018 it took one of his father's former lieutenants to finally deliver Fairfax Media into the hands of the Nine Network, as Fairfax chairman Nick Falloon agreed to a merger deal with Nine which saw the 177-year-old Fairfax brand relegated to history.

Kerry Packer always coveted Fairfax because of the political influence it could deliver him. His son never shared this view. He never believed the Packers could wield the influence Kerry wanted to. 'Dad always envisaged controlling the editorial of Fairfax. I understand that desire but it [was] not going to happen. The reality is I never saw Dad control the editorial of Channel Nine. And in private he admitted to me that he couldn't and wouldn't.'

With the greatest affection for his father's legacy, Packer says Kerry's love for Channel Nine meant he could never have done a deal like PBL Media. It was a generational shift, pointing the company in a new direction by freeing up billions of dollars to expand its gaming interests offshore. While it was undoubtedly the deal of James Packer's life, it also highlighted his penchant for financial engineering and the wizardry of investment banking.

Friends say Packer has always enjoyed an adrenalin rush from deal-making, from making successful big-ticket transactions. But there are dangers in being a deal junkie, as subsequent events in his life have proven. 'When James is on a high, ironically that's when he is most at risk,' says one friend and business associate. 'His dad was a business operator who loved to deal with the day-to-day grind of the business. James is a consummate investor, whose greatest strength is strategy.'

The PBL Media deal would prove the ultimate challenge for Packer to wrestle with his own personality. Full of adrenalin after pulling off the deal of a lifetime, he was unable to pull back and be objective and ruthlessly self-analytical. Instead, the money burned a hole in his pocket.

*

For Eddie McGuire, the PBL Media deal would be the end of a short but eventful road. On the morning of 18 May 2007, he resigned as Nine CEO. Advertising baron and Crown director Harold Mitchell sums up McGuire's departure as: 'Eddie wasn't enjoying it. They weren't enjoying it. And the results weren't there. Time to move on. It was a tough time for Eddie. He probably realised after a time that it wasn't for him.'

McGuire himself says James Packer never forgot their conversation in the former's living room in mid 2006. 'CVC wanted me out. And James went into CVC and said, "If you get rid of this bloke, Seven will snap him up and he will spend the rest of his life completely gutting your business!" And so they came back to me and said, "Let's do this as gentlemen." And I said, "No worries at all, why would I want to slash and burn everything I spent the last twenty years of my life building up? I want you to do well,"' he recalls. CVC later allowed him to return to on-air duties, and he flourished.

In June 2007, PBL sold a further 25 per cent share of PBL Media to CVC for $515 million, giving up control of the company. It was a deal opposed by then CPH CEO and PBL director Ashok Jacob, who like Kerry Packer always believed in the power of the press. He thought Packer should maintain a controlling interest in a key media asset to retain an influence in the public debate, especially where it related to his casino interests. Packer and Jacob had their one and only stand-up fight in PBL's Park Street offices over the selldown, but Packer won the day.

Sixteen months later, after splitting his assets into a gaming company – Crown – and a media company – CMH – Packer wrote down his final 25 per cent stake in PBL Media to zero. The GFC had left CVC with an unmanageable debt burden that ultimately sent broke the assets that were renamed Nine Entertainment Group. 'Eighteen months later it was CVC's choice and they decided to look for a new CEO,' Packer says of McGuire's final days at the helm of Nine.

Packer and McGuire's Channel Nine adventure may not have followed the script, but they remain close. 'I like Eddie; Eddie and I are still friends. I appreciate very much that he has made the effort to keep in touch with me,' the former says.

McGuire acknowledges there were some bruising moments during his fifteen-month stint as a chief executive for the first and only time of his life. 'Was I at times used? Yes, but that's alright. That is part of it. I suppose you're used to being used when you're on air. Your image is used. Your reputation is used. Media is a contact sport,' he says.

Yet he never felt sorry for himself or that he failed James Packer. 'No, not at all. We got a couple of yards into one race and then were in a different one. It was fascinating, and it was the greatest learning experience you could ever have to be sitting at that table,' he says. 'The Packer family gave me enormous opportunities on the Nine Network to achieve really all my dreams in television and the media. And gave me just a huge, huge lift in building a dream life. I have never forgotten it.'

FIVE

Wheel of Fortune

JAMES PACKER IS SO CLOSE to Melbourne businessman Lloyd Williams that when Packer's first son was born on 1 February 2010 at Sydney's Mater Hospital, he was named Jackson Lloyd. Williams has had a deep relationship with the Packer family since the late 1970s, when he owned a string of racehorses with Kerry Packer. They also regularly played golf together and invested in each other's companies. Kerry was an early backer of Williams's property development company Hudson Conway, a partnership with Ron Walker and Sir Rod Carnegie.

The Packers' private company CPH was also a founding shareholder in Williams's listed casino company Crown, which in 1993 landed a controversial $2 billion contract from the Kennett government to build and operate Melbourne's first casino, on the banks of the Yarra River. Despite its later troubles, or perhaps because of them, the casino would forever seal a bond between Lloyd Williams and James Packer. When the Asian financial crisis hit in 1998, the debt-laden and overcapitalised Crown found itself heavily exposed. After three attempts at a takeover of Crown – the first two were stymied by Kerry Packer in the hope of getting it for a lower price – PBL finally snapped it up in 1999 for $1.789 billion, $200 million less than its construction cost. It was a deal that transformed PBL from being a pure media stock and added substantially to the company's annual cash flows. It also put several hundred million dollars of tax losses on PBL's balance sheet, and PBL shares tripled in price in the decade after the deal.

Williams now says it was an acquisition absolutely championed by the then 31-year-old James. 'It was a deal that he drove. He was keen on doing it when I was putting Sydney together. It is well known that we went to America and we got agreement to buy Sydney, and Kerry decided he didn't want to do it after we got agreement,' Williams says of the Packers' decision in May 1997 to pull out of a deal to gain management control of the Sydney casino, then known as Star City. 'At that stage, when James was talking with me, we were going to have Sydney and Melbourne. So James always wanted to do it.'

Kerry was always wary of shifting PBL into gaming. He knew first-hand how much the house could win and lose from the multimillion-dollar hands he played in the world's top casinos. He was also cautious about PBL taking on a struggling asset as Crown Melbourne then was. But he eventually supported it. 'James was fortunate in the Crown transaction in that Kerry liked it,' Williams says. 'Which is different to One.Tel or Hoyts, which he didn't like. The casino business Kerry understood. He was usually on the other side of the table, but he understood [that] if it was run properly, it was a good business.'

James, with the support and encouragement of Williams, was exuberant to do a deal many have described in hindsight as 'a steal'. While James now feels, upon reflection, that Crown was more his father's deal than his own, Jeff Kennett says he shares Williams's view of who should get the credit. '[James] convinced Kerry to buy Crown. It was clearly James's decision,' Kennett now says. 'That was a master stroke in getting an asset that was going to have a long life. That reinforced his astuteness financially.'

The Crown transaction, then the biggest of James's life, was also the first to highlight a stark contrast with his father in their approaches to business and to life. 'James is an optimist; Kerry was a pessimist at heart,' says long-time Packer family adviser Peter Barron. 'That was one key difference between them. James is an optimist about people too. Kerry was the opposite.'

Unlike his father, James also loved financial engineering and complex transactions. With the help of then PBL director and new CPH CEO Ashok Jacob, they came up with an innovative structure for the Crown deal, where Crown investors were offered shares in PBL and the chance to be part of an expanded media and gaming conglomerate. Both Crown and PBL shareholders would soon profit handsomely from it.

Williams eventually became one of the executors of Kerry's will, after the family patriarch in his dying days reportedly told another friend, John Singleton: 'There are only two people I trust to manage my estate and that's you and Lloyd Williams. I am going with Lloyd because you drink too much.' James now says Williams 'has been as good as anyone to me and maybe better. His words are kind and motivating. His actions are grand and generous.' He effuses about the man who for decades has been one of his few true mentors, advisers and confidants: 'I know why Dad loved him so much. He's an incredibly special person. I am continually in his debt.'

In more recent years, as James has spent most of his time offshore, Williams says he has missed the personal contact they had for decades before. 'I love him like a son. There is no doubt about that; I've known him since he was an early teenager. And I worry about him, probably on a daily basis. Just like I worry about my own children. It's the same,' he says. 'My difficulty is I'm living 13,000 kilometres away from him. I was pleased to see Erica and the kids out here in March [2018]. It's difficult when you're a long way away, because there is no touch and feel. I have seen James in person four or five times in the past three years. I do miss him. We did a lot of things together. We talked a lot – he used to come around and sit in my study for hours on end. I don't see him like that now.'

*

JAMES PACKER HAS LONG maintained that his interest in casinos goes back to his childhood. 'As a kid I saw that Dad lost a lot of money in casinos, and I didn't understand that. I thought this must be a great business. At the same time, I saw when I was with him – and I was with him a lot of the time – that this was a really cool business, and it was fun and glamorous,' he told *Forbes* magazine in March 2014. 'As I got older I realised that he knew what he was doing. He was prepared to spend some of the money that he made to make himself feel better by giving himself an adrenalin rush … Some of the happiest times I ever saw my dad were times when I was with him in the casinos and he had a good night.'

James's decision to leave his legacy in gaming in the years following his father's death also stemmed from the terrors of trying to manage Kerry's losses on CPH's balance sheet. He clearly saw there was good money to be made from siding with the house. Ironically, James himself has never gambled in casinos. Crown director Harold Mitchell says James's gaming interest draws from something James knows better than most: numbers. 'In the year after Kerry died, James took an unemotional view that media stocks were overvalued and gaming stocks were undervalued,' Mitchell says. 'He craved nothing of the power of the media that his father had cherished for so long. And he knew a tilt at building a genuine global business would need to be in a global industry like gaming.'

James has long believed that one of the most misunderstood aspects of his life is that he has been determined to have a controlling interest in an operational business as opposed to simply being an investor in other companies. As he told Peter FitzSimons in 1994, when he was only twenty-seven, he would never be prepared to just sit back and bank the hefty dividend cheques flowing from his inheritance. In that interview there was a hint of the vulnerability and fear of the vices that would cause him so many problems later. He told FitzSimons he was worried he would 'self-destruct', through 'gambling, fast cars, alcohol, drugs, whatever it happens to be. If I sat back and decided to sell the product of my father and my grandfather's work, like a leech, you know I wouldn't be able to look at myself in the mirror,' he declared. 'I want to be able to look at my father in ten years' time and say, "I'm proud of you, and you should be proud of me."'

That predilection manifested itself in a passion for deal-making in the decade after his father's death, principally in the gaming sector. Some went well; some went horribly wrong. 'Casinos was JP not KP,' says Village Roadshow co-chief executive Graham Burke. 'I sat on a beach with James in Thailand when he outlined his vision for what could be an incredible business. Much more so than the Nine Network, which was then the family's crown jewel. He had a plan beyond Melbourne, and at one stage Village Roadshow even considered doing [Crown] Sydney with him. The breadth of his vision was extraordinary.'

The appointment of Peter Yates to the CEO role at PBL in March 2001 provided the ideal opportunity for James to look for more deals to further diversify the company's earnings and reduce its reliance on its legacy media businesses. But the key obstacle remained his father. In December 2002, PBL was offered the chance to buy the Brisbane-based gaming company Jupiters, which had casinos on the Gold Coast, in Brisbane and in Townsville. But a debt-wary Kerry refused to borrow the money to pay for it.

James and Yates had also been looking further afield, across the Nullarbor Plain to Perth. The Packers were still haunted by Kerry's disastrous Westralia Square property deal in Perth in the late 1980s, where the Packer family's CPH had lost as much as $200 million. It prompted Kerry to declare 'all West Australians are crooks'. But in September 2002 the Western Australian government agreed to a twelve-month timetable to remove the 10 per cent shareholding cap on the casino and resort operator Burswood, opening the door to a potential takeover.

The decision was in part a response to a clever behind-the-scenes lobbying campaign led by former Labor senator turned Packer operative Graham Richardson. 'I was making sure the government over there changed the rules. The casino was going nowhere; they knew it. They needed to get rid of the shareholder cap and they did,' Richardson recalls.

During the first half of 2003, Yates and PBL's lawyers found a loophole in the WA shareholder cap legislation that would allow PBL to buy 15 per cent of Burswood. 'We weren't necessarily planning to buy Burswood but we'd have it locked away,' Yates recalls in his first public comments on the deal that ultimately cost him his job. 'Kerry was jammed. Because if he didn't allow us to at least secure a foothold on Burswood, then he knew that Crown was going to be an isolated asset, and gaming as a strategy for PBL was gone. And also, Burswood was the largest high-rollers site in Australia.'

Kerry reluctantly agreed to allow Yates to make the Burswood play and agreed on a maximum price that he could offer the company's shareholders. Yates approached WA businessmen Bill Wyllie and Jack Bendat, who between them held 14.2 per cent of the Burswood share register, and went about convincing them to sell. On the eve of the 2003 AFL grand final between Brisbane and Collingwood, Yates secured the signatures of Wyllie and Bendat to sell their holding to PBL at a price 2 per cent above Kerry's ceiling. On 3 October, just days after the Burswood board recommended shareholders accept removing the shareholder cap on their company, PBL announced it had paid Wyllie and Bendat $77.3 million to lift its stake in Burswood to 15.7 per cent. The then WA premier Geoff Gallop declared at the time: 'My point of view is that if Kerry Packer's interested in WA, that's good for WA.' The Packers were back in Perth's good books.

James couldn't believe Yates had managed to pull off the deal. But his father was less than impressed. 'The shit that got poured on me by Kerry for going 2 per cent above his upper limit was like you have never heard. But I did argue that there was no broker involved. If I'd bought stock through the market, we probably would have paid 2 per cent more,' Yates recalls.

Yates says he eventually 'got one of those gruff acceptances' from Kerry that the move had been the right one. 'Kerry then said, "You're not going any further, under no circumstances," because he did not want PBL to have any debt, and to buy Burswood we were going to borrow up to $600 million,' Yates says. 'So James and I'd spent all this time creating all these budgets and outlooks to show that we needed to take on debt and build and buy growth businesses.'

By PBL's March board meeting in 2004, Yates had finalised the company's first ever strategic plan, which showed a vision to grow through a takeover of Burswood. The target was the Perth casino's high-roller income. By organising package deals with Melbourne's Crown Casino, a combined Crown–Burswood could attract a steady flow of punters from Asia. The night before the meeting, the PBL board gathered at Kerry's family compound at Bellevue Hill for its first ever dinner together. After months of quiet lobbying by James and Yates, the directors soon talked up the opportunities for PBL in Western Australia.

'The directors were all primed because at the board meeting the following morning they knew James and I wanted to bid for Burswood,' Yates recalls with glee. 'One by one each of the directors said it was a fantastic idea. [Kerry] had to do it.' It marked the beginning of the end for Yates's job and his relationship with Kerry Packer. But it was another symbolic turning point for James. He might have still been nursing a shoulder injury sustained in a fall from a horse during a polo tournament that had left him unconscious, but twice in the space of six months – first with Crown and now with Burswood – luck had turned in his favour in the strategic battle with his father.

In late April, James and Yates visited the Perth office of Burswood chairman Don Watt and proudly presented him with Crown's hostile bid for the casino. The bid, which valued Burswood at $686 million, was the first major acquisition for Yates as PBL's CEO. But six weeks after announcing the takeover bid, the deal had run into trouble: PBL had received almost no acceptances for its offer from Burswood's shareholders. The Burswood board was digging in for a sweetened offer. Kerry's patience was wearing thin, as his condition for agreeing to the bid in the first place was that there would only ever be one offer. Now Yates was pushing for another. It was the final straw.

On the morning of 9 June, PBL told the ASX that its CEO had resigned 'for personal reasons'. Yates now recalls the event with a wide smile. 'Kerry rang up each of the board members the day before and said, "I don't know if you've heard what's happened to Peter? Well, unfortunately, he's left." He didn't call up and say, "Do you think we should terminate Peter?" It was just done. It was classic.' Under the terms of his contract Yates would get a termination payment of $6.54 million.

James had lost a noble ally who shared with him a genuine love of strategy and he knew it. 'So the next day James called me in. He presented me with the most beautiful note about our relationship and what I'd done and how sad he was,' Yates says.

But James had got what he wanted. Kerry had agreed to raise the Burswood bid price to $715 million in return for the head of the CEO who had dared challenge him once too often. It was enough to win over the Burswood directors. The deal proved to be a master stroke. Five years later PBL had doubled the earnings from the Perth casino. 'Burswood was Peter Yates's finest moment and it's the thing I respect him most for,' James now says. 'He knew if he stood up for his beliefs Dad would fire him. And he didn't budge. Not many people do that.'

Graham Richardson says the Burswood transaction confirmed to James that after the horrors of One.Tel, he could still be a successful deal-maker – and win over his father. 'He was the architect in getting Burswood. His father didn't want it, James pushed for it and got it up in the end. Burwood was very good for his ego, and his ego is important. When you suffer from a bit of depression, you need to have wins. Losses hurt you deeply,' Richardson says.

Yates says Burswood also allowed James to hone his appetite for risk, which would take PBL onto the global stage for the first time. 'Kerry was left with Channel Nine as a toy to play around with. And James focused on Macau,' he says. 'Kerry was a big risk taker but he took it in gambling, not in business. James doesn't gamble, but he's closer to taking more risk in business. James is more prepared to take the risk around the unknown, which has the bigger payout ratio. He makes decisions across a bigger spectrum of opportunity.'

*

THE OFFICES OF LAWRENCE Ho's Asian gaming company Melco Crown Entertainment in Hong Kong tower above a trendy bar and nightclub precinct known as Lan Kwai Fong in the city's Central district. On a clear day, from Ho's relatively nondescript boardroom on the thirty-sixth floor of the building known as the Centrium, you can gaze across Victoria Harbour to the rugged mountain ranges of the Chinese mainland in the distance that encircle the urban precinct of Kowloon.

Impeccably dressed today in suit and tie, with a Starbucks coffee in one hand and a business card in the other, the diminutive Ho bows as he shakes my hand and greets me. As we sit down, he recalls meeting James Packer for the first time in Sydney during August 2004. 'I was meeting with [Crown Melbourne's then chief operating officer] John Williams and James popped in. I had never met him before. It was a chance meeting. It was a total surprise. He then popped out and brought Kerry in two minutes later,' Ho recalls. 'I was fortunate enough to meet Kerry two or three times before his passing. He was very nice to me. Kerry was Kerry; there were some very sharp comments. But he was nice. Certainly not some of the stories I heard about him in terms of throwing people out of the room.'

A year earlier Ho, a former investment banker, had made his first move into the gaming sector of Macau, the once

Portuguese-controlled territory of China where gambling is legal. He started operating his own casino company known as Melco Entertainment under the licence of his father, casino mogul Stanley Ho. The now 96-year-old Ho Senior is known as the King of Gambling in Macau. For forty years, he held a government-granted monopoly on the casino industry there, until November 2001 when the Macau government opened applications for two additional casino concessions. One was awarded to Sheldon Adelson's Las Vegas Sands and the other to US casino magnate Steve Wynn's Wynn Resorts.

By 2003, Ho Senior's oldest living son, Lawrence – one of seventeen children to Ho's four wives – was determined to strike out on his own. He travelled the world looking for partners, which eventually brought him to Australia and the Park Street offices of PBL. Lawrence told Kerry and James Packer that he had secured a piece of land from his father on the island in Macau known as Taipa, where he was building his first casino. They liked what they heard.

Earlier in 2004 the PBL board, at the urging of James, had made the landmark decision to examine gaming opportunities in Macau. James had grown to appreciate the opportunities for Australia provided by China's rising middle class. He was keen for his and other Australian businesses to deepen their ties with the world's fastest growing economy. 'Lawrence came up to Park Street and we sat down in the main boardroom. And he was clearly very impressive,' James recalls. 'After the trauma of what happened with Burswood, Dad was great and my relationship with him improved. When Lawrence came to Sydney, he also met Dad. Dad was more than interested because Stanley Ho was a legendary figure. Dad really liked Lawrence. And he encouraged us to do a deal with him.'

As a result a joint venture between PBL and Melco was formed in late 2004, when the two agreed to unite exclusively to pursue casino developments in Asia. 'What I found different with James and his management team compared to the US operators is that they tried to understand Asian players, their guests, their customers and their preferences. That collaborative spirit was there from day one,' Ho says. 'We always had ambitions beyond Macau; what we had discussed was overall Asia. So having a partner like PBL back then and then Crown was the best bet.'

But the joint venture also opened another door for Ho – a chance to cut the cord with his legendary father. Lawrence had never liked the terms of the deal that was struck for Melco to use the concession of his father's SJM Holdings, and he was wary of the layers of bureaucracy that had developed over decades inside SJM. He was soon in James's ear telling him they needed to be masters of their own destiny in Macau. 'The reason I have never worked in my father's companies, ever – and he is a legend of the industry – is that over the years he surrounded himself with management people. It was too complex, convoluted and bureaucratic,' Lawrence says. 'If we had the opportunity to get our own licence, it was definitely worth it. James was great because he trusted me; he said it was a fantastic idea and that we should pursue it.'

James would also have been wary of allegations that had long been raised about Stanley Ho's association with Chinese organised crime – the so-called triads – and the alleged involvement of his casinos in money laundering, given Macau's history as the Wild West of Asia. SJM had been previously banned from bidding for casinos in not only Australia, but also in the US, Singapore and the Philippines. This could have had implications not only for the new PBL–Melco joint venture, but for PBL itself during probity checks for its Australian casinos.

James also knew of the challenges of running a business in the shadow of a famous father. In the early years of their partnership, James and Lawrence talked candidly about their billionaire fathers and their contrasting experiences of making their way in the business world. This was their chance to forge their own reputations on the global gaming stage.

The timing was ideal. For the previous two years, in an attempt to further grow the gaming dollar in Macau, the government there had been allowing its casino licence concession holders to grant sub-concessions to new players. The new sub-concession holders would be entitled to operate a virtually unlimited number of casinos in Macau until June 2022. By mid 2005 the only sub-concession left to be awarded was by Steve Wynn.

The Packers were well known to Wynn, having been introduced to him by Lloyd Williams. 'I knew Steve back in 1988 and he is still a good friend today,' Williams says. Kerry had been a regular visitor to Wynn's high-roller rooms in Las Vegas and had dined with Wynn at Sydney's Park Hyatt Hotel when the American made a brief visit to Australia early in 2005. Kerry had even been granted a personal locker at Wynn's Shadow Creek Golf Course in North Las Vegas, along with famous names such as former US president Bill Clinton and Microsoft founder Bill Gates.

After Wynn's visit to Australia, where he talked up Macau's prospects to Kerry, Lawrence and James started informal talks about securing the American's sub-concession. 'Steve liked both Lawrence and James. Even though he was a competitor, I remember him saying these words to me: "These young blokes will do well,"' Lloyd Williams says. But they were not alone. Wynn later said he fielded roughly one enquiry per week about the sub-concession during 2005.

The young partners also still needed Kerry's blessing to put serious money on the table, to focus PBL's growth ambitions on the international stage for the first time. 'I remember I went with James at some time in 2005 to talk to Kerry because we knew it was going to be a mega purchase,' Lawrence recalls. 'Kerry was okay with the idea. But I always had the sense that he cared for his publishing and media assets a lot more than the gambling part. It was me and James being somewhat pushy that this was a great idea.'

Kerry's death on Boxing Day 2005 only increased the resolve of his son and Lawrence to push Wynn as hard as they could without blowing their chances. By mid January 2006 James was back on the phone to Wynn, who fobbed him off for a time before in early February agreeing to meet him in New York.

Lawrence was already working on the financing of Melco's new $2 billion City of Dreams casino resort project on Macau's emerging Cotai strip, situated between its two outlying islands of Coloane and Taipa. To discuss the project, Lawrence had already scheduled a meeting in New York with a famous billionaire property developer named Donald Trump. 'We met Donald Trump in the morning and Steve Wynn in the afternoon,' Packer recalls. 'We were talking to Donald about doing a Trump tower together in Macau. He wanted to make the fifth tower of the City of Dreams project an apartment tower. Donald knew Dad quite well and liked him a lot. I had met Donald a few times before. He had taken Jodhi and me for dinner in New York. When Donald came to Australia in 2012 he asked to play golf with me. I was away so he played with Ben [Tilley] instead.'

After Trump they met with Wynn, who was still playing hard to get. But he was clear on one important point: he liked James and if he was going to deal, he would only do it with him personally. The partners left New York knowing US casino giant Harrah's had been negotiating to buy Wynn's sub-concession for less than US$400 million. They also knew that Lawrence's sister Pansy Ho and her joint-venture partner MGM had paid Stanley Ho only US$200 million for their sub-concession. After a long discussion, Melco-PBL agreed to offer Wynn a stunning US$800 million.

Two weeks later James was driving to his Park Street office in Sydney when his secretary Jacquie Murray rang. Wynn was on the phone. He didn't waste words. 'James, US$900 million. But you haven't got long,' he said coolly, before hanging up.

Lawrence recalls then receiving a call from an excited James. 'James was very decisive. The James I know is very passionate and a great numbers person. The negotiation going from US$800 million to US$900 million was a light-switch event. He was like, "Let's do it,"' Lawrence recalls. 'And when James called me up and said the price, knowing my family dynamics and how screwed up those people are, I said it was worth it. And James agreed.'

Before the end of the day James was on his plane to Las Vegas with Crown CEO Rowen Craigie, his legal adviser Guy Jalland and Jacquie Murray. When they arrived at the Wynn Las Vegas resort, which had been open less than a year, they all piled into the same four-bedroom luxury villa for the night. 'We met Steve in Vegas. It was all good except he initially wanted a US$900 million non-refundable deposit. He then thankfully dropped that. And we had a deal ready to be signed within twenty-four hours,' James recalls.

The transaction was announced on 4 March 2006, only two weeks after Kerry Packer's memorial service. It was immediately greeted with surprise, even horror. The critics called it a reckless move by the deal-hungry son who finally had his hands on the keys to his father's multibillion-dollar kingdom. And all it provided was a piece of paper to allow PBL to own and operate casinos in Macau, instead of having to rely on the licence held by Stanley Ho's SJM. Melco-PBL were also paying hundreds of millions of dollars more than their rivals had for their sub-concessions. But as PricewaterhouseCoopers' director of gaming practice David Green told *The Sydney Morning Herald* at the time, giving Melco–PBL some important distance from Stanley Ho and any ongoing probity concerns was worth it.

And for Lawrence personally, the deal with Wynn was especially sweet. 'Getting out of working with my family and my father's company was worth any price … My father was very legendary. But it was not so much him. It was the people surrounding him that were very problematic. The management team. When you look at that company's market capitalisation now, it is half of ours. And they had the monopoly for forty years and a good head start,' he says.

James will never forget the day Stanley Ho ripped up the contract between SJM and Melco and wished him and Lawrence good luck. Two weeks later Ho Senior resigned from the board of Melco and sold all his shares in the company, at the time saying he wanted to avoid any conflict of interest as SJM pursued a sharemarket listing. The listing was subsequently delayed for two years after a legal challenge from Ho Senior's estranged sister. When he next saw Ho Senior in Hong Kong, James says he gave him a lucky gold coin. Meanwhile, Wynn sent him enough flowers to fill his entire Park Street office back in Sydney.

'It was viewed as madness,' James now says. 'But when [Melco Crown] floated [on the Nasdaq in America in December that year] it was a great deal.' The Nasdaq issue of 15 per cent of the company to the public raised a bigger than expected US$1.3 billion and put a $10 billion valuation on the joint venture between the two billionaire scions. And it paved the way for James to try his hand on the biggest stage of them all in global gaming: America.

SIX

The Gambler

STEVE WYNN FIRST MET Michael Milken in 1978 when Wynn was thirty-six years old. Milken, the controversial 1980s Wall Street junk-bond wizard, revolutionised the way companies in America and across the globe were financed. He taught Wynn the secrets to borrowing money in the bond market to drive the growth of what became a multibillion-dollar casino empire. When Wynn introduced Milken to speak at a conference more than three decades later in July 2009, he passionately described him as 'one of those rare human beings who can see into the future. He has gifts intellectually that were not given to most people on this planet. He can look around the corner. Yet he has the capacity to care for all of his friends.'

Milken is now a philanthropist and namesake of a prominent annual conference run by the California-based Milken Institute, which attracts more than 3500 people from fifty countries. At the 10th anniversary Milken Institute Global Conference in April 2007, where the likes of Andre

Agassi, Michael J. Fox and Ted Turner took to the stage, Milken had a chance meeting with James Packer. Global sharemarkets had been on a five-year roll. In America the benchmark Dow Jones index was enjoying its third-longest bull run in seventy-five years. Easy money was everywhere. 'Mike Milken kindly took me aside and told me not to invest in the US gaming market when he heard we were looking around,' Packer now says, noting that Milken knew many of the players and saw it as a trap for new ones.

PBL had more than $4 billion of cash in the bank following the sale of its media assets to private equity buyers a year earlier. Its options were to return some of the money to shareholders or keep it in Crown, which was predominantly a casino company with assets in Melbourne, Perth and Macau. 'At that stage the management of CPH, PBL and Crown all decided that we were not going to return capital to shareholders and that we were going to become a global gaming company. We were already in Macau, so that meant going to America,' Packer says.

The next moment I catch a glimpse of anger on his face. The pain of what was to come clearly still burns deep. 'At CPH and Crown, we made the decision that we knew more about the US gaming market than Mike Milken and that we would continue to look for opportunities in that market,' he adds, deadpan. Milken was banned from the securities industry for life after pleading guilty to a securities fraud charge in 1990, but he knew plenty about risk. His advice to Packer on the US gaming market proved prescient.

Crown would soon pay top dollar to enter the famous US$7 billion Las Vegas casino market in a frantic seven months of deal-making just before the GFC hit. Its first hand was a stake in the Fontainebleau casino resort, and one in the Stations Casino Group, combined worth a cool $500 million.

The second was a $175 million bet on a 2.5 per cent share in the world's largest gaming operator, Harrah's, which owned Caesars Palace and fifty other casinos in the United States. Then followed a half-share in Canadian group Gateway Casinos & Entertainment through a $1.5 billion partnership with Macquarie Bank. In total, Crown shelled out $1 billion to buy into a string of companies where it had no management control and any profits would only come back to Crown in the form of dividends.

But it didn't stop there. Next came plans to build a $5.5 billion Crown Las Vegas casino and hotel complex with private-equity partner York Capital Management and Chris Milam, a Texas property developer. It was followed by the biggest bet of all in December 2007, a $1.75 billion purchase of the Cannery Casino Resorts business in America, with its three casinos in Las Vegas and one in Pennsylvania. It was a manic buying spree, that would prove to be the ultimate disaster.

*

By 2009, as the GFC had taken hold, Las Vegas was in a death spiral. No major US city was more devastated when the subprime mortgage crisis stuck. Americans who had previously had spare cash to gamble in the city's casinos were now using it simply to keep a roof over their heads. Unemployment skyrocketed.

Crown's then new executive vice president of strategy and development, Todd Nisbet, who was based in Las Vegas at the time, couldn't believe what he was seeing. Hour after hour, he was on the phone to Packer and Crown CEO Rowen Craigie detailing the carnage. For the second time in his life, Packer went into meltdown. As he had done after the One.Tel debacle, he fled to the US to visit a Scientology centre in Los Angeles, where the Church of Scientology's then chief spokesman, Tommy Davis, took him under his wing. Davis later went to work for Packer.

'As 2008 neared its end I had a total nervous breakdown. I thought we were going broke. Dad died at the end of 2005 and I had had such a good 2006 with the Macau deals and the sale of PBL Media,' Packer recalls, the pain still clear in his eyes. 'Since then we had invested completely recklessly in the US casino market and [financial services group] Challenger's share price went from around $6 dollars to below $1. Ashok Jacob's [Ellerston Capital] hedge fund wasn't working and our debt at CPH was over $1.5 billion and never seemed to come down.'

It was only months after the birth of his first child, daughter Indigo, to his second wife, Erica. One former adviser to Challenger, in which CPH was an investor and of which Packer was a director, will never forget the lead-up to the Challenger annual general meeting in Sydney in November 2008. 'I remember James almost didn't turn up. He told [Challenger chairman] Peter Polson, 'I'm right on the edge here, I don't think I should come.' He eventually did. But the episode again highlighted his instinctive response to crises, to initially withdraw and hope his problems will go away, before eventually summoning the courage to confront them.

Knowing the Cannery deal could potentially bankrupt Crown, Ashok Jacob and Guy Jalland started working tirelessly to find a way to extricate Crown from it. Jacob even gave up his job running Ellerston Capital for more than six months to work on a fix. The transaction needed to be ticked off by gaming authorities in two states: Nevada and Pennsylvania. While Nevada waved it through, the more onerous regulatory requirements in Pennsylvania were proving challenging for other members of the Packer family.

In November 2008, Packer's sister, Gretel, asked the Pennsylvania Gaming Control Board to let CPH – Crown's major shareholder – withdraw from the licensing process. Gretel asserted that she had not realised the process would require her to disclose sensitive financial information relating to trusts of which she was a beneficiary that were part of the family's complicated CPH network of companies. Her actions meant the Cannery deal could not proceed. 'Ashok was the first person to realise how bad Cannery was. I am so grateful to Ash for everything he did from then,' Packer now says.

The casino's vendors immediately accused Gretel and her advisers of seeking to stymie the deal for the benefit of her brother. But on Black Friday, 13 March 2009, Crown managed to formalise its escape from the deal by paying for a mere 24.5 per cent stake in Cannery worth $US370 million. It was the first time Gretel had been publicly involved in any major transaction involving her brother and it revealed her significant influence in the empire.

Packer still wonders why he did not make Crown's management more accountable for the company's bad US investments. He fell out badly with Crown CEO Rowen Craigie over the Cannery deal even if he acknowledges the buck eventually stopped with him. 'I said to myself never ever, ever again am I going to be in that position.'

The consequences of the disastrous US foray were laid bare in Crown's annual results released on 27 August 2009 as part of what *The Australian* at the time called a $1.44 billion 'scorched earth' writedown program that covered its entire American casino portfolio. The carrying value of its Cannery stake was reduced to just $49.6 million, while everything else was assumed to be worth zero. 'Looking back, it is clear that we completely lacked the capability to go into the US market. That was the biggest mistake of my business life. And its ramifications for me and my business have been lasting and painful,' Packer says. 'And then when we did invest the money in America, we lost it in five minutes. When the tide went out in 2009, we at CPH and Crown were wearing no clothes. I and the previous management of both CPH and Crown were all responsible for that.'

His wealth on the *BRW* Rich List fell to $2.5 billion in the second half of 2008 from $6.1 billion the previous year, as the value of both his public and private investments collapsed. Packer was again petrified by his greatest fear, that he would lose the family fortune.

*

IF THERE WAS ONE corporate deal in Packer's life that disappointed his mother and sister above all else, it was his decision in 2008 to part with the Consolidated Pastoral Company (CPC), the network of iconic cattle stations in the nation's north that had been built up by his father. Every two years Ros Packer would spend a month touring all of CPC's stations, often with her good friend, the company's founder, Ken Warriner. She would base herself at the stunning Newcastle Waters property, then Warriner's home.

But for CPH to survive the implosion of Crown's US casino investments, and with − at that point − no certainty of escape from the Cannery deal, something had to give. 'Dad had spoken to me several times about selling CPC to get CPH's debt down,' Packer recalls. 'Dad, Ken [Warriner] and I had dinner in Melbourne one night in 2004 or 2005 and Dad was going to tell Ken. But Dad couldn't do it. Dad loved Ken Warriner. The problem with Ken was he always wanted to buy another property.'

Packer found an interested buyer in Guy Hands and his British private equity firm Terra Firma. 'He made a very cold business decision,' Hands tells me in his first public comments on the $425 million deal, which was signed off by the Western Australian government on 13 March 2009 – the same day Crown secured its escape from Cannery. 'CPC is not a cash-generative business. It is a capital-gain business. It is very, very seasonal. The weather really does affect it. We have managed to bring in a bit of technology and investment to make it less seasonal and to manage the properties in a slightly less seasonal way. It didn't fit in with what James was trying to do from a business point of view and this was an area that had huge risk. There is no question that for him it was a very good business decision to sell it.'

Packer has subsequently been criticised for not securing a better price for CPC, given Terra Firma reportedly put a $1 billion price tag on the company when it took it to the market during 2018. But Hands describes the commentary as 'totally unfair. We had some real problems with the business over the first five years. We had to put a lot of money in, a lot of wells in, we had to get water to the cattle. We had droughts and we were worried about the cattle dying. We had the Indonesian [live cattle export] bans. For the first five years, it looked like we had done a terrible deal and James had done very well,' he says.

'One of the things people don't get about James is that he thinks very deeply. His thinking ability is way above what he necessarily expresses. You have to spend time with him, get him to slow down and express his thoughts. They are complex and deep. He thinks about business as a chess game. When he sold the properties, he was facing a concern about liquidity in his businesses. James did a major strategic shift in terms of his need for liquidity and the types of businesses he was going to have. I think reducing the volatility was significant.'

In August 2009 James also surprised the market when he resigned from the board of Gold Coast–based property developer Sunland Group. He sold his 11 per cent stake in the group a month later for a significant loss. Sunland was a glamour company James had talked up three years earlier for its opportunities in the key Middle East market of Dubai. His sudden resignation and dumping of his Sunland shares showed his frustration that the company's father-and-son joint managing directors, Soheil and Sahba Abedian, had not delivered what they had promised.

Sunland was another company hit by the GFC, which forced it to curtail its global ambitions. It opened an office in Dubai in 2007 and started building several residential towers, as well Palazzo Versace Dubai with the hotel business of Italian fashion designer Donatella Versace. But the Dubai property market subsequently imploded. In 2013 corporate regulator ASIC also launched an investigation over questionable sharemarket announcements made by Sunland relating to bribery allegations in Dubai during 2009, though it dropped the case in 2016. But Sunland was yet another investment Packer had lived to regret.

*

AFTER THE TERRORS OF the GFC faded into history, Packer made other attempts to build a casino business in the US, especially after his children moved to America following the breakdown of his second marriage at the end of 2013. In April 2014 Crown was offered an exclusive option by then co-CEO of Deutsche Bank Anshu Jain to buy the Cosmopolitan, one of the most expensive casino hotels ever built on the famous Las Vegas strip. The price tag was a cool US$1.5 billion, which Packer wanted to finance by selling a parcel of 40 million shares in Melco Crown while they were trading at almost $40 when the Macau gaming market was at its peak. But, he says, his advisers and management talked him out of it. The following month the asset was purchased by property giant Blackstone Real Estate Partners for US$1.7 billion. It is now worth far more.

The failure of the Cosmo deal also saw Crown in August 2014 purchase a parcel of land on the Las Vegas strip next to a casino owned by Steve Wynn. The plan was to develop what would be known as the $2.5 billion Alon Las Vegas project, Crown's second attempt at building a casino on the famed strip. Crown partnered with former Wynn Las Vegas president Andrew Pascal, with backing from private equity firm Oaktree, to develop the 1100-room resort. The resort was to be based on the same model as Crown Sydney. Showing he had learned from his past mistakes, Packer and his new partners even set up a special-purpose company for the project to reduce the risk. But challenges in financing slowed the planning, and Crown revealed in December 2017 that it was axing the project. At the end of January 2018 the land was sold to Wynn Resorts for US$300 million. Alon has been described by some as another Packer folly.

While Packer is prepared to cop the criticism where he feels it is warranted, on this one he takes issue. He claims the Alon land represented the best remaining site in Vegas. 'We went back [to America] at a time our Macau stake had risen in value to be worth approximately US$7.5 billion. Melco Crown's share price had risen from around US$3.50 in the GFC to over US$40. Although this was an unrealised profit, and Crown subsequently sold its Melco Crown shares at a huge discount to those prices, at the time it had given me the confidence that our international expansion strategy was a success,' he says. 'I was relying on different management at the time, Todd Nisbet as opposed to Rowen Craigie. And Andrew Pascal, who had previously been the president of Wynn, was our local partner. Todd and Andrew were both from Vegas. Oaktree, one of the world's smartest investors, validated Crown's investment by staying in as a minority shareholder.' But the Las Vegas dream again turned to dust. It's now highly unlikely Crown will ever return there.

The critics will always present Crown's American casino adventures as highlighting some of Packer's greatest character flaws. Many still wonder why he did not have some sense of the looming bursting of the Las Vegas gaming and real-estate bubble in 2007, especially after the warning from Michael Milken. While they acknowledge the US casino investments were a collective decision of the CPH and Crown management teams at the time – as Packer highlights – the buck stopped with the major shareholder and chairman. 'James has a decision-making process that is reflective of his mood at the time. Excessive optimism means overpaying and excessive pessimism means selling at the wrong time – both are bad decisions,' says one business associate who knows him well.

Former Ellerston Capital chief executive Glenn Poswell, who was given Gretel Packer's office at CPH's Park Street headquarters when he started work there in 2004, remembers once being asked at the last minute by Packer to be Gretel's date at a Sting concert he was due to attend with her in Sydney. Poswell recalls, '[Gretel] told me that night: "I know you will look after James, he has always been higher than high and lower than low."' Gretel's intervention in the Cannery deal saved the family fortune, and her share in it, from going to ruin. But perhaps she was also saving her brother from himself.

Paul Bassat, the co-founder of Seek and venture capital firm Square Peg Capital – in which CPH is an investor – says Packer has 'really strong business instincts. His decision to exit

PBL, his investment in Macau and his Seek investment are all good examples of this. Critics will point to bad investment decisions like RatPac and the investments he made in US casinos prior to the GFC. I think those examples are less about poor business instincts and more a case of making the right decision for the wrong reasons.'

'My sense is that those investments were more driven by other factors than rational financial factors,' Bassat says. James thought it would be a lot of fun to make movies and hang out in Hollywood with people like De Niro and Brad Pitt. Similarly, I suspect he thought it would be exciting to invest alongside people like David Bonderman of Texas Pacific Group (TPG) in the purchase of Harrah's. He perceived that private-equity legends like Bonderman were infallible, even though he had contemporaneous evidence of their fallibility; great firms like CVC, KKR and Providence were all lining up to buy PBL, and James had real clarity that PBL's best days were behind it. When James makes decisions for purely financial reasons he gets it right much more often than he gets it wrong.'

Bassat only hopes that in the future Packer can better manage his moods and their consequences for his investment decisions. 'When I first met James in 2003 he was emerging from a difficult period in his life after the failure of his first marriage and the One.Tel failure. His investment in Seek was a signal that his drive and motivation were returning. He was chairman of Seek during the GFC and that was also a difficult period in his life, and he has had another difficult period more recently,' Bassat says. 'I'm sure that he'll bounce back from the difficulties he's experienced in the last couple of years. The challenge for James is managing the highs and lows he's experienced, and hopefully in the future the highs will be a bit less high and the lows will be a lot less low.'

Those who have worked with Packer and his father claim that while the latter would never have contemplated the Cannery Casino deal, he also would never have done the deals James did with Lawrence Ho in the Macau casino market – where Crown made six times its money over twelve years. Because Kerry was always loath to move out of his comfort zone, he simply would not have left the safety of his own shores. James also grew up in a different era from his father, one where debt was more available. He has certainly shown a capacity for separating brutal business realities from emotional ties, as highlighted by his decision to sell the cattle stations business. James might view himself as 'soft', but he has arguably made tough decisions about his inheritance that his father would not have made because of his feelings for those businesses.

Which raises an interesting and controversial question: is James actually a tougher and braver businessman than his father? His critics would view such a proposition as laughable. His weakness – which his father never had – has been to rush into decisions. Sometimes he is dazzled by the glamour of being in the company of A-listers, sometimes by the thrill of a big-dollar deal. The impact of those bad decisions and, as he puts it – not 'walking his talk' when it counted – has been brutal.

'I really believed in the internet when [former PBL executive] Daniel Petre introduced me to it in the late '90s. And have believed ever since,' he says. 'As I look back, around that time before the GFC, my two biggest thematics were the rise of the internet and the rise of China. I didn't walk my own talk. To have not reinvested more of the proceeds of selling out of traditional media into internet-related businesses was an enormous mistake.'

*

PACKER'S CRITICS HAVE WONDERED how much the billionaire reflects upon the morality of investing in the gaming industry and the reality that what enriches him impoverishes many. The industry has also long been tainted by instances and allegations of money laundering, drug trafficking and organised crime.

In his book on Packer, *Who Wants to Be a Billionaire?*, Paul Barry devotes a full two chapters to the issue of problem gambling, including the so-called Kakavas legal case, which went all the way to the High Court in 2013. High roller Harry Kakavas sued Crown, claiming the casino company knew he was a compulsive gambler and set out to exploit his weakness by offering him a range of inducements and privileges to gamble at Crown Melbourne. These included being a guest of Crown at the Australian Open in 2005, giving him use of a corporate jet, special rebates and commissions, and free food and beverages. In doing so, he claimed Crown had acted unconscionably. The High Court, whose decision in the case was released after Barry's book was published, found that Kakavas was not a 'victim' of the casino but had willingly turned over more than a billion dollars on its baccarat tables. The Court found that a victim needed to demonstrate Crown's actual knowledge of the disadvantage of a problem gambler such as Kakavas if the company was to be held responsible for 'unconscionable conduct'.

But Barry did ask a prescient question: 'Does [Packer] lose sleep over the damage his huge casinos do to people's health, wealth and relationships? Clearly not, or he wouldn't be investing his family fortune in building more and more casinos. And he wouldn't allow Crown to behave as it does.'

In April 2018 Crown made headlines when it was hit with a record $300,000 fine by the Victorian Commission for Gambling and Liquor Regulation (VCGLR) for the unauthorised use of blanking plates on certain electronic gaming machines. The plates limit the betting options on slot machines so that only two of a possible five are available to a player. The allegations against the company were first raised in federal parliament by anti-gambling crusader and independent MP Andrew Wilkie. While the regulator found Crown's action was not deliberate and made by a small group of staff conducting a trial for which they mistakenly thought regulatory approval was not required, anti-gambling campaigner Tim Costello immediately went on the attack. He questioned Crown's culture and called on the Victorian government to force Packer to sell down his Crown stake.

In August the VCGLR released its 5-year review into the Crown Melbourne licence, criticising Crown for its poor performance in a number of areas including governance, regulatory compliance and its management of responsible gambling. It made twenty recommendations, including pushing Crown to better monitor gamblers to allow interventions to prevent them harming themselves. But again Tim Costello criticised the findings as being too weak, claiming the sanctions from the VCGLR failed to call for specific actions or changes to Crown's licence conditions.

Crown director and former Qantas chief executive Geoff Dixon, who chairs the Crown risk management committee, says the company always takes reputational issues deeply seriously. He also defends the company's governance practices. 'I have never on the board heard of anybody not being concerned about reputational damage. It is a key focus of the risk committee,' he says, before questioning broader allegations – beyond the blanking plates issue – raised against the company over the past year: 'Much of what we hear comes from many unverified sources, much of it under parliamentary privilege. It is harmful to the company and it is difficult to refute, especially where there is a lack of evidence.'

On the issue of problem gaming generally, Packer now says: 'We have to always strive to do better. Unfortunately there will be instances – hopefully rare instances – when we fall short. But we are a casino. A lot of the gambling research has spoken about the difference between destinational gaming [concentrating gambling in fewer, larger venues], and convenience gaming [street-corner gambling in pubs and clubs]. Crown has invested back hugely in non-gaming facilities – hotels, restaurants, retail and convention facilities.'

His comments are echoed by Crown director Harold Mitchell. 'As for gambling, I have no trouble with it. Firstly, it is legal. That might seem a cop-out but that is the reality,' he says. 'Secondly, people will always gamble and an organisation such as Crown does it with a great level of responsibility. Thirdly, Crown is as much an entertainment group as a gambling company.'

Crown now represents 98 per cent of Packer's net worth and 93 per cent of his assets. 'We will employ 18,000 people when Crown Sydney opens. That is a big deal for me. And we have won Employer of the Year from the federal government three times,' he says, referring to Crown's Melbourne and Perth properties being named the Australian Employer of the Year in the Australian Training Awards in 2010, 2013 and 2015.

But others wonder why, given the troubles of recent years, he doesn't simply sell out of Crown and spend the rest of his life building more philanthropic foundations from his wealth. 'I think he'd feel better about himself and finally find real meaning and purpose to having all the money given to him,' one observer says. Another says Packer 'needs to find something to do with his life that is more fulfilling than investing in gambling'.

But David Gonski, one of the nation's most passionate advocates of philanthropy, says Packer is entitled to choose where and how he invests his money. 'I think it is his fortune and he can do with it as he will. It is up to him entirely,' he says.

Packer also argues philanthropy is and will continue to be a big part of his family's tradition. 'Look at the Crown Resorts Foundation. Not many living Australians are giving away as much as our group, and as quickly,' he says. In 2014 the Packer Family Foundation, chaired by Gretel, joined forces with the charitable foundation established by Crown to launch a new $200 million charitable fund. Half of the money has gone to arts programs, while the other $100 million has been supporting charities such as the Father Bob Maguire Foundation, the Salvation Army and Indigenous education programs. 'Gretes does a great job spearheading the Packer family's philanthropic efforts. She is passionate, dedicated, and generous to the causes we support. And she gives her time willingly,' he says.

In a rare public outing for the launch of the fund in 2014, Gretel said philanthropy, especially support for the arts, would always be integral to the Packer family legacy. 'I think the arts really are core to our happiness as individuals,' she said at the time. 'It's not the only thing but arts are enormously helpful, helping us to live a full, rounded life. The arts bring dimension to other parts of our life.'

Questions about the morality of investing in the gambling industry are, of course, matters of individual conscience. Packer seems comfortable with his answers to those questions, even if the critics don't accept his position.

SEVEN

No Sacred Cows

IN THE FIRST WEEK of September 2009, with $1.7 billion worth of losses still red raw on Crown's balance sheet in the wake of the company's failed US casino plays, James Packer was taking refuge on the *Arctic P* in one of his favourite parts of the world: Bora Bora in French Polynesia. With him on board was his old friend from Macquarie Bank, Ben Brazil.

The boyish-faced banker, nicknamed 'Brains' by Macquarie's chief executive Nicholas Moore, had just started a new job at Macquarie – better known as the 'millionaire's factory'. Brazil was to hunt the globe for so-called 'special lending situations', including buying corporate debt at a discount to later sell it for a profit. For years Brazil, the man who had spearheaded Macquarie's unsuccessful takeover bid for the London Stock Exchange in 2005, had moved seamlessly between the Packer empire and Macquarie. He had become renowned for his superb ability to judge risk in markets. At the age of twenty-six he had almost talked Kerry Packer into getting involved in an audacious bid to privatise Qantas. He would try the same with his son – again unsuccessfully – a decade later.

In 2008, as an executive of Packer's private company CPH, Brazil had a bold plan to establish a Packer family hedge fund in London known as Park Street Partners. Unfortunately, its launch was scuttled by the GFC, and Packer now reveals the fallout for the first time. 'I think Ben is as smart as [Caledonia's] Will Vicars or [Magellan's] Hamish Douglass. We were going to own the management company [for the new fund] fifty-fifty. CPH's part was to lock up US$300 million into the fund for five years. We agreed a deal and signed contracts,' he says. 'Ben resigned from Macquarie to start working on the fund. Ben was going to be based in London and started hiring people.'

But as the GFC started to bite, it became clear that CPH couldn't meet its commitments to Brazil and the twenty-five staff he had hired. It had to abandon the deal, and agreed to pay Brazil and his team a US$10 million break fee. It saw Brazil even threaten legal action against his good friend. Packer blamed himself for not being on top of the CPH balance sheet, and Crown's share price was also plummeting because of the disastrous proposed acquisition of Cannery. 'And, to be fair, the GFC changed everything ... But Ben was rightly beyond furious, and went with his team to Macquarie and has had huge success since,' he says. The falling-out was short-lived. 'I thought and think the world of Ben. He is still a good friend today. And [by 2009], in an act of true friendship, Ben had come onto the board of Crown to help me. That was even after I had let him down so badly with our proposed hedge fund that I backed out of our deal on.'

Fast-forward to September, as they contemplated the azure waters of Bora Bora from the deck of the *Arctic P*, only one thing was on their minds: Kerry Stokes.

*

TWO MONTHS EARLIER STOKES'S Seven Network had made a hostile sharemarket raid on the listed pay-TV company Consolidated Media Holdings (CMH), which was then 38 per cent owned by the Packer family's CPH. In 2008 Stokes had quietly built up a stake of almost 5 per cent in CMH, six years after his own pay-TV arm, C7, went out of business. The 2009 raid took Seven's stake in CMH to 19.9 per cent, the maximum allowable by law before it was required to launch a takeover bid.

There was much history between the Packers and Stokes. Kerry Packer had always viewed Stokes as a serial litigant, even though Stokes says he had a special personal relationship with Kerry. They hailed from different lives on opposite sides of the country – Stokes from Perth suburbia, Packer from Sydney's ritzy eastern suburbs. Unlike the Packers and the Murdochs, Stokes was always an outsider in the Australian media. He was a self-made man and a fighter who liked to challenge incumbents.

C7 Sport had been a pay-TV service in Australia owned and run by Stokes's Seven Network. Launched in 1995 and rebranded in 1999, it lasted only another three years because it was unable to secure the one thing any successful TV operation needs: content. Its death knell sounded in 2002 when Seven lost the lucrative rights to broadcast the AFL competition to a powerful consortium of News Limited, PBL, Network Ten and Telstra. The deal saw the Nine and Ten networks carry games on free-to-air, and a new 24-hour football channel established to carry games on pay-TV provider Foxtel. The C7 failure prompted Stokes to launch a massive and highly controversial legal action against his rivals, including News, Nine, Ten, Optus, Austar, the AFL, the NRL, Fox Sports, PBL and Telstra, alleging they had conspired to ruin C7's business. PBL and News were shareholders in C7 rival Fox Sports, while Telstra was a shareholder with PBL and News in Foxtel.

The legal case marked the beginning of a bitter personal rivalry between Stokes and James Packer, which went on for half a decade. It stemmed from a sensational court statement tendered by Stokes during the C7 hearings in September 2005, in which he claimed that when he was PBL chairman, James Packer visited him at his home in Sydney in 2000 and told him of a Murdoch-inspired plot to poach the AFL broadcast rights from Seven. Packer was enraged, given he thought the comment was totally off the record, and he had been trying at the time to broker peace between Stokes and News. At a cocktail party later in 2005, at the Sydney home of then Westpac chief executive David Morgan, Packer confronted Stokes and abused him: 'You are a fucking piece of shit,' he snarled. It was one of his snaps. Stokes said nothing in reply, simply looking down at his shoes.

They did not talk for years afterwards, until Stokes invited Packer and Perth billionaire Tim Roberts to his luxury coastal home at Broome in the north of Western Australia in 2008. Packer had previously visited the property when he was married to Jodhi Meares in the late 1990s. But soon after the Broome trip with Roberts, as the GFC took hold, Stokes's Seven Network ran a series of unflattering stories on its flagship evening current affairs program, *Today Tonight*, about Packer's business and personal woes. He and Stokes were at war again.

In September 2009, on the decks of the *Arctic P*, Packer left Ben Brazil in no doubt that given his history with Stokes, he was determined not to be beaten by him. 'Ben knew the CPH balance sheet and was giving me advice. Ben and I agreed that the CPH debt was still too high even after the pastoral sale,' Packer says, referring to his $425 million sale of CPH's cattle station operations. By then Crown had found a way out of the Cannery deal, and CPH had sold a luxury London mansion and an array of planes and boats, including the $50 million nine-bedroom luxury yacht *Z Ellerston*, the world's largest model of open yacht, famed for coming with a complimentary Aston Martin for the purchaser.

But Stokes looked poised to move on CMH, a company James had spent more than a decade building, at a time when James was in the worst position to fend off his old nemesis. He and Brazil turned their attention to CPH's 21 per cent stake in the sharemarket-listed Challenger Financial Services, long viewed as one of the billionaire's 'babies'.

*

CHALLENGER, A PROVIDER OF annuities designed to give retirees secure income streams, had been part of the Packer family stable for more than a decade. In 1998 CPH took an initial 12 per cent stake in the company, which it later increased to 19 per cent. The Packers were believers in the Challenger story, even when the markets were not so sure. In 2002 they supported a capital raising when rising concerns among investors about the state of Challenger's financial accounts sent its shares plummeting. In a boardroom shake-up as part of the raising, Kerry Packer was appointed a Challenger director. He was later succeeded by James when Challenger merged with the Packer-controlled cash-box CPH Investments, which once held the family's stake in Fairfax.

Challenger then had three divisions – funds management, mortgages and annuities. Packer was most excited about the mortgage business, then run by Brian Benari. The division grew to be the biggest non-bank mortgage provider in Australia, as non-bank lenders grew to account for up to 15 per cent of the mortgage market. That was before the GFC came along, when funding totally dried up and Challenger's mortgage business stopped growing. In September 2008 Dominic Stevens took over as CEO. Benari, who had joined the company in 2003 from Zurich and was known to many as simply 'BB', became the company's chief financial officer as the crisis took hold. While its shares plummeted, through prudent management the company managed to survive the GFC. By September 2009 its shares had rebounded from under $1 to above $3.

On the afternoon of 4 September 2009, the Friday before Father's Day in Australia, Packer and Brazil were outside on the top deck of the *Arctic P*. An unexpected call came through from Packer's trusted UBS adviser and friend Matthew Grounds, who proposed that CPH sell its Challenger shares to bolster its cash position against Stokes and provide it with a war chest to protect CMH. 'Matthew said to me he could place all 120 million of CPH's shares in Challenger. I said to Matthew I would get back to him. I asked Ben what he thought. After a while Ben said to me, "If the world goes well, Challenger would do very, very well." But he then said, "James, I think you should get your debt down because if the world does badly, Challenger will do very badly, as it had shown in the GFC,"' Packer now recalls. 'I assumed Matthew thought I should sell, otherwise he wouldn't have called me. I trusted Matthew completely then. I rang Matthew back and said, "Sell."'

Brian Benari recalls being in Singapore at the time, attending a forum with Challenger investors at the China Club atop the 52-storey Capital Tower, Singapore's premium commercial building. The club is surrounded by 16-metre-tall glass boasting spectacular views across the city. One of the investors had intriguingly asked Benari if Mr Packer was a committed shareholder in Challenger. 'All I said was he had been a long-term investor and you would have to discuss it with him as to his intentions,' Benari recalls responding.

'A few moments later my head of investor relations leaned over towards me and showed me the messages on her mobile phone. They showed James had sold his entire stake.' Moments later Benari's phone rang. Packer was on the line. Benari excused himself from the meeting to take the call. 'James told me, "I love the businesses, I've been committed to the business, but this is a family matter and this is a matter for our family business." He was incredibly apologetic,' Benari recalls. 'I was very matter-of-fact about it [in reply]. At the end of the day, I said: "It's your shareholding and you are free to deal with it in any manner."

'When I went back into the meeting, I asked the investors, "Can I just replay what I said earlier?" and said James had sold his stake. I politely asked them if they knew anything about it, and they calmly nodded and said they were part of the book build [that is, they had agreed to buy Challenger shares in the selldown by Packer]. So even they knew when I didn't!'

James notes he didn't ask Ashok Jacob, CPH's then CEO and chief investment officer, before he sold the Challenger stake. 'And Challenger was Ash's deal. Truth is, the trust between Ash and me – for whatever reason and whoever is at fault – had never recovered from the GFC.' Amazingly, it was revealed in notices to the ASX that week that Jacob, who was a director of Challenger at the time, was actually buying shares at the same time as CPH was selling.

The CPH sale of Challenger shares fetched $396 million, reducing the company's debt from $1.2 billion to $800 million. And suddenly it had the headroom, if needed, to fight Stokes. 'Crown had a relatively good balance sheet after Cannery had been cauterised, and with CMH paying a good dividend, I thought we were safe,' Packer recalls. But while the sale made sense at the time, he now reveals it is one of his biggest regrets. Some say it irretrievably damaged his relationship with Jacob, even if it had been on the rocks beforehand. If CPH still held its Challenger shares today, it would be worth an extra $2 billion. 'Challenger has come good ten years after we bought it. And that is the biggest contribution Ashok has made to the family, and it is not insignificant. And I'm not there for the ride,' Packer laments.

But Brian Benari, now CEO of Challenger, says the Packer legacy at the company will never be forgotten. '[Packer] had been an incredible partner in building Challenger. He was incredibly supportive of the management team and was willing to provide whatever resources he had available to ensure the success of Challenger overall, for the benefit of all shareholders,' he says.

*

CHALLENGER WASN'T THE ONLY prized Packer asset to be jettisoned in the bitter battle to fend off Stokes. The previous week CMH had unexpectedly sold all of its shares in Seek, the darling of the Australian sharemarket, which had stolen the classifieds employment market from media giant Fairfax. Following the dot.com crash in 2000–01, the Packers' PBL had acquired cornerstone stakes in both Seek and Carsales, two new classifieds websites that were in direct competition with newspapers. PBL's rationale for the purchases was that it saw traditional media as increasingly vulnerable to the internet. It proved a prescient move, as James Packer saw the future threat posed to traditional media earlier and more clearly than incumbents like Fairfax.

Carsales had been launched in 1997 by Melbourne entrepreneurs Greg Roebuck and Walter Pisciotta. As CEO and chairman they built it into Australia's leading automotive, marine, motorcycle, construction and equipment classifieds business. In October 2005 Packer convinced them to merge their business with PBL's online auto classifieds operations, leaving PBL with a 41 per cent stake in the merged group. 'I met James for the first time at his office in Crown. I watched him walk in the room, come straight up to me and introduce himself with a great smile,' Pisciotta remembers. 'I watched him do the same with other people. It is so disarming and charming. I have met a lot of successful people in business who have public images, and when you meet them you realise they are just normal people. You just don't find a more charming guy than James. When he wants to be charming, there is no one better at it.'

Pisciotta, who hails from St Louis, Missouri, and came to Australia in 1974 on what he intended to be an eighteen-month working holiday but has turned into a long career, reveals he has an unusual link to the Packer family: his wife's grandfather was a driver for Kerry Packer's father, Sir Frank Packer, whenever he visited Melbourne. He says while James was actively involved with Carsales, he always encouraged – but never unreasonably 'pushed' – the company. 'James is the most numerate person I have ever met. I am good with numbers, Greg Roebuck is good with numbers. But we are not a patch on James Packer. Greg and I have both marvelled at each other that we have never seen anybody do numbers in his head like he does. Anything we ever did, he would remember the numbers better than we did, and I never saw him look at a note!' he says.

Greg Roebuck says he has always believed James will be remembered as 'the smartest of the Packer dynasty. My favourite memory was in a board meeting at Crown; we were talking about dealer reviews and there were two opposing perspectives. Without going into the details of the issues, the thing I admired was James sitting and listening and then saying, "I can see both sides of this issue; however, on balance, I believe we should do x" – it was not about the issue, it was just a great way to move forward without offending either side. It always stuck with me,' Roebuck says.

In 2006 PBL took majority ownership of Carsales, which later that year formed part of the pool of PBL Media assets sold to CVC. 'I sat in his office when he told me he was selling, and he looked at me and said, "I didn't want to sell Carsales in this deal,"' Pisciotta recalls. 'And I said, "Well you had to have some growth assets in there, didn't you?" and he just smiled. Adrian [MacKenzie, then CVC Asia Pacific managing partner] is no dummy. CVC didn't want to buy something that had no green shoots, no bright sparks in it. Carsales clearly was one. It is a great business.'

In September 2009, PBL Media floated Carsales on the Australian Securities Exchange, retaining a 49 per cent stake. While Packer was no longer directly involved in both groups, he had long championed the listing. PBL had invested $100 million in Carsales at a time when it was struggling in the face of heavy competition, and eventually sold its holding, after Packer had ceased involvement with the company, for more than $460 million. PBL's investment in Seek delivered a similar bumper windfall. But the journey for Packer was far more gutting and emotional.

*

PBL HAD PURCHASED A 25 per cent stake in Seek for just $33 million in 2003. Packer soon joined the board and eventually became chairman. Importantly, after the horrors of One.Tel, it was a deal that rebuilt his own self-confidence and his reputation in the eyes of his father. He was also able to outmanoeuvre Fairfax, the media company he so despised.

Seek CEO Andrew Bassat – who at the time shared the role with his brother, Paul – recalls, 'Our experience with James at Seek was very positive. That goes back to when he first met with us and wanted to invest in the business. His reputation was as a tough businessman, that the Packers win the deals. So our starting point was probably negative. But from the moment we met him he was disarming, smart and reasonable. He said to us, "You guys have won; how do we work with you?"' Bassat describes Packer as a 'smart, visionary, incredibly bold, incredibly numerate' chairman of Seek. 'He was willing to take calculated risks and was the first person we met who could see the potential of our business as well [as] if not better than us,' he says. 'James is amazing with numbers. I am not so good with numbers and he frequently caught me out. He will straight away convert from whatever the big picture is to what it could be worth in profit, revenue, at what margin and then what valuation. He knew our numbers much better than I ever did.'

But everything changed in July 2009 when Stokes raided CMH. Packer was at Mount Hotham in the Victorian snowfields when he received a courtesy call from Stokes informing him that Seven had increased its stake in CMH to 19.9 per cent. 'James, I'd like to talk to you about CMH,' Stokes said politely. Packer's reply was swift: 'Kerry, I need a lawyer,' he barked, before the conversation swiftly ended. Packer felt he could no longer trust Stokes after their falling-out in the C7 case.

At the same time Ashok Jacob's Ellerston Capital funds management business was also firmly in expansion mode. In the year before his father passed away, Packer had hired former Deutsche Bank executive Glenn Poswell to manage a new Ellerston fund that would invest the money of wealthy friends of the Packers in funds run by top fund managers. It was known as the Ellerston Master Fund.

In 2007 Packer attended Morgan Stanley's famed annual hedge-fund conference — reserved for the top twenty-five funds on the planet — at the luxurious Breakers retreat at Palm Beach in Florida. 'James was a big supporter of Ellerston. James was prepared to do anything for me and the business,' Poswell now recalls. 'We flew across to the Breakers in his plane. He was putting himself out there for the benefit of the growth of the business. There were not too many other people of his wealth and stature that would do something like that, so it was a real endorsement. It was very successful in attracting US institutional investors.'

Ellerston's fund grew in value between 2005 and 2009 to $4.4 billion. The success prompted the launch of a $600-million listed investment company on the ASX known as Ellerston GEMs, which invested money from wealthy clients directly in the sharemarket. During the Victorian Spring Racing Carnival in 2007, Ellerston paid for the naming rights to a $250,000 stakes race on Derby Day, the hottest corporate ticket on the Australian racing calendar. It also had its own glittering marquee inside Flemington's famed Birdcage, which Packer attended.

A year later, as the GFC took hold, the marquee was gone and Ellerston GEMs was delisting from the ASX, allowing unit holders to redeem their units after they had consistently traded at a discount to the value of the fund's assets. Ellerston GEMs was also being criticised for its poor performance by a vocal investor, Sydney property developer John Dalley. Poswell says, 'It was a difficult time and it wasn't an easy decision. And in hindsight one could argue that it could have been handled in a different way and maintained. I think we were a bit ahead of ourselves in the timing, given the growth of the LIC [listed investment company] sector since. The sector is now worth over $40 billion.' Poswell left Ellerston to set up his own investment business in 2009.

In mid 2011 Jacob also made the landmark decision to move his office out of Packer's Park Street bunker in Sydney to a building around the corner at 179 Elizabeth Street, marking a historic separation from the Packers. Jacob and Packer had grown apart and the former was keen to strike out on his own. The same year CPH agreed to sell down its 100 per cent shareholding in Ellerston Capital, leaving the company 75 per cent–owned by a trust controlled by Ellerston's employees and headed by Jacob, with CPH retaining a passive 25 per cent interest in Ellerston to this day. CPH received $3.6 million in consideration on the selldown of its interests in Ellerston Capital, having originally invested $5 million to establish the business. It made a profit of around $350 million from the investment returns on the capital it put into Ellerston between 2002 and 2011. The value of that capital peaked at $930 million in 2007.

However, losses over the past decade have negated the earlier profits, meaning CPH has to date, on a cumulative basis, made no money on its investment in Ellerston.

'Ashok Jacob said to me more than once that I was the person who had done more for him than anyone in his life,' Packer says. 'Ash is super bright. Way too bright for me. After we had spoken I often was totally confused.' He then gives Jacob another bouquet: 'Ash is an excellent small-cap private-equity investor.'

But back in 2009, after the angst of the Mount Hotham discussion with Stokes, Packer was angry about Ellerston's performance and deeply worried that Seven might bid for CMH, the company he called his own, but of which he only owned 38 per cent. Jacob – who was also CPH CEO – and Packer's legal adviser Guy Jalland quickly gave their boss a clear message: 'You must show the world you still have money! Show you are strong!'

They quietly started buying CMH shares, increasing CPH's stake in CMH from 38 to almost 41 per cent using the so-called creep provisions of the Corporations Act, which allow substantial shareholders in listed companies to buy 3 per cent of the shares on issue every six months without making a full takeover bid. It was an important circuit-breaker. But Packer was still hundreds of millions of dollars from majority control of CMH and sanctuary. He felt he needed more cash, and quickly, to buy CMH shares. He turned his attention, reluctantly, to Seek.

*

PAUL AND ANDREW BASSAT and Seek chief financial officer John Armstrong were at the Sheraton on the Park Hotel in Sydney for their post-annual-results roadshow when dawn broke on the morning of 26 August 2009. Paul Bassat was the first up at 6am, donning his runners for a walk down to the Opera House and then back to the city through the Botanical Gardens. But he neglected to bring his mobile phone. 'When I got back at around 8am there were dozens of messages on my phone. CMH had sold all their Seek shares via a block sale to institutions [for $441 million]. There was a message from James on my phone. And an email saying: "I just tried to call you. I am sorry. I had to sell ... for me,"' Paul recalls.

His brother wasn't up so early. He had been out till 5am after a wake for a friend's father, so he had made sure his first meeting wasn't until 11am and set the alarm for a leisurely 9.30am wake-up. 'And when I woke up there were something like 150 missed calls on my phone. I have never had an experience like that. It took me a little while to work out what was going on,' Andrew recalls.

Paul Bassat says that, with a packed meeting schedule, neither he nor his brother was able to speak to Packer until that evening. 'It was the most emotional I had ever heard him,' he recalls of the phone call when they finally connected. Thirty seconds after Paul started speaking, Packer broke into tears. 'He then made a comment to the effect of: "You know how important the relationship with Andrew and you is for me, but I had to sell. Seek has been my favourite investment but I have to deal with Kerry Stokes [on the CMH register],"' Paul recalls.

The pain is again clear on Packer's face as he describes letting go of Seek. 'I loved the Bassats, and Seek had been totally my deal. We sold for $5 and Seek shares are worth more than $20 today. I was incredibly frustrated that this new problem was appearing [Kerry Stokes raiding CMH, after the issues with Ellerston and the losses on US casinos], and I was determined to do my best not to be beaten by Kerry.'

Importantly, the Seek decision had the backing of Ashok Jacob, who reasoned that the proceeds could be used by CMH to buy back shares, lowering the number of CMH shares on issue. CPH didn't participate in the buyback, so its shareholding in CMH rose to 50.1 per cent – a position of control and sanctuary. Seven also stayed out of the buyback and watched its shareholding rise to 25 per cent. Packer was able to later strike a peace deal with Stokes, facilitated by Matthew Grounds, for Seven to have two CMH board seats.

'James didn't need much convincing on this. I think in his heart he certainly respected Kerry and it made sense for them to make peace,' Grounds now says. 'Their friendship has been important to both of them, in recent times as well.'

Soon after the détente, Packer even suggested to Stokes that they take a tour of Foxtel's North Ryde headquarters in Sydney, chaperoned by another long-time Stokes adversary,

Foxtel CEO Kim Williams. 'James and I took Kerry around and it was very cordial. We had a very pleasant time together. I'd say they were there for over an hour,' Williams recalls. 'I could see that day they were clearly very comfortable with each other. They clearly had their tough times together. But they had worked that through and developed a close and trusting relationship.'

John Alexander is one who has seen more of the Packer-Stokes relationship than most, given he is a director of Stokes's media company, Seven West Media. 'They started off as enemies. But during the battle over CMH, James picked up the phone to Kerry. He told him, "You have always been an outsider; would you like to be an insider for the first time in your life?"' Alexander says. 'James was the person who put Lachlan Murdoch and Kerry Stokes together to the point where Seven and News went from being not the best of friends to being partners.'

*

THE SEEK SHARE SALE wasn't quite the end of Packer's involvement with the company. CPH quietly bought back into the stock during 2011, and by May 2012 had acquired a stake of just below 5 per cent, the threshold for the holding to be disclosed publicly to the Australian Securities Exchange. By then Paul Bassat had stepped down as joint CEO, leaving his brother solely in charge. CPH sold the stake a year later.

CPH also retained a stake in the Chinese online jobs site Zhaopin until early 2017. Along with Seek, it had been an early backer of the Beijing-based company. Packer had long believed in Zhaopin as a bellwether of the Chinese economic growth story and had built up a substantial paper profit on his investment in the company. In 2016, when Seek struck a deal to privatise Zhaopin and remove it from the boards of the high-tech Nasdaq stock exchange in America, James had a choice to stay or go.

'I think James was under a lot of pressure for cash at the time of the process, but he was very fair and reasonable with me. We went to him at the start and asked him if he wanted to sell or hold. He said it was quite timely that he sell. I thought it would be a four-to-six-month process and it went on and on,' Andrew Bassat says.

CPH and other minority shareholders were offered US$18 per share for their stock in the buyout deal, but the process took more than eighteen months, which distressed the again cash-strapped billionaire. 'There is no doubt he had a degree of impatience given that he needed the money and the process kept dragging on, and I did feel bad about not being able to get things done more quickly. But he really did the right thing by us, especially given the pressure he was under, and did not push the option of selling into the market, which could have jeopardised the whole process,' Bassat adds.

The sale eventually netted CPH another $200 million. Bassat credits Packer with helping Seek cement its foothold in China through its Zhaopin investment. 'James's support on China really brought the board along. When we invested in China post our listing in 2005, I used a whiteboard for the first and only time in a board meeting. I wanted them to remember that it wasn't all on me if we screwed up,' he says bluntly. 'I put up that there was a 40 per cent chance we would lose all our money [because of all the risks of investing in China], and only a 20 per cent chance we would end up number one and have a massive business, and some in-between scenarios. But James, who was chairman, said, "Do it."'

While Bassat stresses his overall experience with Packer was positive – he still views him as a loyal friend – he does recall one negative trait that has long been highlighted by friends and critics alike. 'If I am being pressed for areas that James was less strong, the main thing would be openness to challenge sometimes where he has a strong existing view. This is not really reflective of him or a character flaw at all but more reflects how many people behave around him,' Bassat says. 'I have seen a fair bit of it with people trying to please him and win favour to get into the inner circle and [being] less likely to challenge him and contradict him. So when it happens he is not so used to it. I did challenge him a few times and the message I took was not to do that in the future, that it was not my business and not my territory. That would be his only Achilles heel.'

Packer does not dispute Bassat's assessment of him and is full of praise for his friend. 'What [Andrew] has achieved at Seek and the wealth that has been created for all shareholders since he became sole CEO is the most enormous credit to him,' he says. 'Andrew has helped Seek become a truly international company. And its prospects appear to be very, very bright. Of the good assets we sold during bad times, it wasn't just the lost financial opportunity that hurts. It was also dealing with special people. I miss having [Melco Crown CEO] Lawrence Ho, Paul Bassat, Andrew Bassat, Dominic Stevens, Brian Benari, Richard Howes from Challenger and also Rob Woods from Challenger in my life.'

*

DESPITE HIS VISION AND foresight to see the impact of the internet before most others, after selling out of Seek and Carsales, Packer now has no significant exposure to the digital economy. His stake in the Paul Bassat–led venture capital firm Square Peg Capital, which invests in venture and growth-stage online and technology companies, remains his only bet.

In financial services, the fire sale of Challenger and the collapse of his London plans with Ben Brazil have hit hard for almost a decade. 'It is one of my biggest business regrets that we didn't establish a hedge fund with Ben Brazil,' he laments. 'Losing my deal with Ben hurt me as much as selling Seek, selling Challenger or selling our pastoral assets.' Brazil has gone on to make billions of dollars for Macquarie. Last year he received a remuneration package totalling $16.9 million for running the group's lucrative debt-investment business.

Glenn Poswell, who was involved in the work to establish Brazil's new operation – including finding offices for the group in the swish London suburb of Mayfair – says Packer has a 'very high regard for Ben. He felt an indebtedness to Ben to get the fund going and it was emotional for him when he couldn't, given their friendship. He had seen through the eyes of Ellerston what could happen if you had a single manager that was successful. James could not believe the amount of money you could make in this space. We had approaches by Goldman Sachs to take an interest in Ellerston. He could see the potential of these types of businesses,' he says.

When it comes to his business record financially, Packer says there is one inescapable truth that burns deep. 'Within my portfolio, even after the GFC, I had three growth assets. Hindsight makes it easier to realise these things. They were Challenger, Seek and Melco Crown,' he says. 'Selling all these assets or shareholdings all had a logic at the time, but time has proven me wrong. I was chairman or co-chairman of all three of these companies. If I'd held onto them, my other mistakes would have seemed far less significant.'

EIGHT

Crowning Glory

THE $10 MILLION SYDNEY APARTMENT of top-rating breakfast radio host Alan Jones boasts stunning views of the Harbour Bridge and the Opera House. Located on the sixth floor of the controversial iconic 'Toaster' building at 1 Macquarie Street, its walls are adorned with Arthur Boyd paintings and family photographs, while the couches are dressed with Versace pillows. Each visitor to the apartment is welcomed in the Toaster's downstairs lobby by David, Jones's loyal butler, who then ushers them up to meet the most powerful broadcaster in Australia, nicknamed 'The Parrot'.

On a sunny afternoon in early February 2012, David met two extra-special guests in the foyer: James Packer and then NSW premier Barry O'Farrell. He escorted them, separately, upstairs to the apartment where, over lunch, Jones introduced them for the first time. 'James didn't know Barry O'Farrell,' Jones now says, sitting in his apartment with his back to the view of the Opera House, crouched forward at his grand timber dining table. 'So I sat there, Barry sat here and James sat there,' he adds, motioning to my chair and the vacant one opposite. 'It was just the three of us.'

Jones stresses there was nothing untoward about the meeting, the first where Packer personally outlined his vision to O'Farrell to build a $1-billion-plus hotel, casino and entertainment complex on once derelict harbourside land at Barangaroo, and how he wanted to challenge the monopoly of nearby casino the Star. '[Packer] was a fellow who was wanting to do something for Sydney. Is there anything in it for James? Yes. [But] it's something for Sydney as well, a legacy that he wanted,' Jones says. 'And we talked about what it meant. We're trying to grow the state, build the economy. This city's miles behind. It's not an international city by any reckoning.'

O'Farrell immediately liked what he heard from Packer. 'I'm no great fan of casinos,' O'Farrell now says. 'I'm not opposed to them but not a fan of them. What I was an advocate for was a six-star hotel. We were missing out on high-end tourism. Not just those from Asia, but the Middle Eastern tourists who wanted these types of facilities. For me, having an iconic development at Barangaroo would be a confidence boost for the state … I remember James's passion for doing something in Sydney matched the passion I had to do something for major events and tourism.'

But there was a catch: Packer needed a gambling facility to make the project viable. There was only one licence available in Sydney – and it was taken.

*

IT WASN'T THE FIRST time the Packer family had tried to secure a casino in Sydney. During the bidding process for the licence to run the city's first casino in the early 1990s, it is now folklore that a then 26-year-old James phoned a NSW minister on behalf of his father to deliver a blunt message. 'The old man told me to ring … This is the message: "If we don't win the casino, you guys are fucked,"' James reportedly said. But the threat failed. In 1994 the Packers lost the tender to a consortium led by US casino operator Showboat and construction giant Leighton, bidding $80 million less than their rivals.

Kerry Packer took the NSW Casino Control Authority to the highest courts of the land and used his media mates, including Jones himself, to run an unrelenting campaign against the winning bidders in an effort to overturn the decision, but it didn't work. 'James always felt – and it's true – that his father was dudded at Darling Harbour. There's no doubt about that,' Jones now says. But when Kerry subsequently got the opportunity to purchase Showboat, he twice pulled out of the deal, in part because of his paranoia about the probity process and because he thought Showboat's casino – located in Pyrmont Bay – was a poor property. Instead, Kerry always had his eyes on the Barangaroo site, a vision taken up after his passing by his son.

When James moved to act on that dream, he turned to Jones to be his political facilitator. When he met O'Farrell at Jones's apartment in 2012, Packer pointed out a key problem with the bidding process for the original Sydney casino, which had been subsequently solved by governments abroad. 'I said the flaw in the bidding process the first time around was that the main determinate of the winning bid was the [upfront] cash component. But if you think about it, what is more important is the back end, the taxes that you get each and every year off the back of the casino,' Packer now recalls telling O'Farrell. 'I said the back end was actually more important than the upfront payment you're looking for.' He pointed to the process used in Singapore in 2010, where the winners were judged on how much money they were willing to invest in their projects and their economic impact.

Packer says O'Farrell immediately saw the logic in the argument and that he left the lunch feeling content. 'Barry and I gelled. He was interested in the Singapore analogy and analysis. He had heard and continued to hear the difference in quality of Crown Melbourne [compared] to the Star. Macau was being written of and spoken about a lot … He made no promises, of course. But I left lunch thinking it went really well.'

*

THE MARCH 2011 STATE election had brought Barry O'Farrell to power as the first Liberal premier of New South Wales in sixteen years. During the election campaign he had promised a review of the design of the controversial Barangaroo development, which had long been championed by the previous state Labor governments. The project, the biggest urban renewal project in Australia, had three parts: a 6-hectare headland park at the northern end of the site; the 5.2-hectare Barangaroo Central site reserved for cultural and recreational space; and Barangaroo South, a Lendlease development of shops, restaurants, offices, apartments and a hotel.

What worried O'Farrell most was that the centrepiece of Barangaroo South was an 85-metre pier into Sydney Harbour that would house a 33-storey hotel. 'I came to office concerned about one element of Barangaroo. The original tender, which was meant to be for the old port area, included a chunk of the harbour. I think our harbour is one of our great assets. I don't think we should fill it in,' O'Farrell says of his thinking then and now. Unsurprisingly, his new government's review of the project, delivered five months after election day, was opposed to the hotel-over-the-water plan.

Crown's strategy and development chief Todd Nisbet, who had been one of US casino magnate Steve Wynn's most important executives for almost a decade, thought the same. 'Lendlease came to us with their original old hotel-over-the-water idea. I looked at it and didn't think it would work,' Nisbet now says. 'So I went and grabbed the background for Barangaroo Central and [commissioned] a design for it. We came in with a proposition that was more of an image than a design, which put a big building in the middle of Central and a public platform around it.'

What happened next proved to be a turning point for Packer's Crown Sydney dream. 'James shared it with some people in the premier's office. And then, unbeknown to me, he put it out publicly through *The Daily Telegraph*,' Nisbet recalls of the paper's front-page splash on 25 February 2012 carrying the screaming headline: 'Shining jewel in Packer's Crown'. 'I was on a red-eye back from Perth. When I landed I saw the newspaper and thought, "Holy cow!"'

To Nisbet, the move by his traditionally media-shy boss to go public with the design so early in the process highlighted his deep emotional commitment to the project. This deal was personal. 'James leaves a big wake. That is really helpful in circumstances when you are behind the boat. But if you are caught outside the wake it gets choppy,' he says, with another wry smile, of the surprise *Telegraph* headline. '[But] the one thing that was totally understood in all the meetings was that he was totally committed to making it happen.'

Almost immediately Packer was confronted by a powerful and articulate obstacle – the architecture-obsessed former prime minister Paul Keating. Keating was seen by many as the spiritual guardian of the Barangaroo site after his long campaign to recreate the original Barangaroo headland destroyed a century earlier by maritime development at Darling Harbour. He immediately voiced his vehement opposition to Crown's tower encroaching on the land earmarked for public parkland. Packer recalls, of the first of many meetings he had with Keating about the project: 'I went and saw him, and he was very upset because the proposal that was in *The Daily Telegraph* had Crown's casino over Barangaroo Central as well as Barangaroo South. I remember him using the word "treat". He said you can "treat" with Lendlease but you can't be in Barangaroo Central,' he adds of Keating's use of the legal phrase 'invitation to treat' – in other words, a willingness to negotiate. '[So from then on] I was trying to fit in with what Paul had told me to do.'

Alan Jones says Keating was attracted to Packer's vision for the site and for Sydney. Keating saw Barangaroo's towers as a means to reorient the city centre westward and reinvigorate the financial district. 'Paul won't spend five minutes with a shonk,' Jones says of the political leader with whom he fought many famous battles. 'And then he suddenly saw this bloke [Packer] – he didn't quite know him; he knew his father – Paul suddenly saw this bloke had something ... Keating saw the vision.'

By the middle of 2012 Packer had hired Karl Bitar and Mark Arbib, both previously senior figures in the NSW Labor Right faction, as key advisers. They would prove critical in securing the Labor Opposition's and the media's support for the project. Bitar was employed by Crown, while Arbib was paid by Packer's private company CPH, mirroring the roles that former Labor powerbrokers Graham Richardson and Peter Barron once performed for Kerry Packer. Bitar and Arbib knew that having a proposal that fitted Keating's view of the site would be critical in securing the Labor Opposition's support.

But Packer says Keating also gave him some tactical advice suggesting he meet then NSW Opposition leader John Robertson without Bitar and Arbib in tow. Keating felt Packer needed to make the project his own and show this in the meetings with those who mattered. Packer says Keating, as did O'Farrell, also encouraged Crown to do a deal with Lendlease to build its casino hotel at Barangaroo South.

By August the two companies had signed a two–year exclusive agreement for Crown to develop a six–star hotel alongside the three commercial towers that had already been approved for Barangaroo South. As a result, despite previous troubles in the Packer family–Keating relationship over media law reform, Keating became Crown's critically important ally. 'Paul and I built a relationship. I probably saw him fifteen times,' Packer says. But the friendship, like many for Packer in Sydney, didn't endure. 'I haven't seen him for years now,' he says.

*

BARRY O'FARRELL SAYS HE has only met James Packer on four occasions in his life. The first was over lunch with Jones. Two were just chance meetings: once at Sydney's Rockpool Bar & Grill restaurant, when they were dining at separate tables; and then at the Sydney Town Hall in March 2014 as billionaire Paul Ramsay celebrated fifty years of being in the private hospital business.

There was only ever one formal meeting between the two men, on 10 August 2012 at the then premier's plush office in Sydney's Governor Macquarie Tower. 'I saw just how passionate he was about doing something big in Sydney,' O'Farrell now recalls of the meeting. 'It also struck me when we were looking at some of the views from my office … he seemed determined to deliver something his father had wanted. And something his father wasn't able to do.'

Packer now says he is less emotional about the importance of securing Crown Sydney for his father's legacy. 'It's a Packer family legacy. I think my father's legacy speaks for itself. As I sit here today, it is pretty clear Dad was better than me at almost everything. I don't think for Dad owning a casino in Sydney was a big deal,' he says.

It was at that 10 August meeting that O'Farrell informed Packer of a new three-stage framework for infrastructure development that the government had put in place in January that year. It was known as the 'unsolicited proposals process', designed to encourage the private sector to come to government with innovative ideas for infrastructure where, according to its guidelines, 'the proponent is uniquely placed to provide a value-for-money solution'. Importantly, on 17 August, a week after Packer's meeting with O'Farrell, the policy was updated – though Packer's and O'Farrell's critics prefer the word manipulated – to provide that if a private-sector proponent could show its idea was 'unique', it could be considered without the need for a competitive tender.

The process would quickly become the key to unlocking Packer's path to victory over his Crown Sydney opponents. 'I had not met with O'Farrell since the Jones lunch. I went down to see him. My impression was pretty obvious that we were winning his heart and mind,' Packer says of the August meeting where O'Farrell advised Crown to use the unsolicited proposal process for its project. 'I didn't know what it [the process] was but I found out pretty quickly. That changed everything.' Less than a month later, Crown formally lodged an unsolicited proposal for a six-star resort and VIP-only gambling facility at Barangaroo.

O'Farrell now makes no apologies for pointing Crown in the direction he did, noting Crown's subsequent progression through the process was done at 'arms-length, done in an ethical and business-like manner'. He says the two-year exclusivity agreement struck between Crown and Lendlease for Barangaroo South made their project 'unique' because it locked anyone else out of developing an iconic six-star resort hotel in the precinct. But it prompted the critics to claim Packer 'bulldozed' his plan through the NSW cabinet without it going to tender. 'The unsolicited proposal process goes through and tests these things. I ask, what was the tender going to be for?' O'Farrell now says, stressing Lendlease had earlier won a tender to develop the hotel part of the Barangaroo site before striking its deal with Crown. 'Lendlease had the rights to build the hotel. Without a deal with Lendlease, [Packer] didn't have a site. Was the state expected to tender a right that was owned by Lendlease that had already been won in a tender process? I trusted the process. It was signed off by ICAC; I am convinced to this day it was a proper and ethical process.'

O'Farrell also stresses that Crown didn't need the same casino licence as the Star – the former was offering a six-star hotel with an invitation-only high-rollers room, which required a restricted VIP gaming licence that could be implemented through a special act of parliament. But his critics again accused him of playing with words to give Packer what he wanted.

In mid September 2012 the premier gave his public approval for Packer's plan. A month later Labor MPs joined with the Coalition government to back the project. Packer told a business dinner in Sydney the same month that the project's success had not involved any lobbying but was just due the 'strength of a really good idea', drawing a cynical response from his opponents, who claimed it was the result of backroom deals of the finest order. But Packer soon realised he wasn't about to get his way without a fight from the casino arch rival he had been stalking for many months.

*

PACKER'S PLAN A FOR his Sydney casino dream had been to negotiate a deal with Echo Entertainment – which operated the Star – to use its gaming licence for a VIP casino joint venture with Crown at Barangaroo. In February 2012 Crown revealed it had built a hostile 10 per cent shareholding in Echo (half of which was a legacy of buying into Tabcorp, before it spun off its casino operations into Echo in 2011) to use as leverage – or a threat – to convince Echo to cooperate on Packer's Sydney ambitions. At the time it also prompted feverish speculation that Crown was going to make a takeover bid for Echo, which Packer now reveals was never on the cards. 'We couldn't have afforded to do a cash bid,' he says. 'We would have had to do a cash and scrip bid. That would have resulted in me having a much lower level of control [in a merged Crown Echo] – being a 30 per cent shareholder rather than a 48 per cent shareholder in Crown.'

Instead, Crown started an aggressive public campaign – including taking out newspaper advertisements – against Echo's chairman John Story, questioning his performance in the job. It forced the convening of an Echo shareholder meeting to consider a proposal to sack Story and appoint former Victorian premier and Packer confidant Jeff Kennett to the Echo board. Kennett now reveals that despite the headlines of the time, he was never serious about going ahead with the plan. '[Packer] asked me to go on [the Echo board]. I thought about it. I never agreed to it,' he says. 'In my relationship with [James], for better or for worse and because of the respect I had for his father and mother, I don't ever want to be in his debt. At that stage I was still chairman of [mental health support group] beyondblue, so that would have been a conflict. In my heart of hearts I knew I couldn't do it.'

But Kennett's commitment to the Packer plan was never tested: Story resigned ahead of the proposed June 2012 meeting and was replaced by Australian Rugby Union chief John O'Neill. Packer had hoped O'Neill's appointment would herald an era of improved relations with Echo, but it wasn't to be. The two met for lunch on Packer's boat in March 2013, and O'Neill later claimed that Packer had quietly offered to stay out of Queensland, where both companies were also pursuing casino projects, if Echo dropped its opposition to Crown's Sydney casino bid. The competition regulator later cleared both of any breach of cartel laws.

'I thought it would have been better after O'Neill got in there. We had been an activist … We were stirring the pot to make Star look incompetent because, in a positioning sense, one of the things we were trying to show was that what Sydney had was less than it deserved. Let Crown build something Sydney deserves,' Packer now says. '[On the boat trip] they were asking us all sorts of questions about what we were doing. I am too open. What they had not told us in return is that they had put in an unsolicited proposal of their own.' O'Neill and Star declined to comment for this book.

The next month, Echo publicly revealed it was offering to invest $1.1 billion in the Star complex and surrounding areas through the unsolicited proposal process, in return for an extension of its casino licence beyond 2019. O'Farrell then announced that 'because of their mutually exclusive nature', only Crown's plan for Barangaroo or the Star's Pyrmont expansion could proceed to stage three of the unsolicited proposal process. It set up a head-to-head battle between the projects, overseen by an independent committee headed by former Future Fund and Commonwealth Bank chairman David Murray.

On 4 July 2012, Murray revealed the committee had found the economic and financial benefits 'came out strongly for both proposals, but more so for Crown'. In addition to a

$100-million upfront licence fee, the government required Crown to pay a higher than expected tax rate and to deliver licence fee and gaming tax payments to the state of $1 billion for its first fifteen years of operations. But importantly for Crown, local VIPs would be allowed to gamble at the new facility, rather than just interstate and international high rollers. The critics called it a fix-up, decrying Murray's historical links to Packer (he had attended the billionaire's first wedding), but Crown had won the day.

It was the culmination of two years of work for the Crown team, including Todd Nisbet, Crown CEO Rowen Craigie, chief financial officer Ken Barton and UBS adviser Kelvin Barry. The last three had met with senior bureaucrats at the NSW Department of Premier and Cabinet at least twice each month during 2012 and 2013 to deal with all the issues thrown up by the process. 'I've never seen a person who can work with bureaucrats like Rowen,' says one person familiar with Craigie's dedication to the Crown Sydney cause. The three also met twice with Murray. Behind the scenes, Karl Bitar and Mark Arbib both ensured the Labor Party expressed little opposition and supplied selective leaks to chosen media. Crown later sold out of Echo at a loss, but after the Murray decision, its casino rival didn't matter. Plan B had triumphed.

Packer was waiting anxiously aboard the *Arctic P* moored off Bora Bora when Craigie rang him on the afternoon of 4 July with the news that Murray had given Crown Sydney the green light. Todd Nisbet was in Packer's Park Street offices in Sydney with Craigie when he made the call, which lasted five minutes. 'It was extremely emotional,' Nisbet now says. 'You could not have picked a harder melting pot of conflicting issues and problems.'

But for Packer, the decision was bittersweet. As he watched Murray's press conference with O'Farrell on the wide-screen television in the living room of the *Arctic P*, few knew that his public expressions of glee that day were hiding a deep and growing private anguish. 'I was on the boat in Tahiti watching the announcement on the TV when it came out. I was about to hop on the plane to Israel for the first time, with my marriage falling apart. So there was no party,' he says. 'On one hand, I feel I am king of the world. On the other hand, my second marriage is failing.'

*

ON 28 OCTOBER 2012 Sydney's *Sunday Telegraph* splashed its front page with a headline: 'James, Bondi: *Casino Royale* with a six-pack'. It carried a stunning photo set up with then editor-in-chief Neil Breen of a super-fit-looking 45-year-old Packer emerging from the Bondi surf channelling heart-throb actor Daniel Craig in the famous scene from the Bond movie *Casino Royale*. Packer had good reason to feel on top of the world – he had just secured what even he had once thought was impossible: bipartisan NSW parliamentary support for his Crown Sydney dream.

The story explained Packer's stunning shedding of a kilogram-a-week over the previous twelve months, the product of a punishing exercise routine at his home gym in Bondi and at the Hyde Park Club below his office in Park Street, as well as gastric lapband surgery at the end of 2011. His amazing physique even caught the eye of Barry O'Farrell. 'I spoke to James about his weight loss because I had a weight issue too. He told me how difficult it was, because you could only swallow stuff the size of a bread cube,' O'Farrell says of Packer's lapband surgery. 'I had thought about it briefly in the past. I wasn't keen on surgery,' he says, before noting of the 10 kilograms he himself lost over the course of 2012, though without reflecting on Packer's life choices: 'I did it the hard way, which was with discipline and exercise.'

Packer, who had become a regular on Sydney's spectacular Bondi-to-Bronte beachside walk, was looking a million dollars. But inside, he felt anything but. 'All wasn't what it seemed,' he now reveals of the time. 'I got a six-pack [a flat, toned abdomen] because I thought to get the CMH deal [the sale of his pay-TV group to News Corporation] done and to get Sydney up, they were both hard and I needed to be at my best. I was very focused on both deals in late 2012–13.

'I felt good for a time,' he continues 'But apart from that my head was completely muddled. My emotions were absolutely all over the shop. I was taking loads of [prescription] testosterone, which I think arguably cost me my marriage as much as anything else. I was on a diet of testosterone, cigarettes, vodka, lime and soda, and I occasionally would try and eat something. That is how I got Sydney and CMH closed. Then I wanted to run away.'

Packer has always been a private person who eschews the media spotlight, yet the Crown Sydney project put him at the centre of a media storm that raged for more than a year, creating more stress. 'I did [the Nine Network current affairs program] *60 Minutes* in [May] 2012 and [the Seven Network's rival program] *Sunday Night* [in February 2013], which killed me more than people realise. I have always wanted to shy away from publicity. For the first time in my life I was front and centre trying to get it.'

Alan Jones was one of the few who knew of – and so was deeply concerned about – Packer's private turmoil at the time. 'Oh yes, of course. Oh God, I thought that often,' he says, adding he was not surprised at Packer's marriage break-up after the Crown Sydney success. 'That's not uncommon. I mean marriages come together, and then if one of the partners is out there on the big picture and the big project, it is a 24/7 job. And he was at it all the time and absent from the marriage,' Jones adds, while acknowledging it wasn't the only reason for the break-up.

Packer now admits the Sydney Casino project 'took much more out of me than I realised or other people realised. I went public for the first time in my life. I'd given interviews in the past but only when forced to. Now I was everywhere, promoting tourism and promoting Crown. I knew I needed to be fit and to look strong. But inside I hated it. I couldn't walk down the street in Sydney without being recognised,' he says. 'All the papers editorialised in favour of a casino without a tender: [*The Sydney Morning Herald*], [*The Australian Financial Review*], *The Australian* and *The Telegraph*. I knew I had to get to stage three of the unsolicited proposal process and then get out of Sydney. I was desperately unhappy inside.'

*

ON REMEMBRANCE DAY – 11 November – 2013 the NSW government gave its final approval to the $2.2 billion Crown Sydney project. But it failed to silence the critics of a 71-storey tower that had been labelled 'a phallic symbol of greed and kitsch with a vengeance' and an 'opalescent dildo'. *The Sydney Morning Herald*'s Michael Pascoe said it was 'fundamentally wrong' for the government to give approval to the project 'via the back door, avoiding a competitive tender and without the government even pretending to have developed anything like a coherent casino policy', while Mike Seccombe noted in *The Saturday Paper* that 'federal laws and regulations have flexed or melted away in the project's path. Ordinary rules don't seem to apply to James Packer.' Aaron Patrick in *The Australian Financial Review* called Crown's Sydney bid 'a shadowy campaign by political insiders backed by enormous wealth that rewrote planning, health and gaming laws despite deep community concerns about gambling, a deep-pocketed commercial rival and the opposition of the city's planners'. Some money managers have even called the unsolicited proposal route an 'invention'. 'It wasn't best for Sydney. Crown and Echo should have combined their resources. Instead, there was a win-at-all-costs attitude. It was a stitch-up by Crown,' one of them now says upon reflection. Even the casino's VIP gaming rooms were exempted from a smoking ban after Crown struck a deal with the union United Voice.

Micheil Brodie of the Independent Liquor and Gaming Authority later revealed the probity check of Crown took just three months, describing it as 'one of the fastest assessments of a casino applicant in history'. What he didn't mention is that Crown's executives and Packer had been subjected to previous probity assessments by ILGA in 2012 following the company's purchase of its shares in Echo.

But Barry O'Farrell dismisses suggestions that he was too favourable towards Crown or allowed his determination to get a big-ticket tourism project off the ground to ride roughshod over proper planning and regulatory processes. 'I can tell you that one of my senior staff members told me I should have nothing to do with [Packer], because it would be political poison. After I resigned, people said, "Watch out, you will be a director of Crown next." None of that has happened and is likely to happen,' O'Farrell now says. 'I will go to my grave saying that what I was driven by in this was what was best for Sydney and New South Wales. It, like many other controversial projects, will prove itself over the long term.'

Todd Nisbet claims he has never been through a regulatory process like the one Crown had to satisfy for the Sydney project. 'And I have been involved in some of the biggest, large-scale development projects globally in our industry. Emerging markets, the opening-up of Macau, the large-scale mega resorts in Vegas, the opening of gaming markets in Philadelphia,' he says. 'The third-party review with Murray, all the other things that happened in relation to the unsolicited proposal, what we went through to get the planning permit, I haven't seen anything like it. If it was a bad idea fundamentally, it would not have stood up to all the scrutiny. It was a good idea. It just happened to be James Packer, which meant the critics thought it had to be a backroom deal.'

*

PACKER HIMSELF DESCRIBES CROWN Sydney as a 'serious achievement', given it was the first time in his life that he was front and centre of a publicity campaign. 'I am a really good salesman when I have my mojo and believe in what I'm selling. And Crown Sydney means so much to me. I think Sydney makes Crown an Australia-wide casino company.'

In November 2013 *The Daily Telegraph*'s then editor at large, John Lehmann, called Crown Sydney's approval one of the 'cleverest uses of soft power ever seen in Sydney. If his father Kerry was the belligerent bulldozer, James has become the great persuader. Look at his networks and you get the sense he believes he can achieve more by making friends rather than enemies.'

Graham Richardson says it was the best business political achievement he had seen. 'It was a brilliant manoeuvre to get another casino when you had the Star already there. James can be extraordinarily charming when he wants to be. And when you put it with the intellect, he is pretty formidable. That was a big win. When he has a big win, it buoys him. He gets on a real high.'

Packer says he owes a giant debt of gratitude to Barry O'Farrell for doing what he did. 'Barry went out on a limb for me. Without him Crown Sydney was just an idea. I am deeply grateful to Barry. And I believe New South Wales will be better when Crown opens,' he says. Packer also says Lucy Turnbull, a former lord mayor of Sydney – and the wife of former prime minister Malcolm Turnbull – played an important role on the board of the Crown Sydney architectural advisory panel to help the company adopt WilkinsonEyre Architects' design for the project.

Packer also feels indebted to Alan Jones for his unwavering, on-air support for the project and for first introducing him to O'Farrell. Jones says that while Packer doesn't lack self-confidence, he succeeds in difficult negotiations because 'he's not aggressive in presenting himself and he's fastidiously courteous. He's the only person, I think, in the history of industrial development in this country who has managed to get the conservatives onside, the Labor Party onside, the unions onside, local governments, everybody, all through personal negotiation. And it exhausted him.'

Yet Packer still has doubts about Crown Sydney as a business proposition. He's wary of the company making the same mistakes with Crown Sydney that it made in Melbourne and Perth, where he believes it has overcapitalised in spending more than $3 billion over the past decade. 'There is a not insignificant number of astute people who think we are spending too much money for the returns we will achieve in Sydney. It is not something I would say is a no-brainer,' he says, before returning to a familiar refrain. 'That is part of the reason we have got Crown's balance sheet into a shape and form where it can afford to build Sydney. Crown should not be overly stretched even after we build Sydney. Crown should be able to maintain its dividend unless Melbourne and Perth become sunset as opposed to mature businesses.'

But there is an emotional component to Crown Sydney that goes beyond the maths. Packer may be driven in life by numbers and scorecards, but comparisons with his father will always loom large. 'From my perspective, Sydney is a multiple of things. It is a business opportunity. It is also the city I grew up in. I grew up in a family business that had businesses in Sydney, which we don't have [currently]. So I will be back to having a business in Sydney, which means a lot to me,' he says. 'And without being disrespectful to my father in any way, shape or form: ACP has disappeared as such; Channel Nine still exists but it is in a diminished form. Crown Sydney is going to be there for a long time. The licence is for 100 years and I'm hoping it will be there for a long time after that.'

*

In December 2017 Packer splurged $60 million to buy two floors of what are known as the Crown Residences at One Barangaroo, eighty-two luxury apartments within the Crown Sydney project. The purchase price more than doubled the Sydney apartment record price of $26 million set in 2016. Packer's favourite interior designer, Australian Blainey North – who has been involved with several high-end projects at both Crown Perth and Crown Towers Melbourne – has been designing his new apartment. It is an investment not just in real estate, but in Packer's future life. Spending time there will test his resilience and answer important questions about his relationships both with the city of his birth and the people who live in it: family, friends, business acquaintances, competitors and – most significantly – its voracious media.

Now reflecting on the purchase, Packer says: 'My apartment is levels forty-eight and forty-nine. Crown gave me the price; I didn't negotiate, I just said yes. The bottom floor is living. The top floor has four bedrooms: my bedroom and one for each of the kids. I think it is going to be seriously wow.'

Sydney holds so many bad memories, which will be hard to forget. But Packer isn't prepared to give up on the city of his birth. 'I have such a funny relationship with Sydney. I am written about more than anyone other than present politicians,' he says. 'Truth is, I'm scared of Sydney. I'm scared of the newspapers. I don't want to be hit any more. I have fallen out with a lot of people. Too many. Some of the fallouts must be my fault. I worry whether Sydney will ever feel like home again. There is a lot of pain there for me. Crown Sydney is the thing that will draw me back to the city at some time in the future. I will be back to having a business in Sydney, which means a lot to me.'

NINE

The Brotherhood

JAMES PACKER WILL NEVER forget the present he received from his good friend Brett Ratner for his forty-seventh birthday on 8 September 2014. In keeping with Ratner's heritage as a Hollywood producer, it was a short film. But this one was of the spoof variety.

The opening scene sees the camera pan across the set of the Nine Television Network's morning news-entertainment program *Today*, before zooming in on its suited host, Packer's friend the morning-television celebrity Karl Stefanovic. After welcoming the audience, Stefanovic turns to an event in Packer's life four months earlier that made headlines around the world. 'We begin with breaking news, and an extraordinary fight has broken out between billionaire James Packer and Nine Australia boss David Gyngell,' booms Stefanovic, staring down the barrel of the camera.

The film cuts to actual local and international television and radio news reports of the infamous Bondi street brawl between Packer and his former best mate on the afternoon of

4 May 2014. Then, for the next seven minutes – interspersed with some clever animations of Packer and Gyngell in battle in a boxing ring – some of the biggest names in Packer's world at the time, such as the Seven Network's Kerry Stokes, Packer's Asian gaming partner Lawrence Ho, Warner Bros CEO Kevin Tsujihara, Israeli businessman and Hollywood producer Arnon Milchan, Lachlan Murdoch and even then Australian prime minister Tony Abbott, all joke about the fight.

Ho warns that he is a master of kung-fu, 'so James stays away from me'. Stokes declares that the fight was 'more like a *Dancing with the Stars* episode than brawling in the street'. Milchan jokes that Packer might make it in the Israeli army, especially 'guarding the tunnels'. Standing in his prime ministerial office before the Australian flag, Tony Abbott says with a straight face: 'James, I was the first Australian who went to Oxford to learn how to box and from what I have seen, you need some lessons.' In one memorable scene towards the end of the film, Hollywood legends Martin Scorsese, Robert De Niro, Leonardo DiCaprio and Brad Pitt are all seated at a table together, where they joke about the fight and a potential rematch between Packer and Gyngell. Pitt pulls from his jacket a fistful of US dollars and hands them to De Niro, who proudly declares they are his winnings from backing Packer in the first bout. 'I'm on Team Packer [for the rematch],' declares DiCaprio as the camera pans around the table to the others. Pitt soon agrees.

But the appearance of one character in the film comes as a complete surprise: His name is David Liam Barr Gyngell. 'I was just moving, ducking, weaving, he had no chance,' Gyngell says to the camera with a straight face in one short scene, before breaking into a burst of karate chops and kicks. He re-emerges in the final scene with some telling words: 'Pack, I love you with all my heart. Hope you have an amazing day and a great birthday. Take care, brother,' he says before signing off with another series of kung-fu moves, screams and a smile.

'It was all a surprise to me,' Packer now says of the film. 'There was an amazing cast for this video.' But he now struggles to see the humour in Gyngell's performance. 'David must have wanted to be in it as he was the last person in the short film,' he says. 'My bust-up with Erica was in the past, the fight in the street with him was in the past ... I haven't seen David since.'

*

GYNGELL AND PACKER FIRST met at the elite Cranbrook School in Sydney's eastern suburbs before Gyngell dropped out of school in Year 11 and opened his own surf shop in Bondi's main Campbell Parade shopping strip, not far from Packer's apartment. They bonded like their famous fathers, Kerry and Bruce, once had. But while the older generation shared a common interest in television, the younger preferred glamorous women and rugby league. Gyngell was a regular at Packer's apartment, along with Packer's other Cranbrook mates Chris 'Cockie' Hancock, Matthew 'Ched' Csidei and Ben Tilley. James was known to the group as 'Pack' and Gyngell as 'Gyng', the affectionate nature of the nicknames indicating the closeness of the group.

Gyngell accepted Packer's invitation to join Channel Nine in 1999, eventually becoming deputy chief executive at the age of thirty-five. In 2004 Packer was Gyngell's best man when he married Leila McKinnon, the Channel Nine TV presenter, in a ceremony at Byron Bay. That same year Gyngell became Nine CEO, but he lasted less than twelve months before unexpectedly quitting, six months before Kerry Packer's death.

James Packer now reveals he gave Gyngell a special farewell from Nine at the time, a legacy of their shared love of the eastern suburbs Sydney Roosters rugby league team. Packer was a long-time director of the Roosters, which is chaired by rich-lister car dealer Nick Politis. At one point Politis and Packer were joint owners of the blue-ribbon City Lexus dealership in Melbourne. 'When David quit Channel Nine the first time in 2005, when my father had been too much of a weight for him, I gave him a personal redundancy from me – my remaining share of the car-dealership business. It was a lot of money for me at the time. I thought we were brothers,' Packer now says. Gyngell had sold his interest by the time Politis sold the dealership to a local investor for a speculated $15.5 million in October 2014.

After spending two years in Los Angeles as CEO of Granada America, Gyngell returned to Sydney in September 2007 as Nine CEO for a second time, hired by the PBL Media boss Ian Law. By that time Packer had sold 75 per cent of PBL Media to private equity group CVC Asia Pacific. But he says he was still influential in the network, at least when it came to Gyngell. 'I introduced Ian Law to David at my wedding to Erica in France and said to Ian he should hire David. At that time David was living in LA,' Packer says, before lobbing the first grenade to singe Gyngell's feet. 'David would have never got the job to run Nine the second time without my help – just like the first time.' After Gyngell's return, Nine started winning the key viewer demographics prized by advertisers, even though it remained in second place in the overall ratings behind Seven.

Earlier in 2010 Gyngell even joined the board of Crown Resorts. 'I tried to help David whenever I could. He told me he was keen to join the Crown board in 2010 and the directors agreed in June that year. He didn't ask [then CVC CEO] Adrian MacKenzie for permission. Adrian was irked but couldn't do anything,' Packer says.

Later in 2010, during their early-morning training sessions together at Sydney's Hyde Park Club in the basement of Packer's city offices, Packer and Gyngell got talking about the Ten Network and the idea of Gyngell one day running it with Packer as an investor. Packer saw an opportunity to run Ten better, making better use of its new digital channels, and talked of taking Ten back to its low-cost, high-profit model focused on the 16–39 demographic. At the time it was only a thought bubble, but Packer soon got more serious. In late October that year he paid $280 million for an 18 per cent stake in Ten, prompting feverish speculation that Gyngell would follow his good mate to the network as CEO. But it never happened.

Despite Packer's overtures, Gyngell told other friends at the time he felt bound by his contract to run Channel Nine. Then on 2 November 2010 Gyngell was elevated to the role of PBL Media CEO, replacing Ian Law, when the company's private equity owner CVC Asia Pacific sought a big name to front a future $5-billion-plus stockmarket float of the company. As well as overseeing the Nine television stations in Melbourne, Sydney, Brisbane and Newcastle, Gyngell had added responsibility for the magazine business ACP, ticket seller Ticketek and internet portal Ninemsn.

James Chessell wrote in *The Australian* on 4 November 2010 that Gyngell had been in his new job for less than twenty-four hours when Packer got in touch by text message. Packer had seen a provocative quote from the new PBL Media boss that read: 'Channel Ten is a nice little business but it ain't PBL Media.' Chessell wrote, '[Packer] fired back with a message expressing mock outrage at the use of the word "little".'

Gyngell initially negotiated a $2 million annual pay packet with CVC. When PBL Media changed its name to Nine Entertainment Co and floated on the ASX in late 2013, it was revealed Gyngell had negotiated the best remuneration package of any Australian media executive in history. It included a $2.5 million cash bonus for steering Nine to a listing from the brink of receivership a few years before, an additional $2.7 million cash bonus and $11.6 million in long-term incentives. The Nine prospectus for its sharemarket listing put his total potential package at about $32 million. Gyngell said at the time of the float: 'If I get that money – and I'm not saying it's not a lot of money – I think everyone else will be doing pretty well.'

By that time, Packer and Gyngell had grown apart. Their last business deal together, in April 2012, was Gyngell's purchase of a half-share of John 'Strop' Cornell's Hotel Brunswick at Brunswick Heads, for which he borrowed $8.5 million through Packer's private company CPH, paying it back in full just over two years later. By the end of 2013, Packer, with his marriage over, was going global, pursuing his ambitions in Asia, Israel and Hollywood. By contrast, Gyngell had left the Crown board after taking the PBL Media CEO role and was firmly focused on Nine. He was also enjoying life in Sydney and Byron Bay with his wife Leila McKinnon and their baby son Ted.

Packer now describes his falling-out with Gyngell, which led to their fight as 'complex, as I guess all fallouts with former best friends are. Where it manifested was with Channel Ten. David was the biggest advocate that I should buy into Channel Ten. It was while he was running Channel Nine, reporting to Ian Law. The week after I bought shares in Ten, PBL Media terminated Ian Law and gave David the biggest contract a traditional media executive has ever been given in Australia. They were afraid David would come and run Ten for me. So David got the contract of a lifetime off my back after advising me to invest in Ten,' Packer says. 'David made it very clear that he would do his best to destroy Channel Ten after encouraging me to invest in it.'

In May 2011 Gyngell was quoted in *The Australian*'s *The Deal* business magazine, saying that running Ten and managing its board of billionaires – including Packer, Lachlan Murdoch, Gina Rinehart and Bruce Gordon – never tempted him. 'It would be distracting, to say the least, to work for that board,' he said. 'This idea that I wouldn't compete with Ten because my best mate is a shareholder is absolute bullshit. We are like brothers. But like brothers, we are very competitive. I look forward to smashing Ten.'

What apparently worsened the falling-out between Packer and Gyngell – in Packer's view, at least – was CVC's treatment of Ian Law, who passed away after a battle with cancer in October 2013. Packer had got to know Law when West Australian Newspapers (WAN) invested in the Hoyts cinema business when it was owned by Packer's CMH (Law was WAN CEO at the time). He feels Gyngell should have done more for Law, having been the beneficiary of his corporate demise. 'I loved him. He was one of the best people I have ever met in my life. Who knows why things happen in life? When Ian got fired and David got his massive contract, not long after that Ian got cancer,' Packer says. 'It killed him quickly. I tried to visit Ian as often as I could but that's not the point. When Ian died David went on the record with all the papers about what a great person Ian was. I was repulsed.'

Packer says he has always struggled with 'managing' his friends and foes in the Australian media, whether it be the Murdochs, Kerry Stokes, Nine or Fairfax. 'Trying to manage media relationships in Australia, and especially in Sydney more than Melbourne, is impossible,' he says.

He claims his falling-out with Gyngell over Ten was also about Lachlan Murdoch, who bought half of Packer's stake in the network. By taking the PBL Media role and not the Ten job, Packer feels Gyngell forced him to make a choice between two mates. 'Lachlan is a real friend. David was dismissive of him and never thought that Lachlan would become the success that he has,' Packer says. 'David, in effect, forced me to choose between him and Lachlan.'

*

EVEN DAVID GYNGELL'S FRIENDS didn't appreciate the extent of the rage that was building inside him in the lead-up to the afternoon of 4 May 2014. Packer had landed at Sydney airport in his private jet from Jerusalem and was furious to learn from his security team that a Channel Nine van was parked outside his Bondi apartment, apparently waiting to film him (though it turned out its presence was completely coincidental). Packer immediately fired off an abusive text to Gyngell, who was at Bondi Beach only a few hundred metres from Packer's apartment. For Gyngell, who was barefoot and in his beach gear, it was the last straw. He drove his white Audi SUV up the road to Packer's private driveway and waited for his friend to arrive, in the interim yelling at him down the phone, vowing to 'knock his block off'.

When Packer arrived, Gyngell started swinging. Former Nine boss David Leckie, who remains close to Gyngell and stays in touch with him, now says of the moment: 'I think David would agree that he should not have hit him. However, he exploded after receiving several really tough emails from James over a period of at least a year. David was just full of rage about it, and I just didn't know how bad it was until after it happened.'

Packer himself now recalls the incident in detail. 'I was physically assaulted outside my house. As I got out of the car, driving in from the airport as I had just flown in from Israel, David was standing there and started swinging punches as I opened the door. As we know, there was a photographer there and the rest became history,' he says. 'In the hours after, I was worried about my casino licences so demanded David come around the next morning to my house and see me, which he did. He put out a public statement where he took full responsibility. But it was an open-and-shut case of assault. Who gets assaulted outside their house, regardless of the build-up? I got him his job, got him his big contract by buying into Ten on his advice, and saved him his job. Then he stopped talking to me.' Each was subsequently fined $500 for offensive behaviour.

Packer's first wife, Jodhi Meares, now says she viewed the incident as like 'two brothers' fighting in their backyard. 'I thought it was hilarious. I sent James that video [of the Carl Douglas song 'Kung-Fu Fighting']. Everyone on the street thought it was the best thing ever,' she says with a smile. 'I said to James, "Don't worry about it. Everyone will think you are epic legends and the best thing ever." Brothers fight. They fight when they get really angry. That is what happened.'

On the following Thursday, Erica Packer made a surprise trip to Australia from her Los Angeles home. But instead of heading to Packer's Bondi apartment, she drove to the Dover Heights home of the Gyngells. Packer acknowledges that one of the reasons for the fight was that Gyngell thought his friend was responsible for the breakdown of his marriage to Erica. But Gyngell was also angry about the way his best friend was living his life as an international jet-setter between Hollywood, Israel and other parts of the world

Another speculated reason for the fight – that it was also over Packer's alleged relationship with supermodel Miranda Kerr – was subsequently denied by Kerr. 'They weren't fighting over me,' she told the *Sunday Times Style* magazine later in 2014, before adding: 'James and I are friends, but people want to make a story, the public want to put me with someone.'

At the end of January 2015, in an interview with 2GB radio host Ray Hadley, Gyngell said he felt 'ashamed' and 'peeved' at himself for starting the fight. 'We're bad fighters. I put him in more of a precarious situation, which I shouldn't have done, being the person he is and the responsibilities and the governance issues he has,' Gyngell said. 'I was peeved at myself for doing that. I went down to hit him. He didn't come down to my place to punch me, I went down to his place, so it's very difficult to say we were equally to blame.' Gyngell said his wife had called him an 'idiot' when he told her what he had done. Packer himself told a media briefing during a visit to Australia in August 2015: 'I should have never punched Gyngell outside my house.'

While another former Nine CEO, Eddie McGuire, says many people saw the fun of the brawl, he says he 'was really gutted for both because I know how much they genuinely regard each other. The great thing about David Gyngell is that he is a very confident, independent person. I think he'd seen his father's [extremely close] relationship with Kerry. Regardless of how close you can be, you still work for them. David wasn't in that type of relationship with James.' Of the incident specifically, McGuire says: 'When James thought that David had a link van out the front to get shots of Miranda Kerr, I think David was saying, "Mate, you don't own me any more. And, as if I would do that." I think it was just a build-up of two guys who really had a lot of time for each other but were just bursting apart. I hope that they find each other again. But you know, they've got two different paths.'

David Gyngell politely declined to be interviewed for this book, but people who know him echo the comments of McGuire – they say he still 'loves' Packer, but believes they have both gone their separate ways in the world. 'David is now very removed from James's world,' says one.

While they haven't seen each other since the day after the fight, they have been in contact. 'When I was in Argentina, in late 2016 with all my problems hitting home, I sent David an email saying, "You were right about me," or something like that. I was trying to reconnect with him and I needed a friend,' Packer says. 'He replied with a polite but nothing reply. He has never reached out to me since then to see if I'm okay.'

In August 2017 Erica Packer celebrated her fortieth birthday with a lavish medieval dinner in Aspen. 'Erica, I know, invited David and Leila to her fortieth,' Packer says. 'They didn't go to that. It is not as though David has been a friend to Erica, even though what the fight was supposed to be all about was him taking her side.'

Packer still clearly harbours anger and bitterness about the end of his friendship with Gyngell, but Jodhi Meares believes the two still love each other. 'It is like family. And sometimes with family you take things out on each other that you would not do with other people. They still love each other, they are family,' she says. 'You don't [fight in the street] with somebody you don't love. They cannot push you to that kind of upset. I think they are both hurt. They probably miss each other deeply. They will get there.' But again she stresses that her ex-husband is 'allowed to have his human experience. He had a fight with his brother, who cares?'

*

DAVID GYNGELL ISN'T THE only member of Packer's old Cranbrook pack to have fallen out with the billionaire in recent times. Matthew 'Ched' Csidei was previously employed by CPH as the keeper of the billionaire's boats, planes and homes — the so-called 'ministry of fun'. His role included overseeing the construction of the home in Sydney that Packer was going to share with his second wife, Erica, before they split. But Ched mysteriously left CPH's employment in 2017 and has made no comment about it.

The speculated reason had been cost blowouts on Packer's new 107-metre long superyacht, designed by British luxury-boat specialist Redman Whiteley Dixon, which is still under construction at an Italian shipyard in Livorno, near Pisa. Ched, who has been called both 'The Admiral' and 'The Butler', had relocated to Monaco to oversee the project. The $150 million budget for Packer's boat – still taking shape inside a 150-metre-long purpose-built shed – has grown to $170 million in CPH's accounts. The original budget failed to include the cost of the interior non-mechanical fit-out and a tender (a smaller speedboat used by large vessels to shuttle guests to and from the shore). The boat, which will be known as *IJE* – the names of Packer's three children Indigo, Jackson and Emmanuelle, in descending age order – is now not due for delivery until June 2019.

On the subject of Csidei, all Packer will say is: 'I'm incredibly disappointed.'

*

PACKER IS FAR MORE effusive in speaking of one of his other ex-Cranbrook mates, Ben Tilley, who is now his most important male companion and the leader of his new 'pack' of mates. 'Ben has been fantastic and is an unbelievably good friend,' James says. 'He helps organise things. But he is a friend. He is company. He is wonderful. He has my back.'

But Tilley's dedication to his friend has come at a personal cost. The time Tilley spent away from Sydney in recent years, accompanying Packer as he pursued his global ambitions, led to his long-term marriage to his wife Tiffany collapsing in 2017. In early 2018 the couple sold their $20 million Point

Piper residence next door to the home of Malcolm and Lucy Turnbull in Sydney.

Tilley is now employed full-time by James to look after his personal affairs, but he and James were not always so close. During the last few years of his life, Kerry Packer asked Tilley to be his constant travelling companion, impressed by his skill at two of Kerry's greatest passions: playing golf and cards. Kerry played poker with Tilley regularly and took him on gambling trips to Las Vegas, London and on the *Arctic P* as it cruised around the Mediterranean.

Tilley's friendship with Kerry drove James mad for many years. 'Ben and I had a falling-out. We didn't talk for a long time,' Packer now says, 'because Ben was my friend and I couldn't handle it. Perhaps I was being unreasonable because Ben and Dad would go gambling and have fun without me. Without being rude about my father, Dad lost more than he won at gambling, even though that's not the accepted wisdom. So I am sitting there looking at these amounts that are being played for, and I became pretty bitter that Ben was there in the middle of it.' But he quickly adds: 'He's paid it back in spades to me, and did for Dad too.'

So how did they get back on good terms? 'We just started spending time together, and there were a couple of things Ben did that were, you know, very, very good. More personal than business things. We just became closer and closer. When I left Australia when my marriage broke down, Ben started spending a lot of time with me. I think he found it exciting to travel,' Packer says.

Tilley has his critics – from those who wonder what he does every day, to others who say he is a bad influence on James. But celebrity photographer Jamie Fawcett, who has captured thousands of photographs of Tilley by Packer's side, says of Tilley: 'Thank goodness [Packer] has someone who has been prepared to put his life and his marriage on hold in order to help his mate. I think that is great. You would want to help someone like James – he is a nice bloke.'

Packer certainly acknowledges one of Tilley's key roles, above all else, is to provide him with emotional support. 'And there is a depth of friendship that goes back a long time. It has been tested and survived. We care about each other and have good banter with each other. We get on extremely well,' he says. As one who knows them both puts it: 'James is someone who needs company, and Ben keeps him calmer than most.'

Others who remain in Packer's inner circle include former St George rugby league halfback Damien Chapman and professional Argentinian polo player Martin Pepa. Packer first met the man he calls 'Chappy' in the Hyde Park fitness club when Chapman was working with Packer's ex-wife Erica. 'He's in some ways seen more than anyone,' Packer says of Chapman. 'Because you know he was with me almost every day – 24/7 – in 2012–14. When I got in shape, he was my trainer. And that's when we became really close. But he is so much more than a trainer and is exceptionally bright, as is Ben.' The affable Chapman also regularly babysits Packer's children. 'He has done his best to support me emotionally, which is very, very good, and my kids just love him, which is a huge help to me,' Packer says.

The same goes for Pepa, who was introduced to Packer six years ago by champion Argentine polo player Facundo Pieres. 'Martin is a loyal, fun-loving friend, who is great with my kids and who has a terrific sense of humour,' Packer says.

Packer has also been friends for many years with Nine Network television personality Karl Stefanovic, whom some have called the 'court jester' to the billionaire. Stefanovic has been a regular visitor on the *Arctic P* and at Packer's various luxury properties around the world but rarely speaks publicly about his friend.

*

FOR DECADES, PACKER AND UBS's star investment banker Matthew Grounds were inseparable. Grounds was the man Packer always turned to for advice on his public and private affairs, including the break-up of his marriage to Erica in 2013. Grounds even became the executor of Packer's will and godfather to his son, Jackson. In an interview with Grounds for *The Australian Financial Review Magazine* in August 2012, Pamela Williams quoted Packer as calling Grounds a 'rock star' and 'a smiling assassin'. The latter comment was never explained.

In more recent years their relationship has cooled. For one, he is no longer executor of Packer's will. Grounds, along with David Gyngell, Paul Bassat and Erica Packer, were also all in Packer's ear in the second half of 2013 and the early part of 2014 telling him to slow down as he pursued his ambitions in Hollywood and Israel. Packer was always uncomfortable that Grounds's wife, Kimberley, was too sympathetic to Erica following their split. He was also exercised at times over the handling of negotiations to split the family estate with his sister during 2015, in which Grounds initially played a major role, though Grounds was also involved in bringing the siblings back together in March 2018.

In October 2017 Packer made his first ever public swipe at Grounds – even though he didn't explicitly name him – when he revealed his anger at his 'advisers and management' for talking him out of Crown bidding for the Cosmopolitan Casino in Las Vegas back in 2014. The next week *The Australian*'s 'Margin Call' column followed up on Packer's comments, noting: 'Keen followers of Packer's business career will be aware that his most trusted adviser is the boss of UBS in Australia, Matthew Grounds, who was by Packer's side in the recent aborted attempt to privatise Crown, as well as the difficult negotiations with Gretel Packer over the settlement with her brother over their late father Kerry Packer's estate.'

Packer and Grounds went skiing together on the slopes of Aspen in early 2018 before having a friendly lunch the same day. Yet in the weeks that followed, Packer was still brooding. On 17 February, he asked his top numbers man, Mike Johnston, to compile a table of the fees Crown and CPH had paid to UBS since 2006. It showed UBS had been paid $115 million in total fees – $86.7 million by Crown and $28.3 million by CPH (the latter being largely share-trade brokerage) across more than twenty transactions. The largest payment to Crown was a $20.09 million consulting fee to help the casino group secure regulatory approval for its Crown Sydney casino resort development in 2013. The numbers incensed Packer and he sent them to Grounds.

But the tension between them had further consequences. On the evening of 5 March, Packer was at his luxury villa perched atop the exclusive One & Only Resort in Cabo San Lucas, Mexico, when CPH used Goldman Sachs to sell just over $100 million worth of Crown shares, the first time either Crown or CPH had transacted without UBS in a decade and a half. Packer had negotiated the trade with Goldman Sachs partner Andrew Rennie, whom he had met when Rennie was working in Hong Kong. It amounted to a public sacking of Grounds and was highlighted as such by Joe Aston that evening in *The Australian Financial Review*'s 'Rear Window' column.

Grounds eventually made contact with Packer, and they agreed to put their differences aside. What had been done out of anger, Packer now says he regrets. 'Matthew is a lot more important than me these days. And I was stupid to fire him the way I did. Matthew has been a good friend to me,' he says. Then comes a sting, however. 'But on the whole, I think I gave more than I got. And I like now being non-exclusive [meaning Crown and CPH are no longer wedded to UBS] with Andrew Rennie at Goldman's. Hopefully the inbox will be busier,' Packer says, hinting that more deals may come his way in the future. 'The fact Matthew never put CPH into one ECM [equity capital markets] trade hurts as I look back. Making money for CPH was clearly never a priority for Matthew. I am sure UBS have clients who paid them a lot less, who made money from the ECM desk.' Ouch.

But Grounds resists the temptation to bite back. 'James has been very good to me and we have shared many happy and fun times together,' he says, declining to comment about what happened in March 2018. He prefers to look at the bigger picture. 'James has been an extraordinarily loyal client for many years, and whilst he hasn't necessarily always been the easiest client we have always tried to do our best for him. He's not your everyday traditional corporate client, let's say, and so things often get interesting and you do have to stay on your toes, as he is usually a step or two ahead.'

Grounds also acknowledges that Packer has been more than just a client. 'James can be seriously funny. He does have a brilliant mind and there's not many topics he can't cover or have a relevant statistic on. So over the years he's been great company and of course very kind to my family,' he says.

Packer has been more willing than most wealthy scions to cop his share of the blame for his mistakes. But some of his friends who are self-made multimillionaires say they stick by a simple rule in life when things don't go their way: Never blame your advisers.

*

IN HIS DARKEST MOMENTS in recent years, Packer has lamented that he has no friends left in the business community in

Australia. Yet plenty were prepared to praise him for this book, including the nation's richest man. 'James is one of the most generous businessmen I have ever met. His word is his bond, and I completely trust him,' says paper, packaging and recycling king Anthony Pratt. 'He always errs on the side of generosity. He is a very good bloke.'

Packer acknowledges Pratt is someone he looks up to and respects. 'Anthony has succeeded in building a business in America where I failed,' he says, before also praising fellow Melbourne billionaires Solomon Lew and Lindsay Fox, whom he also describes as friends.

Nevertheless, Packer has a familiar refrain when you talk to him about friends, especially those in Australia: that many have been better to him than he deserves. It is hard to tell how deep these apparent feelings of a lack of self-worth run, but they suggest a degree of vulnerability, a lack of confidence that does not fit with the traditional Packer family image. Perhaps it again reflects how his personality was shaped by his relationship with his father. Maybe it also draws from the deep paranoia he has developed about the city of his birth, Sydney.

Tellingly, he says there are many days he wishes he had moved to Melbourne with Erica and his children before they broke up. 'Melbourne and Sydney are so different. I remember talking to Lachlan [Murdoch] once about how different the cities were,' Packer says. 'We wondered to ourselves whether it went all the way back to the start – Sydney, the only major global city founded as a convict settlement; Melbourne, a [largely] free settlers city. In some ways they seem that different to me today. Their media is that different. Melbourne, to me, is civilised. Sydney, to me, sometimes resembles a bear pit.'

That view hasn't stopped Packer keeping up some friendships in Sydney business circles, most notably with the billionaire Lowy family.

Packer also laments losing touch with former UBS Australia boss Chris Mackay, who was once on the boards of PBL and Crown. Mackay also helped Packer at CPH, including advising him to invest in the financial services powerhouse Magellan. Packer reveals that Mackay resigned from the Crown board in March 2008 because he didn't believe in the company's US casino strategy. 'Losing Chris in my life was, looking back, a serious loss. He's amongst the best bankers I've ever met and Magellan speaks for itself. I wish I listened to him more,' Packer says. Mackay went on to join the board of Kerry Stokes's Seven Group Holdings, which is now run by Stokes's son Ryan, who Packer says is doing a 'fantastic job'.

And it is Kerry Stokes who has the telling last word on perhaps the most important friendship in Packer's life that has not endured. The loss of David Gyngell, the friend Packer long called a brother, is perhaps the greatest casualty of Packer's now dashed global ambitions. 'That was very damaging,' says Stokes of the Packer–Gyngell fight. 'They were both very long-term friends. They are not any more. That is a shame. You don't make that many friends in your life, [that] you can afford to lose them like that.'

TEN

Dancing with the Stars

IT IS KNOWN AS Hilhaven Lodge, a stunning stone and redwood 91-year-old mansion at the end of a well-guarded private lane in the prime lower Benedict Canyon area of Beverly Hills. Once home to Hollywood luminaries such as *Casablanca* star Ingrid Bergman and *Vertigo* actress Kim Novak, its neighbours now include casino magnate Steve Wynn, TV talk-show host Jay Leno, rock star Bruce Springsteen and soccer legend David Beckham.

The houses in this plush celebrity precinct of towering front gates, long, meandering driveways and sprawling estates in the Westside region of Los Angeles are not normally for sale – you have to wait for someone to die before you can buy one. Hollywood film producer and director Brett Ratner did just that in 1999 when he purchased Hilhaven from the estate of *Grease* film producer Allan Carr, who succumbed to liver cancer at age sixty-two.

What won Ratner over was the full-scale discotheque Carr had installed in the basement for his extravagant anything-goes parties, which were legendary in Hollywood. After buying the house, Ratner added an old-fashioned black-and-white photo booth, into which he subsequently enticed a host of A-list celebrities, including Michael Jackson, Britney Spears, Colin Farrell, Heath Ledger, Heidi Klum, Shaquille O'Neal, Edward Norton and Salma Hayek, to pose without make-up, wardrobe or lighting. He compiled the photos into a published hardcover book he titled *Hilhaven Lodge: The photo booth pictures*. At the launch party for the book in May 2003, Michael Jackson told a reporter: '[Ratner] is the nicest person I've ever met. He's so sweet it makes me cry.'

When I arrive at Hilhaven on a balmy early-spring afternoon, walking past three Teslas, a Mercedes and bunch of other flash cars along the steep driveway, the man famous for directing such films as *Rush Hour, X-Men: The last stand*, and *Red Dragon* is initially preoccupied. Dressed in a tee-shirt, tracksuit pants and slippers, the curly-haired, bushy-bearded, slightly dishevelled-looking Brett Ratner is talking at a million miles an hour into his mobile phone.

With his loud, brash American accent, I can't help but overhear that he is on about his health. 'But I've been eating vegetables for five days!' He barks at the person on the other end of the line, who I presume is his doctor. The next minute his mother rings on the landline, and he politely tells her he will call her back, before resuming the mobile call. When he finally finishes the conversation, he stands up and shakes my hand, apologises for the intrusions and explains to me that his protein levels are, mysteriously, too high. Tonight he is departing on a whirlwind trip to Hong Kong, Shanghai and Beijing, and he wants to know if he should continue with his new vegetarian diet.

I quickly notice that on the dark polished-timber wall behind him, seemingly peering over his left shoulder as we talk – perhaps strategically so – is a large framed photo of pop music songstress Mariah Carey. Ratner, who has directed a number of music videos for Carey and calls her a close friend, first introduced her to his then business partner James Packer at the end of 2013. Their whirlwind eighteen-month romance, ending in a broken engagement, was subject to intense media scrutiny.

I eventually ask Ratner if, after all that has happened, he and Carey are still close. 'Of course,' he shoots back, before swigging a mouthful of his staple drink, iced tea. On the table between us sits a bottle of his Hilhaven Lodge whiskey, which he launched in 2007, though he's never touched a drop – he's always been a teetotaller. Of Carey, he quickly adds: 'But when I say close, I haven't seen her. She has a new boyfriend so maybe she feels uncomfortable. I still consider her my friend and consider James my friend.'

*

PACKER FIRST MET BRETT Ratner through Miami property developer Jeffrey Soffer, now supermodel Elle Macpherson's husband and heir to the Turnberry Associates multibillion-dollar real-estate empire in America. Soffer was Packer's business partner on the doomed Fontainebleau casino in America, and he had invited Packer to his fortieth birthday spectacular in December 2007 at the Fontainebleau Aviation hangar at Miami's Opa-locka Executive Airport. The party, organised by Ratner, saw rock legend Prince perform all of his greatest hits. Prince even invited the audience members at one point to join him on stage for a group dance.

Ratner was no stranger to Australia. In 2002 he travelled to Sydney to promote his Anthony Hopkins thriller, *Red Dragon*. In 2008 Ratner became an investor in beauty products business, Jurlique, owned by Packer's private company CPH, and at the end of July that year turned his house into a day spa to promote Jurlique's new biodynamic skincare line, with Salma Hayek, Rosanna Arquette and even Paris Hilton turning up for the relaxed afternoon event.

After James sold Jurlique at the end of 2011, a deal that made Ratner more than three times his money, the two caught up to celebrate early the following year in Los Angeles. That night, as they were listening to the Four Seasons' hit song 'December, 1963 (Oh, What a Night)', they came up with the idea to form a film production company. It would be known as RatPac, both an amalgam of their names and a reference to Frank Sinatra's famed Hollywood Rat Pack, including Dean Martin and Sammy Davis Junior, who hung around and often performed together throughout the 1950s and '60s. Importantly for Packer, RatPac gave him a business in America, later allowing him to spend more time with his children following his separation from Erica in 2013. During this period, Packer initially lived in the presidential suite at the Hotel Bel-Air in Beverly Hills, also a favourite of Steve Wynn, before moving into Warren Beatty's guest house.

RatPac made the Hollywood big time in October 2013 when it signed a four-year, US$450 million deal with former hedge-fund leader and Goldman Sachs veteran (now US Treasury secretary) Steven Mnuchin's Dune Entertainment group and movie giant Warner Bros to fund as many as seventy-five of the studio's films. 'While negotiating a film slate–financing facility with Steven Mnuchin of Dune, one of his key partners was going to be [Hollywood producer Arnon Milchan's] New Regency. For a number of reasons it turned out that New Regency wasn't going to participate,' recalls Warner Bros CEO Kevin Tsujihara, who became a good friend of Packer's. 'That's when Steven introduced RatPac as a replacement for New Regency, and that's how I met James,' he adds.

As part of the deal RatPac was given the bungalow at Building 95 in Warner Bros' Burbank studio complex that was originally built in 1963 for Frank Sinatra, featuring a fully stocked bar and a display of Sinatra's bulging typewritten phone book. 'Some people have said I put Kevin and James together,' says Village Roadshow co-chief executive and Hollywood aficionado Graham Burke. 'This is not accurate, but when Kevin called me and had met James, I extolled him as the good guy that he is.'

The first film the new partners financed was Sandra Bullock and George Clooney's space action thriller *Gravity*, which was released in October 2013. It took US$723 million globally at the box office on a budget of US$100 million and won seven Oscars, including best director, at the 86th Academy Awards in 2014.

Packer was on top of the world, having befriended – through Ratner – the best of Hollywood's A-list, including Martin Scorsese, Robert De Niro, Leonardo DiCaprio, Ben Affleck and Brad Pitt. On the night before the 2014 Oscars, Packer and Ratner had been invited to the opulent fiftieth birthday party for Steve Wynn's second wife, Andrea Hissom, at the Wynn casino in Las Vegas. The event starred Australian performer Hugh Jackman (Ratner directed the second Wolverine movie, starring Jackman) and featured more than seventy dancers and musicians for an audience that included Quincy Jones and Steven Spielberg. The dress and decor was, as they do in Hollywood, a *Great Gatsby* 1920s theme.

'This has only happened to me once in my life,' Packer recalls of the night he was one of the most eligible bachelors in the room. 'We were on this table. There is this woman in her mid forties. She is stunning. She has just broken up from her husband. We get talking, we get on well, and we leave to have a drink.' They disappeared for so long that Ratner, who was also on Packer's table, started to get worried. After calling his friend several times to no answer, he decided to go on a search. When he eventually found the pair back at Packer's hotel room, his phone started ringing.

'And it's somebody from the party going, "Hugh Jackman has called your name six times to come up to the stage!"' Ratner recalls with a wide smile. Jackman knew Ratner and Packer were both in the audience and had called to them from the stage, but when the spotlight fell upon their seats, there was nobody in them. 'So I'm saying, "James, James, they're saying that they're calling my name! Hugh Jackman is calling my name." Steve [Wynn] is blind, he can't see if I'm there or not, but they just keep calling. So James says, "Oh shit, that's embarrassing, let's get the fuck out of here," and we go straight to the airport and we leave on his plane,' Ratner adds.

Packer will never forget what happened next. 'So we take off. When we land there are messages. I check my voicemail. There is a message from Steve Wynn,' Packer says, before lapsing into a rendition of Wynn's trademark deep vocal tones. "Jamie, it's Steve Wynn. I want to say this slowly, so it is very clear. I want you to lose my number!" Steve said. And hung up.'

'The next day I write Steve an email – I said, "I'm sorry to have caused you offence but I thought you would be happy I met someone at your party. If you don't want to speak to me again, no problem." It was a bit more cutting than that, but that was the gist of it. Then he sent me a cutting email saying, "You are not your father," meaning Kerry would never have – as some might say – done a runner at an event to which he'd been invited.' They have since made up, with

Packer in early 2018 selling Wynn a strategic parcel of land on the Las Vegas strip after Crown abandoned its ambitions to build a casino there.

The Vegas birthday event highlights the high life James was then living. He was quoted in an article in *Forbes* magazine that very week as saying: 'Business is good right now, but now my personal life is a disaster.'

In May 2014 RatPac teamed up with the so-called Wolf of Wall Street, Jordan Belfort, to produce a *Mad Men*–style television series about the excesses of the New York finance industry in the 1980s. Belfort served twenty-two months in jail for defrauding more than 1500 investors before his bestselling novel about his Wall Street career was turned into the hit movie *The Wolf of Wall Street*, starring Leonardo DiCaprio. With Packer, Belfort also attended the Australian Open Tennis tournament in Melbourne in early 2014 and later the Philippines casino resort owned by Packer's Asian gaming partner Lawrence Ho's Melco Crown Entertainment.

Ratner says he felt Packer was somewhat wowed by the stars of Hollywood. 'Somehow I think James got seduced a little bit by these guys. They were all around. But that was part of my normal thing. You know I was just like, "Yeah, come around to my house." Mick Jagger's there, Warren Beatty's there, DiCaprio, whatever,' he says. Indeed, Ratner has one of the best contact books in Hollywood, with many stars on speed dial.

But he says Packer always viewed RatPac as a business investment, a chance to create a successful company rather than a way to gain access to the Hollywood celebrities club. 'This is the thing about James,' says Ratner. 'Anybody who is an outsider and has money has got into movies for the wrong reasons. I think James genuinely, really believed in me. I think he was in a new chapter in his life,' he says. He recalls Packer flying to meet him in Hungary in mid 2013 to talk about the filming of RatPac's big-budget version of *Hercules*, starring Dwayne 'The Rock' Johnson. 'James flew from Australia at the time to Budapest to just sit and look me in the eye and say this is really happening, we're doing this,' Ratner says.

In addition to Hollywood's superstar actors, Packer also befriended some of their key backers, including billionaire American record executive, film producer, theatrical producer and philanthropist David Geffen. 'David was good enough to take an interest in me. We began talking about things. He said to me I could contact him at any time and that he would be happy to get to know me better,' Packer recalls.

'The last time I saw David Geffen was in August 2016. He invited me to his house in LA for another one-on-one dinner. After dinner I was due to fly to London and then on to Israel. I was asking David about his career and his life and his investing. And he was kind and generous. He said two things to me that night that I will remember forever. David knew [Apple founder] Steve Jobs well and so never felt he could buy Apple stock. But he told me that his only position in the sharemarket at that time was a significant holding in Apple shares. They were selling at US$100. Today they are almost double that. The other thing he talked about was Amazon. He started to explain why it is such an amazing company. Then he said to me, "Jeff Bezos is going to be the richest man in the world." Since that night Amazon shares have more than doubled.'

Packer says he tells the Geffen stories with regret. In the horror year that was 2016, he was so leveraged in his private company that he couldn't follow Geffen's investment advice, which would have made him a small fortune. More importantly, it would have given him some growth investments for a life after Seek, Carsales, Challenger and Melco Crown.

*

As RatPac rose to the peak of its powers, its founders talked up the potential of making it a genuine global entertainment brand – a play on the purported synergies between Hollywood and the casino industry. Packer talked of plans to stage exclusive celebrity events at Crown's future Sydney casino, using a model borrowed from Las Vegas, where casinos such as the Bellagio were the centrepiece of blockbusters such as George Clooney's *Ocean's Eleven*.

RatPac also moved to target Chinese consumers through a partnership with a Chinese company called China Media Capital, including an investment in Chinese-language movies, TV, digital and live entertainment. Packer wanted to use RatPac to bring together Western and Eastern cultures.

But RatPac also had a huge social side. During 2014 and 2015, social media was littered with posts of Packer and Ratner together in locations across the world, especially aboard the *Arctic P* in the waters of the Mediterranean. Many called them Hollywood's odd couple, given the different worlds from which they came – and the fact that the rotund Ratner stood at only 1.7 metres tall compared with the then slim and muscle-packed Packer's almost 2 metres – but they had seemingly become inseparable. For two years running, Ratner joined the *Arctic P* when it was moored in the waters of the French Riviera for the Cannes Film Festival in May. In 2014, at a party on board reportedly attended by *Gravity* director Alfonso Cuarón, Russell Crowe, Edward Norton and Naomi Watts, *The New York Post*'s celebrity gossip column 'Page Six' claimed Ratner had accidentally dropped his phone into one of the fancy toilets and was spotted putting the device into a bowl of rice in a vain attempt to revive it. The next year in Cannes, a photograph of supermodel Miranda Kerr in an affectionate embrace with Ratner was posted on his Instagram page from an after-party, fuelling further speculation about a romance between her and James.

The RatPac partners were photographed at the Australian Open tennis in early 2014, while a month later they were at the opening ceremony of the winter Olympic Games in the Russian city of Sochi. In September they were snapped by the paparazzi walking the streets of New York in matching tracksuit pants. Ratner was still in tow eighteen months later when the then newly engaged James and Mariah Carey stepped out on the red carpet at the annual G'Day USA tourism event in Los Angeles, which was also attended by the Seven Network's Kerry Stokes and Australian foreign minister Julie Bishop – who became a friend of Ratner's.

With CPH's support RatPac went on to directly co-fund more than fifty films, which reaped more than US$10 billion at the box office and picked up twenty-one Academy Awards from fifty-one nominations and seventeen BAFTAs. In addition to *Gravity*, its hits included *Birdman*, *Creed*, *The Lego Movie*, *American Sniper*, *Kong: Skull Island* and *Godzilla*.

Packer also forged other famous friendships in Hollywood, including one with superstar actor Robert De Niro. In mid 2014 De Niro launched a documentary called *Remembering the Artist*, a portrait of his father, the esteemed figurative painter Robert De Niro Senior. The launch function was an intimate affair – for Hollywood – of only 200 guests at the Museum of Modern Art in New York City. Actors Christopher Walken, Denis Leary, Josh Lucas and Whoopi Goldberg were there, as were James and his good friend and personal trainer Damien Chapman, who travels with him almost everywhere.

De Niro and his father had a complex relationship, much as Packer did with his own father. Chapman recalls, 'Bob took to his feet at the front of the room and gave a deep and meaningful introduction to the film. Then he wandered up the side, shuffled next to us and sat down on the chair next to James. It just verified the fondness and the connection that James and Bob had for each other. And I also felt James was connecting with someone who also shared a complex relationship with his dad.'

Packer says De Niro and his wife Grace 'have been very kind to me', though he quickly adds, 'but I have also been very kind to them. I lent them my boat a number of times, willingly.'

Sixteen months after the New York event, Crown Resorts agreed to pay US$141 million for 20 per cent of the high-end Japanese restaurant and hotel chain Nobu, which De Niro owns with businessman Meir Teper and chef Nobuyuki 'Nobu' Matsuhisa. The deal in October 2015 was announced just days after the opening of the Hollywood-themed US$4 billion Studio City casino resort in Macau, which was attended by Packer and De Niro. Crown's purchase valued Nobu at US$500 million and was immediately attacked by some Crown investors, such as Australian fund manager Colonial First State, complaining that it highlighted the Crown board's inability to say no to the whims of its biggest shareholder. But Packer now declares that Crown 'will make money on Nobu. Nobu is a good deal for Crown. Bob and Meir and Nobu Matsuhisa were very good to have invited us in. They could have invited in a number of other people at the same price who would have said yes,' he says.

Packer also went into business with another of his Hollywood friends, actor Leonardo DiCaprio, when in 2016 RatPac teamed up with director Martin Scorsese to make the DiCaprio-championed documentary *Before the Flood* about climate change. The film, which received mixed reviews, showed DiCaprio visiting various regions of the world to explore the impact of human-made global warming. 'Climate change is Leo's passion. He did this film with me at RatPac when he could have done it anywhere. We actually made a bit of money on this film,' Packer says. 'It was a real act of friendship for Leo to do this with me.'

*

PACKER LIVED IT UP and on the edge in Los Angeles for more than three years, but he sometimes forgot one important lesson: nothing comes for free in Hollywood. Despite the friendships he forged, friends say he too often – and sometimes naively – allowed his deep pockets to become a lure for hangers-on and free-loaders. He also shows a striking vulnerability when talking about this period in his life, almost as if he feels unworthy of the genuine kindness some of the stars of Hollywood showed him. The critics would say they were simply after his money – and some undoubtedly were – but for others, like De Niro, the connection was clearly deeper.

By the second half of 2016, things had turned bad for RatPac. The group had earlier formed RatPac Entertainment, an independent production and financing entity separate from its Warner Bros and China ventures. It secured a first-look deal with Brad Pitt's production company Plan B. With Arnon Milchan's Regency Enterprises, it scored a big hit with the film *The Revenant*, which won Leonardo DiCaprio his first Oscar.

But the misses for the independent venture surpassed the hits. Russell Crowe's directorial debut, *The Water Diviner* – which was financed independently by RatPac in partnership with the Seven Network in Australia – did well at the box office in Australia and Turkey but struggled elsewhere, while *Aloha* and *Assassin's Creed*, both produced with Regency Enterprises, fell flat at the box office.

But the biggest disaster was the box-office bomb *Rules Don't Apply*, Warren Beatty's first screen-acting role in fifteen years, where he played reclusive billionaire Howard Hughes. RatPac was its biggest backer, along with New Regency and a bunch of billionaires. The film's financiers considered striking a distribution deal with streaming giant Netflix before deciding to distribute the film through 20th Century Fox and New Regency Pictures. When released in late November 2016, the film received mixed reviews, the critics decrying its style over substance, but it was a clear flop financially, reportedly grossing US$3.9 million while costing $31.1 million to produce and $23.2 million to distribute.

'It was basically a movie where the distributor had not a nickel in it. The financiers that came in were all very, very good people who were interested in making a good movie. James, Brett and RatPac were well-meaning and supportive financiers,' Warren Beatty now says. 'Then when you get into the marketing phase of a movie, that is a whole other story. I have learned now that if you are going to make a movie for theatres, you should make it something [the public] are familiar with. That it gives people a reason to get out of the house and have an idea of what you are going to see. It is very difficult, if you make a [US]$30 million movie, to say we have to spend $50 million to make people aware of it because they don't know who [the central characters in the film] are, we don't know the story or whatever.'

The box-office failure of *Rules Don't Apply* also created bad blood between all involved. In December 2017 Milchan's Regency Entertainment and Monarchy Enterprises filed a lawsuit against Beatty and the investors in the project, seeking US$18 million in unrecouped distribution costs. The suit alleged that Beatty was so obsessed with getting the film on as many screens as possible that he ignored contrary advice and bad preview screenings. Then in March 2018 the investors in the film, including RatPac, filed a US$50 million fraud complaint against Milchan, saying the film flopped because he failed to market it properly.

For Packer, the whole episode was an embarrassment, given his close relationships with both Beatty and Milchan, and marked the beginning of the end of his business association with Ratner.

Beatty says that even after all his experiences in Hollywood, he took away lessons from what happened, and remarkably it never affected his friendship with James. 'The whole business of financing a movie – if it is not a tent pole, a theme park or a water slide – can be very complicated if you are doing a subject that is not a sequel,' he says. 'One of the many things that has changed with this technology is that there is now such a proliferation of themes and people and news … That it takes something to get people to get into their car to drive to a theatre at the time of a theatre owner's choosing. Not to have their cell phone used during that experience, unable to go to the toilet without missing the movie, and to not know what it is [about]. To do a movie that is a low-priced movie – less than US$30 million – it is going to cost you more to open it properly than it is to make it.'

He laments that because of the technology now available, people in the future will treat movies more like books. 'If you are bored with a book you can put it on the bedside table. You can pick it up three days later and it is no longer boring. That will happen more and more with movies,' he says. 'What will be missing is the communal experience. That silence that can exist with 1000 people that teaches you something while you are sitting there, or the laugh or the fear.'

James stirred the pot in Hollywood when, in his interview with me in *The Weekend Australian* in October 2017, he claimed

RatPac lost most of its money on movies picked by Ratner. He confirmed in the interview that he lost US$100 million on the venture. He still stands by the comments, but unsurprisingly Ratner disagrees. 'Well, I'll dispute that. If you look at that slate of movies they're all Regency movies. I wasn't managing the movies, I was just making the investments,' he says. 'I'm happy to take the blame, but we only did movies with New Regency. I didn't go make movies outside of New Regency.'

*

IT WAS A COOL mid-winter morning in Los Angeles on Thursday 19 January 2017 when the Hollywood Chamber of Commerce proudly honoured Brett Ratner with the 2599th star on the Hollywood Walk of Fame. Along for the show were Australian foreign minister Julie Bishop, Dwayne Johnson and comedian Eddie Murphy. But James Packer was nowhere to be seen.

Eight days earlier Ratner had visited Packer at his luxury home in the heart of Aspen's ski fields. He had both good and bad news to share. The bad news was that RatPac would need to find at least another US$200 million in cash. The good news was Ratner wanted to try to find a business partner to buy his friend out of RatPac. 'I went to see him in Aspen. I said, "You want to go first or should I go first?" He goes, 'You go first and I said, "I want to buy you out,"' Ratner recalls.

He says Packer snarled in reply: 'How the fuck are you going to do that?'

After the horrors of 2016, Packer was not in a good place, especially with Ratner. Friends say he felt disappointed his friend and business partner never apologised for the millions of dollars they lost in RatPac, even if Ratner never took a salary for his work. Packer was also agitated about the high overheads at the RatPac office in Los Angeles, which was being shared by then CPH CEO Robert Rankin.

Friends say Packer was also deeply conscious of the big Jewish presence in Hollywood. When he was drawn into the corruption scandal involving Israeli prime minister Netanyahu in the second half of 2016 – even though it was eventually proven he did nothing wrong – they say it only made Packer's life harder in Hollywood. The last thing Packer wanted was to be frowned upon unfairly over what was happening in Israel.

Now, with Ratner's Aspen offer, at least he had a solution that could put an end to the losses on the investment, even if there would be no goodwill in the sale price for his interest in a venture that had once been the hottest property in Hollywood. Ratner recalls, 'I've seen how anxiety-ridden James is when his debt is up. I said, "I don't want to be a burden but there's some huge obligations coming up." My idea was to get my friend [British billionaire] Len Blavatnik to buy James and [Steve] Mnuchin out. That was my strategy. When James gave me [the price he wanted], which was a big number, I said, "Great, thank you, love you."'

Ratner then told Packer he needed six months to do the deal. Packer gave him two weeks. 'When I left I called Len from the plane. I said, "I'm coming to New York; when can I see you? I'll be in my pyjamas but come over,"' Ratner recalls telling Blavatnik. The deal was eventually done in April 2017, when CPH formally sold its RatPac stake to Access Entertainment, a part of Blavatnik's Access Industries.

Warner Bros CEO Kevin Tsujihara says Packer's Hollywood ambitions were a victim of the problems plaguing Crown and CPH in Australia – namely, the debt issues facing CPH and the scandal that engulfed Crown following the arrest of its staff in China in 2016. 'James came in with a strategy to brand RatPac and his casinos. He envisioned marrying the glamour of Hollywood to a global network of casinos,' he says. 'When James turned his focus to his Australian holding, the investment strategy changed, and holding RatPac no longer was a viable part of it.'

He also says the timing of CPH's exit was unlucky. It has been the story of the billionaire's life: think of his investments in Seek, Carsales, Challenger, Magellan and, most significantly, Macau. 'We had a very good run on the film side after James exited, but investing in a slate is always a portfolio-model approach,' Tsujihara says. Slate financing is commonplace in the film industry, where an investment is spread across a wide range or 'slate' of productions. The theory goes that there will be a sufficient number of hits within the slate to offset those projects that flop.

Ratner is now adamant that RatPac's turn for the worse was just bad timing. 'When we started RatPac, we knocked it out of the park in the first picture with *Gravity*. But our failure and our success weren't controlled by us. We were a passive investor in Warner Bros. Warners had its worst year in the year we first went in with them,' he says. While some early movies backed by the RatPac–Dune venture didn't do well, the losses were later offset in 2016 by marquee titles including *Batman v Superman*, *Suicide Squad* and *Sully*. After Packer sold out, RatPac–Dune had other winners in films such as the action hit *Wonder Woman* and Christopher Nolan's epic World War II drama *Dunkirk*.

Village Roadshow's Graham Burke says, 'The losses from my observation were not in the Warner deal. Warner Bros was a slate deal with lower risk and lower returns but would average out over time and be very powerful in a portfolio. Warner are the best distributors in the business and having access to their product was a brilliant move by James.'

James managed to part on good terms with Kevin Tsujihara. 'James is a great person and a really smart guy who reads a lot and has a great sense of global and economic trends. James recognised very early the power of China and how technology is changing the world. As a person, James is incredibly generous and has a huge heart. James's word is better than any contract I have ever signed,' Tsujihara says. 'He is one of the most passionate people that I know. When he has conviction for something or someone, he's all in. It's rare to see someone with that level of decisiveness who follows up on it as often as he does. And I would say he is right far more often than he is wrong.'

Graham Burke says movies only work as a result of good people, hard work and – most importantly – luck. 'RatPac was not a folly for James. Raising money in Hollywood is all about reputation. Reputation is a long-term record of doing what you say you will do. And James has that in spades,' he says.

But Burke won't say the same for Ratner. He isn't alone among some of Packer's friends, who claim the celebrity producer was not the person Packer needed at the centre of his life as his world fell apart after the breakdown of his marriage to Erica. She, for one, is no longer on speaking terms with Ratner. Burke says, 'Ratner, in my view, took advantage of one of James's flaws – misplacing loyalty in people not deserving. Ratner was "Hollywood" and James was real. The losses at RatPac were due to the profligate and "Hollywood" overhead style of Brett Ratner coupled with poor development and lousy choices of projects, some of which would have been complete dead losses.'

Packer himself also says his relationship with Ratner was 'more complicated than that [people suggesting he was a bad influence]'. When I put it to Ratner that some believe he brought out the worst traits in Packer, he shrugs it off, claiming it is the first time he has ever heard such a suggestion. 'I don't think I can get the blame for James. He's pretty independent,' he says, calmly. 'I think James has to be responsible for James. I don't think anybody can influence him. He's fifty years old.'

He then adds a comment that could be interpreted as a reflection on Packer's lifestyle choices, though not intended as such: 'I've never had a sip of alcohol, never had a coffee, never had a cigarette in my life.'

While not directly reflecting upon the comments of Burke, Packer says of Ratner's critics: 'There's also a lot of jealousy. RatPac could have worked. Everyone thought I was mad backing Lawrence [Ho in Macau].' Macau and RatPac were big risks. The latter might have been successful in the long run. But he then quickly acknowledges: 'We will never know.'

*

BRETT RATNER NOW FINDS himself engulfed in a crisis of his own. In November 2017 the *Los Angeles Times* detailed sensational allegations from six women, including Natasha Henstridge and Olivia Munn, accusing the Hollywood producer of sexual harassment or assault. The allegations, part of a number that have flowed out of Hollywood since the Harvey Weinstein accusations were made in October 2017, have had serious consequences for Ratner. Warner Bros has severed ties with the filmmaker, having opted not to renew RatPac's production deal and taken away Ratner's office on the studio's Burbank lot. His whiskey brand, Hilhaven Lodge, has also been discontinued by spirits company Diageo.

Packer called Ratner with some reassuring words when the story first broke. It was their first contact for many months. 'I don't know, maybe 20 per cent of it was like, "Let me hear Brett grovel because I've been suffering,"' Ratner says sarcastically with a wide smile. 'But he was great, his words were great, it meant a lot. I said, "God, this is so difficult."

James said, "One thing you're going to realise is who your real friends are." And that was the best thing he said to me. What he said to me just made a lot of sense.'

Ratner says he misses his friendship with Packer, even if it ended badly when the latter hit rock bottom. 'I loved being with him. I loved doing business with him. But it wasn't like I had a full-time partner. His other businesses took precedence,' he says. 'This is where I think his brilliance is. He always kind of somehow sees the future. He's always about a bigger picture. He doesn't focus on the small things.'

Packer says his relationship with Ratner is now 'improving'. They got in touch again in mid 2018, but he still bears scars. 'Let's just say I did more for Brett than he did for me. And Brett should really still be calling me his best friend. But I hope it will be good between Brett and me in the end. He is a force of nature, so anyone writing him off is making a mistake,' he says. 'I'll admit we had a lot of fun. If we had got lucky we could have raised money at higher valuations. We were everywhere for a minute, and we were everywhere for $100 million. Then things didn't work out for me. Brett's new backer is a lot richer and smarter than I am.'

The critics will always view Packer's Hollywood experiment as foolishness, where he enjoyed a playboy life and lapped up being a Tinseltown A-lister. More significantly, it showed his poor judgement in choosing friends and again ignoring the dangers of doing business with them. Whenever I raise criticisms such as these concerning his judgement, whether it be about RatPac, One.Tel or Channel Ten, I sense Packer is on a short fuse.

I can literally see the hairs standing up on the back of his neck when the memories of Jodee Rich, his infamous partner in the One.Tel failure, come flooding back. But on this occasion, he is prepared to concede at least one thing about

Friends forever – With first wife Jodhi Meares in 2000. She still sees James regularly and says they will always remain friends. *Newspix/Jamie Fawcett*

Ties that bind – With mother Ros, sister Gretel and ex-wife Erica. Erica says she remains very close to Ros and Gretel, especially since the passing of her own parents. *Newspix/Noel Kessel*

Brothers in arms – With former Macau business partner and friend Lawrence Ho, who regrets that they no longer see each other. *Brigitte Lacombe*

Paradise found – With former Crown chairman Robert Rankin, actor Robert De Niro and friend Damien Chapman on the Caribbean island of Barbuda, where James and De Niro want to build a luxury resort. *Supplied by James Packer's private staff member*

Filling big shoes – With Lachlan Murdoch outside Yad Vashem, Israel's official memorial to the victims of the Holocaust in Jerusalem. *Supplied by James Packer's private staff member*

Enemies no more – With Kerry Stokes in Aspen, where Stokes rescued his friend from the brink by sending him to Israel in February 2016. *Christine Stokes*

In royal company – With Warren Beatty, the man dubbed the 'Prince of Hollywood', who was at the centre of a remarkable fortnight of James's life in October 2016. *Supplied by James Packer's private staff member*

Talking politics – Former American ambassador to Australia Jeffrey Bleich was a regular visitor to Warren Beatty's guest house in Los Angeles when James was in residence. *Supplied by James Packer's private staff member*

Time out – With Thom Knoles, overlooking The Himalayas at the mountaintop temple 'Kanjapuri Devi' during a visit to Rishikesh, India. *Supplied by James Packer's private staff member*

'Casino Royale' – Photographed while emerging from the Bondi surf in October 2012. Tabloid headlines compared him to actor Daniel Craig in the hit James Bond film. *Newspix/Damian Shaw*

'My Way' – With Brett Ratner in Frank Sinatra's historic Hollywood bungalow on the Warner Bros studio lot in Burbank, California. *Supplied by James Packer's private staff member*

Homecoming – With ex-wife Erica and their children outside Sydney Airport just days before Christmas 2014. *InStar Images/Jamie Fawcett*

Packer whacker – Squaring up with best friend David Gyngell outside his Bondi home in May 2014. *Brendan Beirne/Media Mode*

Israeli connection – James turned heads when he was a guest of the Netanyahu family at the Israel Prime Minister's address to the US Congress in March 2015 and at the UN (pictured) in October that year. *Timothy A. Clarey/AFP/Getty Images*

Love birds – With Mariah Carey in July 2015. James says in their good times together she was kind and took an interest in his life. *Supplied by James Packer's private staff member*

Lady in red – Wearing a striking fishtail dress, Mariah Carey boards billionaire David Geffen's superyacht off the coast of Capri to celebrate American Independence Day on 4 July 2016. *InStar Images*

Burning deep – Seeing Iván Capote's work 'Mantra occidental' in Cuba's Galería Habana in late May 2016 drove James to tears. *Iván Capote, courtesy Galería Habana*

Floored – James tries to pull himself together outside the Galería Habana. *Supplied by James Packer's private staff member*

Presidential party – Former Israeli president Shimon Peres celebrates his 93rd and last birthday at James's house in Caesarea, Israel in August 2016. *Supplied by James Packer's private staff member*

Six-pack style – With his assistants Nat (left) and Val (right) at Ellerstina at the end of 2015, the last time he was super-fit. *Supplied by James Packer's private staff member*

Billionaire company – With his good friend Shari Redstone, the vice chair of American media giants CBS and Viacom, in Aspen in early 2018. *Supplied by James Packer's private staff member*

Father's day – With his children Indigo, Emmanuelle and Jackson during an afternoon cruise on the Sea of Cortez off Cabo San Lucas in March 2018. *Supplied by James Packer's private staff member*

Family time – On *EJI* near Ibiza to celebrate Indigo's tenth birthday in July 2018. *Supplied by James Packer's private staff member*

Sanctuary of the sea – James says he has always enjoyed the escapism of taking to the ocean. He named this 55-metre superyacht *EJI* after his children, Emmanuelle, Jackson and Indigo.
Damon Kitney

More than mates –Damien Chapman (left) and Ben Tilley (right) have become James's two closest friends and confidants, travelling with him around the world. *Splash*

Taking things slowly – In the streets of Aspen with current partner Kylie Lim, who has reportedly played a critical role in getting James back on his feet in 2018. *Splash*

himself. 'People have compared Brett to Jodee Rich,' he says. 'I loved Jodee Rich and Brett. I should not have loved either as much as I did.'

More generally, he agrees with a telling comment made by former CPH boss Brian Powers in Paul Barry's book *Who Wants to Be a Billionaire?*. Powers claimed Packer too easily 'falls in love' with people in business. 'It can be a strength and a weakness. If you're going to take big risks you need to back people to the hilt, but if you're the boss you've also got to exercise some discipline if things are going wrong,' he told Barry.

Packer responds: 'That quote has proven to be prescient. That quote is fair. Lawrence Ho was my biggest bet … I fell in love with Brett [Ratner], that is fair. But I think I was realistic about the prospects of the business and I cut my losses.'

Other unnamed sources quoted by Barry in his book claimed Packer is too often 'bedazzled by people he thinks can bring him a pot of gold'. Responding to this claim, Packer says: 'Perhaps I am impatient and perhaps that works against me. Perhaps I fall in love with people in business and end up being too loyal to those people. There is part of me that doesn't think I can be a rainmaker on my own. I have to find somebody to help me do things.'

As he speaks, you get a feeling that this sort of self-reflection is not something you were ever likely to hear from his father. Packer may be his father's son in many respects, but he is also someone for whom self-doubt is a fundamental part of his character. It may be a weakness, but the ability to question himself and his own judgements – if he can learn from his bad experiences – can also be a strength for the future.

ELEVEN

The Israeli Affair

JAMES PACKER FIRST MET Israeli billionaire and Hollywood producer Arnon Milchan at the upmarket Botanical hotel in the swish inner-city Melbourne suburb of South Yarra in early December 1993. The occasion was Milchan's forty-ninth birthday, for which his good friend and Village Roadshow co-chief executive Graham Burke had organised a private kickboxing event starring then Australian cruiserweight champion Tosca Petridis. At one point in the evening the bespectacled Milchan even got into the ring and started mock-sparring with Petridis. 'When he left the ring Arnon told me, "I knew he wouldn't hit me because I had my glasses on,"' Burke now recalls of the evening.

Burke had also invited along another Hollywood film producer who was in town, Meir Teper, known for the films *From Dusk till Dawn*, *Everybody's Fine* and *What's Eating Gilbert Grape*. That night Teper met Packer for the first time, and Crown Resorts later became a partner in the Nobu Japanese restaurant chain with Teper, actor Robert De Niro and Japanese celebrity chef Nobu Matsuhisa.

But for Packer, that night became all about Milchan. 'Arnon is maybe the most charming and deadly person I have ever met. By the end of dinner I was totally captivated and I thought Dad should meet Arnon,' Packer now recalls. James suggested he, Burke and Milchan fly to the Packer family's Ellerston property in the NSW Hunter Valley the next day, where his father would be waiting.

It was blowing a gale in Melbourne when dawn broke. Kerry's beloved DC-8 jet was unserviceable, so he sent a smaller private jet to fly his son and friends to Scone, from where they would take one of his helicopters to Ellerston. But Milchan, a nervous flyer, initially refused to get on the plane. Eventually, he agreed to fly on one condition – that Burke bought him a bottle of wine for the journey. 'I had to go to a local grocery shop to get Arnon his wine. It was the roughest flight I have ever had in my entire life, but we made it,' Burke says. Packer couldn't believe what he witnessed on the flight that morning. 'Said with love, on the plane on the way to Ellerston at 10am Arnon drank a bottle of wine,' he now says. 'When we arrived, Arnon charmed Dad.'

Born in Rehovot, south of Tel Aviv, into an Israeli family that had lived in the region for more than 500 years, Milchan started out in business transforming his family's bankrupt Israeli fertiliser company after taking it over at the age of just twenty-one in 1962. A star professional soccer player for Maccabi Tel Aviv and Israel's national team, Milchan's biggest claim to fame for many years in Israel – although he did not confirm it for decades – was working as a liaison for Israel's secretive Bureau of Scientific Relations, known as Lekem.

As a weapons procurer through the 1970s and '80s, he ensured the Israel Defense Forces received the very best from the big American defence contractors, including prized weapons such as the Hawk and Patriot missiles. The latter was famously used by the United States to foil Saddam Hussein's more primitive scud missiles in the 1991 Gulf War.

In 1991 Milchan also turned his hand to movies, founding film production company New Regency and the associated firm Regency Enterprises. New Regency became a Hollywood powerhouse, involved in over 140 full-length motion pictures, including such classics as *Pretty Woman* and *JFK*, and more recent Oscar winners such as *The Revenant* and *12 Years a Slave*.

Kerry Packer enjoyed his time with Milchan at Ellerston so much that a few weeks later, at the Australian Open tennis tournament at Melbourne Park in January 1994, he approached the Israeli businessman, who was about to leave town in his helicopter. 'Kerry comes up to me and says, "I've always wanted to be in the movie business. You and I are going to be partners,"' Milchan recalled of the time in one of his rare public interviews in September 2008, with the American magazine devoted to cigars, *Cigar Aficionado*. 'I laughed and said, "How is this possible? I don't have stock for sale." He [Packer] moved quickly with his team of lawyers and accountants and within a few weeks bought out my outside shareholders and acquired new stock in Regency. He ended up with 25 per cent of Regency Films, for somewhere in the US$200–220 million range.' Packer's fellow investors at the time included German TV baron Leo Kirch, former Italian prime minister Silvio Berlusconi and Korean electronics giant Samsung. Rupert Murdoch also later bought into the company.

In 1996 New Regency invested in then troubled German sporting-goods company Puma, paying US$60 million for an initial 12.5 per cent interest, which later grew to a 42 per cent holding worth US$150 million. Milchan once said: 'I hope to transform Puma into the Julia Roberts of the athletic world.' He followed his words with action. Milchan told *Cigar Aficionado* that when his Puma stake was sold in 2002, it was worth around US$800 million. It did so well that a single Puma profit distribution the Packers received as a Regency shareholder covered their entire initial investment. 'We were in for free,' James Packer now says, describing the Puma investment as 'a massive success. I loved Arnon even more.'

Graham Burke says he watched the friendship between James and Milchan blossom over time. 'I was thrilled to have put them together because I was witness to this lovely friendship between an Israeli and an Australian. I felt like a matchmaker,' he says.

After his father passed away on Boxing Day 2005, James Packer invited a select group of confidants to join a loosely framed advisory board for his private company CPH. Milchan was one of them, along with Ashok Jacob, John Alexander, former UBS head Chris Mackay, then ANZ Bank chief executive John McFarlane and then Qantas chairman Margaret Jackson.

When PBL later split itself in two to form Crown and CMH, following the sale of Channel Nine and ACP magazines, Packer decided an interest in a Hollywood film studio didn't have a place in the empire. He announced that his New Regency stake was non-core and put it up for sale. 'I hadn't spoken to Arnon [about it] and understandably he was upset. He was the only buyer for a minority stake in Regency. We were holding our stake for free because of the Puma distribution. There were no other buyers. Arnon came back and bid over US$200 million. He didn't have to,' Packer now says. Indeed, history records that Milchan paid US$324 million for the Packers' 25.4 per cent stake in New Regency Productions in April 2008. Packer has never forgotten it.

*

PACKER HAD NEVER BEEN to Israel when Milchan took him there for a week-long visit in mid 2013. Melbourne businessman and Seek co-founder Paul Bassat, who visited Israel with the billionaire on three occasions, remembers his friend being 'blown away' by his experiences. 'I have spoken to many people who have visited Israel for the first time and have been completely blown away by the country. The sense of dynamism and energy, and the way it deals with the existential threats it faces inspires many people. Israel is a global leader in disruptive technology and its entrepreneurial talent is extraordinary,' Bassat says.

Milchan was superbly well connected in Israel after years of working deep inside the Israeli establishment, and was keen to show off his links with the most powerful figures in Israeli politics. So Packer received an exclusive introduction reserved for an elite few. 'James's first visit to Israel wasn't the normal tourist visit; he met the president, the PM and the finance minister [Yair Lapid], and was welcomed as a friend. It isn't surprising in that context that he immediately fell in love with the country,' Bassat adds.

Packer will never forget his first private dinner at the presidential palace in Jerusalem – there were just two other people at the table: Milchan and Israeli president Shimon Peres. 'The president and Arnon went way back, and that was very clear. There was huge mutual respect and affection between the two of them. I don't know what Arnon did for Shimon when Arnon worked for him starting from the '60s. Arnon usually told me everything and vice versa, and we did everything together. But he wouldn't tell me that,' Packer says.

Packer soon developed a good friendship with Peres, a Nobel Peace Prize winner who by then was in his nineties. In June 2016 Peres made Packer a director of his prestigious Peres Center for Peace and Innovation, an Israeli educational facility encouraging the development of innovation promoting peace, describing him as 'one of the world's most successful young visionaries'. Through Peres, Packer also became the first non-Jew to become a trustee of the Simon Wiesenthal Center, a leading international Jewish human-rights agency. 'Getting to know President Peres was one of the highlights of my life. He honoured me beyond my wildest dreams with his friendship. In the times I met President Peres the thing that stood out most was he was always looking to the future: scientific breakthroughs, flying cars, things that sounded impossible today. He believed in technology and in progress,' Packer says.

Remarkably, Peres had his last birthday dinner on 2 August 2016 at the beachside home Packer had purchased in Israel, next to the private residence of Israeli prime minister Benjamin Netanyahu. The birthday celebration was a low-key affair. 'There were seven of us for dinner: President Peres, Yona who looked after him, Arnon, his wife Amanda, myself, Chappy [Packer's friend Damien Chapman], and Nat [one of Packer's personal assistants] who looked after me,' Packer says. 'What an amazing honour for Shimon to choose to have his birthday dinner at my house.'

Peres passed away almost two months later, on 28 September 2016. 'I went to the funeral on September 30 and sat in the second row, and as fate would have it I sat directly behind Peter Cosgrove who was representing Australia,' Packer says. His relationship with Peres was matched by the friendship he developed with Prime Minister Netanyahu, one of the most formidable and controversial leaders in the country's history. The night after Packer dined with Peres in mid 2013, he sat down for a meal with Milchan and the prime minister at the PM's official residence in Rehavia, an inner-city neighbourhood in Jerusalem.

Paul Bassat remembers going to dinner with Packer and the Netanyahus on two consecutive nights when they both were in Israel eight months later in February 2014. The first dinner was with Benjamin and Sara Netanyahu, the prime minister's then chief of staff Ari Harow and Crown executive chairman John Alexander. On the second evening, it was just the prime minister, Harow, Packer and Bassat. 'James was in awe of the PM and there was a palpable mutual affection between James and the Netanyahus. He had first met Bibi [Benjamin Netanyahu] less than a year earlier through his friendship with Arnon Milchan, and their friendship had blossomed since then. It was apparent that James saw Bibi as having extraordinary talent and personality, and that made the friendship particularly special to him. James's life had changed pretty dramatically in a very short period of time and it must have been an exhilarating experience for him,' Bassat recalls.

'James frequently referred to Bibi as having the hardest job in the world. My superficial impression was that Bibi was a normal person, albeit a highly intelligent and charismatic person, in a job that required superhuman capabilities. He also appeared to be a person with all-too-normal frailties. There was a sensitivity and insecurity that surprised me, given his public persona of self-confidence and assertiveness. He was clearly sensitive to the criticism that his wife and he frequently received from the media, and made frequent mention of how unfair the criticism was. James has often expressed similar views about the media, and there was a mutual empathy on this issue.' But Bassat also recalls a degree of normality and informality about the conversation – talk of family, movies, business and a range of other topics. Netanyahu even spoke with great affection about his deceased brother Yoni, who was the commander of an Israeli hostage rescue team in Entebbe,

Uganda in 1976 and died during the rescue. Netanyahu himself had been shot in combat while serving as a soldier.

After dinner on the second evening, Packer and Bassat drove back to Tel Aviv together. Packer was exhausted but invigorated by the two dinners. 'I went into our dinners with a more sceptical view [than Packer] about the prime minister, and those views weren't significantly altered by meeting him, but James's feeling of warmth and affection was contagious and easy to understand,' Bassat recalls. 'It was an intoxicating environment.'

Another friend of Packer's says the billionaire once told him he couldn't imagine two human beings being closer than he and Netanyahu, who always called him 'Jamie'. Packer became so entangled with the Netanyahu family that he sat with the official party when the prime minister made historic addresses to the US Congress in Washington in March 2015 and the UN General Assembly in New York in October 2015. He was even present in the backstage green room at the UN with Netanyahu when he was rehearsing his speech, again with Milchan by his side. He described both events to friends afterwards as like being at top football games, except better.

With Packer at both events was Netanyahu's son, Yair, who had also forged a friendship with the Australian. Yair had introduced his public relations consultant friend Roman Abramov to Packer. Then CPH CEO Robert Rankin organised for Abramov to take a job at Packer's private company.

Packer now publicly repeats the comments he made in private in early 2014 over dinner with Netanyahu and Bassat in Jerusalem, to highlight his admiration and affection for the prime minister. 'He has one of the hardest jobs in the world. And he is so impressive. You look at Israel today compared to twenty years ago. He has been PM for twelve years and was finance minister for five years. My impression is the whole time Prime Minister Netanyahu has been prime minister he's been carefully managing the economy,' Packer says.

'People talk about what Israel was like twenty years ago and what it's like today on an economic basis. I understand he believes that the job of leadership is to increase the standard of living of the populace. So I think he's got a multifaceted job in the sense he's running an economy, the domestic economy, and takes it incredibly seriously. But then he's got a foreign policy realpolitik reality that he has to manage. If you look at where that is today, America and Israel have probably never been closer. Saudi and Israel have never been closer. I think he gets the credit for it – the runs are on the board.'

*

ARNON MILCHAN ALSO INTRODUCED Packer to other big names in Israel. One was former British prime minister Tony Blair, who became the peace envoy for the UN, US, EU and Russia – the so-called 'quartet' – in the Middle East. Blair would often be at Milchan's house in Tel Aviv. 'Tony was always kind and generous to me and included me in the conversation. Winning three elections in Great Britain in a row is an amazing political achievement,' Packer says.

Another was Yossi Cohen, the current director of Mossad, the national intelligence agency of Israel. Packer got to know Cohen before he joined Mossad, when the latter was head of Israel's National Security Council (NSC) under Netanyahu. 'Yossi Cohen is one of the most impressive men I've ever met,' Packer says. They got on so well that, after he left the NSC, Cohen was even set to run a new cybersecurity operation for Milchan's security business, Blue Sky International (BSI), on a salary of US$10 million a year. That was before - unbeknown to Packer and Milchan - Netanyahu made Cohen an offer he couldn't refuse to run Mossad, and the Blue Sky job never eventuated.

BSI was established by Milchan after the November 2008 terror attacks in Mumbai in India, and Packer invested $15 million in the company. Its backers were Milchan's New Regency Group and India's Tata Group, and its clients included Tata subsidiary Taj Hotels, Philip Morris International, Chevron oil operations in Africa, the presidents of the Ivory Coast and the Dominican Republic, and top Spanish soccer side FC Barcelona. At one point BSI even provided security checks for Packer's Crown casino in Melbourne, showing that it could shut down the whole casino far more easily and quickly than any of its staff had ever imagined. The firm was engaged to do a security analysis on Crown, both cyber and physical, which the casino failed on both fronts. BSI was then employed to help improve the casino's systems.

In mid 2015 Packer publicly revealed that he wanted to build a cybersecurity company with Milchan, because 'Israel now has the highest start-ups per capita in the world and this will provide major opportunities in the future.' Packer even made a cybersecurity pitch to former Commonwealth Bank of Australia chief executive Ian Narev. But by late 2015 BSI had been wound up by Milchan, with Packer repaid his $15 million.

Paul Bassat says Packer's desire to invest in Israel was unsurprising given his love of the country and his passion for disruptive technology. His biggest move was through his funding of venture capital fund Square Peg Capital, co-founded by Bassat. In June 2015 Packer joined a delegation of Square Peg investors on a visit to Tel Aviv and Jerusalem that included Bassat's brother Andrew, former Telstra CEO David Thodey, Evans & Partners founder David Evans, then Carsales chief Greg Roebuck, and Square Peg co-founder Justin Liberman and his cousin Josh Liberman. During the trip Square Peg announced its fourth investment in an Israeli company, leading an $8.1 million Series B equity raising for technology firm JethroData, in partnership with existing investor Pitango Venture Capital.

Square Peg also had investments in early-stage Israeli storage and database software technology businesses, including Feedvisor, the world's first algorithmic pricing and business intelligence platform for online retailers. Square Peg co-founder Dan Krasnostein moved to Tel Aviv in 2014 to lead the firm's expansion plans. Former Cisco executive Arad Naveh also joined Square Peg as a venture partner based in Israel.

In 2015 Krasnostein, Bassat and Packer met with Arnon Milchan to discuss the potential for Square Peg to pursue ventures with Milchan's companies in Israel. The trio visited Milchan's home at Beit Yanai beach, considered by many to be one of Israel's best beaches, forty minutes north of Tel Aviv. While Milchan was great company that day, Bassat and his team were wary and eventually decided his lack of exposure to and interest in venture capital would not be an ideal fit for the Square Peg business model.

But the decision didn't trouble Packer, who remains close to Bassat. 'Paul Bassat is a quality, quality person. We have remained friends even though we haven't seen each other much in the last few years,' he says. 'Paul has under-promised and over-delivered with me on a consistent basis.'

*

For a time in 2015 and 2016 Israel became Packer's official place of residence, after he bought a thirty-year-old mansion on a 1000-square-metre beachfront block adjacent to the Netanyahus' private residence. It was in a wealthy gated community in the ancient beachside town of Caesarea, forty-five minutes' drive north of Tel Aviv. Packer immediately started renovating the property, with plans for an additional storey, a new 7-by-16-metre swimming pool and a large entertainment area. Such was the close proximity of Packer's and Netanyahu's homes that they even once talked about installing what Australians might colloquially call a 'back gate' linking both properties.

Packer became so enamoured with Israel that his lawyers at one point informally sought clarification from the Israeli tax authorities about him becoming an Israeli resident. He was required to spend 120 days a year in Israel to be treated as a resident for tax purposes, which offered significant tax breaks for ten years for people relocating there. But he did not spend the necessary time there in either 2015 or 2016. In reality he was spending much more time living in the US, which is where his children and then fiancée, Mariah Carey, lived and where Ratpac was based. By 2017 he had changed his formal place of residence to Aspen, Colorado. Packer also toyed with the concept of seeking Israeli citizenship, but abandoned the idea once his advisers realised the bureaucracy involved and the laborious nature of the process.

Despite this, his film producer partner and friend Brett Ratner falsely claimed Packer had become an Israeli citizen during a speech at the Beverly Hilton hotel in April 2015, where he was being honoured by the Anti-Defamation League (ADL) Entertainment Industry Awards. The ADL is an international Jewish organisation that aims to stop the defamation of Jewish people and secure justice and fair treatment for all. 'James Packer is not Jewish,' Mr Ratner told the audience. 'Though he actually recently became an Israeli citizen … James, you are now the first non-Jewish Zionist in history.' It forced Packer's advisers in Australia to publicly deny that one of the nation's wealthiest men had become a citizen of Israel. Ratner now admits he just made an honest mistake.

In mid 2015 Charles Miranda, who had been a foreign correspondent in Europe and the Middle East for Australia's News Limited for a decade, spent some time with Packer at his Caesarea home. Miranda says the billionaire looked completely at ease the three times he met him over the space of a fortnight. On each occasion a super-fit-looking Packer had been out running on the beach that morning. 'It was just like having a chat to a mate. And I'm obviously not his mate. It was that level of conversation,' Miranda now says.

He recalls that Packer's personal assistant in Tel Aviv, Hadas Klein – who was also Arnon Milchan's PA - would often tell him how much her boss was enjoying his Israel home, especially given his then blossoming romance with songstress Mariah Carey in the second half of 2015. 'He loves it here, he really does,' she once told Miranda. 'He feels at home, he can relax and be himself and he doesn't get recognised all the time like he does in Australia and he has many, many friends. That's why he is here, it's good for him, and also because he can see [business] opportunities.'

When Miranda sat down for his formal interviews with Packer, he found a subject deeply in tune with world politics outside the realm of business. 'He spoke at length about what was going on at the time with Iran. It wasn't just back-of-envelope stuff, he was quite detailed in his musings,' Miranda recalls. He says Packer's views were, unsurprisingly, very pro-Israel, and Miranda felt Packer was 'very embedded in the world conspiracy according to Israel'. When Benjamin Netanyahu slammed the Obama administration's nuclear deal with Iran, Packer publicly echoed Netanyahu's hardline position, telling journalists in mid 2015 that it was 'the stupidest thing I've seen in my life'.

Miranda says Packer also expressed strong views on the decline of US power in the world, the rise of China and the importance of technology. 'He spoke of the advances in Israel which Australians could only ever dream of. He also spoke about his love for Jaffa. And he also spoke a lot about Gaza,' Miranda says.

The billionaire was seemingly in his element, immersed in global politics. At times he even saw himself as a player on the geopolitical stage. 'I think Bibi is probably the smartest leader in the free world and is incredibly seductive and brilliant, and he speaks better than anyone in the world about what James is fascinated with,' Brett Ratner now says. 'Before he met Bibi, all James talked about was global politics. I met [Australian foreign minister] Julie Bishop through him. Julie and I became really good friends. Every conversation James wants to have, I don't care who it is with, it is about global politics.'

*

BUT BEING SO PUBLICLY critical of the Obama administration on the Iran nuclear deal and his outspoken support for Israel also put Packer on edge. One of his favourite movies became a 2016 American documentary directed by Alex Gibney called *Zero Days*, which focuses on a piece of self-replicating computer malware called Stuxnet. It was allegedly let loose by the US and Israel to destroy a key part of an Iranian nuclear facility but instead went global, backfiring on the Israelis and the Americans.

In July 2016 Packer's Hollywood film production company with Ratner, RatPac, pulled out of financing a film with American filmmaker Oliver Stone about whistleblower Edward Snowden, who in 2013 leaked classified information from the National Security Agency to the media before seeking political asylum in Russia. 'I love politics. I think it is fascinating. Geopolitics is the most fascinating politics of all. Oliver and I were having dinner and he was telling me about Snowden and the movie he was about to make. I was spellbound,' Packer recalls.

'Oliver said we should do it as a RatPac movie. I agreed. Oliver and I shook hands that we would do Snowden together. The two people I was closest to in Hollywood and listened to were Arnon and [Warner Bros CEO] Kevin Tsujihara. Both of them said the same thing to me: "James, you just can't do this movie, it is too hot." I was shattered. It was the first and only script I ever read.'

Afterwards, an angry Stone told US entertainment magazine *Variety* that Packer had pulled out of the venture after being 'warned by an Israeli friend of his that he wouldn't get a visa to go to the United States'. Importantly, it would have prevented Packer from visiting his children in Los Angeles.

But Packer's Israel adventure and his relationship with Netanyahu were about to embroil him in one of the deepest of all Israeli political scandals.

*

IN OCTOBER 2016 PACKER took the *Arctic P* for its first and only visit to the waters of the southeast Mediterranean off the coast of Israel, but his timing wasn't good. The political heat in Jerusalem had reached boiling point in a high-drama political corruption scandal involving both Benjamin Netanyahu and Arnon Milchan. Netanyahu was being accused of corruptly accepting lavish gifts from both Packer and Milchan, breaching a law that bars Israeli state employees and elected officials from accepting gratuities. The Israeli media were even speculating Packer could be charged in the saga that became known as Case 1000.

After protracted negotiations over many months between his lawyers and Israeli investigators, Packer eventually agreed to provide testimony, reportedly on the condition that his evidence would not be used against him.

In November 2017 he flew to Australia from America for a single day in his private jet to be interviewed by officers from the Australian Federal Police while Israeli investigators listened in. The next day, after Packer had left the country again, a Federal Police spokeswoman unusually revealed the interrogation had taken place. She confirmed Packer was a witness but declared he was not a suspect in the case and had given his full cooperation.

Packer will make no comment on Case 1000 or his testimony, but it was later reported by Israel's Channel Ten that he had told the police he had not asked Netanyahu for anything in return for the gifts. 'I admire Prime Minister Netanyahu and am happy that I was given the opportunity to be his friend. I was happy to give him presents, many times at his request and his wife Sara's request,' Channel Ten reported Packer as telling investigators.

On 13 February 2018 the Israeli police confirmed what followers of the case had expected for some time: that they had found 'sufficient evidence against the PM on suspicions for the offence of accepting bribes, fraud and breach of trust regarding his connection with businessman Arnon Milchan'. They recommended charges be laid against Netanyahu and Milchan, but not Packer.

At the end of June 2018 they also charged Sara Netanyahu for allegedly using public money to pay for meals from top Jerusalem restaurants that were delivered to the PM's official residence. Like her husband, she stridently dismissed the allegations.

Packer appears to have escaped any legal consequences from his brush with the Israeli authorities, arguably among the most fearsome on the planet. Although, depending on the outcome of the case, he may yet be exposed to claims of bad judgement and reputational damage.

*

ASK PACKER WHY HE pursued what many have viewed as a strange life in Israel, and his reply is instant. 'I was taken in in the most kind and generous way,' he says, noting he never showed any interest in Judaism and was never pressured by a single person to convert to the religion. Instead, it seems his Israeli excursion was the product of an infatuation with a seemingly surreal world and the larger-than-life personalities Netanyahu, Peres and, most importantly, Milchan.

Former American ambassador to Australia in the Obama administration Jeffrey Bleich never travelled with Packer to Israel but spoke to the billionaire many times while he was there. 'He was really enjoying it there. He developed friendships that were real friendships. He also formed this very close bond with Prime Minister Netanyahu,' Bleich says, before making a telling observation. Like Kerry Stokes and Warren Beatty, perhaps Bibi became more than just a friend. 'I haven't been a great advocate for Netanyahu,' Bleich says, 'but I think James saw Bibi as something of a father figure.'

The same goes for Milchan, according to former Ellerston Capital chief executive Glenn Poswell, who has spent plenty of time in Israel and has met with the Hollywood film producer. 'I think Arnon had James's good intentions at heart. I think in some ways Arnon was like a father figure to him. I saw that. I sat down with them together, I met Arnon's wife. Arnon always called himself a seventh-generation Israeli. I don't think he ever maliciously tried to mislead James, ever,' Poswell says.

Milchan's detractors are not so sure, saying they were always wary of his friendship with Packer and what it might mean for the billionaire. It can be argued that Packer's Israel sojourn again showed his lack of judgement and even a naivety about the complexity and brutality of Israeli politics. That is certainly the view of his critics, but even his friends were wary of him being drawn into dangerous places. 'James was very close to Bibi, and Bibi loved him understandably because he's so bright and he's successful,' Brett Ratner says. 'But James got seduced and again, as smart as he is, he can sometimes be a little naive. Because I said, "James, this is Israeli politics."'

Packer's friend and former Australian treasurer Peter Costello, who has dealt with Netanyahu over the years and got to know him, describes Israeli politics as 'very vigorous. It is every bit as vigorous as Australia, and in many respects they are playing for bigger stakes. I have spoken to James about Israel, and he has recounted to me some of his relations with Netanyahu. At the time he was very positive about Netanyahu,' Costello says, before making an observation that has – in hindsight – rung true for Packer: 'It is a dangerous thing for an outsider to be caught up in Israeli politics.'

Packer clearly plunged into his relationship with Netanyahu wholeheartedly and without caution. His admiration is apparently unqualified, despite the Israeli PM's controversial and in many ways problematic track record as an uncompromising, hardline leader – one now accused by the Israeli authorities of corruption. The complexities of Israeli politics, of the Palestinian question and Netanyahu's settlements policy, of his ruthless approach to Israel's security and what critics regard as his dangerous stand against Iran, seemed to trouble Packer little.

What he saw in Netanyahu was a pro-business mover and shaker, a man of conviction and a fighter for his country, which has few friends in the world beyond its most powerful ally, America. He clearly deeply admired – and still admires –

Netanyahu's strength and decisiveness, qualities he long respected in his own father.

*

PACKER STILL HAS BUSINESS links with Israel, albeit indirectly. In May 2018 the Nobu restaurant and hotel chain announced that it was establishing a luxury boutique hotel in central Tel Aviv. Canadian billionaire Gerry Schwartz and his wife of thirty-six years, Heather Reisman, are partnering with Nobu in the venture. But Packer knows he cannot return to Israel any time soon, if ever. One friend says, 'For James, Israel was a place for privacy like nowhere else, a central place in the world where he could be protected. It is gone now. He will never be able to go there again.'

But despite what has happened, Packer will never forget Arnon Milchan. They spoke for the first time again in more than a year in July 2018. 'Looking back, Arnon has opened doors for me. I might have fallen through some of them. Or I might not have succeeded, like with RatPac. But I cannot begrudge him,' Packer says.

Milchan declined to be interviewed for this book, but did provide a quote via email from his villa at the luxury resort he recently purchased at Bora Bora in French Polynesia, one of his favourite spots on the planet. It is known as Bora Bora One, a 7.5-acre private islet on Bora Bora's Motu Piti Aau island.

'I was introduced to Kerry and James by my friend Graham Burke. Kerry and I became business partners and we had a long and successful relationship together,' he says. 'During those years James became my best friend. And still is.'

While Packer hasn't spoken to Netanyahu in more than two years, he still gives him one of the highest accolades in his extraordinary life, describing him as 'the most impressive man I've met. And one of the kindest. My time in Israel was in many ways some of the most special times in my life. Israel's actions and words exceeded my every expectation. Israel was better to me than I was to Israel. Israel will never be the same for me. Too many things have changed. It's a bigger loss than my bad business deals.'

TWELVE

Blood Battle

James Packer was doing his best to blend into the bustling crowd at Sydney international airport when he sauntered into the arrivals concourse six days before Christmas 2014. Dressed in jeans and sporting a pair of designer sunglasses, he waited patiently for his Los Angeles–based ex-wife Erica and their children to emerge from the customs hall after their long Qantas flight from America. They were home for a Christmas rendezvous with their father and unsurprisingly, after a tip-off, the local paparazzi were there waiting to meet them. After greeting his family with kisses and hugs, as the photographers swirled around them in the airport car park, a beaming Packer uncharacteristically called out: 'Go for it … It's fine.'

'I remember seeing James at the airport that day standing behind a phone box. So I went up and chatted to him. He said he was fine if I took a picture,' recalls Sydney celebrity photographer Jamie Fawcett. 'He had a driver but otherwise just looked like a punter waiting for his family. When they came out he went over, kissed Erica on the cheek, kissed the kids and picked up one of them. Then they started walking out and we got the photo. It was beautiful.' *The Sydney Morning Herald*'s Andrew Hornery reported at the time that within an hour the photos had been the subject of a bidding war that quickly reached five-figure sums.

But Packer's happiness was short-lived, with other family matters about to become much more problematic. His older sister, Gretel, had remained very much in the shadows in the nine years since their father's death. For decades it had been common knowledge that the Packer women played second fiddle to the men of the empire. 'Kerry could not accept the remote possibility that Gretel could do anything in the business,' Phillip Adams recalls.

That was about to change.

Named after her father's mother, Gretel Packer had been educated at the prestigious eastern Sydney private school Ascham. After graduating she worked at Ansett Airlines in the catering department, before joining the family business in the ACP magazine division, where she spent four years being groomed by then *Cleo* magazine editor Lisa Wilkinson. Gretel and James spent a couple of months living together in London before Gretel met and married British financier Nick Barham in 1991 – though her brother was never close with him. Gretel and Barham had two children, Francesca and Benjamin, before the marriage ended in 1999, when Gretel returned to Sydney with the children. In 2001, after the One.Tel collapse, she was persuaded by her father to return to ACP, where she worked under the guidance of CPH chief executive and PBL director Ashok Jacob. She was also later briefly married to her spiritual adviser, Sydney-based philanthropist Shane Murray. James was, again, not a fan of his brother-in-law. Gretel and Murray had one son, William, before divorcing in 2007.

By mid 2014, Gretel was a single mother with three children to support, and she was worried about the family fortune.

She had watched on from afar as her then Los Angeles–based brother made a big splash in Hollywood with his RatPac film production business. She had read with interest the speculation swirling that year about James dating supermodel Miranda Kerr and reportedly giving her a $100,000 pair of diamond earrings for Christmas. Gretel had also watched her brother pursuing what many viewed as a strange life in Israel. His Israel and Hollywood adventures saw him becoming less involved in the company that held most of the family fortune, Crown Resorts.

In May 2014, Gretel approached Sydney fund manager Will Vicars, the chief investment officer at boutique investment firm Caledonia Investments, to ask him if he would be prepared to broker an agreement with her brother to divide their father's multibillion-dollar estate. Vicars accepted the challenge, having known Gretel since she was five. He had also attended the same school as James, the exclusive Cranbrook, leaving two years before him. Despite their age difference, they had become friends at school.

In 2013 James had made headlines when he followed Caledonia's lead to make a surprise $330 million investment in US property start-up Zillow. The theory was that the rush by real-estate agents in Australia to advertise properties online was set to happen in the US and that Zillow, with over 70 per cent of online listings in America, would be the biggest beneficiary. James thought Zillow could replicate his stunning investments in Seek and Carsales, and he became the second-biggest shareholder in the website, taking 9.4 per cent of the company. James also viewed his Zillow purchase as an act of faith in his friend Vicars.

'It was an awkward process, because I had been representing James on Zillow and his sister had asked me to help her in negotiations with her brother. I had known Gretel for decades and she trusted me,' Vicars now recalls.

On Sunday 4 May 2014, James arrived back in Sydney from Israel and headed to his apartment in seaside Bondi. Waiting for him in the street was his best friend David Gyngell. What followed was their now infamous brawl that made global headlines.

That same day Gretel took a deep breath and called her brother. She told him she finally wanted to be paid her share of the family fortune left by her father. Before James had arrived back in Australia, Vicars had arranged to come to his Bondi apartment on the morning of 5 May to discuss the Zillow investment. After Gretel's Sunday call, this meeting would carry extra significance — it would be the first to discuss a division of Kerry Packer's estate. 'The process started on an unfortunate date, given it was the day after James had his altercation with David Gyngell,' Vicars now says.

In the months that followed, James made an informal offer to his sister. But Gretel and Vicars were suspicious and dismissed it. It set the scene for the tumultuous negotiation that followed. James now says about Gretel's move: 'I think my sister thought RatPac was a folly. I think my sister was probably confused about my time in Israel. Mostly, I think my sister thought she could do better than me in business. And she is doing a very good job of it.'

On Christmas Eve 2014, a package of documents arrived in the hands of James's lieutenants, CPH directors Guy Jalland, Ashok Jacob and Mike Johnston. They carried a series of written demands by Baker McKenzie legal partner Steven Glanz, on behalf of Gretel. She wanted to break up the complex network of trusts that held together the Packer family fortune, alleging that Jalland, Jacob and Johnston had not been behaving in the trustees' best interests. And she wanted to divide the family fortune. Her brother was livid.

*

JAMES SAYS THE TIMING of his sister's demands could not have been worse. He'd sold all of the family's media businesses — bar a stake in the struggling Ten television network — and reinvested the proceeds in the Crown casino business. The value of the shares of Crown's key growth asset, the Macau-focused casino company Melco Crown Entertainment, had halved during the course of 2014 as the Chinese government's corruption crackdown took hold. As a result Crown shares had also fallen in value by almost one-third during the year, which had a massive impact on the value of CPH's half-share in the company. At that time, all CPH owned — apart from an array of boats, planes, and city and rural properties — was the Perisher Blue ski resort in the NSW snowfields, the Pretty Girl fashion chain, and stakes in the Ellerston funds management business and Chinese online employment site Zhaopin.

But Gretel was in no mood to be fobbed off. She had resolved to tackle her brother head-on, even briefing a London QC to contest her father's will at London's Privy Council. (The ultimate holding company of the CPH empire is the Bahamas-domiciled Consolidated Press International Holdings Limited. The Privy Council is the highest appellate court of the Bahamas after the North Atlantic island nation's Court of Appeal.) Tactically, Gretel wanted to show she was prepared to fight for what she believed were her entitlements, through the highest courts of the land — and abroad — if necessary.

Formal negotiations started in early 2015 to divide the family empire, but the structure of Kerry Packer's will — administered by Kerry's closest friend Lloyd Williams and lawyer and investment banker David Gonski — was complex. Because of Frank Packer's concerns about estate tax, his will had unusually left his estate not to his son, but to his grandchildren James, Gretel and Francis, the only son of Kerry's brother, Clyde. Clyde had been the original heir to the Packer empire until his spectacular falling-out with his father in 1972, which saw him angrily quit the family business and move to America. Clyde never had a high regard for his brother and asked to be bought out of the business, which Kerry duly did, taking charge of the family's $100 million controlling stake in PBL.

Because of the structure of his father's will, Kerry never owned any shares in the trusts controlling the family estate, but he was left with a lifetime interest called a governing directorship. This meant that during Kerry's life, even though the shares and the equity in his company were equally owned by James and Gretel, he could still do as he saw fit. In the latter part of his life Kerry subscribed for 1 per cent of the trust's equity, and when he died on Boxing Day 2005, he left James that 1 per cent share and the governing directorship. On his passing, CPH had a net worth of $5.1 billion and $1.5 billion of debt. James nominally had 51 per cent of the shares and Gretel 49 per cent, but the governing directorship meant Gretel's effective interest was below 49 per cent.

'The will was based upon Kerry having absolute faith in James and his business abilities, and gave him control as a result. But it also entrusted in James the responsibility to look after the family,' David Gonski now says. 'I didn't detect any falling out at the time of Kerry's death. Everybody acted with enormous decorum. From day one, James and Gretel acted incredibly properly.'

Yet Gretel came to feel she was entitled to 50 per cent, which is why she took the action she did on Christmas Eve 2014.

James was initially advised in the negotiations by CPH finance boss Mike Johnston – a former senior partner of Ernst & Young who had advised Packer's private companies for more than fifteen years – Guy Jalland and UBS Australia chief executive Matthew Grounds. James and his advisers took legal counsel from Minter Ellison. Gretel was advised by Vicars and Sydney financier Michael Triguboff, the nephew of property developer Harry Triguboff.

The initial negotiations for what their advisers have since termed a 'framework agreement' to divide the family fortune took six months. They weren't pleasant, as James became aggressive towards Gretel and her advisers, believing that his sister was seeking to take advantage of him at his weakest moment. At times, rude emails were exchanged.

In early 2015 CPH borrowed $630 million in long-dated money on the US private placement bond market, an alternative to borrowing from traditional banks and public bond markets available to American and foreign companies. Unlike bank debt, this sort of money is expensive and can't be paid back early. The money would be used to pay Gretel out. But at the same time, James also had an eye on the potential privatisation of Crown, which would have required significant borrowings.

With the debt crisis that had hit CPH six years earlier still strong in his memory, James started a fire sale of family assets in a frantic effort to reduce his borrowings to more manageable levels. In March he ended his family's 43-year association with Perisher Blue by selling it to the US-based Vail Resorts for almost $180 million. Three months later he sold his 52-metre superyacht *Seahorse*, which had been purchased in October 2012 to mark the arrival of his youngest daughter, Emmanuelle, for almost $50 million. In August he and ex-wife Erica set an Australian house-price record when they sold their Vaucluse mega mansion La Mer in Sydney for $70 million to Australian-Chinese billionaire businessman Chau Chak Wing.

A week later CPH sold a half-share in the Packer family's luxury Hunter Valley retreat Ellerston, excluding the polo and agricultural parts of the property, to Crown for $60 million. Crown said at the time it intended to use the luxury facilities at Ellerston to helicopter in high rollers from its new casino resort being built at Barangaroo. The so-called related-party transaction raised eyebrows among investors and corporate governance experts, many wary of seeing a Packer family asset sold to a public company controlled by a Packer, though it was eventually ticked off by a committee of Crown's independent directors. And for James, it delivered much-needed cash.

When a landmark agreement with Gretel was finally documented, a day after James's forty-eighth birthday on 8 September, it was reportedly worth $1.25 billion and included a lump sum worth more than $200 million. Christine Lacy and I subsequently reported in *The Weekend Australian* that, under the deal, Gretel and her children would also receive a series of smaller secured cash payments over the coming years and retain a minor residual interest in CPH. What wasn't reported at the time was that the deal also provided Gretel with personal guarantees over all of the family's assets – which she had demanded and which allowed her to sell any asset the family held if her brother defaulted on an obligation – sending a debt-laden James further into panic.

*

WHEN JAMES AND GRETEL agreed to pose for a photograph for *The Daily Telegraph* newspaper at Sydney's Rockpool restaurant on the evening of 19 October 2015 – two days after news of the settlement of their father's estate broke – the atmosphere was tense. They had agreed to the shot at the insistence of *The Daily Telegraph*'s then editor, Paul Whittaker, and its editor-at-large John Lehmann. The siblings were also keen to portray a public image that relations between them were amicable.

While the shots published the next morning showed them smiling at each other, inside they were doing anything but.

According to *The Sydney Morning Herald*'s 'Private Sydney' columnist Andrew Hornery, the photographer that night, Richard Dobson, was reportedly told by James he had 'ten seconds to take this fucking photo and then you can fuck off' before launching into a NASA-like countdown, bellowing, 'Ten … nine … eight …': '[Private Sydney] hears James was none too pleased to see the lights being erected for what he described as "just a fucking photo", ordered his sister to sit down and "don't pose for the fucking photo" after she stood in readiness for the photographer,' Hornery wrote.

What the public did not know at the time was that negotiations between the parties had recommenced four weeks earlier, after James decided he wanted to pay his sister early rather than staggering the payments over future years. He was especially incensed by terms of the deal obliging him to provide Gretel with hundreds of millions of dollars of payments – plus interest – at set dates up to ten years into the future. By the middle of October he was deeply frustrated, claiming Gretel was dragging out the negotiations to put him under more pressure. He told Gretel and her advisers at the time that he was being 'tortured'. But Gretel was angry that details of the confidential agreement they had struck in the middle of the year and formalised in September had found their way into the media. She was also wary of James's blossoming relationship with pop star Mariah Carey.

And there was another catch. On the table in the negotiations was now a quarter-share of the Ellerston property, where their father is buried. Both siblings have a special affection for the property. While James had been out of the country for almost two years, Gretel had been a frequent visitor to Ellerston and maintained a close friendship with Robert Teague, Ellerston's long-serving general manager, and their sons had worked together as jackaroos in the Northern

Territory. Yet James believed he had as much entitlement to Ellerston as his sister. Or more, given he had paid for its upkeep for many years. He was especially angered by media reports in November 2015 that his mother and Gretel had taken the reins – literally – at the family's Ellerston horse stable, leasing the polo grounds that were owned by Crown. In his darkest moments that year, James even threatened to employ security guards to bar Gretel from using the property.

By Christmas Day, eight months ahead of Gretel's fiftieth birthday, a revised $1.25 billion deal was finally agreed, running over a shorter time frame. Importantly for James, it reduced CPH's debt to $1.5 billion from the $2.3 billion it had risen to under the original deal. It had been $1.5 billion when his father died in 2005. Christine Lacy and I reported in *The Australian* that Gretel emerged with stakes in the listed Crown Resorts and Zillow – then worth $100 million and $200 million respectively – as well as cash holdings, a residual interest in CPH and ownership of the Packer family's long-time seaside retreat at Palm Beach north of Sydney.

But, tellingly, the recut deal also gave Gretel a one-quarter share of Ellerston, and this is where James and his sister really fell out. He made his first visit to Ellerston in two years in January 2016, while the ink was still drying on the revised agreement with his sister. On New Year's Eve he had introduced his then girlfriend Mariah Carey on stage at a gala concert at his Crown Casino in Melbourne. On 2 January the couple took a helicopter ride to Ellerston. It was the last time he would visit the property.

In an interview with me in *The Weekend Australian* in October 2017, James publicly confirmed rumoured tensions with his sister for the first time. 'Stages of the negotiation with Gretel were difficult, but a framework for future resolution was achieved,' he stated, carefully. It was code for the fact the siblings had been at war. Asked about their relationship in the wake of the talks, he replied at the time: 'We have not spent a lot of time together. She is getting on with her life and I am doing the same.'

He now acknowledges that even after the second agreement, 'CPH's debt and obligations were at a level I could not psychologically deal with.' Says one observer from the time, 'Some people were saying, "James, why are you getting so worked up? These obligations are not for years." But he kept saying to them they were still obligations.'

So the asset sales continued. In May 2016 Crown sold a $1 billion stake in its Macau-based joint-venture casino company, Melco Crown Entertainment. Later that year Crown sold the rest of its Macau holding, after nineteen Crown staff were arrested in China, and ditched its plans to build a casino in Las Vegas. The special dividend declared by Crown from the proceeds of the Melco sale and the sale of Crown shares by CPH in August 2016 brought to almost $1 billion the size of the cash pile James had raised since the second Gretel deal had been concluded at the end of 2015. But the negotiations between the siblings were still not over. And by this stage, James had dispensed with his advisers. He wanted to finish the talks with Gretel and Vicars himself.

*

GRETEL VISITED HER BROTHER in Aspen on 17 and 18 February 2017 to talk about a resolution for the final tranche of the settlement, but it did not go well. An important topic was on the table – the future ownership of the *Arctic P* superyacht, a beloved Packer family asset. The 88-metre vessel, originally built as an icebreaker, was converted by Kerry Packer into the ultimate pleasure craft, complete with helipad, cinema, glass-bottomed swimming pool and jacuzzi. In 2006, US magazine *Power and Motoryacht* listed the *Arctic P* as the fifteenth-largest private vessel in the world.

After his father's death, James used the *Arctic P* all over the world to entertain friends, celebrities, politicians and business associates. But in Aspen, he came to the emotional decision to part with the craft his father had purchased more than two decades earlier. It would be sold to his sister, who jumped at the opportunity to keep the boat in the family. Still smarting from two years of negotiations, James now wanted to bring all his future obligations to his sister forward and cut the cord between them once and for all.

Two weeks earlier in Aspen, he had cut ties with two of the people who had been closest to him for the previous two years. The first was Robert Rankin, who spent a week with James in Aspen before they agreed to go their separate ways.

'Post the selldown of Crown's stake in Melco Crown in mid December 2016, James and I agreed to meet in Aspen early in the new year. We mutually agreed that I would step down as CEO of CPH and Chairman of Crown and remain on the Boards of Crown and Melco Crown,' Rankin now says. 'I have always been and remain a long-term friend and supporter of James, CPH and Crown. It was an extraordinary period and I only wish James the very best.'

Rankin was replaced at Crown by cost-cutter John Alexander. On 11 January, the day Rankin left Aspen, James agreed with his movie-making partner Brett Ratner to quit their RatPac joint venture.

Immediately, Alexander and Jalland both looked at culling other non-core assets. Over the coming months one of those identified was Crown's stake in Ellerston. When James made his first visit to Australia in two years for the Crown annual general meeting in Melbourne in October 2017, he and

Gretel lunched at the exclusive Koko Japanese restaurant, but remained at odds over the final tranche of their settlement. Ellerston was again the sticking point. Gretel wanted more of it, but James was resisting. He could not bring himself to give up control of it.

But by the end of 2017, with the assistance of John Alexander, he had agreed that Gretel could eventually move to take full ownership of both her brother's and Crown's stake in Ellerston to give her 100 per cent control. In an ASX announcement that it was selling Ellerston back to the Packer family, Crown revealed its stake in the property was valued at $62.5 million. This price implied James's stake was worth around $30 million, meaning Gretel agreed to pay around $90 million to take full ownership of the property. The company that now owns it, Ellerston Leisure, is run from Gretel's family company office at Sydney's Hudson House in Macquarie Street, the same building that houses Vicars' Caledonia Investments.

The final settlement between James and Gretel was also said to include other liquid assets and property. James declines to comment on its details because of a confidentiality agreement. Rather, he simply says: 'Ellerston is a painful subject for me. Gretel has exclusive rights to it now and in the future will own it 100 per cent. It is where my father is buried. Will [Vicars] and Gretel won it from me.'

But, he says, allowing Ellerston to be in the deal with his sister was the price he had to pay for reducing his debt and allowing him to keep his half-share of Crown. 'My father once said to me, "Son, the problem with the English is they sell their businesses to keep their properties. Sell your properties to keep the business,"' he quips.

After looking at the respective valuations put on the fortunes of James and Gretel in the latest edition of the *BRW*

Rich List, it appears she received more than 20 per cent of the net worth of the family estate, including an interest in Zillow, a key growth asset. In the two years after the second settlement between the siblings at the end of 2015, Zillow shares more than doubled in value on the Nasdaq in America before falling in value from mid June 2018.

Ros Packer was not a direct party to the agreement between James and Gretel, having been provided for separately in Kerry Packer's will. But broadcaster Alan Jones believes she was deeply hurt by the bitter battle between her children. 'It is wounding for any mother to find these gaping chasms in the family. She has a deep affection for James … and Gretel,' he says.

Jones says he was 'disappointed' to hear about the dispute. 'I'm simply looking at it from the point of view of James, who has had to endure all the slings and arrows. He had to cop it all. He had to live through the GFC. Had to live through all those things that really caused him trauma. But I understand Gretel believes that was her entitlement,' he says. 'And no matter how good or how bad people have been, they are family. They've got to move on. They've got to build bridges, not blow them up. And [James] is a good bridge builder.'

The Seven Network's Kerry Stokes adds another perspective. While he has never spoken to Gretel about the issue, he believes the battle with her brother had its genesis in the fact that 'James had started to want to walk away from control [of Crown].' Gretel had always had confidence in her brother's business acumen, but she knew he ruled Crown by his charismatic personality and his daily thirst for data about the company's performance. Without him focused, there was a danger the company could become rudderless. 'When he [walks away], that is when things fall apart,' Stokes now asserts.

Former Victorian premier Jeff Kennett remembers meeting with James in Perth when he returned to Australia briefly in October 2017 to attend the fiftieth anniversary of Channel Seven's Telethon, an event dear to Stokes. 'I told him in October, you have to let this thing with Gretel go. You can't be aggro to Gretel. He at that stage was blaming her for everything. It was unbalanced,' Kennett says. 'I said to him, "At the end of the day, the only people that will be standing around your death bed will be your family. I know it has been uncomfortable, but it is not as though you are down to your last shekel."' Kennett describes James's comments about Gretel in my interview with him in *The Weekend Australian* as 'awful'. 'I understood where he was coming from but that was sad. I was so saddened by that,' he adds.

Lloyd Williams describes the battle as 'difficult. I think it would have been nice to have the situation settled without it being as public as it was. It is not something I want to go into in great detail. But obviously, being the executor of the estate and knowing a lot of the background to it, I just thought it was unfortunate. It created a division in the family. I hope that division heals,' he says. 'I am sure they will heal. Ellerston is a famous place; Kerry Packer is buried there. For Ros Packer's sake and for both her children, I hope that situation does heal itself over a period of time.'

*

JAMES NOW SAYS HE HAS DEEP REGRETS about what happened but wants to make clear that his actions were better than his words. 'Even though we have a framework arrangement that spans many years, I separately arranged, without obligation, to make funds available to Gretel and her children early. To do that put me under financial pressure,' he says. 'I accept at times my words were unforgivable to Gretel and Will. I hope my actions were better than my words. I can understand my sister wanting to be bought out. I can understand my sister saying, "James, Will Vicars is going to be a better custodian of my money than you." I just wish we had all done it better, and I certainly take my share of the blame for that.'

In March 2018, the two siblings agreed to finally put the past behind them and make peace. Ros Packer is said to have played a key role in the reconciliation when she visited her son in Aspen in the first part of 2018.

'My sister and I have made up. I want to thank David Gonski, Matthew Grounds and my mother for helping both Gretel and me make peace. I'm so happy. I love my sister,' he declares, before adding with a smile, 'even if I get jealous at her Zillow shareholding.'

Gretel Packer's first public comments on the battle appear genuinely heartfelt. 'I love my brother very much and am very happy that he and I have been able to negotiate this settlement,' she tells me in an email. 'I don't think there was ever going to be an "easy" time for us to do this and it was always, more likely than not, going to be difficult. The short-term easier option would have been to leave it for our six children to work out … and that would have been unfair to them and lazy of us. The fact that we didn't take that route is something I think we should both be proud of.'

David Gonski, whom James describes as 'the king of Sydney', is said to be quietly determined to ensure the peace holds, even if others are not so sure it will last given the bitterness of the battle between brother and sister. 'David brings people together and makes difficult things happen. My father was hugely fond of David. David was one of the few people whose advice Dad listened to closely,' James says. 'David is making Australia a better place with his philanthropic and artistic pursuits. In business he's at the top of the corporate table. He's a dear friend of mine and someone I look up to completely.'

Gonski says he always felt it was a good thing that a brother and sister, both of whom were hitting their fifties, should sort out their independence. 'I think that was a correct thing for them to do,' he says. He acknowledges he played a role in their reconciliation, but declines to go into specifics. 'Sure, I spoke to both sides, and I am delighted that they settled their issues,' he says.

Matthew Grounds says the same. 'I'm just happy for James and Gretel that it has been resolved and they are in a good place right now,' he says. 'I respect both of them. I would want for them to be able to live and work very happily together. They deserve full happiness from this.'

After a nasty falling-out with Will Vicars during the Gretel negotiations, which included James sending a barrage of emails sometimes laden with expletives to his former friend, James says he has also agreed to make peace with a man he now describes as a 'formidable negotiator. Will Vicars is a better steward of my sister's money than I am,' he says. 'I sold out of Seek and Magellan to go into Zillow [in 2013]. That was an act of faith in Will Vicars, [because] Seek and Magellan had been very good to me and were both very dear to my heart,' he says.

'[Vicars'] actions and words [in the Gretel negotiations] were better than mine. He out-negotiated me every time. He fought for Gretel on every point right till the end. Gretel couldn't have had a better adviser and friend taking care of her interests and holding her hand. Even when I tried to be generous, Will still fought for a better deal for Gretel, which infuriated me at the time.'

James says Vicars is 'a self-made man, whereas I inherited all my money. Will and I have made up. It makes me very, very happy. I'm glad we've put all the bad blood behind us. Will was right about Zillow, it's just that he was early. My balance sheet changed when my new Gretel obligations were added to CPH's existing debt. Rightly or wrongly, I decided to sell everything I could to keep control of Crown. I hope I have learned lessons from the last twelve years. It's too painful to have to do this again.'

Vicars agrees it was a long, drawn-out, emotional process negotiating the division of a whole range of assets that were dear to the hearts of both siblings. 'A lot of things were said that both sides wish were never said, but that's what can happen in the heat of the moment. That moment went on for quite a while,' he says. 'At the end of the day, everyone is now talking again; the emotion has washed through. The pain of dealing with emotional assets and large sums of money has passed. Both parties are back to being more like brother and sister. James and I are in contact again, and our relationship is back to where we started.'

*

JAMES PACKER SAYS MORE than two years of brutal negotiations with his sister reminded him of the value of the three people who have stuck by him through the toughest of times: Mike Johnston, Guy Jalland and John Alexander. 'Mike Johnston has been with me for a long time. He's a good friend and has also shown complete loyalty to me and my family. I am deeply appreciative of Mike's work and dedication to CPH,' he says.

Johnston, Jalland and other Packer executives have often been viewed by some as simply yes-men, prepared to only tell Packer what he wants to hear. On this point the billionaire bristles. 'I don't think Guy is a yes-man. I don't think JA [John Alexander] is a yes-man. Nor is [CPH strategy and business development boss and former federal Labor minister] Mark Arbib,' he snaps in reply.

'Guy Jalland has been with me for decades. He worked for Dad and has been the most loyal friend and colleague imaginable. Guy and I sat down two years ago and agreed we were going to go down a path towards a debt-free CPH. I'm sure we have missed good opportunities, but we've also missed bad ones. Guy is a special person and I am eternally in his debt,' he says.

Packer also confirms what many have long suspected about John Alexander: that he should get enormous credit for the cost-cutting job he did at ACP before it was sold to private equity in 2006. 'It allowed us to get the price we got in the CVC deal. JA also served as chairman of CMH and was closely involved as a director of Foxtel and Fox Sports until News bought CMH. John now chairs Crown and has my full support. JA has been a great friend and has shown true and lasting loyalty to me,' he says.

In response Alexander declares himself to be 'a loyalist at heart'. 'James has been extraordinarily generous to me over the years. He has often been inspirational in his thinking, in his capacity to see the big picture. He saw the internet much earlier than anyone else and thus pursued the two big plays on jobs and cars. He saw it was time to get out of traditional media when no one else was seeing it. Then out of so-called new media: pay-TV. Very few people in the world were making those plays at that time. His brain and instinct were ahead of the curve. That sort of capacity inspires loyalty.'

Alexander still has his critics, though. Some wonder why he didn't pay a greater price for his involvement in Packer's disastrous US casino foray before the GFC. Others say he is still living off the legacy of his ACP turnaround and call him a 'divide-and-conquer leader' who revels in playing internal corporate politics. But there is no doubt, Alexander knows how to make businesses more efficient.

Kerry Stokes, who has Alexander on the board of his own media company, Seven West Media, is one who has appreciated Alexander's penchant for cutting costs. 'In casinos it is hard to keep costs under control,' Stokes says, before adding with a chuckle: 'When John took on the executive role at Crown he said, "I'd really like to leave [the Seven board]." I said, "You can't." I am grateful he stayed and he is an invaluable member on our board.'

But Packer's negotiations with his sister also reminded him of the immense complexity of CPH's corporate structure, a legacy that goes back to his grandfather and father. It is something he now has Guy Jalland and Mike Johnston addressing.

As a result, Packer quit twenty-six boards across CPH and Crown before 30 June 2018. 'I have been taken through our corporate structure ten times. I have tried hard to understand it but I don't understand it. One of the jobs I've got for Guy is to work with Mike Johnston to dramatically simplify it. We are a holding company for Crown. We have $70 million of private equity assets. And there are shareholder assets I own,' he says.

The review will include further reducing CPH's head office costs. In 2016 the group ended its association with its legendary Park Street headquarters in Sydney, moving to the premium ANZ Centre on Pitt Street. In the future the corporate office of CPH could potentially end up at Barangaroo, the site of Crown's $2.4 billion luxury hotel-casino complex. 'CPH is not an operating business, we own shares in Crown,' Packer says.

'As someone who has sold good assets at the worst time in both 2008–09 and 2016–17, Warren Buffett's words about leverage in his last shareholder letter ring incredibly loudly, truthfully and painfully to me.' He is speaking of the mantra of one of the world's top investors, the legendary long-serving boss of US investment firm Berkshire Hathaway. In his annual letter to investors in February 2018, Warren Buffett warned against borrowing to invest in stocks because it can accentuate panic during periods of volatility. 'There is simply no telling how far stocks can fall in a short period,' Buffett wrote. 'Even if your borrowings are small and your positions aren't immediately threatened by the plunging market, your mind may well become rattled by scary headlines and breathless commentary. And an unsettled mind will not make good decisions.'

Packer says Buffett's mantra now underpins his ambition for a debt-free existence for CPH. 'We will invest only out of cash flow. With this approach we will no doubt miss and have missed great opportunities, but we will fully own what we buy,' he says. 'I freely admit a hard truth being that I do not have the temperament to make my best decisions when I am under maximum pressure.'

But Packer now appears to have forgiven his sister for her actions, which he has previously claimed left him 'terrified'. Gretel is believed to have done the same. Whether the peace will hold remains to be seen, given that the wounds of both run deep. Those closest to them, led by their mother, are praying it does. Perhaps the regard they share for the man they called Dad – who they both know would surely have wanted them to be close – will continue to draw them back together. 'My father was the largest and most important figure in my life. He was the most remarkable man, and it's only with time that I more fully realise the breadth and scope of his huge achievements and accomplishments,' James says. 'I believe that Gretel would share some, if not all, of those sentiments. Her actions demonstrate that, with her ownership of so many places and things Dad held dear – from her shareholding in Ellerston, to *Arctic*, to Palm Beach. I have no doubt Gretel loves and loved my father dearly.'

THIRTEEN

Rocked to the Core

I<small>T WAS A TYPICALLY</small> clear mid-autumn morning on the calm waters of the Ionian Sea on 26 September 2016 when James Packer left the *Arctic P* moored off Greece's northwest coast. His destination was the Ioannis Kapodistrias international airport, near the town of Kerkyra, on the Greek island of Corfu, where his private jet was waiting. It took him on a short flight to the Israeli city of Tel Aviv, where he stayed for the night, before heading to the Chinese gaming province of Macau for a board meeting of his Asian gaming joint-venture company Melco Crown Entertainment.

Packer had been to Macau and China more than sixty times over the previous decade to help his Chinese business partner and good friend Lawrence Ho build the operations of Melco Crown into a multibillion-dollar enterprise, as Macau became a casino mecca bigger than Las Vegas. He had been just one of thousands of Australian business leaders who had recognised the opportunities presented by the extraordinary rise of China over the decades since former prime minister

Gough Whitlam's groundbreaking visit there in 1971. By mid 2016, he had become one of the few to actually build a successful business on the ground in China.

But the 27 September board meeting in Macau would prove to be his last, marking the beginning of the end of his China dream and the severing of his relationship with Ho. The two billionaires have not seen each other since. By mid December 2016, Crown Resorts had sold almost half its 30 per cent stake in Melco Crown for $1.6 billion, and Packer had resigned as deputy chairman and a board member of the company. By June 2017 Crown had completely sold out of Macau, just as the territory's fortunes were on the rise again. What had started as a bold venture and became a lucrative one had turned into an ugly mess of politics, finger-pointing and miscalculation.

The trigger was the shock arrests in late October 2016 of nineteen Crown staff by the Chinese authorities, including its head of international VIP business, Jason O'Connor. They were charged with 'gambling crimes' as part of a crackdown on foreign casinos marketing their properties directly to Chinese citizens on the mainland. Gambling is illegal in mainland China, so foreign operators can only promote the hotels, restaurants and entertainment facilities located within their resorts. The crackdown was part of the Chinese government's Operation Chain Break program, aimed at cutting off the flow of cash out of China to foreign casinos. In 2015 it had snared Korean operators Grand Korea Leisure and Paradise Co, arresting their staff in China. They were released after spending about sixteen months in custody.

To this day no one knows the real reason Crown and O'Connor were targeted. Nor do we know exactly who approved Crown's decision to beef up its marketing push in China at a time when the authorities were cracking down hard. Crown had received solid legal advice that its marketing team was acting in accordance with the loose conventions used by it and the other major casino operators in Australia, the Star and SkyCity, to ensure they stayed within the Chinese rules. But something clearly went wrong. 'It is heartbreaking to me what happened there,' Packer now says of the arrests that rocked his world.

Melco Crown was viewed as one of the best examples in the global gaming industry of a successful cross-cultural collaboration. In the shadows of their legendary fathers, Ho and Packer had forged their reputations on the global stage with the success of their joint venture. 'If you look at the gaming world, partnerships have never worked. Because there are such big egos and legendary figures involved, they have never worked out. But James and I have very similar backgrounds,' Ho says.

The China arrests were not the first time the Packer–Ho joint venture had struck trouble. After the pair joined forces in 2004 and their company floated in late 2006, the following year their first casino – the upmarket but poorly located and poorly designed Crown Macau (now renamed Altira) – had a terrible start. 'It was the worst opening I have ever had. We rushed it. It was four months ahead of when we should have opened it. The property wasn't ready. In 2007 [before the GFC and as Macau gaming revenues boomed] there was a mad rush to open properties. James was very supportive of me, even though it was my decision to open,' Ho recalls. Eleven years on, Altira now generates good profits for Melco Crown.

The same problems hit the partners' flagship City of Dreams (COD) casino resort development after its opening in 2009. As the GFC took hold, critics described COD as a ghost town offering the wrong product in the wrong place. In the development phase the construction bill for the COD project also blew out to a stunning $4 billion. Melco Crown was saved from going broke by a string of capital raisings backed by the major shareholders and a US$1.75 billion syndicated loan facility. The then group treasurer of Packer's private company CPH, the late Ray Fleming – a chartered accountant who had worked for the Packer family for fifteen years – sat with Guy Jalland in Macau working around the clock for five weeks in 2007 to get the facility signed off by its lenders just before the GFC took hold.

Ho says, 'I was thirty back then, super young. The [Melco] management team really only came together at the time of the IPO [initial public offering] in December 2006. Back then it was literally as thin as a piece of paper. Melco International didn't have the expertise that CPH and Crown had. During the COD financing, it was tough. We were having monthly board meetings because it was such a dire time. I appreciated James for his experience. For me I was going through a very serious financial crisis for the first time.'

The COD financing introduced Ho to an investment banker at UBS in Hong Kong named Robert Rankin, who was already well known to Packer. Rankin was a smooth-talking former Sydney-sider, who graduated from Sydney University with an economics–law degree before joining the Sydney offices of law firm Blake Dawson Waldron as a securities and mergers and acquisitions lawyer. In 1990 he turned his hand to investment banking, joining UBS's predecessor firm SBC Australia. Later he ran the Asia-Pacific operations for both UBS and Deutsche Bank. At the latter he played a key role with ANZ Bank in helping put together the US$1.75 billion COD loan facility for Melco Crown, something Packer has never forgotten. 'Ever since Rob did that for me, I had a very high regard for him and a close personal relationship with him,' Packer now says. It proved to be the dress rehearsal for Rankin's main performance.

*

YEARS EARLIER IN 2001, Packer had surprised the investment world when he hired Macquarie Group banker Peter Yates to run the family's media and gaming company, Publishing and Broadcasting. In late 2014 Packer did it again when he convinced Robert Rankin to leave his job as Deutsche Bank's then London-based co-head of corporate banking and securities to return to Hong Kong and run CPH. At Deutsche, Rankin was running a business with 25,000 staff spread across fifty countries and a trillion-dollar balance sheet. On paper he looked to be a good choice to be Packer's right-hand man, even if CPH had nowhere near the same number of staff or assets.

To CPH Rankin also brought his trio of loves: sport, wine and the arts, particularly contemporary art from the Asia-Pacific region. But, more importantly, he talked Packer's language of financial engineering and deal-making. One of his key early briefs after starting work in 2015 was to examine a more efficient structure for Crown, Melco Crown and CPH. In August 2015 he was elevated to the position of Crown chairman when Packer decided to relinquish the role and become just a director of the casino company, allowing him to focus on his life in America. Packer also told friends at the time that he simply wanted a break and trusted Rankin to be in charge.

By then – with Packer's blessing and with Crown shares falling to their lowest level for three years – Rankin was working on his first top-secret deal, a plan to remove Crown's listing from the Australian sharemarket. Listed companies are usually privatised to help streamline their operations, restructure parts of their businesses and reduce their reporting requirements. In theory, being private also allows a company to better focus on long-term goals, rather than shareholders' short-term demands. But the company or entity that privatises a company must be prepared to pay the public shareholders a premium, which can come at a significant cost – usually from borrowings.

Rankin held preliminary talks with US private equity firms Blackstone, TPG and Apollo as well as several Canadian pension funds about bankrolling Crown in the deal. But the most serious talks were held with another well-known US privateer, Hellman & Friedman (H&F). In early 2016 Rankin, Crown CEO Rowen Craigie, Crown chief financial officer Ken Barton and UBS's Melbourne boss Kelvin Barry met with H&F deputy chief executive Patrick Healy – who had once worked for CPH – in the Italian capital of Rome. H&F was then given access to Crown's financial statements for a time – a process known as due diligence – and its boss, Brian Powers, became involved in the process. Powers, a former managing director and chief executive of CPH and PBL from 1993 to 1998, also met with Crown founder Lloyd Williams to get his view on the transaction.

But his meeting with Packer on the deal in Las Vegas did not go well. In the end the deal, which would also have allowed CPH to take advantage of significant tax losses within its corporate structure but required it to take on significant levels of debt, could not be done at a price Packer found acceptable. His instinctive fear of over-borrowing had resurfaced after paying out his sister at the end of 2015.

Another stumbling block to the deal was Rankin himself, who had requested that CPH be paid a management fee to run Crown once it was delisted. It illustrated one of the challenges for Packer of having an investment banker at the helm of his company at what critics claim was precisely the wrong time. 'Rob came from a different world, a high-leverage world, where debt was viewed in a different way,' says one person familiar with Rankin's work.

In mid 2016, with Packer off the Crown board and distracted by Israel, Hollywood and his romance with Mariah Carey, Crown's directors then proposed to split the company in two in a bid to improve its valuation on the sharemarket. It was another piece of financial engineering known as Project Skycatcher. One company would house Crown's Australian casinos in Melbourne and Perth and its future Sydney project, while the other would hold its investment in Melco Crown. The theory was that the Australian assets would be valued higher on their own and be closer to the rating given to Crown's rival, the Star, with its Sydney, Brisbane and Gold Coast properties. The split would also remove the discount being applied to Crown by investors because of its volatile investment in Macau. The plan also included a potential public listing of a 49 per cent interest in a property trust that would own some of Crown Resorts' Australian hotels. But not everyone at CPH and Crown was convinced of the merits of the deal – most importantly, Packer. CPH still had $1.4 billion in debt on its balance sheet and the only thing on his mind was reducing it.

For the previous two years Macau had been hit by a Chinese government crackdown on corruption that had stemmed cash flow to its gaming tables. Melco Crown shares had been on a steady decline, and the Crown board and Packer were worried they would fall further. To put the fall in context, the share price of casino magnate Steve Wynn's Wynn Resorts at the beginning of 2014 was US$260, and at the start of 2016 it fell below US$58. In May 2016 Crown decided to take some Macau profits off the table when it collected $1 billion in cash following the selldown of its interest in Melco Crown from 33 per cent to 27 per cent.

The sale had opened a dialogue between Packer and Ho about looking at opportunities for the latter to further cement control of Melco Crown while helping the former with his balance-sheet issues. 'Even during the discussions of the selldowns, our intentions were clear. Macau was just coming out of the tough economic conditions it had been experiencing. It shook the confidence of many, but I thought for the long term it was the best bet possible,' Ho now says. 'At the same time I fully understood what James wanted to do. Over the years we had talked about him wanting to reduce debt at the CPH level and the Crown level. This gained momentum when Rob joined. He was looking at ways to restructure his balance sheet.'

Then the mid October arrests of nineteen Crown staff in China changed everything.

*

As Packer tried to come to terms with the biggest crisis facing Crown in its history in the weeks following the arrest of its staff in China, he, his board and their advisers knew they had to play their cards carefully. Crown's crisis management team, led by Robert Rankin and assisted by former Labor Party political operatives Mark Arbib and Karl Bitar, had learned much from the way another Australian firm, Rio Tinto, had handled the arrest of some of its China-based executives, including Stern Hu, eight years earlier. Rio had initially publicly defended Hu and his colleagues, saying it believed they had acted 'properly and ethically'. But that had proved to be a red rag to the Chinese bull.

By contrast, Crown's deliberate strategy in the early weeks of the China crisis was to be cautious and refrain from attacking the Chinese legal system and authorities. Instead, it chose to accept and respect the fact the alleged offences had taken place in a foreign country where it had to play by the local rules. Days after the arrests, as he battled his own personal problems in Los Angeles, Packer went public with his response to the arrests, putting his name to a statement saying he was 'respectful' of the sovereign rules and 'investigative processes' of the authorities in China.

Behind the scenes, Karl Bitar, Crown's executive vice-president, group marketing and brand strategy, immediately started making secret visits to China. By the time Crown's staff were released nine months later, Bitar had travelled to Beijing and Shanghai fifteen times. He played a key role, along with a group of lawyers and a crisis management firm, in dealing with the employees' families and the authorities.

Given his knowledge of China, Rankin's role was also significant. 'Rob did an important job behind the scenes and was sensitive to the China authorities in resolving that issue and deserves credit for that,' says Crown director and advertising-industry legend Harold Mitchell.

The Crown board was also facing a multitude of issues. Revenues from its high-roller business collapsed in the weeks following the arrests, and the directors were concerned that the arrests could have serious consequences for Crown's licences not only in Macau, but also in Australia. They recalled the actions of Steve Wynn's Wynn Resorts in 2012 when it pushed its co-founder and former partner Kazuo Okada out of the company and forcibly sold his US$1.9 billion worth of shares over allegations he had bribed Filipino gaming officials. But the board reasoned that having nineteen people in jail in China charged with gambling crimes meant there was little chance of their release unless they pleaded guilty. As one observer familiar with its thinking at the time puts it: 'They knew they were playing by different rules in China. It was all so opaque.'

Former Australian treasurer Peter Costello said at the time: 'When you invest in China, when you trade with China, you think you know how it operates and you do – right up until the time there is a corruption investigation or there's a power shift and things can turn on you very quickly.'

Project Skycatcher – bold and adventurous – quickly morphed into what might be termed the 'save the furniture' strategy of what was code-named Project Alpha: the stunning move by the Crown board, supported by its biggest shareholder CPH, to sell out of Macau. Crown shareholders, who would have received a share in a volatile international business in the original demerger deal, instead got cash in hand and a bigger share in a far less risky Australian business. Eight months later, experts said the share sale was part of the reason Crown 'got off lightly' when it accepted a $1.67 million fine for its misdemeanours.

Jason O'Connor and Australian–Chinese dual nationals Jerry Xuan and Jenny Pan Dan received relatively lenient ten- and nine-month jail terms. All the other Crown staff also escaped hefty jail terms. Given the time O'Connor had served in prison in Shanghai, the decision allowed him to return to Australia immediately.

The critics argue that Packer's response to the scandal was too hasty, yet another example of him panicking under pressure. Or that the Crown board was again unduly influenced by the demands of the company's major shareholder to sell. But upon reflection, Packer still feels the company had no option. 'Selling out of Macau hurt the most. I had sold my [US online real-estate company] Zillow shares so I could keep Macau. I would still be leveraged but Macau was my baby,' he now says. 'Lawrence and I had built Melco Crown into being one of the most valuable integrated resort companies in the world. When the arrests occurred I was not on the Crown board but I agreed with their decision that we had to sell.'

Crown joined the long list of Western companies gambling big in China and losing. There was some solace for Packer and his investors, given that Crown's initial investment of $700 million in its Macau sub-concession had been turned into $4.5 billion, returning the company more than six times its money on its venture. But it could have been so much more.

*

PACKER AND HO STILL call each other 'brother', despite the personal trauma and wasted opportunity of the scandal that destroyed their business relationship. 'I think we will be friends forever, even if we don't stay in touch. I'd love to do business with Lawrence again. Of all the partnerships I've had, it is the one I'm most proud of. Lawrence never broke his word, he never did anything to harm me, and was a twenty out of ten partner. But I don't want to go back to Macau or Hong Kong; there are too many bad memories,' Packer now says. 'The China arrests and Crown's sale of its Melco Crown shares just gutted me. It was too painful. I had lost again,' he adds, referring to the rapid rise in Melco shares after his decision to sell.

But since mid 2018 the Melco Crown share price has fallen dramatically, which provides some solace for Crown shareholders. 'Hindsight is 20/20 and should always be used with care, but Crown has out-performed MCE since the December 2016 selldown,' Robert Rankin now says, before adding: 'This could change over time.'

Ironically, Crown's selldown of its shares in December 2016 took place on the tenth anniversary of Melco Crown's listing on the Nasdaq. Ho was in New York to mark the occasion, ringing the bell for the market opening. He says he was simply lucky Melco Crown shares rebounded the way they did in the months after his purchase, even if Packer's critics would argue there were genuine signs of a recovery of gaming revenues in Macau before Crown cashed in its chips.

Ho's Melco International now has majority control of Melco Crown. 'I was happy to continue to creep up in terms of my shareholding. Naturally, it worked out great for me given the timing of it. But who knows, the timing of these things is pure luck,' he says.

Law firm Maurice Blackburn has since initiated a legal class action on behalf of aggrieved Crown shareholders, accusing the company of not telling investors that it was flouting Chinese laws prohibiting the promotion of foreign gambling junkets in mainland China. The law firm claims Crown should have known that promoting junkets in China was illegal from February 2015, when the Minister of Public Security held a press conference and announced the gambling crackdown. The Crown share price fell 20 per cent on the news of the arrests.

Lawrence Ho says he felt powerless to help his partner at the time he most needed it. 'There weren't many ways we could help. We offered to find lawyers. There wasn't much we could do. When people get arrested in China, it is hard to navigate through it,' Ho says. 'I do feel bad for James. I haven't done enough research on what those people did specifically in China that got them arrested in such a high-profile manner. I know the Koreans were arrested sixteen months earlier.'

In a mid 2017 newspaper interview, after Crown had sold out of Melco Crown completely, Ho made global headlines when he criticised foreign casino operators for 'deliberately spitting in the face' of Chinese authorities in 2016 by engaging staff in China despite a ban on the marketing of gambling. Many interpreted it as a direct criticism of Crown, and the comments initially bemused Packer and his executives and board. Commentators at the time claimed it reinforced perceptions that Ho was embarrassed by his Crown partner and was happy to buy him out. But Ho now says he 'absolutely' regrets what he said. 'I emailed [James] right away. I think I was set up. We listened to the recording sixty times. [The reporter] totally took it out of context. I even wanted to send James the recording, that section of it. I certainly regretted that comment. When I listened to the recording, I wasn't talking about Crown,' he says.

Was Ho worried the authorities would have considered the conviction of Crown staff when it came time to decide whether to renew Melco Crown's Macau licences in 2022? While he says the licence issue was not on his mind at the time, he now acknowledges that 'in hindsight, potentially it could have been problematic'.

So does Ho think Crown needed to sell out of Macau, as Packer has suggested? 'It is a hypothetical and really hard. But given 90 per cent of our EBITDA [earnings before interest, tax, depreciation and amortisation] comes from Macau and China, I guess I would agree with him,' Ho says. 'James could be right. He was doing me a favour as well. China or Macau never put any pressure on me … I am a phone call away [for the authorities] … I never got the phone call.'

Ho also dismisses the claims of conspiracy theorists who suggest Melco had a hand in the arrests – even that it reported Crown to the authorities – to stop the Australian company luring Chinese gamblers out of Macau. 'I wish I had that power in China,' Ho says with a wry smile. 'I would never do that. James has done so much for me. Even if I had the power – and I don't – you don't do that to your friends and brothers.'

Ho says he would not hesitate to work with Packer again on another project. Melco International is now building Europe's biggest casino complex in Cyprus, and if the Japanese government legalises casinos – as it is currently in the process of doing – Ho would seek to spend as much as US$10 billion to build a casino resort in a major Japanese city such as Osaka. Packer has publicly played down the prospects of Crown pushing for a casino licence in Japan, and although the company was actively working on a bid proposal during 2018, it has recently been shelved. Ho says, 'I would not close the door to being partners again. [James] is the best partner I have ever had. Everywhere we have been at Melco, we have worked well with partners. I would not hesitate for a moment to do anything together with James. He was amazing. I love him like a brother. I miss him. I do. I am a very private person and I don't socialise that much. But I really enjoyed my time with James.'

*

ASK FORMER QANTAS CHIEF executive and Crown director Geoff Dixon his perspective on Crown's China scandal, and he chooses his words carefully, describing it as 'an unfortunate episode'. But Seven Network mogul Kerry Stokes, whose comments on China carry extra weight given his long history of investments in the country's media and earth-moving industries, is far more forthright, describing it as 'totally the result of poor management. In retrospect it should never have happened,' Stokes declares. 'It was not as if there were not signals [for example, the Koreans]. If there had been proper governance, it would not have happened.'

Part of the blame for Crown's China disaster has been laid at the feet of Robert Rankin, even though Rankin hadn't been working at Crown when the Korea arrests happened. Rankin travelled regularly in Packer's private jet between his homes in London and Hong Kong and to other parts of the world. Investors were always concerned that he did not spend much time in Australia until the final part of his tenure. Stokes says Rankin was 'not the right man for the job. James knew he was hiring a merchant bank person, not an operational leader. He did not spend much time in Australia.' Harold Mitchell agrees: 'Rob just didn't fit in and it didn't work, but the company moved on.'

But Rankin notes that when he was hired by James, Crown already had a strong management team in place in Australia to run the operations. He says he was hired to be James's proxy globally. 'When I joined CPH and Crown, the priorities set by James were international expansion and growth. It was an exciting time. However, circumstances and priorities rightfully changed such that debt and cost reduction became key,' Rankin says.

Rankin also notes his travel schedule was related to his work on the potential privatisation of Crown, the sales of Crown's Melco Crown shares and Crown's proposed demerger.

Choosing his words carefully, Packer now echoes Harold Mitchell's line, saying in hindsight that 'Rob Rankin and I didn't work. The Crown China arrests happened on his watch. CPH's overhead costs went up a lot. And we agreed to having personal guarantees against me [in the settlement with Gretel] when that should have never happened,' he says. Packer has previously said he 'felt let down' over the China scandal, without naming Rankin or Rowen Craigie. But both stepped down from their roles in January and February 2017, only months after the arrests were made.

In response, Rankin won't comment directly on what he thinks happened in China that led to the arrests, but says: 'The detention of the Crown employees occurred whilst I was Chairman. It was the most difficult and challenging of periods and I led a small team [including Mark Arbib and Karl Bitar] entirely focused on their release and well being.'

Packer does give Rankin credit for giving him an important piece of advice, unrelated to China, which he ignored to his detriment. 'To be fair to Rob, he never thought I should have sold any Zillow shares. If I had listened to that advice I would be hundreds of millions of dollars richer than I am,' he says.

The Zillow shares were sold as part of the second settlement with his sister, which was negotiated in part by Rankin in his capacity as CEO of CPH.

Back then Packer was fixated on a story told to him by Rankin when Rankin first joined CPH as its chief executive in April 2015. It was a piece of advice Rankin received from Hong Kong billionaire Li Ka-shing, one of the thirty richest people in the world: that your net debt should never be more than 15 per cent of your net worth. Yet in September 2015, Packer's total net debt (being CPH's debt and his share of Crown's debt) was $2.3 billion compared to his net worth of $4 billion: a stunning ratio of 55 per cent. In hindsight, the timing of Rankin's arrival at CPH could not have been worse. As Packer told me in *The Weekend Australian* in October 2017: 'What was hard for Rob was my balance sheet fundamentally changed from the time I employed him – December 2014 – and then we were forced to deal with Gretel literally before Rob started work. My balance sheet went from one with a bit of spare capacity to one which was overstretched. That made it difficult.'

During his tenure Rankin had the discretion to spend $1 million of CPH's funds without needing to seek permission from his boss. CPH's overheads under Rankin surged to almost $50 million at their peak during 2016 (they are less than $20 million today), after CPH opened five offices around the world, including one in Santa Monica, west of downtown Los Angeles, to assist Packer's work with the RatPac film production group, staffed by former Scientology spokesman Tommy Davis.

Rankin also thought that, given the size of the Mariah Carey entourage in LA, Packer needed extra staff there. One person familiar with Rankin's thinking at the time says, 'Rob thought they had no one on the ground or any infrastructure in LA compared to Mariah's machine. It was the same in Israel; James wanted to invest there so Rob thought it best to give him extra support.'

Yet people who did business with CPH during Rankin's tenure say they found the CEO hard to track down. One says, 'James I found always very easy to deal with. James would always return a call or an email, and he would always give you an answer. Rob you could just never get on to. And it would take one, sometimes two, months to organise a call or a meeting with him.'

So why, I ask Packer, did he decide to put another investment banker like Rankin (after Peter Yates in 2001) in charge of his company in late 2014? Although, Rankin would argue he was more than just a deal-maker when he was appointed, given his significant managerial role at Deutsche running a global corporate banking and securities business. 'I think Peter Yates did a reasonable job. Peter got [Crown's successful takeover bid for] Burswood up,' Packer replies. 'It comes back to a mindset that perhaps I inherited from my father. Brian Powers was an investment banker, Ashok Jacob was a markets person. I had become used to having someone, in the first instance, as an interface with my father that was a sophisticated markets person.

'I hired Peter at a time when I thought PBL was going to be a telecommunications and internet company as well as a traditional media company. Peter had gaming experience too – he had advised on the original Crown deal and other gaming transactions. Rob, I thought, was a China expert, which was partly why it hurt so much that we got into the trouble we did in China.'

Critics have particularly questioned Rankin's lack of focus on the operational side of the Crown business. One observer says, 'At the outset Rob vowed he would bring structure and discipline to Crown and CPH. And they started having monthly meetings. But there was only ever one meeting.' Rankin, however, was the company's non-executive chairman, and Crown boasted a star-studded board of directors and an experienced managing director in Rowen Craigie. Craigie also had a difficult relationship with Packer during the final years of his tenure. Their relationship had never recovered from the Cannery disaster in America.

Kerry Stokes believes the turning point for Crown came with Packer's decision to step off the board in late 2015 due to potential conflicts arising from any privatisation of the company – which never happened – and to pursue his business interests in America. Packer was always a domineering figure in the minds of his executives and without him, Stokes says, there was less certainty as to who was actually in charge. 'It is easy to come back and blame people. I know Rob Rankin in James's mind takes a lot of the blame. But the real issue is James stepped back,' he says. 'In stepping back, there was no clear leadership in the rest of the group. James, his father, they have always been thoroughly strong, visible leaders. People knew the objectives and outcomes. Suddenly there was a vacuum. In my experience, vacuums are filled by problems.'

Geoff Dixon agrees Packer's departure left a vacuum but disputes suggestions it wasn't filled. 'James is a strong person. He has very, very strong arguments and views on the direction he wants for Crown. But I don't think the place in any way, shape or form – and this is not a self-serving comment – went off the rails or anything like that,' he says. Dixon is careful not to comment directly on the China issue given the class action at hand, but notes that companies with the size and heritage of Crown 'are going to have the occasional misstep, if that was a misstep. It was, for want of a better word, an unfortunate episode. We did a very good job in resolving it.'

The China arrests also brought into focus the role – or lack of it – in the affair of Crown's star-studded board, which, in addition to Dixon and Harold Mitchell, includes John Alexander, former AFL boss Andrew Demetriou and former Liberal senator Helen Coonan. The company's response to the crisis reinforced the concerns of some in the investment community who had long questioned whether Crown's strategy was too often driven by the needs of Packer as the major shareholder. In this case, Packer needed cash to cut the debt levels of his private company. 'There has been nothing that has crossed the line, but it can be uncomfortable,' says one market player. 'Also, a different board may not have changed the final decision on things, but there may have been some directors who were prepared to give James an alternative view.'

Harold Mitchell stresses no one on the Crown board is there for the money. 'There is no one on that board who needs to be there. All have their independence and are there in the interests of all the shareholders. In my case, it is all the shareholders, including the interests of James Packer. Directors need to be concerned for shareholders, the entity and the employees,' he says.

Geoff Dixon will not comment directly about the Rankin era, but stresses the Crown board has never been a rubber stamp for the wishes of the major shareholder. 'James would attest to the fact that I am an independent director. And I mean that in the meaning of the word. Where I think it is necessary, I speak my mind,' he says. Dixon says his relationship with Packer has largely been good, but they have had their moments of conflict. 'At one stage it was about people that we both knew. Some mutual friends. It was a disagreement away from the board. A personal issue. That was patched up pretty quickly,' he says, before politely declining to go into the details. 'And I wouldn't say there has been conflict on the board. But have I disagreed with some ideas at board level? Of course.'

While governance experts have often taken the view that the primary role of directors in a company with a major shareholder like Packer is to look after the interests of smaller retail shareholders, Dixon stresses the wishes of the owner can't be ignored. 'While it is hugely important to look after the minority shareholders, for want of a better word, it is also very, very important to consider the issues put up by someone who owns such a huge stake in the company,' he says. 'I don't agree with the view that when you have a 47 per cent shareholder, you have to stand and fight the battle for the rest of them. We do have battles occasionally, not many. This is very much a company that came out of the Packer family. That is important to remember.'

The Crown board and management have been reviewing the company's high-roller strategy, and in the year following the release of its employees from a Chinese jail, its revenues have rebounded, albeit not as strongly as those of its biggest rival, the Star. This financial recovery is of little solace for former accountant Jason O'Connor, who was in the wrong place at the wrong time, and has since returned to his home in Melbourne suburbia to rebuild his family life with his wife and two children. But for Packer, the rebound in the VIP business and the rejuvenation of Macau is confirmation of his belief in the China economic growth story. 'Despite what happened in China, my record of on-the-ground investing in China, be it in Melco Crown or [the Seek-backed Chinese online jobs site] Zhaopin, is one of the best in Australia,' he says.

While the China–Australia relationship is one of mutual economic benefit, it is also one of geopolitical complexity given Australia's strong historical strategic relationship with the United States. Australian leaders – corporate and political –

have a delicate and potentially problematic path to tread. But Packer, despite his troubles in China, is very clear where he stands on the issue. 'The fact the prime minister and the foreign minister have not visited China for over a year is highly unfortunate,' he says. 'If Australia thinks [Chinese president] Xi Jinping is going to change his behaviour because of anything we do, I believe that is naive.'

FOURTEEN

A Hero No More

It is known as West Buttermilk Estate. Just minutes from downtown Aspen, the winter playground of America's – and some of the world's – richest and most famous people, its ceiling-to-floor windows offer sweeping views of the scenic hills of the picturesque Colorado snow country of Mount Daly, Mount Sopris and and Owl Creek Valley. Some say they are the best mountain views of any property in Aspen. Built in 2007, the 18th-century-inspired property offers seven spacious bedrooms, seven bathrooms, a state-of-the-art kitchen, a medieval-style dining room, and a theatre room, steam room, games room, gym and library.

It was purchased for more than US$20 million by James and Erica Packer in 2013, a few months before they separated. They quickly turned one part of the home into a children's wing, complete with six timber double bunk beds, and built an outdoor waterslide for their children to play on during the warmer months. It is attached to a swimming pool that doubles as a super hot tub during winter. Little did they know that just after Christmas that year, almost four months after their formal split, it would play host to a union that would live with Packer forever.

In the dying days of 2013 Packer was in Aspen with his good friends Ben Tilley, Brett Ratner and London-based French financier Arpad 'Arki' Busson, the ex-partner of Australian supermodel Elle Macpherson. On Busson's arm during his Aspen sojourn was his then fiancée, Hollywood actress Uma Thurman. Also in town was one of Ratner's closest personal friends and collaborators, world-renowned pop star Mariah Carey. Ratner had directed her 1999 music video 'Heartbreaker'. Late one evening between Christmas and New Year, at the invitation of Ratner, Carey and her entourage, led by her Russian manager Stella Bulochnikov, pulled up at the front door of Packer's home at around 11.30pm. They quietly tiptoed in their high heels through the snow into the living room, threw off their coats and warmed themselves in front of the spectacular gas fireplace.

It was party time and Ratner was master of ceremonies. 'Brett was a very good host,' remembers one of Packer's friends who was there that night. 'He put everyone in the group at ease. They were playing music, and he was playing YouTube videos of things that had happened in his life. He played this YouTube video of him and Michael Jackson. Then he was playing Mariah Carey songs. Brett had been the filmmaker or the director of a couple of the videos so he was talking us through them. It was a real fun, casual night.'

It was the start of a most unlikely relationship, one that would stun the world.

*

PACKER AND CAREY WERE TOGETHER again seven months later at the TCL Chinese Theatre in Hollywood, when Ratner invited Carey to the Los Angeles premiere of the RatPac-produced hit movie *Hercules*. It starred Dwayne Johnson, who made headlines on the night when he gave Carey a kiss on the cheek. Carey was the gala star of the event, showcasing her figure in a tight, low-cut little black dress, paired with white heels and a silver butterfly ring. Also on hand was Russian model Irina Shayk – Johnson's co-star in the film and then the girlfriend of footballer Cristiano Ronaldo – as well as comedian Eddie Murphy and Australian singer Kylie Minogue. Carey later told *The Steve Harvey Show* in America that she and Packer 'hit it off' that night. 'We were talking and laughing and people were getting mad at us and stuff like that,' she said.

Packer himself is reluctant to talk much about Carey when we sit down together fifteen months after their break-up, in the same room in Aspen where they first met. In October 2017, in his first public comments on their relationship, he described it as a mistake. 'I was at a low point in my personal life. Documenting the negotiations with my sister was taking longer than expected,' he told me in an interview for *The Weekend Australian Magazine*. 'Brett Ratner put Mariah and me together. She was kind, exciting and fun. Mariah is a woman of substance. She is very bright. But it was a mistake for her and a mistake for me.'

Today in Aspen, three months after that interview, he sticks to the same line. But as he munches on cheese sticks and sips his preferred drink of lemon-lime Gatorade between a steady stream of cigarettes – he is prepared to offer a few extra reflections on the times they had together. Like Carey, he has fond memories of the *Hercules* premiere in July 2014. 'I was sitting next to Brett and [Mariah] was on the other side of him. [American writer and filmmaker] Oliver Stone was sitting behind us and kept telling us to be quiet,' he says with a smile, followed by a puff of smoke.

After that meeting they stayed in touch, exchanging regular emails, before in February 2015 Packer headed to Parañaque in the Philippines for the official opening of the City of Dreams casino complex in Manila with his Asian gaming partner Lawrence Ho.

Packer was due to return to the US after the Manila opening, but opted instead to spend some time on the *Arctic P* in the Mediterranean. Rumours swirled that his romance with supermodel Miranda Kerr was on the rocks. By the start of the northern summer, at Packer's invitation and with Ratner's encouragement, Carey had joined him on the *Arctic P*, along with her twins, Monroe and Moroccan. 'By May 2015 the deal with my sister is two months overdue, and four months from happening. And I am thinking I can't do anything until the deal is done. I'm feeling trapped,' Packer now recalls. 'So Mariah arrives on the boat, I am not in a good place. She is not in a good place; she has only recently publicly split with the father of her children. So she stays longer than she indicated she would, which makes me happy.'

Fast-forward to 19 June and the couple were photographed strolling hand-in-hand for the first time around the Italian isle of Capri, including outside the Pasticceria Da Alberto on the Via Roma. Carey wore a striking red summer dress and Packer a plain polo top, casual pants and his trademark Ray-Ban sunglasses. Later in the day they returned together to Packer's boat. Twenty-four hours later Carey was posting photos on Instagram with her twins aboard the *Arctic P*, while Packer's children were also aboard. The pictures made a dramatic impact around the world. For some friends, business associates and gossip columnists back in Australia, the relationship was almost shocking, the ultimate folly for Packer, dating one of the most watched and photographed women on the planet.

But to others it confirmed his penchant for dating high-profile women. 'Having once romanced Sylvester Stallone's American on–off girlfriend Jennifer Flavin, it's possible Packer developed a fascination for American women, though it's more likely he's developed an appetite for what they can deliver to him – in this case the ear of Hollywood powerbrokers and the attention of the world,' wrote Annette Sharp in *The Daily Telegraph*.

Former Channel Nine boss David Leckie, for one, couldn't believe it. 'The one thing James always asked when I was running Channel Nine was, "Please make sure you stop any publicity about me." Then he goes and dates Mariah Carey! I was shocked,' Leckie says. 'I always thought the last thing in the world he wanted was publicity.'

The once media-shy casino mogul suddenly looked to be relishing being pursued by the paparazzi swarming over the Mediterranean. After two failed marriages, a bust-up with his best mate David Gyngell and a failed romance with Miranda Kerr (though neither publicly acknowledged their less-than-secret union and then apparent break-up), and now living far away from the country of his birth, Packer, the critics reckoned, had totally lost the plot.

*

THE DAY AFTER NEWS broke of the blossoming romance between Packer and Carey, the union received an important and somewhat surprising endorsement from an unlikely source: Packer's first wife, Jodhi Meares. In the early hours of 22 June in Australia, Meares posted on her Instagram an awkward-looking photo of herself, Packer and Carey posing together on board the *Arctic P*, captioning the post 'Amore' with three love hearts. Packer was grinning widely in the shot. It turns out

Meares and her sister were in Capri at the same time as Packer and Carey, so joined them on the *Arctic P.*

When I ask Meares about the photo, she rolls her eyes and smiles, before noting that it was Carey who insisted Meares put the shot on her Instagram page. 'I don't really have a strong opinion,' she adds when I ask her view on the romance. 'If James loves somebody, then I love them. Unless they hurt him, and then I despise them vehemently. If James is happy, I am happy and I will be respectful of his choices in that area.'

But was she surprised her ex-husband would date a diva like Carey? 'I thought it was unusual. But then I thought these are two people who have had some extraordinary experiences and that is how they connect. That is how it made sense. She is Mariah Carey. I was like, "Wow." She is extraordinarily creative, she is an incredible singer, I grew up with her [music], we are both the same age. She might be the biggest star I have ever met. She was lovely to me.'

Days later Packer and Carey partied at a private concert in Cannes headlined by English singer Sting, before heading to Israel. There they stayed in the presidential suite of Jerusalem's famed David Citadel Hotel, which had recently hosted American celebrities Kim Kardashian and Kanye West. Their trip to Jerusalem included an emotional visit to the Western Wall and dinner with Benjamin and Sara Netanyahu at the prime minister's residence.

As it gathered momentum, the romance was soon dubbed PaRiah, JaMimi and Cacker by comedians. Packer might have subsequently called it a 'mistake', but he stresses that he and Carey were good friends. 'It was fun to begin with. Wherever we went we were on the top table and that was because of her, not me. She was kind and she took an interest in my life. RatPac was still gathering momentum. So in the entertainment industry, I was having some impact,' he says.

A mutual friend agrees. 'She is very bright. She tried her best to provide advice and support to James and was extremely supportive of him,' they say. 'She's the first to admit she's a diva. She might be a diva but her heart, I think, is decent. She was always very respectful of James.'

*

PACKER SAYS CAREY HAD 'amazing friends, artistically and commercially. One of the people that I got to know with Mariah who made a big impression on me was David Geffen,' he says. The billionaire American record executive, film and theatrical producer and philanthropist is famed for founding Geffen Records, which launched the careers of bands like the Eagles, Aerosmith and Guns N' Roses. He was also one of the founders, along with Steven Spielberg, of film production company DreamWorks.

Geffen took his luxury yacht, *Rising Sun*, to the Mediterranean in the northern summer of 2015. The US$300-million, 138-metre boat was built for Oracle founder Larry Ellison, but he found it too big and sold it to Geffen in 2010. Packer says, 'David was wonderful to me. Arnon Milchan and Kevin Tsujihara and Lachlan Murdoch had all told me how formidable he was. I knew David a little, but Mariah said we should go and visit him on his boat. His guests were Tom Hanks and his wife Rita, [Disney CEO] Bob Iger and his wife, and [Apple Music executive] Jimmy Iovine. Mariah was always wonderful in a room. She has the most wicked sense of humour – and is lightning fast. For me to be able to sit around a table with those people was humbling and hugely exciting.'

Packer also started going to Carey's concerts. 'She has had more number ones than anyone except the Beatles. Eighteen. She wrote them all herself. The fact she can write those lyrics, let alone her voice … She is insanely bright – that is before you get to the voice, which is out of this world. I probably went to ten of her concerts and they were all fantastic,' he says.

In July 2015, while performing at the Colosseum at Caesars Palace in Las Vegas, Carey chose to dedicate one of her most emotional hits, 'Hero', to Packer. 'I've got a new heart,' Carey told her Las Vegas residency audience. 'James is in the house.' Friends say it made Packer feel amazing. One says, 'She hadn't dedicated that song to many people. At that time his Macau business was still getting worse, he was feeling as though he had way too much debt before the second deal with his sister. I think he thought it was a special feeling hearing her singing that song to him.'

On the evening of 18 August, Carey performed for the first time in Israel at Rishon LeZion's Live Park, fifteen minutes south of Tel Aviv. She was reportedly paid more than $500,000 for her performance, which started shortly before 10.30pm and finished almost two hours later, for 12,000 fans sweltering in the 30-degree summer-evening heat. Sara Netanyahu attended the concert, as did Yossi Cohen, now the head of Israel's intelligence agency Mossad. The Israeli Civil Service Commission subsequently launched an investigation, as part of its corruption inquiry into Prime Minister Netanyahu, into suspicions that Cohen had received the tickets, worth thousands of shekels, for free.

Packer declines to comment on the controversy, but says he will never forget the evening for a different reason. For the first time he was able to sit on the stage to watch his girlfriend perform. He couldn't take the smile off his face. 'I went to the concert with my friend [the journalist] Ari Shavit. We were taken to the backstage area by one of Mariah's assistants. Ari had a great seat just off the side of the stage. They said to me I could go on stage just to the side of where the band was performing,' Packer says. 'I was looking out over the crowd and getting the view that Mariah and her back-up singers were getting. The concert was fantastic. For the time of that concert, I think for the first time, I understood what it must be like to be a rock star.'

Packer also learned from Carey about listening to music, and that the version of the performance of a song can be just as important as the song itself. One of his favourites is British pop band Coldplay's performance of its hit song 'Fix You' at the Glastonbury music festival in 2016. Friends say 2016 was such a horror year for Packer and his business that he didn't watch the YouTube video of the Glastonbury performance for almost a year, finally summoning up the courage to view it again just after Christmas 2017. When he did, he cried uncontrollably.

In September 2015 Packer celebrated his forty-eighth birthday in Los Angeles, and Brett Ratner threw him a surprise party at Ratner's Hilhaven Lodge mansion. The guest list that night read like a who's who of Hollywood: Carey, Al Pacino, Mick Jagger, Warren Beatty, Eddie Murphy, Ben and Casey Affleck, and Arnon and Yariv Milchan. Leonardo DiCaprio was a late arrival at around 10pm. Also in the crowd were casino magnate Steve Wynn's ex-wife Elaine, Warner Brothers boss Kevin Tsujihara, Viacom vice-chair Shari Redstone and Steve Mnuchin, who was one of the original backers of RatPac and is now the US Treasury secretary. Ratner did not forget Packer's Australian roots, also inviting Jodhi Meares, Crown chairman Robert Rankin, CPH executive Sam McKay and Perth rich-lister Tim Roberts.

Ratner remembers Packer being miffed at one point during the evening when an off-colour joke apparently upset the birthday boy. 'He got really mad at me. It was actually Mariah's fault,' Ratner says with a wide smile. 'Mariah is friendly with this guy Jeff Beacher, who has a cabaret, and he had midgets and obscure characters within the show. So we had a midget Mariah. I think James thought she got offended or something. But Mariah has been my friend for twenty-five years. I can never offend her.'

Ratner believes Packer was smitten with the songstress. 'I saw it that night at the birthday party. She's very charming. She's very beautiful,' he says. 'I've never seen James pursue a woman. Meaning, James is all about business. Women are not part of his thing. Girls are not his thing. It's business. That's all he thinks about – and global politics.' So was he surprised Packer and Carey became a couple? 'I was surprised. I think it's timing. It's like James wanted somebody by his side. Mariah was lonely,' he says. 'I was on many of those trips [in the Mediterranean]. And, you know, he was great to her. He is very warm and affectionate. Kind and generous. There's no doubt he is the most generous person I've ever met in my life.'

*

THE GLAMOUR COUPLE MADE their red carpet debut in September 2015 at the Tribeca Film Institute's Annual Gala Benefit for the New York premiere of the film *The Intern*. A month later they were in the Chinese gaming province of Macau for the launch of Packer's new $4.4 billion casino resort Studio City with his partner Lawrence Ho. Packer and Carey appeared happy, holding hands and smiling for the cameras as they posed together on the event's red carpet.

Hollywood stars Robert De Niro, Leonardo DiCaprio, Brad Pitt and director Martin Scorsese were also in Macau that night for the premiere of their US$70 million 'short film' *The Audition*. The fifteen-minute production, directed by Scorsese, was an elaborate marketing campaign for Studio City. It was Scorsese's first film to feature both De Niro and DiCaprio. De

Niro, DiCaprio and Pitt reportedly pocketed US$13 million each for the four-day film shoot.

Lawrence Ho says that while the film was Packer's idea (though Packer said at the time it was actually De Niro's brainchild), he supported it. 'Studio City is a Gotham, Hollywood-themed property. I went to some of the Hollywood meetings [on the film] with James originally. He was introducing me to Warren Beatty, Kevin Tsujihara and Robert De Niro,' he says. 'He knew I had a passion for watching movies. I love movies. I have a great knowledge of movies. So I was interested when he was doing the RatPac thing. I went to the filming of the project in New York. When the idea came together, I thought it was fantastic,' he says.

Packer's critics have described it as the ultimate 'vanity' project: the best illustration that his chequebook had been captured by the bright lights of Hollywood, and that his ego was out of control. When confronted with the claim, Packer initially responds: 'That may well be true,' before launching into a strident defence of the project. 'There were $5 billion of casinos [that year] for which there were cinematically themed openings. I remember showing [the film] to Lachlan [Murdoch] and he said it was worth every cent of what it cost. It was the best short film that has ever been made. But when you are Icarus and you are flying close to the son, there is a lot of jealousy,' he snaps. Packer is also critical of the broader investment returns from Studio City since its opening. 'I don't think Macau Studio has been as successful as it should have been for the amount of money that was spent on it,' he declares.

Lawrence Ho chooses his words carefully, but says of the cost of the film project: 'I think, in hindsight, for US$70 million, probably the money could have been better spent,' before quickly adding: 'When we opened Studio City it was the worst possible time to open a property, in October 2015. The worst possible time in Chinese politics and the Chinese economy. No matter what we did it would not have mattered because of the constraints people were feeling in China about going to Macau.' Ho was referring to the controls the Chinese government imposed for a time on its citizens travelling to Macau to gamble. 'If we had done it more economically, it would have been better. But it was the biggest stars in Hollywood. I still think it was a super cool project. And we didn't just do it for the Studio City opening. We did it for our project in Manila and [it also detailed] our ambitions in Japan and beyond.'

At the Studio City opening, Packer and Carey were photographed together with Ho and his wife Sharen Lo Shau Yan, granddaughter of the founder of Vitasoy, Kwee Seong Lo. It was the first and only time Ho met the pop star. He openly volunteers that he wasn't sure at the time whether the Carey relationship was the best thing for his good friend. He says he and his wife missed the friendship they had developed with Packer's second wife, Erica. 'I think [Carey] lives up to her diva reputation,' Ho says. 'I liked the feeling I had with Erica where she was fantastic for James. I wasn't quite sure on Mariah. She wasn't that interested in talking to me [that night] and I wasn't so keen to please either. I was just like, "Sure." When [James] and Erica separated, I thought it was a shame. My wife and I both liked Erica. Erica was a good balancing force for him. Erica is one of the nicest, kindest people. She didn't have any of the "I am Australia's richest man's wife" [attitude]. You never had that with Erica.'

Crown director Harold Mitchell, who was also in Macau for the event, will never forget the entourage that trailed Carey. 'I remember we were sitting in the private lounge at Macau airport as they swept in. There were two mini buses full of support staff for Mariah and they took over the place,' Mitchell says.

Despite the misgivings of many of his friends, as the year drew to an end, Packer's romance with Carey was in full swing. A month after Carey and ex-husband Nick Cannon spent Thanksgiving together – for their children's sake – in late November, Cannon told American radio personality Howard Stern that it was 'awesome' his ex had found a soulmate in Packer. In mid December Packer and Carey returned to the house where they had first met in Aspen to celebrate Christmas, where they were famously photographed together walking in the snow. Packer, wearing his Ray-Ban sunglasses and red earphones, looked smitten.

After Christmas they boarded Packer's private jet bound for his homeland for a gala New Year's Eve concert at Crown in Melbourne. It would be the first and last time they would visit Australia as a couple. Carey was the star attraction on New Year's Eve, wearing three different outfits during the show, including a white diamond dress with a plunging neckline, for a crowd that included Ros Packer, Lloyd Williams, and foreign affairs minister Julie Bishop and her partner, property developer David Panton. 'Spectacular, handsome' was how Carey described her beau to the audience at the start of her show. 'I don't even have words for the man who introduced me tonight. We'll just say the amazing Mr James Packer,' she breathlessly enthused. Again, she dedicated her performance of the song 'Hero' to him.

On New Year's Day the entourage headed to Packer's home town of Sydney, where they joined Sarah and Lachlan Murdoch aboard the media heir's superyacht *Sarissa* for a tour of the harbour. The paparazzi were in their element. 'James introduced me to Mariah when he came back to Australia with the kids and went out on a yacht with Lachlan and Sarah. I think it was more being a gentleman that he wanted to introduce me to the kids,' remembers photographer Jamie

Fawcett. 'He was being the ultimate gentleman. Everything seemed to be okay, nothing seemed wrong.'

That evening the couple visited Packer's Bondi apartment, even mingling with the crowd at the nearby local ice-cream parlour, before heading in Packer's jet to Tamworth airport. From there they went by helicopter to Ellerston for a few days of rest and recuperation with their children. Ellerston had always been one of the places where Packer chose to retreat from the world. Yet as Packer lounged around by the pool in shorts and tee-shirt, one Ellerston staffer remembers Carey getting dressed up to the hilt each morning. 'I remember telling her, "No one can photograph you here, you don't need to worry about the paparazzi." But she simply responded with words to the effect of, "This is me."'

*

PACKER DID HIS BEST to turn a blind eye to Carey's diva whims, which included bringing along her personal stylist, hairdresser and make-up artist when they travelled together. In late January 2016, *The New York Post*'s celebrity gossip column 'Page Six' reported that a few days after she flew from New York to Los Angeles with Packer, Carey flew her Jack Russell pet dogs Cha Cha and Jill E Beans in their own seats on an American Airlines flight. Each was also accompanied by its own staff member. 'Page Six' also claimed she spent at least US$45,000 a year on spa treatments for her beloved pooches. Australian gossip magazine *Woman's Day* later reported that while she was dating Packer, Carey was spending $100,000 a month ordering exotic flowers from around the world to be delivered wherever she happened to be.

Packer and his staff also did their best to tolerate the whims of Carey's personal assistant and manager Stella Bulochnikov.

Bulochnikov took Packer ring shopping in New York, where he purchased a massive 35-carat Wilfredo Rosado–designed engagement ring from her uncle in the city's jewellery quarter on 45th Street. Packer chose the New York three-Michelin-star restaurant Eleven Madison Park to get down on one knee and propose to Carey on the evening of 21 January. It would have been the third marriage for both of them. Plans were made for the couple to be married on Bora Bora in French Polynesia on 1 March 2016.

But trouble was brewing. 'There were already problems trying to negotiate our prenup,' Packer recalls, without commenting further on the details.

Carey told *Complex* magazine in July 2016 that she was in favour of a prenup. 'We would like for [a prenuptial agreement] not to be a big thing, but the reality is it has to be. Because there's things that are specifically mine, and he's got huge friggin' conglomerate stuff, and I'm not looking to take that from him. So it has to be dealt with. Anytime you get married to somebody [it does] – and I should know. This'll be marriage No. 3.'

Celebrity news site TMZ subsequently described the agreement as an unromantic, 37-page document stipulating that Carey would receive $115,385 per week in the event of a divorce, up to a maximum of $30 million, adjusted pro-rata on a weekly basis. But it was never agreed on.

In early 2016 Packer was in panic mode after having concluded a $1.25 billion agreement to divide his family empire with his sister on Christmas Day 2015. Shares in his Macau casino company were still falling and Crown shares had slumped to their lowest level in two years. The GFC had been a deeply traumatic event for Packer, testing his judgement and his nerve in ways which revealed elements of his character that few would have expected in someone with such a privileged life and immense personal wealth. He became depressed, put on weight and took up smoking again. He became fanatically obsessed with the money he was losing at the time, petrified that less than five years after inheriting a multibillion-dollar fortune, he might lose it all.

In the years that followed he vowed to never again be caught with too much debt. Yet by the end of 2015, he had again taken on more debt than he could psychologically handle in an effort to pay Gretel out. More threateningly, in light of the fallout between them, he had agreed to Gretel having personal guarantees over all his assets. He was terrified she could one day take everything from him.

The life of dating a diva was also starting to take its toll, and Packer's friends were seriously concerned about his mental and physical welfare.

Packer now recalls sitting at his home in Aspen in February 2016 when the house phone rang. 'It's a call I will never forget. It was from a man I once knew who lived in Israel. I thought the world of him. He said, "Jamie, I'm worried about you. You're unwell." He told me to rely on my friends nearby to tell me what to do next. That was code for [relying on] Kerry Stokes,' he says.

Stokes had been spending the American ski season, as he does each year, at his hunting lodge – a two-storey, six-bedroom, six-bathroom penthouse for which Stokes had paid US$15.5 million for in 2002 – at the exclusive Beaver Creek in Vail, Colorado, two hours' drive from Aspen. In the years following their détente after the battle for CMH, Packer had often been to see him there. This time Stokes returned the favour and turned up with his wife, Christine, on Packer's doorstep in Aspen. Also there was Packer's good friend Thom Knoles, a maharishi (or master teacher) of Vedic meditation, a mental technique for relaxation developed 5000 years ago in India. Knoles, who is based in Phoenix, Arizona, had a meditation practice in the leafy eastern Sydney suburb of Woollahra for twenty-nine years, where he worked with other rich-listers, including construction tycoons Bruno Grollo and son Daniel (whom he had introduced to Packer more than two decades earlier).

'My wife, Christine, and I went up to Aspen. We took a fair bit of time out of our schedule. We cared for James. When you are close to somebody, you have to try to help them,' Stokes says. In this vein he then made a remarkable decision: to unilaterally take charge for a time of Packer's personal affairs. 'It just needed to be done,' Stokes says, without flinching. It was a remarkable move by someone already chairing his own public companies, Seven West Media and Seven Group Holdings.

'With due respect, those around James and those executives (like Robert Rankin), they accepted I did have authority (to manage James's personal matters). I made the decisions,' Stokes says. 'It was easy for me to say, "No, you are not spending $250,000 on a wedding dress. No you are not moving this here. You are not doing that."'

Stokes also rearranged CPH's small internal board of directors. 'All I did, in effect, was put in place some controls that made it easier for people there to do their jobs. It was never envisaged previously that James would not be there,' Stokes says.

Rankin, who was not on the CPH board, continued overseeing the business interests of the company, including chairing Crown. But Stokes had little to do with Rankin. 'He avoided me at that point in time,' Stokes says before one of his trademark grins. 'I didn't see much of Rob.'

After having endured the horrors of the GFC, Packer's debt phobia was beginning to have telling physical effects, which were horrifically apparent to Stokes and Knoles in Aspen.

'I was in a bad way, a bad way,' Packer recalls. A blizzard in West Buttermilk meant his Global Express jet couldn't make it into Aspen airport. Instead it flew into Rifle, an hour and a half's drive away. Stokes helped a panic-stricken Packer into the front seat of Knoles's car, which Knowles then drove the 70 miles to Rifle where Packer's plane was waiting to take him to Israel. Knoles recalls of the day: 'I thought, "Now we are going to get somewhere." I felt, "Now we are at the moment of truth, now we are going to get some decisions made."'

Stokes says Packer, at the time, was 'confused. We agreed it would be good if he spent some time in Israel. Away from all the controversies and the pressures and the intensities … My concern was that [he and Mariah] were both in bad places and that James needed some space. He had friends in Israel who were concerned about his welfare. I felt comfortable he would be looked after there.'

Stokes was always worried that Packer and Carey had both fallen into the relationship on the rebound from bad break-ups. And he was concerned about their fast-paced lifestyle. After Packer's arrival in Israel, Stokes organised for Packer's pilots to take his plane in for unscheduled maintenance to ensure Packer wouldn't be able to leave Israel quickly. 'He wasn't happy at one stage. In good humour, of course. But I certainly incurred the wrath at the time of his fiancée and her agent. They were threatening to go to the police for me kidnapping James. There were some strong words said. They wanted to charter a plane from Las Vegas to Israel, and I wouldn't approve it. I was accused of separating the lovebirds,' Stokes says, before adding with a proud grin: 'I said I was prepared to pay two economy fares to Israel if that was helpful.' Packer's memory of the time is hazy, but he recalls, 'Mariah was very upset when I was in Israel because I had just disappeared.'

Stokes also did more than physically separate the then not-so-happy couple. In hindsight, it proved to be the ultimate act of friendship from a one-time adversary. 'I did postpone his wedding,' Stokes volunteers without flinching. 'We did have some issues at the time because Mariah's agent was most insistent that they would not be separated and the wedding take place … James was upset at not seeing [Mariah]. But he wasn't sure. He was obviously engaged to her. He was obviously emotionally involved. The fact that it was postponed, he was happy to get the chance to get himself into a better place.'

When Packer eventually returned to America in March to be reunited with his fiancée, he still had wedding bells on his mind. But Stokes had quietly ensured the moment had passed. 'James was still reasonably intent on marrying her [after Israel]. But the boat had been moved, the occasion had been cancelled, circumstances had changed. To restart it all was not easy. During that process it [the wedding] all fell apart,' Stokes says. 'In retrospect that was good for James. James's welfare was paramount. He needed care at that stage.' Stokes stresses he had nothing against Carey. In fact, he liked her and enjoyed her company. 'I saw Mariah and James together. The times they were together, they seemed truly happy with one another. I just thought it had moved too quickly for James and he was being railroaded. I was more concerned about the influence of her agent, Stella,' he says.

The cancellation of the wedding didn't stop the Packer and Carey entourage returning to the Mediterranean for the northern summer of 2016 to party. In early July they were back on Capri, the spot where they had been first photographed together a year earlier. There they again boarded David Geffen's luxury yacht to celebrate American Independence Day on 4 July. Photographer Jamie Fawcett, who was in the Mediterranean celebrity-spotting at the time, recalls Carey in full flight on that day. 'There was a big party there. David Geffen's yacht was there. She wore this amazing red fish-tailed dress. She wanted to be the centre of attention. There were buckets of people on that yacht that I didn't recognise: billionaires, squillionaires, barons and whatever else,' he recalls. '[Earlier in the day, Mariah] was on the back of the deck working out to her own music playing on the screen. She loved it and wanted to be the centre of attention. I sold that photo several hundred times.' That evening Carey put on Instagram a photo of herself clad in a slinky, cleavage-baring crimson gown with a glass of red wine in hand, next to a grinning but weary-looking Packer.

Jamie Fawcett says he could see the chemistry between Packer and Carey through his camera lens during the weeks he spent in the Mediterranean that year. On the evening of 24 July they were photographed in an intimate embrace on the dance floor at a Capri nightclub. 'To me it looked like there was some genuine affection and that he was besotted by her,' Fawcett says. But as a member of the paparazzi who had watched hundreds of celebrity couples at close quarters, Fawcett could also sense all was not well. 'She also came with Stella Bulochnikov, the friends and the entourage,' he says, before recalling the moment he got a more direct sense of Packer's frustrations at the time. 'When James was ready to go ashore [from the *Arctic P*] they would get the tender boat ready to go. Usually you might be waiting for a few minutes, you'd get on and off you'd go. Mariah would keep them waiting there. They would be holding the ropes in the rough seas for half an hour. And sometimes she would be in the tender and wouldn't get off,' he says. 'I had this very impromptu discussion with James on the Isle of Capri one night when he was kept waiting. He seemed a bit embarrassed about the whole thing because everyone was waiting around.'

Doyen of the private equity industry and Packer's friend Guy Hands – who spent some time with Packer and Carey in the Mediterranean in the summer of 2016 – also recalls the 'extraordinary' entourage Carey carried with her. Like Jamie Fawcett and Kerry Stokes, he could see the chemistry between the couple, but Hands feared that Mariah's world was never a good fit for his friend. Like Stokes, Hands stresses he has nothing against Carey. He describes her as an 'extraordinarily powerful and charismatic woman. James is incredibly intelligent, emotional and a very generous human being. It was a bit like a moth and flame, and I wasn't sure which was which. They attracted each other and it was painful for both of them. When I saw them together, they seemed very happy together. I mean this in the nicest possible way: Mariah is a professional performer; James isn't. James wears everything on his sleeve. I don't think he could pretend if he tried. That always worried me – that was her job, to perform. Were they both reading the same things in each other?'

Another friend who spent time with them agrees that they clearly cared about each other, even if, as was widely reported, they never slept together. 'Their moments were surprisingly normal,' the friend says.

But Carey was also clearly doing it tough. When it was released in late 2016, her reality show *Mariah's World* aired an intimate conversation she appears to have had with Bulochnikov about Packer in the second half of that year, in which Carey laments not being able to spend quality time with her fiancé. 'I don't know how we're gonna be able to put this together because we keep pushing things and we'll be upset,' she tells Bulochnikov, who goes on to question why Packer 'shows up for five minutes and then he goes'.

'Everybody has their own thing, I mean, and he's busy, and it's just like I just wish I had more time to give him. Like, more quality time to be with him, but I really don't have that right now. This is a very demanding schedule,' Carey says.

'James has so many responsibilities, it's not really easy for us to spend time together. I feel like life is really about balance and I'm not – I've never been – like a good juggler and, like, I really wouldn't be good on that tightrope: yet that's what I walk every day. I don't know, it's making my stomach hurt to think about it.'

*

PACKER AND CAREY WERE last photographed together on the island of Mykonos in Greece in late September 2016.

'We were there between the 15th and the 20th of September. Mariah is there and I'm not drinking. I'm still on the very strong medication [he was put on in Israel] and I'm the worst company in the world,' Packer says. 'She's the opposite. [But] Said with respect, she's understandably strung out and stressed out about her own things. It is not as though she hasn't got a lot of pressure and a lot on her mind … It's not a good trip. I see the pilot video of *Mariah's World*. I have to go to the next Melco board meeting in Macau and agree with her to meet in Naples.'

Packer and the *Arctic P* featured prominently in the rough cut of the show's first episode, which was set to debut on the E! entertainment pay-TV channel in America on 4 December. It was 'Lifestyles of the Rich and Famous'.

'And whether James was in it specifically or not, it became apparent to him that it was going to be a billionaire husband/ boyfriend thing and that was going to be a significant thematic,' says one friend. 'That was going to be a complete nightmare for him, given his [business] interests in Macau, Israel and RatPac, let alone Crown.'

Despite his dalliance with Carey, Packer wanted to be viewed as a serious global businessman. But the friend stresses that Packer never asked to be edited out of the series, as has been suggested. His lawyer, Guy Jalland, apparently asked for Carey's people to show him the signed consent forms from Packer allowing his image to be used in the series. They never materialised. 'James is not someone to invite cameras into his personal life,' says another friend.

It was widely reported that Greece was the site of their relationship break-up. When news broke a month later of their separation, *People* magazine reported a 'representative' of Carey claiming that the pair's Greece vacation in September had taken a turn for the worse.

But Packer says it happened later. He left the *Arctic P* when it was moored off the Greek island of Corfu on the morning of 26 September, bound for Macau for a regularly scheduled board meeting of Melco Crown Entertainment. The day of the Macau board meeting, Shimon Peres – former president of Israel, who in early August had celebrated his ninety-third birthday with an intimate private dinner at Packer's home at Caesarea – passed away after battling complications from a stroke two weeks earlier. Packer made a flying trip to Tel Aviv for the funeral, where he sat in the second row, before leaving Israel the same day to return to meet Carey on the *Arctic P* that evening when it was docked in Naples.

'I then head back to the boat, Mariah and I break up and Mariah gets off the boat,' is all Packer will say of the break-up. On the evening of 1 October 2016 Carey and her entourage – including her children – left the *Arctic P* in Naples to fly to Los Angeles.

His friends say Packer took full responsibility for the split. 'James felt he needed to cut the cord,' says one. 'He just felt like they seemed like different people compared to when they first met.'

It has been speculated Packer spent a multimillion-dollar sum on Carey in eight months, including a US$4 million engagement ring. Packer himself will not confirm any numbers, but Carey's camp has denied the spending was one of the reasons for their split.

Since Packer and Carey had never formally settled on a prenuptial agreement, after the break-up, the advisers of both sides quietly worked towards finalising a settlement centred on a sum of around US$5 million. That was thrown out the window when *Woman's Day* magazine in Australia broke the news of the break-up on the morning of 28 October. Suddenly, Carey's camp was reportedly demanding US$50 million, believing Packer's side had leaked the story. They also wanted to see her compensated for moving her family in early 2016 to Calabasas in California to be with Packer in an 1700–square-metre house they rented for US$250,000 a month, because Packer had insisted on remaining based in Los Angeles to be close to his children, who lived across town with their mother, Erica.

Things then got nasty. TMZ reported that Carey's people claimed Packer had done 'something really bad' involving an unnamed assistant to Carey, which a Packer spokesperson vehemently denied. Other gossip websites gave Packer the movie moniker 'Shrek' after the animated ogre character voiced by Mike Myers (critics had apparently given Packer the label earlier in his life). They claimed Packer used his casino connections to get Carey's former back-up dancer Bryan Tanaka – whom she dated after the split from Packer – banned from Caesars Palace in Las Vegas. Packer says it never happened. TMZ also reported leaks of emails exchanged between Packer and Carey where he referred to her as 'MCP': Mariah Carey Packer. One he wrote in August 2016, under the subject line 'Will U marry me soon MCP pls -:)))))', said: 'I'm in love with you and can't wait to get married and be together forever.'

When the storm eventually passed, the two sides managed to formalise a settlement reportedly worth around

US$8 million in February 2017. Carey kept her engagement ring, which she then reportedly sold in May 2018 to a Los Angeles jeweller for $2.7 million.

Packer's dalliance with Carey was viewed by many as a foolish phase for him. But as the man himself and his friends have attested, they did enjoy each other's company – even if they both seemed to be living in a fantasy land for the sixteen months they were together.

Jodhi Meares says that for the sake of her ex, she was upset to hear about the break-up. 'James is so smart, and he sees the good in people, especially if he loves you. Or he will make excuses even if he sees something not quite right. He has such a great EQ [emotional intelligence] and an incredible capacity to understand people.'

Brett Ratner reckons Carey, with whom he remains friends, would be disappointed. But he claims he has not spoken to her about Packer – and he won't. 'I think he was good to her. I don't think she can complain. I mean a man's got pride, a woman's got pride. I think it's hurtful, it's a public thing. It was such a public thing when they broke up,' he says.

Packer's good friend Arki Busson says in the beginning he felt a real romance was possible. 'I thought the entourage surrounding her was quite surreal. If there was any chance of something real happening, the entourage was incredibly toxic. I don't think they ever really had a chance because the entourage turned it into a business deal,' he says. 'He was coming off a difficult time from the break-up with Erica. Having gone through that myself, I think you are always trying to find something or re-create something. To bring back what you lost. He wasn't able to find that. In the end I am glad he came back to his senses in that he regained control of the situation.'

Stella Bulochnikov and Carey have since parted ways and the former has sued the latter, accusing her of sexual harassment and of having a substance abuse problem. Bulochnikov is reportedly seeking damages and interest, also alleging that she is owed money because she was fired by Carey in the middle of a three-year contract. Carey is vigorously defending the action, claiming Bulochnikov was terminated due to her failure to perform her job effectively. However, Bulochnikov and Packer have apparently made peace since his split with Carey.

By contrast, Packer and Carey have not spoken since the day they last saw each other on the *Arctic P* in Naples more than two years ago. They apparently have no plans to.

When asked about Packer's whereabouts in early 2017, Carey replied pointedly: 'I don't know where the motherfucker is.'

By March this year her attitude had apparently softened. That month she revealed in an interview with *People* magazine that she had been diagnosed with bipolar disorder in 2001, a condition associated with episodes of mood swings ranging from depressive lows to manic highs. In that interview, the little she said of Packer indicated that time might healing her wounds. When asked why she had been engaged to a billionaire like Packer, she replied: 'I wonder what I was thinking as well. The whole situation was a whirlwind. But I definitely wish him the best.'

FIFTEEN

Crown of Thorns

THE HAVANA RESTAURANT LA Guarida is a Cuban gastronomic institution. The communist nation's only Oscar-nominated movie, *Fresa y chocolate* (*Strawberry and Chocolate*), was filmed there in 1993. When Hollywood great Robert De Niro made a flying two-day visit to Cuba at the end of May 2016, he dined there three times, so significant was La Guarida to him. With him then were two companions – James Packer and his best friend Ben Tilley. De Niro and Packer had been regular visitors together to the Caribbean and the tranquil island of Barbuda, once Princess Diana's favourite hideaway, which they had been – and still are – considering as a site for a luxury holiday resort. But this time they were holidaying much closer to De Niro's American homeland.

In Havana on the morning of 26 May, they visited the famed Galería Habana, the city's leading showcase for star Cuban artists. There Packer had an experience he will never forget. It left him in tears. 'Whilst in Cuba I saw this piece of art and it affected me very deeply,' Packer now says of Iván

Capote's work titled 'Mantra occidental' (Western Mantra), a simple metallic sculpture made up of three letters, O, W and N. Protruding from the letters, like daggers in flesh, were fourteen incense sticks. Packer saw them as arrows.

But he saw more than the artist intended, especially as the font of the letters was identical to that used in the logo of his company. 'Through my eyes I saw two things and there are two questions I asked. I saw the Crown brand that I had worked so hard to build. But the C and the R were missing. To me they were missing because I didn't fully own Crown. I mean by that the C and the R were owned by the debt holders, my leverage in both CPH and Crown, and the rest of the OWN was mine,' he says. 'The arrows were the pain Crown has caused me. And this was before the [China] arrests. It was true then and became even more true as the year unfolded. Then OWN. It hit me like a sledgehammer. Do I own Crown or does Crown own me? I went outside and started crying.'

Through the tears Packer quickly came to a frightening realisation. 'Crown owned me,' he says. 'I still had close to a billion and a half of debt at CPH and was cash-flow negative, and I was running out of assets to sell. All I wanted was to own my business, not be owned by my business. I wanted the pressure to ease. I had tried so hard. It was too much for me.'

*

IN THOSE HORRIBLE MOMENTS James Packer might also have reflected upon what he has since termed the 'wild' two and a half years he spent away from Australia's shores, splitting his life between America, Israel and his private jet. It was a period when he turned his back on the country of his birth in a quest to prove to himself and his critics that he could become a truly international businessman, after telling his second wife, Erica, in 2013 how much he wanted to leave Sydney, scared of its spotlight, pained by its judgement. By January 2014 he had risen to such prominence that he was on the cover of *Forbes* magazine in Asia, his dream to build a casino in Sydney had finally become a reality and the share price of his casino joint venture in Macau had hit a record. He had graduated to the inner circle of friends surrounding the controversial Israeli prime minister Benjamin Netanyahu, his Hollywood RatPac business was in full swing and he was dating a supermodel in Miranda Kerr. It was a world with seemingly no boundaries.

Former Nine Network CEO Eddie McGuire reckons his friend even had his eye on heredity as he pursued his global dreams. 'When Kerry had his big heart attack on the horse, I think he was around fifty. And I reckon James almost had one eye to the clock,' McGuire now says of the time. 'He set himself huge time frames to achieve massive things. I think he was enormously proud of his father and everything that his father and grandfather and great-grandfather had done in Australia. But he wanted very much to have a go internationally.'

But other friends were worried. One who decided to make his concerns known was Seek co-founder Paul Bassat. 'I spent a few days with him in Aspen in December 2013. Life was exhilarating for him; his close friendship with Bibi [Netanyahu] and RatPac were new and exciting. Brett Ratner was staying at Aspen at the time, and he was a charismatic guy who clearly operated at a pretty frenetic pace,' Bassat recalls. 'James told me that the people who had been the closest people in his life, like Erica, David Gyngell and Matthew Grounds, thought that things were going off the rails for him. He clearly rejected their perspective and felt they didn't "get it". There were a lot of things that I didn't have visibility on, but it was clear their concerns were well placed. I didn't feel there was much chance he would listen to me, given he wouldn't listen to the most important people in his life, but felt I should tell him what I thought.'

Bassat's key piece of advice was that everyone had a speed limit and that Packer needed to be careful not to exceed his, even if his dial was calibrated differently from most. 'His speed limit was not necessarily the same as Arnon Milchan's – who I hadn't met at that point – or Brett [Ratner]'s. He replied forcefully: "You don't understand, PB. You don't walk in my shoes." I told him he was right but that what I (and others) had was a degree of perspective and objectivity that he was lacking. He rejected my views out of hand. I assumed that the whole conversation had pretty much washed over James, but he subsequently brought it up with me a few times over the next year or two.'

Indeed, Packer now acknowledges Bassat has, at times, told him things 'that I might not have wanted to hear. But [he has] done so in a way that was constructive and kind. I have felt, rightly or wrongly, in dealing with a lot of people – especially in Australia – that there was a degree of competition in relationships. I have never felt that tension with Paul.'

Another friend describes being 'pretty outspoken' with Packer at the time he was in Hollywood as to what he thought he was doing 'right and wrong. In most cases, if you are telling him something he doesn't want to hear, it is one of two reactions that I personally saw. One was an acknowledgment and a changing of the subject. And the other was ignoring it. I never got into an argument with James. But I have seen him in heated arguments with other people.'

By May 2014 Packer's best mate in Australia, David Gyngell, had become so annoyed with his friend's wild ways that he infamously decided to try to 'knock his block off' outside Packer's own house in Bondi.

After that incident, Packer became even more agitated about being in Sydney. When he appeared at the Dally M rugby league best and fairest awards at The Star at the end of September 2014, he was on a short fuse. He'd flown in from Los Angeles after a long lunch with Leonardo DiCaprio at the invitation of his good friend Russell Crowe, who was doing the Dally M medal countdown for the second year running. Crown was the main jersey sponsor of the South Sydney Rabbitohs, partly owned by Crowe.

When Packer sat down at the head table next to Treasurer Joe Hockey, he ordered several vodka, lime and sodas in quick succession, at one stage complaining to the waiter that the service was too slow. Under the table his legs were often shaking, seemingly uncontrollably. When league star Jarryd Hayne was being interviewed on stage, Packer ignored the proceedings and instead held his own loud conversation at the table with then *Daily Telegraph* editor Paul Whittaker. It prompted then ARL Commision chairman John Grant to interject, asking Packer to be quiet, prompting a visibly agitated Packer to abuse him before he left the table and went outside for a cigarette.

When he returned he apologised to Grant and did the same in a phone call to him the next morning, but the incident alarmed others on the table, including then NRL CEO Dave Smith and his wife Emma and News Corp CEO Julian Clarke.

Fast-forward to Easter 2015, and suddenly Packer's life had become a mess again: Miranda Kerr was gone, he was fighting with his sister over the family fortune, and the share prices of his key investments were falling.

Then he fell in love with a celebrity pop singer in Mariah Carey. It opened the door to a lifestyle that was the absolute antithesis of the private world he had so long coveted. The critics were again out in force.

By the end of 2016, Carey was gone, Packer's staff were under arrest in China and the recurring nightmare that had repeatedly haunted him – that he was going broke – had returned. Packer's mood plumbed new depths. He was tearing himself apart.

Those who had seen this before were sympathetic. 'James is a human being; he is entitled to have a human experience and go through things,' says his first wife, Jodhi Meares, who walked out on their marriage after Packer's first nervous breakdown following the collapse of One.Tel. 'There is all this judgement on his human experience being wrong. It is ridiculous. You have to be able to experience your life. It is absurd the amount of judgement made on him,' she says. But she also has an important piece of advice for her ex. 'I would like to see James be less hurt by his experiences. He should focus more on the amount of good he does and what an incredible person he is.'

Eddie McGuire agrees that Packer focusses too much on the negatives. 'I've seen the pressure on James from media. I've seen the enormous pressure he puts on himself. I see a guy who is genuinely brilliant and wants to go to the next level, [to show] that he was prepared to take on the world,' he says. 'I think James is too hard on himself. I think he holds on to the mistakes along the journey as opposed to celebrating the victories. I think he sees the victories as something that should happen because he is so smart in his tactics. I think he sometimes beats himself up too much on his Packer legacy and therefore he completely beats himself up when something doesn't quite happen right.'

*

THERE IS A TRUTH about Packer that so many close to him had wondered and worried about. But it was a truth about which they dared not speak for fear of how he might react. Or what it might trigger. They saw it most during his attacks of debt phobia, when assets and investments — some of which were visionary and hard-earned — were unemotionally discarded in dashes for cash. They saw it in his mood swings, from manic highs to the lowest of lows, and in the different James Packers who would confront them, depending upon the time of day — one was smart, charming and generous; the other angry, depressed and foul-mouthed. This changeable personality made them wonder about his mental condition. At the end of 2015, as Packer sat on his favourite cream couch in the living room of his Ellerstina polo ranch in Argentina, it was the latter persona who was firing off searing emails to his closest advisers and friends, screaming: 'How the fuck do I now have $4 billion of debt??? We all said never again, never again!'

Packer now seeks to explain the time. Such is his grasp of numbers, he reels them off as though it were yesterday. 'In late 2015 and early 2016 I was suffering from severe mood swings, feeling very depressed and extremely nervous,' he says. '2015 had been a bad year, where I'd had to deal with a falling Crown share price, a falling Zillow share price, the framework arrangement with Gretel, and then the second Gretel deal, which took a lot longer and was a lot more difficult than it should have been. Towards the close of that year, when CPH's net debt was approximately $2.2 billion, I felt under the most enormous pressure and stress. Crown additionally had approximately $3 billion in net debt and had the commitment to build Crown Sydney, which was budgeted to cost over $2 billion. In addition, there was Vegas and the Queensbridge project in Melbourne, both of which were multibillion-dollar projects.'

Packer always considered that his share of Crown's net debt needed to be added to that of his private company, CPH, to get to his real and underlying net debt position. 'As I owned 53 per cent of Crown, then it amounted to another $1.6 billion of debt. So $2.2 billion of CPH debt and $1.6 billion of Crown debt meant I considered my underlying net debt to be $3.8 billion. I had been at Ellerstina and had been working out hard. That was the last time I had a six-pack.

'The thing that upset me most was that some of my creditors had insisted on getting personal guarantees from me on my debts to them. My chief executive at the time, Robert Rankin, and my advisers should have never let me agree to that.' (Although Rankin only joined CPH in April 2015, after the guarantees had been included in the first Gretel deal. The problem in James's mind was that Rankin then failed to have them removed.) 'It meant that if the world collapsed completely I wouldn't even own a house. I wouldn't have a million dollars. I would have nothing. I had no safety net. When I looked around at the people who worked for me or advised me, none of them had a situation like that in their own lives. I felt unnecessarily exposed and I just hated it. I hated it with all my being and it consumed me.'

Other manic emails on topics like Australia's foreign policy or the nation becoming a republic went to a wider circle, including Prime Minister Malcolm Turnbull. In March 2018 *The Sydney Morning Herald* reported that Packer had 'fired off the emails to the Prime Minister with an intensity that prompted worries about his health at a time when he was under pressure in his personal and professional life. The Prime Minister responded to the emails with a quick decision to speak to Mr Packer over the phone to find out what was worrying him.'

In his personal life, Mariah Carey and her entourage were pressuring Packer for the couple to get married. In January 2016 Packer proposed to Carey and the wedding date was set for 1 March. 'Mariah wanted to get married in March, which was a stress as well,' Packer now recalls.

But by mid February, money and debt were again front of mind for Packer when Crown received a $362 million bill from the Australian Taxation Office, relating to the tax treatment of some of the financing for Crown's investment in Cannery Casino Resorts in the US and other investments in North America. It was a brutal blow and it pushed Packer over the edge.

At the insistence of Kerry Stokes, he flew to Israel to visit a mental health facility. 'There, I was diagnosed with a mental health illness,' Packer now recalls. He was manic and paranoid, plagued by unpredictable mood swings and an inability to manage stress. He was put on powerful medication to help his condition. 'It was really strong. I can't describe the feeling it gave me but six to eight months later, it was so powerful I could barely function.' In Israel he was also diagnosed – utterly unbeknown to him, because he had experienced no symptoms – as having had two mini-strokes during 2015. 'I was in Israel for three weeks [after Kerry Stokes had sent him there],' he says. 'I ended up spending a lot of time there in 2016 and was sober the whole time. I had my house [in Israel] at that stage and was very comfortable there.'

Former US ambassador to Australia Jeff Bleich, who was then based in America, was on the phone to Packer regularly. 'Jeff Bleich was a great comfort to me and friend. He would check in often and was always supportive, caring and the best friend you could hope for. We disagree on politics but agree on life. He was there for me when I needed someone to hold my hand,' Packer says.

Bleich won't go into detail about the time, and notes he never actually visited Packer in Israel, but says he spoke to him often. 'What I tried to talk to him about was issues relating to perspective. What really matters in life: family, friendships, your health. You can worry as much about a $50 problem as a $50 billion problem,' Bleich says. 'I guess I'm lucky in that I have had the ability to step back and appreciate the benefits of having a profile and high-tempo jobs, like at the White House, but also being lucky enough to have a quiet and relatively anonymous life. Especially compared to James. If you have always lived in a fishbowl, it is easy to lose perspective about the things that matter.'

In March 2016, Packer returned from Israel to Los Angeles where a worried Carey was waiting. 'Everyone was very worried about me because of the two strokes. But I had an MRI and they found that I hadn't even had one stroke, so that was a relief,' he recalls.

Crown then sold its first tranche of shares in Melco Crown, cutting its debt from $3 billion to $2 billion. 'At that point CPH's debt had gone down from $2.2 billion to $1.55 billion due to CPH paying, distributing and eliminating liabilities. So we've made a good start,' he says. Then in August CPH sold a tranche of Crown shares, cutting its debt to around $1.2 billion from $1.6 billion. 'So our actions in 2016 were in line with the words that Rob [Rankin], Guy [Jalland] and I had agreed at the end of 2015. We were doing what we said. We were getting the debt down, getting the debt down, getting the debt down,' Packer says.

In early September, after spending more time on the *Arctic P* in the Mediterranean with Carey, David Geffen and other friends, Packer returned to Los Angeles. He remembers being invited to a surprise birthday party for Lachlan Murdoch at Murdoch's house in Brentwood. 'I went with Arnon [Milchan]. Arnon and I were meant to have a drink afterwards. I say this with huge love and I do have huge love for him, but Arnon would always be the first person to encourage me to start drinking again if I'd been off it. I was incredibly depressed and almost unable to function properly because of the medication.

I left the party after an hour and said to Arnon, "I just can't do it." And I went back to [Warren Beatty's guest] house on my own.'

Later in the month Packer flew to New York to visit his American doctor, one of the world's leading experts in the neurobiology and treatment of mood and anxiety disorders. There he was again diagnosed as suffering from a mental illness. He received a similar diagnosis in Los Angeles a month later, from the doctor recommended by Warren Beatty, and then from a third doctor in Argentina in November.

It has been suggested Packer suffers from bipolar syndrome, the same condition afflicting Mariah Carey. Packer won't use the same words to describe his condition. 'I have wrestled with mental health issues at times in my life – depression and anxiety – especially in times of extreme stress,' he says. 'I have big mood swings.'

'This is the third time I've been in a really bad spot. The first two times were really bad, really bad. It's not like I was imagining it,' he says. 'I'll never be an international businessman again. I just won't be. My chance was in the casino business and I got close. I got close. And what happened in China wasn't my fault. I wasn't on the board of Crown. Something went wrong somewhere. And it was devastating for the people involved.'

By the end of October 2016, he now acknowledges for the first time, he was 'having a complete nervous breakdown. And you know, I'm still not right,' he says.

*

PACKER'S LONG AND WINDING road of battling his mental demons reached a decisive point in March 2018. In the early hours of 21 March in Australia, a short and abrupt email from Packer landed in the inboxes of Crown chairman John Alexander and CPH executives Guy Jalland and Mark Arbib. He told them he would be resigning from the Crown board, effective immediately, because he was suffering from 'mental health issues'.

Jalland, who had been face to face with Packer at the exclusive One & Only resort at Cabo San Lucas in Mexico in the previous forty-eight hours, had been terrified as he watched the deterioration in Packer's condition. That afternoon in Mexico he double-checked with his boss in person that he really wanted to drop such a bombshell publicly. But Packer was adamant.

When Arbib woke up in Sydney, he and Jalland got to work on finalising the form of words to go public from CPH. The statement was then sent to Alexander, who forwarded it to Crown company secretary Mary Manos and other Crown senior executives. They formulated a short response. On the stroke of 9am, Crown released a statement to the ASX saying Packer had resigned from the board for personal reasons. With it was the statement from CPH: 'Mr James Packer today resigned from the Board of Crown Resorts Ltd for personal reasons. Mr Packer is suffering from mental health issues. At this time he intends to step back from all commitments.'

No one at Crown or CPH had any warning of Packer's move. Packer had complained of feeling unwell to those who had communicated with him in the days beforehand, but none knew of the panic attack he had experienced, leaving him feeling completely paranoid and his thoughts totally scattered.

'I have been sober during 2018. In March this year I was experiencing major panic attacks and felt extremely depressed and paranoid. It was scary, very scary – especially as I was sober and thought I had been improving. It is very hard to come to any other conclusion than my problems and condition were not getting better; it felt like they were getting worse. I was desperately worried. That is why I got off the Crown board and why I said what I said publicly,' Packer now says. 'I feel fine now. There are a lot of moments where I regret getting off the Crown board, because I think I am fine. But I have crossed that bridge and I know I can't keep jumping on and off the board. Maybe I still have one more run left in me.'

Paradoxically, Packer had seemed to be in good spirits when I visited him two weeks earlier in Mexico for a series of interviews for this book. The day I arrived in Cabo he had been out on the water with his children, even posing for a photograph with them. That night he took them to dinner at the trendy Flora Farms restaurant in the foothills of the Sierra de la Laguna Mountains. The largely outdoor restaurant, which in 2014 hosted the wedding of pop singer Adam Levine of band Maroon 5 and celebrity model Behati Prinsloo, pioneered the farm-to-table dining scene in Cabo. When Packer's children left the next day to return to their home in Los Angeles on his private jet, his eldest daughter, Indigo, was FaceTiming her father on her iPhone even before they arrived at the airport, clearly already missing him.

When Packer and I talked in Cabo, I also realised how much interviews for this book were taking out of him. He told me as much. Reviewing the darkest parts of his past had been a deeply emotional and painful experience. The interviews with him in Mexico were hard work for both of us, as they had been in January when I met him in Aspen.

And there was an additional stress in Cabo. There Packer was on edge as he publicly sacked his good friend, the UBS banker Matthew Grounds, a move that was documented in detail in the pages of the 'Rear Window' column in *The Australian Financial Review*. The short-lived falling-out with

Grounds came at the same time Crown revealed it was being investigated by the Victorian gambling regulator for alleged tampering with poker machines at its Melbourne casino, which was another added stress for Packer.

On 15 March, Packer also decided to spend his first night in Los Angeles since October 2016 after lunching earlier in the day with Warren Beatty. He stayed at the Peninsula hotel after visiting his children and their mother, Erica. It was an exciting but stressful event given the bad memories of his turbocharged life in Hollywood and the failed romance with Carey. An additional source of stress was the Easter travel plans for Erica and the children, who were heading to Australia, the country he had grown to fear.

I had a clue something was amiss in a series of emails I exchanged with Packer on 18 and 19 March. In one he told me, 'I've had very little sleep these last few days and am feeling unwell.' After that our communication ceased for several weeks.

*

AFTER GOING PUBLIC ABOUT his illness, Packer immediately checked himself into the exclusive Boston mental health facility at the McLean Hospital, called the Pavilion. It is renowned as one of the top psychiatric hospitals in the US, with a list of patients including Nobel Prize–winning mathematician John Nash – whose struggle with mental illness was depicted in the film *A Beautiful Mind* – and best-selling, five-time Grammy-awarded music artist James Taylor. Packer's mother, Ros, and new girlfriend Kylie Lim visited him there.

The good news for Packer from his fortnight of treatment at McLean was that the doctors believed that the mental condition from which he has been suffering was both treatable and manageable. Their opinion was that, provided he was serious about his recovery, he could live a completely normal life in the future.

'I was only in the Boston clinic for two weeks. As soon as I got there, I felt fine again. They put me on new medication straight away. And now I'm feeling okay,' Packer says. But he says he is still on more prescription drugs than he would like. 'For me it is an introduction to the American medical system. I feel very dulled, very dulled. I have an appointment with a psychiatrist once a week that I do over FaceTime. Changing my medications is something that my doctors take very seriously. I am not sure I really see a light at the end of the tunnel in terms of getting off the medications I am on. Which sort of reminds me why health is 18 per cent of the US GDP. You get caught on the treadmill,' he says.

Lifeline Australia chairman and former NSW Liberal leader John Brogden, who once tried to take his own life after battling severe depression, was one of the first to support Packer's move to go public about his illness. Brogden recounted an occasion when Packer had told him he wanted to support Lifeline and suicide prevention because of his own experience with mental health issues.

The reactions of Packer's friends to his public revelation were mixed. Some were completely taken aback. His former Macau casino business partner Lawrence Ho says, 'I was very surprised. I never thought he had mental health issues, ever. I sent him an email right away. He replied. My wife and I are very fond of James and also Erica. I felt sad if anything. I felt really sad. A friend and brother that all these years was struggling and I never knew it. I just knew him as being very passionate. I didn't know there was more behind it.'

Some were worried it could mean his business will more likely be in the control of others in the future.

But his ex-wife and the mother of his children, Erica, says she felt nothing but pride for her ex-husband's decision. 'I feel very grateful that we live in a time where mental health issues are no longer stigmatised and that, whoever you are, it's okay to stick your hand in the air and say, "I'm not doing so great … I need help,"' she says. 'I'm proud of James, and that he put his hand up.' She recalls a sketch she saw on Twitter from British artist Charlie Mackesy to mark Mental Health Awareness Week in the UK in May 2018. It depicts a boy asking the horse he is riding: 'What is the bravest thing you've ever said?' The horse replies: 'Help.'

Packer's first wife, Jodhi Meares, also supported his decision to go public about his private battles. Unlike some, she is not concerned about her former husband being stigmatised by revealing his mental problems. 'I don't have a strong view on this, other than to say I just hope James does what he needs to feel okay in the world. And to find some joy and some peace. Peace is the highest happiness. Who wants joy? We just want peace. That is what he needs and deserves. And I think he is making his way there,' she says. 'I think he will come back, 100 per cent he will. This does not represent James not coming back. This is part of him coming back; he has a lot of stuff to work through, because he has had such a complicated life.'

Packer's good friend and broadcaster Alan Jones says he was relieved. 'I've had people [in] far worse [shape] than James and I've had people take their own life. And there are other very successful people, and you would know who they are if I mention their names, they've recovered in private,' Jones says. 'To actually admit that took a lot of courage, to resign from Crown took a lot of courage. It was very, very public. I'm not too sure that it was even necessary. It's part of his demeanour, also, of being a bit of a panickster. He could have continued on the board of Crown. At the end of the day there are some simple things that have to be done. Self-esteem is the thing with him. His size, his weight is a factor that affects his self-esteem.'

Another friend, private-equity guru Guy Hands, says he is not a fan of ascribing mental health 'labels' to people. 'I think every great person is on a spectrum. What makes you successful can also destroy you. [But] I think what James has done is be very honest about his emotions and how he feels. Whether it is a turning point or not depends upon how much space he is given … I think it is more about whether the world, and particularly Australia, will give James some space or not,' he says. 'He tried in recent years to erect a bubble around himself, to almost try to escape from it. Now he has said, "I am going to be honest and tell the world it does hurt. And please let me get on with my life." The world wants these honest, colourful people but they don't tend to treat them very well.'

Alan Jones says there will be one strange but significant challenge for Packer over the next period: boredom. Packer has said he intends to simply 'take it easy' before the opening of Crown Sydney, which is still three years away. 'That is one of the problems with the current set-up. In a way, the projects are in place so there are no battles. He needs battles. He needs something to fight for,' Jones says, before adding that he thinks Packer needs a full-time job and should continue his rehabilitation in Australia. 'To be comfortable, to know that not all the media are ready to tear you apart, that there are a lot of good friends in the public place here who would support him.' Jones has told Packer as much. He and Lloyd Williams once called Packer from Williams's farm near Macedon outside Melbourne, urging him to come home to his real friends and family.

Eddie McGuire agrees with Jones that despite what Packer thinks, he has no shortage of friends back in his homeland. 'I can tell him that "There's a lot of people who actually love you. Who genuinely think you're a good bloke. Not looking for a ride on the *Arctic P.* Not wanting to join you in Argentina or any of those places. Who actually just think you're a great bloke,"' he says.

But Crown director Harold Mitchell sees it as a positive if Packer sits still for a period, especially after a tumultuous five years. 'I once said to James at the end of 2017, sometimes when there is nothing to do, do nothing,' Mitchell says. 'And business can be boring. James has battled with that his entire life.'

Lachlan Murdoch says the key priority in the mind of all of James's friends is for him to be happy and healthy. 'His bravery and honesty about confronting mental health is unique and something to be commended. All of his friends want him to succeed in this battle. That is primary above everything else,' he says.

'It shows what an amazing person James is that he has confronted his issues with such honesty and transparency for the whole world to see. That is not something many of us would measure up to. I have been worried about him, of course. There have been darker times in the past when we have had to reach out to help him, which haven't been as public. With mental health, the thing I know is the first step to treatment and therapy is understanding that you have an issue.'

Lachlan has no doubt his friend can come back. 'Yes, 100 per cent. He has a unique brain and he is a beautiful person,' he says. 'He has incredible strengths, he has some weaknesses, but if he can control them he is one of the great businessmen in the world today.'

*

SYDNEY PSYCHOLOGIST JOEL CURTIS told *The Australian Financial Review* in March 2018 that being both wealthy and famous could be a 'double whammy' to heighten feelings of depression. Curtis claimed that while poorer people worried about paying the bills, and middle-class people were trying to get ahead of the bills to pay off the mortgage, the seriously affluent were preoccupied not with what they had done, but how to keep it that way. For decades Packer has found it impossible to talk about his private demons without sounding like a rich whinger, or like he was offering excuses for bad behaviour or for, as his father once called One.Tel, 'fuck-ups'.

But on 20 March 2018, he decided he had to face up to his problems, regardless of how it looked or what people said about him. Mental health issues are viewed by society these days through a different prism from what they once were, even until very recently. James Packer has the good fortune to be living in a time when the kind of confession that he has made is, largely, greeted by feelings of compassion and respect. His genuine friends hope that putting his battle with mental illness on the public record will set him back on the path to happiness. And in the wider community there is a feeling that the honesty of someone of the billionaire's stature about his condition might inspire many others to follow his lead and be upfront about their own challenges.

'I've seen the knock-on effect all around the world, business executives saying, "Shit, James Packer was honest. I am going to be honest too,"' says Packer's spiritual adviser, Thom Knoles. 'On its own it had a worldwide ripple effect of people honestly addressing and publicly dealing with issues they have had. James paved the way for that. I saw it everywhere after that. It was a relief that somebody in James's position can actually speak openly about how he was feeling.'

In Packer's case, it was also a surrender to reality, a surrender to the certainty that without openly and bravely accepting the need to seek help, he faced a bleak and increasingly lonely future. 'Some people handle pressure well and some don't. I don't. I don't know if that is because I am wired that way. Or if it is because bad things have actually happened to me,' Packer says. 'I am tired of being on this roller-coaster. I don't want to do it any more. I'm ready to put my hands up for a few years. I really am.'

Whatever the complexities of his relationship with his father and its contribution to his character, Packer recognised that the most honest thing he could do to honour his father's memory was be brave and confront the truth of his own life. Kerry Packer was a hard man, but he respected guts, and there is no question it took courage for James to go public about his mental health problems.

David Gonski reckons that if Kerry were alive today, he would have nothing but admiration for his son. 'Kerry was not a person who was secretive. He was an incredibly open person. My own view, having watched them over thirty-five years, was that he was very proud of James, which links in to how he structured his will,' Gonski says.

'He would have said publicly that if anyone can beat the demons, James can.'

SIXTEEN

Above and Beyond

O N THE EVENING OF 7 October 2017 at Packer's Argentinian polo ranch Ellerstina, as the silver light of the full moon spilled across the perfectly manicured but now darkened turf of the Field of Dreams, Packer retired to the property's guest house after a barbecue dinner to relax on its expensive cream couches with a few friends. Their gaze was on the giant flat-screen television normally hidden inside the elaborate timber cabinet that dominates the room. Packer's girlfriend, Kylie Lim, was trying out the new virtual-reality headset on display, a fiftieth birthday present to Packer from Warner Bros CEO Kevin Tsujihara.

Packer had declared to his friends for weeks beforehand that he had no intention of leaving Ellerstina for many months after enduring the horrors of the previous two years. He wanted to remain a recluse, hidden from the world, thousands of kilometres from his homeland while he recovered his sanity. He had reaffirmed that intention earlier that day.

But in the back of his mind was an invitation from his good friend Kerry Stokes to attend a gala dinner in Perth later in the month to celebrate the fiftieth anniversary of the Seven Network's annual Western Australian charity fundraiser, known as Telethon. So too was a more pressing engagement, the annual general meeting of Crown Resorts scheduled for 26 October in Melbourne. It was going to be Packer's first annual general meeting since returning to the board in January 2017, yet Crown's staff and board were preparing to explain his absence to the hundreds of shareholders who would attend the meeting.

But as the moon rose over the Field of Dreams that evening, Packer did what has become something of a trademark of his complex life: he unexpectedly changed his mind. As he watched his headset-clad girlfriend cleverly navigate her way through a virtual city on the big screen, he proudly declared to Lim and friends that in two weeks he would make his first trip to his homeland in two years.

The interview he had given to me earlier that day for *The Weekend Australian* magazine – a gruelling and emotional conversation – had clearly been cathartic. Memories he tried hard to forget had come flooding back. And then there was Stokes. 'You always want to be respectful to Kerry,' Packer replies upon reflection when I subsequently ask why he changed his mind that night. He was soon on the phone to Crown chairman John Alexander, arranging to meet him in Perth. There he would spend the week based at the luxurious chairman's villa at Crown Towers, with its stunning views of the Swan River but comfortable distance from the attention of the city centre.

Packer had been to Perth for Telethon on numerous occasions. On his arm in 2011 was his then wife Erica. In 2015, despite their having separated thirteen years earlier, it was his first wife, Jodhi Meares. When he arrived at the Perth Convention and Exhibition Centre on the evening of 21 October 2017, he was on his own. Lim had business to attend to back in her Canadian homeland. Instead, a nervous-looking Packer was trailed only by his best friend and minder, a tuxedo-clad Ben Tilley.

They were confronted by an A-list crowd sipping champagne and nibbling on canapés, including Prime Minister Malcolm Turnbull, WA premier Mark McGowan, finance minister Mathias Cormann, foreign minister Julie Bishop and a host of Perth's corporate elite, among them Packer's good friend and Telethon trustee Tim Roberts, and Wesfarmers chairman Michael Chaney. 'I'd always been unsure of what to think of Michael Chaney. I'd never really meet him but, you know, I'd heard lots of things about him. Mostly good. Chaney and I had a conversation before dinner and he went out of his way to be charming, humble, generous and kind to me. And it really quite affected me. I hadn't been in Australia for two years,' Packer now recalls.

Dressed in a black tuxedo and sporting a fuller figure since his sixteen-month relationship with Mariah Carey had ended, Packer soon made a beeline for the evening's host, Kerry Stokes. Their reunion in Perth was deeply symbolic, the culmination of an, until now, untold personal journey over the previous two years through the ski fields of Colorado, the azure waters of the Mediterranean and the bustling freeways of Los Angeles and Tel Aviv.

So long the enemy of the Packers and the Murdochs, Stokes had bullied his way into their pay-TV companies in 2009 after a decade of hostilities, before exiting with a handsome cheque when he sold into the Murdoch's $2 billion takeover offer for the Packer-controlled CMH. Packer will never forget how his relationship with Stokes changed after he struck a truce over CMH and welcomed his long-time adversary into the tent.

They developed a remarkable friendship, which associates say ultimately helped Packer stay sane – and even, during his darkest moments, alive – during 2016, as it was Stokes who had sent Packer to Israel to get treatment for his mental health condition and had helped cancel his wedding to Mariah Carey after taking over Packer's personal affairs. Where Stokes went was far beyond the call of duty of a friend.

*

AFTER A WEEK SPENT enjoying the hospitality of Crown Perth, Packer had his first meeting with Stokes on the evening of 20 October, the night before the Telethon event, during a private cocktail party at the swish West Perth offices of Stokes's private company Australian Capital Equity. 'Kerry took me aside and said, "You're on my table tomorrow night." I wasn't expecting to be on the head table. I felt as though Kerry was being very protective and a great friend,' Packer now recalls.

Earlier in the week Packer had reconnected with a few other friends, including former federal treasurer Peter Costello – who by chance was staying at Crown that week – and former Victorian premier and director of Stokes's Seven West Media, Jeff Kennett. 'I spent an hour with both of them and it couldn't have been nicer. Both instances. It made me so happy to see them both,' Packer says. 'Jeff has been very good to me personally when I've been low.'

Asked about his meeting with Packer, Costello now says: 'I thought he was good. This was the first time he had been back to Australia for some time. We had a lovely chat.' For the first time Costello got a first-hand sense of what Packer had been going through for the previous eighteen months, which ultimately led to his decision to go public about his mental health battles five months later in March 2018. 'I thought it was a very brave thing for him to come out and say what he did,' Costello says. 'I believe that's part of the healing and I just hope this enables him to come to grips and get a good recovery. As I understand it, part of getting yourself fixed up is acknowledging the problems.'

Kennett, a former chair of health advocacy organisation beyondblue, says he was not surprised about Packer's honesty. 'In one sense he is a very innocent soul. So it didn't surprise me at all. He never held back from those around him how he felt. He has always been terribly open,' he says. 'If you break your arm, everyone is sympathetic. If you have a mental illness, it is different. But things are changing. If you come out, especially if you are a high-profile person, there is a lot of sympathy because so much of the public have been in the same boat.'

But few knew as much as Stokes about Packer's private battles with his weight, alcohol and prescription drugs. Stokes knew the true tale of the pressures on Packer's business interests flowing from the billion-dollar settlement with his sister and the arrest of his staff in China. And he knew – more than anyone has ever appreciated – about the fallout from Packer's whirlwind romance with Carey. Stokes says he recognised the importance of inviting his good friend to the Telethon evening to allow him to reconnect with the world again. 'James and Crown have been big contributors to the [Telethon] charity ever since he got involved in Crown Perth. It was a wonderful gesture to me,' Stokes says of Packer's decision to attend. 'He had put on a bit more weight, but he was in very good form. I think he was surprised that he got such a warm reception in Perth. James had an opportunity to meet other people and I know he felt very good about that.'

Stokes had become acutely aware of Packer's resort to many vices when his marriage to Erica fell apart in the second half of 2013. Many times during the six-year marriage, Stokes had invited the couple to his lavish ski lodge at Beaver Creek, a two-hour drive from Aspen. When he was staying with Stokes, Packer would often fly his jet into Eagle County Regional Airport in Colorado and park it next to the one owned by Stokes before taking a chauffeur-driven, half-hour car trip to Beaver Creek. 'Where I'm most grateful to Kerry is the way he helped both Erica and me through my marriage breakdown. And the way that he helped me at the end of 2015,' Packer says slowly, before a long pause to light another cigarette. 'At the time I was doing the separation with Gretel. I needed good friends.'

The public got a rare glimpse of the emotional connection between Packer and Stokes when photographs were published of them in a long embrace on the lower deck of the *Arctic P* as it cruised the waters of the Mediterranean at the end of June 2015. On the deck above was Mariah Carey. It was only days after her blossoming romance to Packer had become public.

'Kerry also helped me on Crown Sydney. Chrissie [Stokes's fourth wife, Christine Simpson] and Kerry spent time with Erica, made her feel welcome. Our marriage had broken up. And Kerry spent time with Erica, gave her support, made her feel as though she was not cut out or excluded,' Packer says. Stokes had done the same for Jodhi Meares, inviting her and Packer to his luxury Broome property in the years they were married. The mansion is set in acres of bushland fronting the world-famous Cable Beach. It features a swimming pool that surrounds a luxury gazebo, a tennis court, separate guest quarters, manicured gardens and a dirt-bike track.

Stokes says he and wife Christine both now enjoy the company of Packer's children. 'We have had them in Broome on a couple of occasions. We were as disappointed as anybody when [James and Erica] split. We thought it was a really good marriage. But when it did happen, we continued to take an interest in Erica and the kids. We tried to help Erica put things in some perspective,' Stokes says. 'When your life gets turned upside down and shattered, it is always difficult to work out what is real and what isn't. In her case, she has always had the children and has always been grounded in the children.' Like Packer, Stokes backs Erica's decision to live in Los Angeles. 'It has kept the kids away from all the publicity they would have otherwise attracted. She has been a wonderful mother. James has been extremely lucky and fortunate she has kept his goodwill with the children to the degree she has. That is a great outcome and not easy,' he says.

Stokes won't go into details, but he acknowledges Erica was deeply hurt by the break-up. 'Of course. [Seeing] James's name associated with any woman … would hurt Erica. Everything was raw and sensitive. But in addition Erica would genuinely love James to find the right person. She would feel very happy if he did. She is worried he will continually attract the wrong person because he is wealthy and vulnerable. It is great for both of them that Erica and the kids are in the position they are in,' he says.

Jeff Kennett is also wary of the types of 'hangers-on' Packer attracts. 'I've always been very aware he has surrounded himself with many advisers, people doing things on his behalf. Because of your position in life, if you are not very careful, you can support an army of people, some of whom are good and very bright but others are indebted to the individual who is their patron,' he says. 'I told him a long time ago that I didn't want to join any of his boards. I never wanted to be indebted to him. I never wanted to prejudice the advice I was giving.'

*

PACKER SAYS THAT DESPITE their past battles, there is one small thing he will never forget about Stokes. 'You know something with Kerry, a little thing that is self-indulgent on my part. I gave Kerry a watch for his seventieth birthday, and Kerry must have fifty watches, and you know sometimes when I have seen Kerry, he's worn the watch,' he says. 'It's a little thing, but it's a really nice thing.'

It has often been written and remarked that Stokes, who turned seventy-eight in 2018, became the father figure James Packer never had. But both men dispute this assessment. 'Kerry would think I'm incredibly lucky to be my father's son,' Packer says. 'People saying Stokes has been a father figure to me misunderstand our relationship. I would describe it differently. I'd say over the past five years I haven't had a better friend.'

Stokes has a similar view. 'No, no,' he chuckles when I ask Stokes if he has filled the shoes of Packer's late father in James's darkest moments. 'I had an interesting relationship with his father that few people understood or knew about. We had quite a close relationship privately. He interviewed both my sons at one stage when they were at Scots [a Bellevue Hill private school] and frightened the lights out of them!'

Now Stokes is looking forward to his good friend returning to being the world-class businessman he has long known and admired. 'James did so much adventurous and good stuff. Challenger, Carsales, Seek, Macau – these were epic investments made at risk. He was really right. It has to be recognised,' he says. 'He is a talent. My objective would be to see James back as the James Packer he can be. I have every confidence we will see him back.'

*

PACKER'S RETURN TO AUSTRALIA for the Telethon event in October 2017 allowed him to connect with many friends he had left behind during his whirlwind years in Hollywood and Israel and his reclusion in Argentina. When he flew to Melbourne for the Crown annual general meeting, he caught up with the venue's founding father Lloyd Williams, former Crown director Ben Brazil, UBS chief Matthew Grounds, AFL chief Gillon McLachlan, rugby league legend Phil Gould, former Nine Network CEO Eddie McGuire and ex-wife Jodhi Meares. He even had an awkward lunch with his sister Gretel at Crown's Koko Japanese restaurant, which ended in a fight.

Tellingly, he did not visit Sydney, the city that in three years will become home to his $2.2 billion Crown Sydney project. His love–hate relationship with the city of his birth – and its media pack – remains firmly in the negative. 'Getting through the trip to Australia and getting through the [Crown] board meeting and then getting through the annual general meeting were much more at the top of my mind [at the Telethon dinner]. And how I went reconnecting with people I had not seen for some time,' Packer says. 'I'm trying to be honest here, I wasn't sure I would be strong enough. It ended up being a good trip and I was reminded that I've got good friends.'

To many it might seem remarkable that this giant of a man, who stands nearly 2 metres tall and is one of Australia's highest-profile businessmen, could make such a comment. How had someone with the vast wealth, privilege and extraordinary range of contacts Packer has enjoyed come to the point of having such fear of his homeland?

But Packer goes on to explain. 'In truth, I'm scared of Australia. Leave aside whether if I've got a thin skin or my skin's not thick enough. As a person, I'm very soft. I think that's why I get hurt. I think that's why I react. As a default setting I'm not a hard man, I'm soft,' he says. 'I'm scared of the media, I'm scared of the attention, I'm scared of the judgement. If you think about where I've been spending my time, whether it was even Israel or Argentina, I'm anonymous. Aspen, I'm anonymous. Tahiti on the boat, I'm anonymous.' It is a stunning revelation coming from the son of Kerry Packer, one of the hardest and most ruthless people in Australian corporate history, a man who was contemptuous of weakness. But perhaps that provides an explanation.

Carsales co-founder Walter Pisciotta, for one, believes those traits in the father explain the trials of the son. 'I'm a keen observer of Australian politics and business, and have been for the forty-odd years I have been here. Having got to know James as well as I have and having witnessed what Kerry did to him in that One.Tel scenario, I think that is responsible for James's demons. I really feel for the guy over that,' he says. 'I think he is one of the brightest, quickest, warmest individuals I have ever met in business, or generally. I mix with many people who are not wealthy. Everybody has an opinion about James Packer. And I have had the pleasure of watching a number meet him and tell me afterwards what a great guy he is. And they are very cynical about him before they meet him. Very cynical. Once they meet him they are charmed. No one can have a father like Kerry Packer. He has been the biggest public figure in my forty-five years in this country.'

Pisciotta says when he saw Packer's announcement in March that he was resigning from the Crown board citing mental health issues, 'I went back to Kerry in my mind. It is probably a hurtful thing to say, and I don't want to hurt Ros, who is a lovely person, or Kerry's memory – he did some great things in his life, including for his son – but I have never gotten over the way he treated James after One.Tel. And I have always felt [that] the burden of being the third generation of a massive family fortune, perhaps the most public family fortune, is a huge burden for anyone. And then to be massively attacked, embarrassed, annihilated by your father in front of the world, I have never understood that. I relate every one of James's problems back to that, I really do.'

Is it reasonable to expect members of the public to sympathise with a person like James Packer? After he went public about his mental health crisis, one reader of *The Australian* commented: 'I care and respect this guy just as much as he cares and respects me. Zero. Why do so many people feel they have to express concern for super rich celebrities they will never actually know? It's weird.' Another welcomed Packer to 'the real world. The world where household debt in Aus is at 200 per cent. I am sure that keeps a few people awake at night. So sad that you have been able to retire to your polo ranch. Others don't have that safety net.' Another said, 'Buck up James, look how the world really lives, consider yourself bloody lucky, and get on with it. Maybe put a pack on your back and get out in the real world. Spend your money giving others a leg up and reap those rewards.'

But for all the critics, a growing number have been commending Packer for publicly acknowledging his demons. One reader of *The Weekend Australian*, after my interview with Packer in Argentina was published in October 2017, commented: 'For all his failures and acts of poor judgement, it can't have been that much fun growing up a Packer and under the harsh and unforgiving criticism of his father, let alone the media and the rest of Australia's gaze. For all his wealth he admits not having done a very good job building on what he inherited and to being responsible for the failure of his marriage. Perhaps at fifty there's an opportunity for personal growth.' Another commended Packer for taking huge risks and pushing himself in business and in life. 'You have had success and failures and in that course you have provided employment for thousands of Australians and Macanese. You have also lived a pressure-filled life that your father thrived on, he was a different personality to you. You don't owe anybody anything other than to be the best father you can be to your kids.'

Jeff Kennett still struggles to fathom his friend's siege mentality when it comes to his homeland. 'He thinks the Australian public and the media are against him. But they are not. Get fit, get involved. They are a very forgiving mob, the Australian public. Yes, they will haul you over the coals from time to time. But it is one of the good natures of the Australian community,' Kennett says. 'There are so many good qualities in him. There really are. And the saddest thing is to see the journey he has had. With James, I felt, as some others did, that we failed, because we didn't change the intensity of the way he was living his life. I have been able to change the lives of hundreds of people [through beyondblue]. He still wouldn't allow himself to take some of the simple steps that would have given him a better social life.'

Broadcaster Alan Jones, who refers to Packer as a 'dear friend', is equally supportive. And bemused. 'People love you. They love you. There's more love than you can handle. Let them love you. Bring them into your life,' he implores of Packer. 'Not all the hangers-on. Write down the list of the people you've never given ten bob to who still want to be there for you, and there's a stack of them.' It seems Packer is conscious of how much people like Jones want to help. He describes Jones as 'a better friend than I deserve. He has been simply wonderful to me. Every time. No matter the circumstances. I have no words to express how much I love him and to say how grateful I am,' he says.

One public relations company executive says Packer gets all the press he does 'because he is rich, but he is flawed. A lot of people quite like him. They feel he is quite hard done by. And he actually cares whether people love him or not, and that is his problem. Criticism hurts him and when he is down, it really hurts him.'

Stokes says Packer too often forgets his own standing in Australia, which he claims remains exceptionally high. He reckons his friend doesn't get as much recognition as he should, especially for the work he does in the philanthropic and Indigenous spheres. He says the tall poppy syndrome, which affects prominent people across the spectrum of Australian society, remains alive and well. 'James has also become very sensitive to what is written about him. He and his family have always been magnets for publicity. It has got to a stage where in his mind it is more amplified,' Stokes adds. 'I would hate to be the subject of that sort of publicity. Sometimes it makes him feel like he is not wanted in our country.'

*

ANYONE WHO MET PACKER during the two weeks he spent in Australia during late spring 2017 was immediately struck by his physical state. Unflattering photographs taken outside the Crown annual general meeting showed a puffy-faced, slightly flushed billionaire who had clearly regained the 35 kilograms he had lost after undergoing keyhole gastric lapband surgery in late 2011. Throughout his life Packer's weight has shown a close correlation to his mood and mental state. 'My weight and my fitness are a barometer of how I am,' he says. 'When I lost the weight I was working out, I was on a diet of testosterone, cigarettes, vodka, lime and soda, and I occasionally would try and eat something.'

The lapband surgery in 2011, with all its risks including heartburn, reflux, dehydration and constipation, represented an attempt by Packer to break a vicious cycle. The surgery involves wrapping a silicone band around the upper part of the stomach to create a small pouch. His doctor now adjusts the band to change the pouch size when it becomes too tight. It can also be removed. Packer's decision to undertake the operation was inspired by the experience of his friend Harold Mitchell, whose weight halved from 165 kilograms after undergoing lapband surgery in 2009. But in 2014 and more recently, it became clear to Packer that it wasn't the medical miracle he had hoped for. 'It is very hard to digest good food and the only thing that goes down well is bad food. Because you have a band there that is quite tight, so things that are greasy go through,' he says, referring to his diet in Argentina during 2017 of crisps, ice cream, pizza and meat pies. 'So I am not sure how sustainable the band is. I don't know whether I will keep it or not. It is like a false economy.'

Those who have travelled with Kerry Packer on his legendary private DC-8 jet, and have also travelled on his son's Global Express, says James is definitely his father's son. 'What is bred in the bone comes out in the flesh,' one says. 'His father was exactly the same way. You get on the plane and there are two bowls of Twisties and doughnuts. We saw his father basically smoke himself to death, yet [James] smokes, including in the jet. It is an unusual thought process, hard to get your head around … His father never did a day's exercise in his life. But James is capable of getting fit when he puts his mind to it, no doubt.'

While Packer was never a heavy drinker in his younger years, in more recent troubled times alcohol has become his vice. His favourite tequila was Don Julio 1942, a small-batch 'Añejo' or aged tequila named after its founder, Don Julio Gonzalez-Frausto Estrada, who first distilled tequila at the age of just seventeen in 1942. Before that he was partial to French-made Grey Goose vodka, one of the bestselling premium vodka brands in the United States.

Packer drank heavily right through the first six months of 2017, until he spent time on the *Arctic P* in July and made a pact with his friends not to drink again. When he returned to Australia in October, he started drinking again in Melbourne when he shared a bottle of red wine during lunch at Neil Perry's Rockpool restaurant at Crown with *The Australian*'s editor-in-chief, Paul Whittaker. 'I drank for two months after that. By the end of that period I really felt depressed and so started to think probably more seriously than I had before about the impacts of drinking versus not drinking,' Packer says.

He stopped drinking again in Aspen in January 2018 and has been off alcohol since. So far so good, even if he still has his doubts that he can sustain it. 'I'm not strong enough or good enough to sit here and say to you on the record that I'm never going to have another drink again,' he says. 'I don't know if that is the reality or it is not.'

SEVENTEEN

Everglow

JAMES PACKER CALLS IT 'the best Christmas I've ever had'. In December 2017, he and his ex-wife, Erica, spent their first family Christmas – with their three children, Indigo, Jackson and Emmanuelle – in the Aspen house they jointly own, West Buttermilk Estate. A week later, the day after his children headed back to Los Angeles, his first wife, Jodhi Meares, arrived in Aspen with her sister Sophie Morgan. James's mother, Ros, was also there for the New Year period, spending some precious time with her only son.

Remarkably, through the horrors of recent years, as everything else spiralled out of control, James's greatest comfort came from his contact with these three most important women in his life. He still calls his ex-wives, whom he affectionately refers to as 'Eri' and 'Joda', his 'best friends', while he calls his mother 'Mummy'. Over recent years, another name has been added to the list of his closest female confidantes – his current partner, Canadian-born model Kylie Lim. James says he hopes to have the same 'magical' experience with Erica and his children in Aspen for Christmas 2018. It's a fair bet Meares and his mother will visit again at some stage, as will Lim.

Sitting in the living room of that very house, with its spectacular backdrop of magnificent Colorado snow country visible over his shoulder through the floor-to-ceiling windows, I ask him how he has managed to stay friends with both his exes. There is a long pause before he eventually answers; it is clear this is tough terrain. 'Erica is my priority. She is the mother of my kids. And the kids are my priority,' he says, slowly. 'Jodhi is a great source of happiness and friendship in my life. I talk to Erica multiple times a day. And I think Jodhi is an incredibly special person. I'm just so lucky to have them both in my life.'

*

JAMES DESCRIBES HIS WEDDINGS as 'epic and different'. After a four-year romance – punctuated by a short period apart – he and Erica married at the majestic Hôtel du Cap-Eden-Roc in Cap d'Antibes on the French Riviera in June 2007 in a lavish $6 million affair. They invited 182 guests to the wedding, and 180 turned up for the big day, including Rupert Murdoch and his then wife Wendi Deng, Lachlan and Sarah Murdoch, Tom Cruise and Katie Holmes, Lloyd Williams, Alan Jones, cricketer Shane Warne, TV host Karl Stefanovic, and Packer company executives John Alexander, Chris Anderson and Ian Law. Erica wore a $100,000 Christian Dior gown. Hundreds of thousands of flowers were flown in specially from the Netherlands. Erica's sister, Joanna, was her bridesmaid, while then Channel Nine chief executive and James's best mate David Gyngell was his best man. But this was not a show wedding. It was a strictly private affair. The guests were asked not to take photos on their phones or post anything from the event on social media. One attendee recalls it was hard to hear the ceremony for the drones of the paparazzi helicopters circling above seeking to get an exclusive shot of the billionaire couple.

Friends say that throughout their subsequent marriage, Erica, who was born in the NSW country town of Gunnedah, was always important in 'grounding' James. In a 2007 profile of her in *The Sydney Morning Herald*, journalist Neil McMahon described her as someone who was smart and 'laughs a lot', with 'an infectious and very girly giggle'. One of her friends later called her 'very welcoming, open and non-judgemental, with a wicked sense of humour'. But there was much to their relationship that suggested a deeper need in James. One friend of his suggests the billionaire always hoped Erica 'would be another mother for him like Ros was'.

Former Nine Network CEO Eddie McGuire describes Erica as 'one of the most wonderful people you could ever meet. Erica is somebody who is attuned to the limelight and is understanding but is compassionate and grounded. She is a great foil to James,' he says. 'She is a wonderful person in a corporate setting as well. Erica is equally adept at making everybody feel welcome at a major business dinner and then at the karaoke bar after the Derby Day at Crown. If you ever meet James and Erica's children, they are the most polite and well attended, beautiful kids. They've been brought up in extraordinary circumstances, but they are grounded and wonderful kids.'

To those around them, the Packers appeared solid and stable through good times and bad, even as James suffered his second nervous breakdown following the intense pressure of saving his business from the brink of disaster in the wake of the GFC. After his recovery he began to travel the world again to oversee new casino projects in Macau, the Philippines and Sri Lanka. But the stresses of growing his businesses began to take their toll, especially as he worked to get the green light – and public approval – for his controversial Crown Sydney project. At the same time he was also trying to conclude the sale of his pay-TV investment company, CMH, to Rupert Murdoch's News Corporation.

In 2012 UBS chief Matthew Grounds arranged for James to meet Thom Knoles, a maharishi of Vedic meditation. Grounds was concerned for his friend's welfare, as was Erica. James now says, 'Thom came very highly regarded to me on the recommendation of Matthew and [his wife] Kimberley Grounds. Thom has had one of the most interesting lives of anyone I have met. Emmanuelle Packer had just been born, my third beautiful child. Erica was the best wife a man could hope for. Yet I was unsettled. Matthew thought Thom could help. It was the start of another adventure.'

Grounds says of the time: 'I guess the context was that we were looking for something a little different to help, given where things were at at that time. I thought meditation might be helpful, to slow things down a little!"

Knoles says James had been working very hard on his fitness at the time and was 'remarkably open' to the idea of learning to meditate. 'I have to say he was religious about it. I was only with him for five days, every day for about ninety minutes. Then I went back to Arizona. We resolved to see each other at least once a year for ten days,' he recalls. Round two, as Knoles calls it, was at the end of 2012 in Aspen. 'James's friend Orly [Orlando] Bloom was there. So were some people from the Fairfax press. We had our meditation sessions.'

Knoles advised James to visit Rishikesh, located in the foothills of the Himalayas in northern India. It is known as the yoga capital of the world, where non-vegetarian food and alcohol are prohibited. James went there in March 2013 and stayed for twelve days. 'He had been to India before, but this was the first time he had been there for himself. He loved it. I took him down to the Ganges River. We were doing what we call rounds of meditation. At our peak we were doing eight rounds per day,' Knoles says. 'I think it was pivotal to him, frankly. He was in a crucial period of change in his personal life. It gave him a kind of inner strength to get on with embracing change, which he knew he had to do. I am not going to say after India he was the best, most regular meditator. But he had a shot at it.'

James will never forget the experience. 'That was when I meditated most seriously and most deeply. It was for a decent period of time. It was the only time I have ever done yoga,' he says. 'I wish I had dedicated myself to a meditation practice more than I have. It would have been good for me, and it is something that I hope in the future I will come back to.'

James later attended clinics in Israel and Switzerland, on the advice of Grounds, Erica and Kerry Stokes. But nothing could rid him of his troubles.

Several friends remember him being 'simply miserable' at the time. He would constantly tell Erica how much he wanted to get out of Sydney. One friend recalls, 'He used to say to Erica: "Can't we live somewhere else? Why do we still live in Sydney?" He didn't have a business in Sydney any more after the CMII sale.'

James reveals he would even get sick in his private jet when it flew into the city of his birth. 'When I used to fly back into Sydney, sometimes I would get physically ill. Erica saw it happen,' he says. 'I'm very soft. Too soft. I hurt easily. I have the most privileged life. I'm not complaining at all. I inherited all my money. I am so lucky. But I didn't want to be in Sydney. It was too rough a city for me.'

James and Erica had spent more than three years expanding their Vaucluse home La Mer, with its rooftop lap pool, gymnasium, soaring 6.2-metre ceilings, twenty-seat cinema, internal lift, soundproof twenty-car garage, and bedrooms for guests and staff. But James never felt comfortable there, and he and Erica lived together in the house for only a month after moving in around April 2013. They were drifting apart and fighting over email, as Erica spent an increasing amount of time in Los Angeles. She rented a $100,000-a-month Beverly Hills mansion featuring seven bathrooms and a separate guest house in a high-security gated community, one of the most expensive estates in Beverly Hills.

Everything came to a head at Bora Bora in French Polynesia in mid 2013. Eventually, James asked for a divorce and Erica agreed. The news was announced to the world on the afternoon of 6 September. In a short statement, the estranged couple said: 'We remain deeply close friends and incredibly proud parents, and our children are our priority going forward.'

Forty-five days later, supermodel Miranda Kerr announced her marriage to Orlando Bloom was over. Almost immediately James and Kerr reportedly started dating, a relationship James has never confirmed or denied. In fact, he will say nothing on the subject when asked. But friends of Erica say she was hurt by the liaison, given she and James had been friends with Kerr (also a Gunnedah girl) and Bloom. They had even all holidayed together in Tahiti in May 2012.

When James and Erica sold La Mer for $70 million in 2016, breaking a property record for the most expensive home ever sold in Australia, Erica received half of the sale proceeds. She now has an apartment in Paris, which she visits regularly, in addition to her base in Los Angeles.

She initially agreed to talk to me face to face for this book during one of her visits to Sydney, before James went public about his mental health battles. After that she preferred to talk over email. 'I love Sydney,' she writes to me from Los Angeles of her decision to move abroad in 2013. 'But I wanted to escape the hothouse pressure and start again somewhere I wasn't the subject of gossip. I had three kids under five years old and was still breastfeeding Emmanuelle. So I really wanted to gather up my babies, try to heal and find some silence from all the noise. James didn't want to be in Australia at that time either so it worked for both of us.'

She had always resented the intrusion of the media into her life as a Packer wife, and it affected her deeply. One family friend says, 'Erica always had the blinds drawn at James's Bondi apartment. She also never went on the balcony because of her concern about the paparazzi.'

Erica says she chose to move the family to Los Angeles because 'it was far enough away, but only one flight away if I needed to get home'. In LA she wasn't a public figure. 'I knew less than a handful of people here when I moved but since I arrived, this sprawling town has welcomed me and the children, and we've all made some great friends. LA offers a really great lifestyle, and the sunshine is truly glorious. I've made some wonderful friends and life is fun, but much more quiet,' she writes. 'James travels around a lot, but LA is also fairly central to his life. The kids love it here and have access to so many fun activities and great experiences. They were all so young when we moved here, but I've made sure they have a very strong connection to Australia and still define themselves as Aussies.'

The family visited Australia over the Easter break in late March 2018, when they travelled to both the Packer family's estate Ellerston and Erica's home town of Gunnedah. In Sydney, where they stayed at the Vaucluse mansion known as Coolong, the children visited Taronga Zoo, climbed the Sydney Harbour Bridge and took a boat ride on the harbour on Lachlan Murdoch's luxury yacht *Sarissa*. One evening Erica even welcomed some of her old Sydney friends to Coolong, where late into the evening they were dancing – wine glasses in hand – on the street. 'I do miss Australia and I miss my Aussie friends enormously. One by one I'm luring my Aussie friends to come and live in LA! But who knows what the future brings? Five years ago I would never have thought I'd be living in Los Angeles on my own with the kids. I've given up trying to plan!' Erica writes. 'James and I will always figure out together what is the best for our children and go from there.'

They both share a friendship with actor Russell Crowe. Crowe and Erica dated for six months in 2001 before the latter met James, while James bought into the South Sydney Rabbitohs rugby league club with Crowe in October 2014. James says, 'I like Russell a lot. He was great friends with Dad and I used to get so jealous of him. The actor of his generation in my view: *Gladiator* to *A Beautiful Mind*. Dad's favourite team was always Souths, even when he was with the Roosters or Manly. When the chance came up to be Russell's partner, I took it and am glad I did.'

Despite the breakdown of the marriage, Erica remains proudly close to both James's mother Ros and sister Gretel. 'Families come in all shapes and sizes and they are absolutely part of my family. The kids adore their grandma Ros and she comes to stay with us a couple of times a year – and we all try and see each other at any and every opportunity,' Erica says. 'Family is of the utmost importance to me. Since my mum and dad have passed, Ros never fails to be there for me and for the kids. Gretel is one of the most interesting and special women in the world. I adore them both immensely.'

She says it has been fundamentally important that she and James remain close, especially for the sake of the children. 'We are a family no matter what. As I said earlier, families come in all different shapes and sizes and my family is my highest priority; the kids always come first.' Erica explains that she still has a deep regard for James. 'I first fell in love with James for the following characteristics: his kindness, curiosity, tenacity, and enthusiasm for life,' she says. 'These traits are the fundamental reason why James and I continue to have a loving and respectful relationship.'

Despite speculation to the contrary, James has not sought in recent times to reconcile with Erica. Rather, Erica's friends say she just wants James to be a happy and healthy dad for their kids. James himself says he felt in 2013 and continues to feel 'enormous guilt' about the failure of their marriage. He adds, in his characteristically self-critical way: 'It was entirely my fault. I followed [Erica] to America in my own way. I knew I should be near her and the kids, and our break-up is my biggest failure. I think in some ways I have never gotten over it.' So what does he believe are the prospects of a reunion? His reply is short: 'I'm not sure Erica would want to.'

*

IT IS A STUNNING late-autumn morning in Sydney when Jodhi Meares agrees to meet me for coffee at her favourite park, the Camp Cove Reserve in harbourside Watsons Bay. It's just up the road from the quaint timber fisherman's cottage with a baby-blue facade that she purchased for a cool $2.75 million in June 2017, after selling properties in Point Piper and Paddington following her split from photographer husband Nick Finn Tsindos.

When I arrive a good twenty minutes late, a victim of Sydney's perennial eastern suburbs traffic snarl, Jodhi looks anything but stressed. She's been playing in the park with her monster-looking dog named Soda Pop, a cross between a Great Dane and a French mastiff. She's dressed in a light summer dress and her bare feet are covered in mud after kicking around a half-chewed basketball with her canine friend on the dewy morning grass. She greets me with a hug and, halfway through our chat, casually lights up a cigarette.

Meares, who was formerly known as Jodie – she changed her name in April 2002 reportedly due to her commitment to numerology – was twenty-eight when she married James in October 1999, a year after he had separated from his former fiancée, Kate Fischer. James and Fischer had spent five years together, including a two-year engagement. Fischer, who is now known as Tziporah Malkah, revealed in May 2018 that it took her almost a decade to get over the break-up, and that she had often fantasised about reuniting with James. She claimed her fiancé's huge work commitments had prompted her to call off their engagement. In mid August 2018 Malkah told *Daily Mail Australia* that she would welcome rekindling a friendship with James.

When James was romancing Jodhi, he would often take her on a Friday evening for dinner at the Sydney dining institution Kingsleys Steakhouse, a former candle factory with cathedral ceilings and stone walls near the city's King Street Wharf. One friend of the couple recalls, 'His driver had the producer's number for Richard Mercer's "Love Song Dedications" program on FM radio in Sydney. He would always organise for a dedication to be played to Jodhi on the radio on their way to the restaurant.' Jodhi was reportedly attracted to James's vulnerability, and around her he often lapsed into what friends described as his 'baby voice'.

Their wedding ceremony was a $10 million affair that saw Elton John perform for 720 guests spread between three marquees in pouring rain at Kerry Packer's eastern suburbs compound. To make room for one of the marquees, Kerry even ordered his gardener to uproot an old tree in the yard, which died when he subsequently tried to replant it. James's best man and groomsman were David Gyngell and Chris Hancock. (After James and Jodhi were married, Hancock and his actor wife Dee Smart lived with them for a year in James's Bondi apartment.) Jodhi's bridesmaids were her sisters, Kirsty and Sophie.

Jeff Kennett, one of the wedding guests, recalls: 'The tents were two-storey. I was sitting with Ros [Packer] and Felicity [Kennett's wife] that evening. They had brought out from England all the family's silverware [the Packers were originally from the Reading area in the Thames Valley] for the candelabras [and the cutlery] on the tables and they were absolutely amazing.' Another guest that night, Crown director Harold Mitchell, remembers then Nine sales boss Graeme Yarwood collapsing at their table from the allergic condition anaphylaxis after mistakenly eating a peanut. 'He got rushed into a makeshift operating theatre in the house, where they gave him an injection. A little while later he was back at the party!' Mitchell recalls.

Yarwood now gives a bit more detail to the story. 'My allergic reaction to peanuts was starting to take effect during Elton John's performance. I thought I was being particularly discreet trying to manage the reaction. But there were people there who knew my name, identified I was in some distress and escorted me to an area in the house where Kerry's doctor was set up,' he recalls.

'The doctor was straight on to it. He was fantastic. He then said to me, "I guess you would like to see the rest of Elton," and said the best way to do that was to have an injection straight into the vein of my hand, which he did. That gave me immediate relief and I was soon back at the table.'

Eddie McGuire served as MC for the evening, and it is one he will never forget. 'I have never had a more attentive floor manager in my life than Kerry Packer was that night,' he recalls. 'He knew exactly how he wanted it to look and how he wanted it to be.' McGuire recalls a few memorable Kerry anecdotes from the evening, which he describes as a night for 'Australian royalty. The time comes for me to get up and to make the first introductions. I'd been given no run-down, no speech notes, no nothing. So I get the microphone and I go, "Good evening, everybody." There's no sound, no audio. There is no audio at James Packer's wedding with Kerry in full flight!' McGuire gives a wide smile.

'We worked out in a flurry of behind-the-scenes activity that it was the prime minister [then John Howard] and his secret service people blocking all the frequencies. So we had to go up to the security of the prime minister's detail and ask him to turn it off for two minutes. They said there was no chance. And I said, "Well, you go and tell Kerry!" So even the fear of Kerry turned off the PM's security,' McGuire says, affirming that when it came to deciding whether to confront Kerry Packer or compromise the PM's security, placating Packer came first.

McGuire also remembers Kerry's impatience to get his star international attraction, Elton John, onto the stage. 'So I'm standing backstage and things were a bit behind time, and Elton was being a perfect gentleman. They had these dancers on the stage. I looked from behind the curtain and all I could see was this laser-like look coming from Kerry again. I get this nod of the head. Then another nod of the head. Then I get a finger-point and he says, "Hey, you!" So I go over and he says, "I want Elton on now. Everybody is ready to go." I said, "They've got about another two dances left." He said, "Are you deaf? Don't you hear me, son? Get them off!"'

Some might say this was bully Kerry at his most obnoxious, but McGuire sees it differently. 'To me it was just such an important night for Kerry. He was so proud. He was so hospitable. And there was a genuine pride and love in what was happening that night for his son and for his family. To me it wasn't him being a control freak. It was him being so giving of himself and his family and his house for this to be perfect that he took such a hands–on role.'

Jodhi herself describes the night as 'extraordinary. Kerry gave me away, which was really beautiful. I adored Kerry. I couldn't have imagined [the wedding] would be that big. It was amazing. In torrential rain, James and I had to shake the hands of 720 people at the door.'

Harold Mitchell now declares, looking back: 'It looked like a marriage that was going to last.' But Jodhi struggled with what it meant to marry into what was then Australia's richest family. She constantly wrestled with the burdens and responsibilities of being a Packer wife. After three years, it all became too much. 'That world was a lot for me. I am a girl from Merimbula ... I don't think I realised how complicated the life was going to be. That is not an excuse, but it really was like moving to a different planet for someone like me,' she says. 'I don't think I understood there would be seven dinners a week. I didn't understand what that might be. I didn't know anyone in the corporate world, not even anyone who wore a suit. It wasn't my life – most of my mates were surfers, plumbers and working in bars. It was extremely foreign, that kind of life. James had a huge amount of pressure. I came to understand that during the few years we were together. But I think that [to separate] was the right decision for both of us at the time.'

Kerry Stokes says that when the marriage broke up in 2002, hastened by James's nervous breakdown following the collapse of One.Tel, James was 'very hurt. But I don't think over the longer term Jodhi could have lived in his world. James's world is full of pressure. Any successful person's world has that pressure. They tend to generate a lot of energy. I never thought of Jodhi as being comfortable in that environment. For example, when I saw her a few times in Canberra, she didn't look comfortable.'

As was to be the case with James's second wife, Erica, he and Jodhi stayed close after their three-year marriage ended. On the day their split was announced in a newsflash on the Packer family–owned Nine Network, they issued a statement saying: 'We will remain the best of friends.' During the GFC, Jodhi even agreed to forgo $5 million of her $10 million prenuptial agreement to help relieve the pressure on her former husband.

More than a decade after their split, in October 2015, with Packer firmly in his new relationship with Mariah Carey, Jodhi and James turned heads when they arrived together at the annual Telethon Lexus Ball in Perth. 'He trusts her,' says Stokes, who was at the ball that night. Carey was reportedly directing a movie in America at the time. Two months earlier James and Jodhi had been photographed arm in arm for the Adopt Change charity event in Sydney. That night on Instagram, Jodhi had shared a quote from author Charles Bukowski: 'I will remember the kisses our lips raw with love and how you gave me everything you had and how I offered you what was left of me.' She clearly still had feelings for James, even if she knew she could never be a Packer wife again. She now hints at the softness in his character, which has endeared him to women. 'We are quite similar in many ways … He is such a kind person. He would never be someone who you wouldn't remain friends with. He would not allow that to happen. That is not in his nature,' she says. 'He has really evolved in that way. The way he can see things. He really doesn't have any sort of bitterness. He does not have that in him.'

Their relationship has also continued at a business level. In 2017 James doubled his stake in Jodhi's fashion enterprise, the Upside Corporation, to 40 per cent, buying out the 20 per cent holding of his Israeli billionaire businessman and movie producer friend Arnon Milchan. He is now helping her take the brand global. Her first swimwear company, known as Tigerlily, was sold to international surf brand Billabong in December 2007 for $5.8 million. In February 2017 Billabong sold the brand to private equity firm Crescent Capital Partners for $60 million. James says, 'I believe in the Upside. I believe in Jodhi as a businesswoman. Tigerlily is a big success, and I believe Jodhi can and will do it again.'

Jodhi says they have no problem separating their friendship and business relationship. James, for one, is not on the company's board. 'We have two people from CPH who sit on our board, Mark [Arbib] and Sam [McKay]. So that is enormously helpful. My role with the company is as creative director. Crunching the numbers I need a lot of help with, and the strategy of where you go,' she says. '[James and I] respect each other so much that there are clear lines and they would never be crossed. Ever. It would never happen.'

While Jodhi has been an important confidante for James in his darkest moments — especially in the past two years — it has been a mutually supportive relationship. In June 2014, Jodhi was arrested for drink-driving after crashing her 4WD into three parked cars in Sydney's eastern suburbs (she pleaded guilty and had her licence suspended for twelve months). In February 2015 her engagement to former Noiseworks rock singer Jon Stevens came to a very public and abrupt end following a three-hour domestic dispute to which the police were called. Reports in the aftermath claimed James repeatedly rang Jodhi during the break-up, offering his support.

'We all do some pretty heavy things in life,' Jodhi now says. 'With me, without James, I don't think I could have gotten through them. He was really extraordinary. I don't think I would have been able to pick myself up without James's emotional support and his refusal to judge me. And telling you, "It is okay."'

I ask Jodhi if she feels her ex is protective of her. 'Definitely,' she responds immediately, declining to comment about her break-up with Stevens (whom she hasn't seen or spoken to since their split). But, as with James, she says she now remains on good terms with her most recent ex-husband, New York City–based photographer and actor Nick Tsindos. 'Nick is in my life and always will be. I don't regret marrying him, or the experience, and he is a beautiful person,' she says. 'He is one of my best friends now and we talk to each other every day. He was just too young for me.'

Despite speculation of previous tensions between the pair, Jodhi says Erica was a 'wonderful wife' for James. 'They had three beautiful children together. I adore Erica. She is a great woman and she is a really incredible mum. James's kids are a testament to both of them,' she says.

Jeff Kennett, who has long counselled James about his personal and professional life, says he is greatly saddened that his friend went 'off the rails' in his relationships with both Jodhi and Erica. 'I, from a friendship point of view, felt terribly sorry for them all, the children included,' Kennett says. 'The demise of [James's relationship with Carey] that led to his current [mental] condition, reinforced his many failings, his insecurities in terms of relationships.'

Kennett identifies the pressures of being prominent public figures as a key factor in the break-ups. He says James and his female partners and wives have always suffered from the fact that their personal lives are 'part of their public standing, that they are on display'. Kennett had his own short public split from his wife, Felicity Kellar, in 1998 – it was reported at the time as a six-month trial separation – before they reconciled and are still together. 'There are many people like James who have inherited wealth who don't have successful family relationships,' Kennett says. 'I would love James to have had a happy family life with Erica and the children. So that he would have got the full value of his commercial success.'

*

EMMANUELLE PACKER'S DRAWINGS TAKE pride of place on the wall next to the fireplace at the Packer family home in Aspen, as do the photos of her with siblings Jackson and Indigo on the desk of her father's study. On numerous occasions during my interviews with James – whether it be in Argentina, Aspen or Cabo – our discussions are interrupted by FaceTime calls to his iPad from his children. In those precious moments suddenly he is a dad. The burden of being a billionaire and son of one of the toughest fathers of them all is lifted, the great weight of expectation gone. Unlike the hundreds of hangers-on over the decades who asked for and – more often than not – were given plenty but delivered little in return, his children continue to give him something money cannot buy: unconditional love.

'Erica has never poisoned the children [against him], even one-millionth of one per cent. For that I am incredibly grateful,' James says. 'But my family lives in LA and that is just the reality of things.' He says he is determined to play a part in their lives – Erica wouldn't have it any other way – even if the painful memories of his wild life in 2012–13 in Sydney and Hollywood still burn deep.

Financier Arki Busson, who first met James when he came to London in the early 1990s – they were introduced by Damian Aspinall – says he has 'never heard or seen Erica do something non-supportive towards her kids being close to their father. Even in moments where she could have said,

"Let's wait for a moment." I have never seen that from her, and I commend her for that. Even in moments where James was fragile, when sometimes as a mother you could say, "It is not the right moment," she has encouraged them to see him. I think that has been a great support to him.'

Busson brings a unique perspective to the issue, having been through a nasty, public New York courtroom battle in 2017 with his ex-fiancée Uma Thurman over custody of their then four-year-old Luna. 'There is nothing worse than going through a period like that, and then on top of it having barriers put in the way of you accessing your children. For me it was clearly one of the most devastating things I ever went through,' he says. 'Going through these different stages, Pack [as Busson calls James] has always been open to seeing [his children] and embracing them. When you go through these periods it is not that easy. It really isn't. You need to be able to take care of yourself before you take care of anyone else.'

Busson visited James on his boat off Saint-Tropez in the south of France in late June 2018, where they both spent time with James's children, who were staying in a rented property in the town with their mother. 'We saw his kids and they were super attached to him. They were screaming when Daddy walked in. You could also sense the anxiety in them too when Daddy was going to leave. That is a tribute to both James and Erica that they have got to that point,' he says. 'I think where he does an amazing job is really juggling everything. I think sometimes he is too much of a people pleaser. I have a bit of the same issue. At the end of the day we don't really take care of ourselves when we should and think more about the outside.'

In December 2017 James also flew to LA from Argentina to watch his eldest daughter, Indigo, perform in a play. In January 2018 he and Erica attended an interview for Emmanuelle's new school in LA.

James's gratitude to Erica is clearly something he wants known publicly. 'I just want to say what an incredible job Erica is doing bringing them up,' James told me in Argentina in October 2017. 'I always thought she'd be a good mother and she is proving that every day … LA is a really terrific place for them to be. There is a lot of positive energy, a lot of positive affirmation there. And there is not the Packer fishbowl that there would have been in Sydney. They have anonymity there that they don't have in Sydney. That is really healthy for them.'

He claimed then that his decision to step down from the Crown board in December 2015 was about his kids and not his then blossoming relationship with Mariah Carey. 'I was attempting to build a business in North America to be closer to my kids,' he told me. 'The travel was unsustainable.' He now says that whether they will eventually move to Australia – when James makes one of his family homes his apartment in the new Crown Sydney development – is entirely a decision for their mother. 'That is a decision for Erica, and a question you will need to ask her. But at the moment, I think that will be unlikely. I think that Los Angeles is a lot less public for her and the kids,' he says.

He adds that ten-year-old Indigo has ambitions to be an actress. 'My eight-year-old [Jackson] is a sensitive soul who is doing the best to find his way. My five-year-old [Emmanuelle] is very confident for a five-year-old, I think,' he says. He says he hopes one day his children will take an interest in the Crown business, before adding: 'But it is a long, long way in the future for them at the moment.'

I put to him one of the final, telling comments from Paul Barry's book *Who Wants to Be a Billionaire?*. It asserts that James's whole life has been about business and materialism. 'All he cares about is creating wealth and making money because that's all Kerry ever taught him. And he didn't have a lot of options, because he had to do what he was told,' Barry wrote. James's response to the comment is telling: it is reflective rather than combative. He says he has become more risk-averse as his children are getting older. You get the sense he is finally starting to see the consequences of pursuing his big ambition to be a global businessman. And the little people that, for a time, he left behind.

Now it seems he has a powerful need to make up for that lost time in spades. 'All you can do in life is your best. Dad wanted me to go into the business, I wanted to go into the business. I have seen more of the world than most people would ever imagine. How that fits into being purely materialistic I don't know. I have had a life where I have seen things that are different from just business,' he says. 'People change when they have kids. The kids have changed my outlook on life. Even if I let my marriage fail when I shouldn't have. Your priorities change. It is a priority for me to be around my kids when I can be. They are my favourite people.'

For all the wreckage that has been left behind in his closest relationships, he still has a group of women and a loving family who play a fundamental role in his life. In this sense, James would always acknowledge one important point: that despite his turbulent past, he enjoys a fortunate life.

EIGHTEEN

The Corridors of Power

I T IS KNOWN AS one of the bluest of blue–ribbon Liberal
seats in federal parliament. Taking in the leafy Melbourne
suburbs of Hawthorn, Kew and Camberwell, the electorate of
Kooyong in the city's inner-east has been held by the Liberals
since it was created in 1901. It was the prized seat of the party's
founder, Sir Robert Menzies, and before him Sir John Latham.
After Menzies, for almost three decades it was held by former
Liberal leader Andrew Peacock.

When Peacock announced his retirement from parliament
in August 1994, a big-name candidate was quietly touted by
party powerbroker Michael Kroger as his replacement: James
Douglas Packer. Packer enjoyed a close friendship with the then
Victorian Liberal president and through him met Jeff Kennett
and Peter Costello. 'I have always been interested in politics. In
the early '90s I had become good friends with Michael Kroger.
When Andrew Peacock announced his retirement from
politics, Kroger encouraged me strongly to run for preselection
for the seat of Kooyong,' Packer now recalls. 'Michael assured

me I would have his support in the preselection contest if I ran. I was interested. I spoke to my father about it. My father said to me that it was a seriously bad idea, in perhaps even more colourful language than that.'

Packer would have been following a long tradition of his family's support for the Liberals. His uncle, the late Clyde Packer, was even a NSW Liberal MP. In 2003, while his father was still alive, James joined the Liberal Party to help support Malcolm Turnbull's bid to win preselection for the federal seat of Wentworth. But back in 1994, Kerry Packer – who his friends claimed voted Labor more times than Liberal during his life – saw red at the idea of his son becoming a member of parliament.

James recalls Packer family adviser and former Labor senator Graham Richardson coming to visit his father in the CPH offices to discuss Kroger's Kooyong plan. 'Dad invited me into his office and asked Richo to give his opinion on my political idea,' Packer recalls. 'Richo said words to the effect that he agreed with Dad that it was a ridiculous idea. I especially remember him saying words to the effect of, "You don't realise what Paul Keating would do to you. He would tear you from limb to limb and then spit you out."' Keating, then prime minister, had a passion for using the parliamentary stage to destroy his opponents.

Richardson remembers the day well and is now even more adamant that if James had gone into politics, the weight of expectation on him would have been massive – and impossible to bear. 'No one could live up to it. For a man who has never liked publicity, it would have been a disaster. I think the advice at the time was right. It's not that he couldn't be a good politician, it's just he couldn't have been as good as people would expect him to be. The charm is amazing when he turns it on. But he also has that temper,' Richardson says.

Former Liberal federal treasurer Peter Costello also recalls James raising the Kooyong idea with him, noting that he was obviously genuinely interested in a political career. 'I strongly advised him against it. I said it was a stupid idea. I said, "You can be a businessman or politician but you can't be both. And if I were you I would be a businessman,"' Costello says. He felt Packer had no sense of the nitty-gritty of what was involved in being a federal member, including attending evening branch meetings to talk about issues like local roads. He also questioned Packer's political ambitions and what he would be trying to achieve by becoming an MP – did he want to be a minister, treasurer, even prime minister? 'Maybe in the back of his mind was the fact his uncle Clyde had been a member of the state upper house in New South Wales. But that was a different time. You couldn't be the heir to a media empire and a politician,' Costello says.

James now says he has no regrets about being talked out of the Kooyong opportunity. 'I think, as I look back, I'm not quick enough,' he says of his suitability for political career. During the approval process for the Crown Sydney development, he also finally got to know Paul Keating in person after the former prime minister and the Packer family had fought a public war of words fifteen years earlier over the controversial issue of media law reform. Keating is known as the spiritual guardian of the Barangaroo site where the Crown Sydney casino project is being built. While he eventually supported the plan and location of the project, it was not without a battle for Crown and Packer. 'Paul Keating is Paul Keating. A giant of a man. He could have killed me in one second. One second,' James says with a smile. 'I think he should be listened to more.'

*

JAMES PACKER MAY NOT have pursued a political career, but that never stopped him developing a deep interest in politics, following in his family's tradition of relishing wielding influence in the corridors of power. Kerry Packer's widow, Ros, has a long history of donations to the Liberal Party, while her late husband used his media outlets for political gain for more than three decades, and was both respected and feared by all of the nation's state and federal MPs.

His key backroom operatives were legends of their craft. One was Peter Barron, who, after working for Neville Wran when he was NSW premier, became one of the most influential advisers in the Hawke Labor government. Another was the impeccably connected Graham Richardson. Kerry Packer's immense ability to pull political strings behind the scenes ensured that for decades the nation's free-to-air television networks, led by his number-one-rating network Channel Nine, were long protected from competition by Australia's media laws.

Kerry Packer did make public waves, though, when in 1995 he appeared on Nine's *A Current Affair* evening program to declare that Liberal leader John Howard would make an excellent prime minister. Howard subsequently defeated Paul Keating at the 1996 election, and Keating publicly accused Howard and Packer of doing a secret deal to repeal the cross-media laws introduced by Keating during his prime-ministership, which had stopped the Packers buying the Fairfax media empire.

Howard's attempts to review the laws, which also limited foreign ownership of the Australian media, were shelved in 1997 after an unexpectedly passionate party-room backlash. But in 2004 the Howard government included a renewed commitment to reform media ownership laws in its re-election platform. In October 2006 it was able to secure the support of

Family First senator Steve Fielding to overturn the twenty-year-old laws, paving the way for James Packer, on the same day, to announce the sale of Channel Nine and the ACP magazine business to a private equity firm for $5.5 billion.

Packer says his interest in politics grew out of necessity. 'I suppose in the first instance from a business perspective, our businesses were historically regulated so there was a necessity to be in touch with the politics of the day that affected the regulation of our businesses,' he says. 'I spent a lot of time trying to develop relationships during the time that our businesses were regulated. My record as a lobbyist in Australia is pretty good.'*

He developed a close relationship with federal communications ministers Richard Alston and Helen Coonan in successive Howard governments, with Coonan later joining the board of Crown Resorts. Packer at one point even secretly lobbied then prime minister Kevin Rudd on behalf of pay-TV operators Foxtel and Fox Sports, of which his CMH held interests of 25 per cent and 50 per cent respectively. At issue was the Rudd government's review of the 'anti-siphoning list', which mandates that certain major sporting events must be shown on free-to-air television. The review was considering whether Foxtel would get exclusive access to broadcasting more sporting events. The pay-TV industry had long felt the free-to-air stations used the anti-siphoning regime to hoard a range of sports rights and broadcast the events when, or even if, they wished.

'In 2009 [News Limited CEO] John Hartigan and I began to have a limited dialogue. I had not spoken to him for three years. I had stayed close to [then Foxtel CEO] Kim Williams. Kim and I had always got on well. So I was on top of the issues that were going on in Foxtel at the time,' James now recalls. 'John Hartigan – for the first and only time – asked if I could go down and lobby on behalf of all the Foxtel shareholders to then Prime Minister Rudd. So I went down to Kirribilli House to see him.'

At the time Rudd believed News Corporation, which owned 25 per cent of Foxtel and 50 per cent of Fox Sports, had been waging an unrelentingly personal and ideological campaign against him, especially through the pages of *The Australian* newspaper. Rudd was threatening to do whatever he could to hurt News, and Hartigan was worried. 'John had a really ferociously severe session with Rudd, when Rudd had let fly about News Corp, in a way that was entirely unconstrained,' recalls Kim Williams. 'I think John was genuinely shocked by Rudd's animosity. He was concerned this might prove to be a really major issue in terms of the upcoming AFL rights.'

But Packer was also concerned about his company becoming collateral damage in the war. 'I had only seen Kevin once before as PM, at Andrew Forrest's Generation One launch at Kirribilli House. I'd known him before he became PM. We had dinner at Bellevue Hill with Dad once or twice. He would also come into the office in Park Street to see Dad,' he recalls. 'At Kirribilli, I told him I was worried as a Foxtel shareholder about being roadkill in a situation where the main players are above my pay grade. The AFL was the issue on the table. And I started to make my case why the AFL should be allowed to do a deal with Foxtel.' As part of a review of the anti-siphoning list, and in the rights negotiations for a new five-year broadcasting deal with the AFL, Foxtel wanted to be guaranteed better quality matches.

Rudd told Packer in the Kirribilli meeting how much he despised Rupert Murdoch and News Corporation, but Packer had some advice for the prime minister. 'I said to him, "John Hartigan once said to me, 'Don't have a fight with someone who buys ink by the tonne.' These guys have hit me over the years, too, so in my own little way I understand what you are talking about." But I then reiterated to him that he should remember about not fighting with people who buy ink by the tonne,' Packer says. After that meeting, Packer spoke with Rudd by telephone on several occasions, urging him to meet with Hartigan to make peace. That meeting ended up happening in North Queensland, with Hartigan even cutting short his holiday to attend. And it was a success.

Kim Williams says Packer's intervention was significant in helping Foxtel securing unprecedented access to matches in the next AFL deal. When the deal was announced in early 2011, Fox Sports had secured the right to provide live coverage of every AFL game, except the grand final, uninterrupted by advertisements. It later secured the same deal for its coverage of the NRL. 'I have no doubt James's representation was very important in the process,' Williams says.

Packer had managed to emulate his father's brilliance in practising the art of politics behind the scenes. But a significant victory on media policy wasn't a guarantee of wider influence on the Rudd government. During the GFC, Packer personally lobbied then federal treasurer Wayne Swan to extend the government guarantee for mortgages given to the big four banks and Macquarie Bank to non-bank lenders like Challenger, in which his CPH held a strategic interest. His view was that if the banks were to have their mortgages guaranteed by the government, non-bank lenders should be allowed to compete on the same terms. But this time, the political power of the Packer name failed.

'Challenger was a prudentially regulated life company but the government would not provide the guarantee. So our capacity to raise capital in the markets to fund the mortgages was harmed dramatically. It absolutely constrained the business,' recalls Challenger CEO Brian Benari. 'It was an incredibly difficult time. The government guarantee was unpopular and the government was working frenetically to secure the banks, especially the smaller banks. All the government was thinking about was how to stabilise the sector rather than inhibiting growth of [rival] companies.'

Packer believes, in hindsight, that the decision cost Challenger billions and made the mortgage market significantly less competitive in Australia. The failure to influence Swan on this issue did not mean the end of Packer seeking to influence political outcomes. While many corporate chiefs find state and federal politics either unfathomable or a dirty business, the Packers have never had any compunction about getting involved.

For Crown Resorts, influence in the halls of political power is a now never-ending quest to protect the interests of its gambling franchises. In 2011 Crown was a major beneficiary of then Western Australian premier Colin Barnett's decision to build the new Perth football stadium next to the new Crown Towers development on the city's Burswood peninsula. It followed a meeting three months earlier between Barnett and Packer, although Barnett subsequently claimed the meeting was to discuss Packer's hotel plans, not the stadium location.

Then, during the federal Labor government's attempt to introduce a mandatory precommitment on poker machines in 2012, a move driven by independent MP Andrew Wilkie that would have cost Crown tens of millions of dollars in annual revenue, James secretly met with Prime Minister Julia Gillard on three separate occasions to dissuade her from the plan. Details of the meetings never leaked. For that battle Crown also hired former Labor Party national secretary Karl Bitar as its government relations manager, as well as appointing Helen Coonan and the politically connected Harold Mitchell to its board. Graham Richardson also played a role in heading off the reforms, which were eventually released as a watered-down package, importantly excluding mandatory precommitment. The measures were later repealed by the Abbott government.

In August 2014, Packer again played a personal hand in helping Crown secure bipartisan support for an extension to its Victorian licence. But his biggest lobbying success was undoubtedly securing bipartisan support for a second casino licence in Sydney in 2013 – something he once thought was an impossible dream. Graham Richardson called it one of the greatest political achievements of all time. In the jargon of lobbyists, James never had any qualms about 'getting his hands dirty' on behalf of his corporate interests. In fact, even though his father and his better judgement put paid to his political ambitions, he is – like his father was – undoubtedly a political animal. One confident enough of his own political judgement to mix it with the nation's, and subsequently some of the world's, biggest decision-makers.

*

ONE OF THE KEYS to Packer's mastery of the political lobby is that he knows how to play both sides of the field. He may have considered a career as a Liberal politician and joined the party at one point to help a friend, but he has been careful to keep the channels open to all sides of politics. Ask him who is the best Australian prime minister he has seen, and he hedges his bets. 'Hawke, Keating and Howard are equal best. Keating was also a brilliant treasurer,' he says, before adding an important footnote. 'I think Peter Costello would have been there too if he had become PM.'

Costello and Packer have forged a close bond over the past twenty-five years. They were once regular dinner companions in Sydney and Canberra. James says Costello was the one politician he was closest to for many years. 'I had a lot of one-on-one dinners with Peter. They were mostly dinners out of friendship, not out of business, and at that time it's fair to say I was extremely close to Peter,' he says. 'We'd invariably sit down at the table and complain about our bosses. I still think the world of him. I can't wait to see him again. He's one of the funniest and smartest people I've ever met.'

Costello and his wife have even been guests of Packer on the *Arctic P* as it has cruised the world. The former federal treasurer stresses there was 'nothing clandestine' about his meetings with one of the nation's richest people. 'I never sought anything from James. It certainly wasn't done for political advantage. I just genuinely liked his company. I have always found him an interesting, friendly person. And he had great perspectives on Australian politics,' Costello says. 'I was also very interested in what was going on in the business world. There was a frustration about his boss, who happened to be his old man. He used to share with me a lot of stories about Kerry. Kerry was not someone to be messed with. I found James a lot softer than Kerry.'

James Packer also still has a clear affection for former Liberal prime minister Tony Abbott, describing him as 'someone I look up to' and 'one of the most decent people I have ever met'.

While Packer still knows how to pull political strings, his interest in the domestic political scene and the ongoing battles between the major parties has waned in the wake of selling his media assets, and as he has grown more distant from his homeland in recent years. Graham Richardson says, 'James has always loved politics, but when he sold Nine, he stopped being influential in politics. When you have a television station, you have influence. You have a very powerful weapon. He doesn't have that any more. He hasn't taken the same interest in domestic politics of late.'

Instead, with the evolution of his business interests in Israel, China and America, James has become much more an aficionado of global politics. 'There's not much that is more interesting politics than Israel, the Middle East and China,' says one of his friends. 'When you are suddenly in the centre of the politics of talking to world leaders, anyone given that sort of political insight would be intoxicated by it.' His interest in international politics, and especially the role of Israel in the Middle East and the world – flowing from his friendships with Israeli prime minister Benjamin Netanyahu and former Israeli president Shimon Peres – saw him develop a close friendship with Jeff Bleich. They first met when the Democrat-aligned Bleich was appointed US ambassador to Australia by President Barack Obama in 2009 for four years.

Bleich says he has always been intrigued by how he and Packer have looked at issues from very different perspectives. 'You can always learn from people who think the way you don't,' Bleich says. 'James grew up in the business world with a very fierce private-sector mindset and not a lot of focus on the public sector. A lot of people raised in families that have the kind of business holdings of that scale go either one of two directions: they are focused on developing good relations with regulators and governments and treating them as partners, or they treat government as an obstacle. I think he views government as an obstacle. Our initial conversations were on those issues.'

But Bleich says, over time, Packer's political views became more nuanced, 'because he found political mentors, people who are significant figures in global politics. I don't think there was a great love of politicians or institutions of government when he was growing up. But when you grow to discover this world, it can really draw curiosity for people like James. And he is unique in the sense that he forms friendships with people like me and Robert De Niro, who are on the left side of the ledger. Plus, among my friends, there are relatively few who were as firmly in line with believing that Donald Trump would be successful in his campaign [in 2016].'

Packer even apparently asked one of his advisers to lay a US$500,000 bet on a Trump win before the November 2016 poll, but the best they could get was a US$100,000 wager, so he abandoned the idea. Fellow billionaire Anthony Pratt famously became so convinced about a Trump victory that before the third presidential debate in October 2016 he placed a US$100,000 bet at the juicy price of $4.50.

Bleich adds, 'James was prepared to accept some of the claims that were being made. Those that were being ridiculed in the media. And James was right. I've learned a good deal from him.'

*

THE CODE NAME WAS Project Suzie, an audacious bid in October 1998 by the Packer family to bankroll a private equity takeover of the formerly government-owned national airline, Qantas. It was the brainchild of Macquarie banker Ben 'Brains' Brazil, who had convinced American billionaire David Bonderman's giant TPG to join Macquarie and the Packers' CPH in a bidding consortium to privatise the airline. At the last minute, an ever debt-averse Kerry Packer got cold feet, as did his son, James, and the deal fell through. But it heightened the interest of the Packers in Qantas.

There are few more politicised companies than the national flag carrier. But knowing James Packer's political connections, affections and his love of political and corporate strategy, in 2004 then Qantas chairman Margaret Jackson asked him to join the Qantas board. It was an unprecedented move – no

Packer had ever sat on the board of a listed company in which the family did not have a significant investment. 'Margaret Jackson was very kind to me after One.Tel. She convinced the other directors that I would be a good director,' James now recalls.

Her decision was supported by her chief executive, Geoff Dixon, who also felt Packer could give the company greater sway in the corridors of power in Canberra and could provide valuable strategic advice to the board and management. Packer was close to both Jackson and Dixon. Jackson was invited to join a loose advisory board of CPH soon after Kerry Packer's death, while she and her husband, Roger Donazzan, were invited to James's second wedding in 2007. Dixon also agreed to join the board of PBL when James Packer restructured it after his father's death.

'I do remember Margaret came to me and said James would be a very good board member. And she was right,' Dixon recalls. But Jackson and Dixon first had to ask Kerry Packer's permission. Initially it did not go down well. 'Shortly after we had asked James to join, Kerry rang me and said "Why are you doing this? This guy has enough on his plate." I said it would be very good for him to see how some of these companies operate,' Dixon adds.

Eventually, Kerry relented. '[He] rang a year after and said "I think it's been alright,"' Dixon says. He says James Packer became a valuable director. 'I thought he was very decisive. As I have said before, he was incredibly numerate, knew the numbers,' he says. One Qantas director remembers a board meeting where Packer managed to stump the then chief financial officer Peter Gregg with a difficult question about a set of numbers buried deep inside a pack of board papers. It was the first time he had ever seen Gregg, who knows numbers better than most, caught out.

Packer now describes Qantas as 'an interesting business. It took me a fair amount of time to understand Qantas as a business. Qantas doesn't make money, it makes planes. At the end of the year, the fleet goes up by ten planes. There is no money in the bank. Or at least there wasn't when I was a director. And those extra planes get valued by an accountant and that is the profit. There is never any cash because the [capital expenditure] never ends. Maybe it has changed now. And Alan Joyce has done a super job.'

In late 2006 Packer was a Qantas director when Macquarie and TPG again came knocking with a second takeover bid for the airline. Where the first bid never made it to the start line, this one almost made it all the way to the finish. This time round, Macquarie and TPG had Australian finance houses Allco Finance Group and Allco Equity Partners, as well as Canadian private equity firm Onex, in tow. They came together in an entity known as Airline Partners Australia (APA), which pitched an $11.1 billion friendly takeover offer for the airline. In contrast to 1998, on this occasion the bid was made public. It generated a massive political controversy, notably around concerns over Australia's national airline being owned by an American- and Canadian-backed investment group looking to pump up its returns by injecting a big chunk of debt into the airline. Under the APA plan, the airline's bank debt was to rise more than four-fold to $10.7 billion.

But Packer, who was also one of Macquarie Bank's largest individual shareholders at the time, after CPH had bought a stake in the stock they call the 'millionaires' factory', supported the bid. He thought the $5.45-a-share offer – which, including a 15-cent dividend payment, was $1 above the level Qantas shares had been trading at before the bid – was convincing. It raised questions about his conflict of interest, which were deflected by Jackson and Dixon. Dixon recalls, 'Obviously the APA bid for

Qantas had its supporters and its opponents. I remember James saying to me, "This is crazy, this is too good an offer to knock back." He was very supportive, as was Margaret and a few other board members. There were other directors who thought there would not be enough safeguards. And because of the airline's special place in society, it should not happen anyway. That was not a view I held. I thought it was about the shareholders. And some ultimately knocked it back.'

In May 2007 the bid collapsed at the eleventh hour after it was blocked by two key investors, Australian fund managers Balanced Equity and Integrity Asset Management, who wanted a better price. In hindsight, the takeover could have sent the airline broke during the subsequent GFC. Jackson paid the ultimate price for the bid's rejection, resigning her position two weeks later after fifteen years on the board, seven of them as chairman. Packer opted to resign at the same time in solidarity with his good friend. While he won't comment on the reasons, it is believed he was annoyed with the way some of the Qantas directors turned on Jackson after the failure of the APA bid. 'James felt she put them all on the board and she had done the right thing supporting the takeover,' says one observer familiar with Packer's thinking at the time.

Geoff Dixon says Jackson's departure could have been handled differently. 'It was no one's fault particularly. As often happens in Australia, the press were calling for heads to roll. I was a bit surprised mine didn't roll. But I think the board felt there needed to be some stability,' he says.

(In 2014 Packer joined Jackson and Hollywood actor Robert De Niro in bankrolling the global expansion of a super premium Australian vodka brand known as VDKA 6100, produced by a Melbourne company called Artisan Spirit Merchants. Packer reportedly put $10 million into the venture but has since sold out of it.)

He says his time on the Qantas board was invaluable, allowing him to see big-company discipline and governance up close for the first time. He will never forget it. 'It was a fantastic experience for me,' he says. 'I was lucky to be a Qantas director.' Dixon says he believes Packer used his Qantas experience 'to get a bit of an idea dealing with a big public company. I am not sure he liked the public company thing, but who does these days?' he says.

But it also confirmed to Packer a truism for life – that there is only one listed public company worth being in: one you control.

*

THE GREATEST POLITICAL REPORTER for the Packer empire was Alan Reid, known as the Red Fox, who worked for Frank Packer's *The Daily Telegraph* and for Kerry Packer's *The Bulletin* magazine, retiring after fifty years in Canberra shortly before his death in 1987. Reid was both a journalist and a political player, advising political leaders such as Sir Robert Menzies and playing a significant behind-the-scenes role lobbying for the Packer family's business interests.

Despite his deep involvement in politics, Reid always resisted the temptation to go into parliament, once likening politics to a circus and the politicians to the circus animals. While he said it was great to watch the circus, he would never have wanted to be one of the animals. James Packer has enjoyed the political circus but he must surely be content that he also chose, like Alan Reid, never to become one of the animals.

'James is a private man, born into a public life'
– Peter Barron

The Pursuit of Happiness

THE EARLY-SPRING AFTERNOON SEA breeze is howling as James Packer steps out of his chauffeur-driven black SUV and gazes out over the Sea of Cortez, on the southern tip of Mexico's Baja California Peninsula. Dressed in jeans and runners and sporting designer sunglasses, he's standing in the middle of a sun-drenched 2-acre vacant block, about ten minutes' drive from San José del Cabo, one of the Mexican playgrounds of America's rich and famous. One of Packer's good friends who travels the world with him, Damien Chapman, has joined us for today's site visit. 'It is like the Mexican version of Bondi when it is busy,' he says of the stretch of sand in front of the block.

Here Packer will build a dream property, a stunning ten-bedroom beachfront mansion with a five-car garage. The home will feature a wide, flat expanse of beachfront grass for his children to play on, encircled by a 40-metre infinity pool that will also surround a spectacular fire pit. Packer purchased the three blocks that make up the development site from three different owners over the past year, and the new multimillion-dollar residence is taking shape under the direction of Packer's best friend Ben Tilley.

The site overlooks Palmilla Cove, home to one of Cabo's few patrolled swimming beaches and once a favourite of General Abelardo Rodríguez, interim president of Mexico in 1932–34. In 1956 the former president's son, Don Abelardo Rodríguez, the pioneer of tourism development in the Los Cabos region, founded an intimate fifteen-room resort at Palmilla where guests could arrive only by boat or private plane. Over the years its elite clientele has included John Wayne, Bing Crosby, Lucille Ball and Desi Arnaz, Dustin Hoffman, Ernest Hemingway and President Dwight D Eisenhower. Today the luxurious resort is known as the One & Only Palmilla.

The property's Villa Cortez residence – a four-bedroom beachfront villa featuring a media room, gym, spa suite and its own infinity pool overlooking the ocean – has in recent years become Packer's Mexican sanctuary, after he was first introduced to Cabo in 2014 by one of his doctors, the Los Angeles–based cardiologist Alejandro Junger.

'Aspen and Los Angeles are both around two hours away and because I am lucky enough to have a plane, that makes it perfectly manageable for the kids to come for a weekend,' he says. 'It makes me think of Greece here. And the fact that it works for the kids was the biggest part of my thinking. Here and Aspen are really nice experiences for them. I am happy they are living in LA, for a whole series of reasons. Aspen and Cabo are as good as, if not better than, anything you can get in

Australia. The weather here is fine 340 days a year – the best weather you can get anywhere.'

Packer plans to retain Ellerstina, his Argentinian polo ranch, the site of his low-key fiftieth birthday celebration in 2017, with its four luxury guest rooms, pool, spa, stables, eighteen-hole golf course and play equipment nestled among the trees, for his children. He will now have only one apartment in Sydney, at the new Crown Sydney. The other, his pre-marital home on Campbell Parade in Bondi, was sold in August 2018 for $29 million.

At the end of July Packer also made another important property play, one of his most significant personal decisions since going public in March 2018 about his mental health battles. The painful memories of his wild Hollywood life and his break-up with Mariah Carey stopped him from spending more than a few hours on the ground in Los Angeles for more than eighteen months, but the time has come to return.

It is ultimately his family that has drawn him back. 'I have just bought a house in Beverly Hills and will base myself there for the time being. It is where my children live,' he says. The purchase will be funded by the sale of Bondi and the sale of his new yacht, *EJI*. 'Even though I have been out of Australia for the past four years, I haven't had a base that has felt right. And I think it is important to have a proper base until I return to Sydney.'

Packer intends to make Los Angeles his official place of residence, subject to satisfying US immigration rules.

*

PACKER MIGHT BE PLANNING to base himself in LA for the coming years, but the many seas that separate the three continents in which he owns properties will still provide him with the sanctuary and solace that a billionaire has the means to enjoy – whether it be cruising each northern summer through the azure waters of the Mediterranean Sea, or fleeing an Australian winter to the idyllic South Pacific island of Bora Bora northwest of Tahiti in French Polynesia. 'Bora Bora is an amazing corner of the world,' Packer says. 'Arnon Milchan first told me about it. The water is so blue and the lagoons are so calm. I just love it there and find it so peaceful.'

Bora Bora's waters are matched by those surrounding the Caribbean island of Barbuda, where Packer and actor Robert De Niro have been working on plans to build a US$250 million luxury resort called Paradise Found Nobu. But since the category-five Hurricane Irma tore apart the island in September 2017, the local community has been battling property developers over the island's future shape, so Packer is now hedging his bets on what he does with this opportunity. 'Barbuda, unlike Nobu, looks like a tough deal today for me. Bob [De Niro] is more optimistic than me about it. Having said that, I put up the money. Bob is very passionate about it. He is a tourism ambassador for Antigua and Barbuda,' Packer says. 'We need to raise significant monies for the development to proceed forward; I won't be putting in more money. Bob's dream is to build one of the world's best resorts in Barbuda, and location-wise there are lots of wealthy people nearby. Let's see.'

After selling the *Arctic P* to his sister in 2017, Packer in mid 2018 took delivery from Netherlands boat builder Amels of his 55-metre superyacht, which he named *EJI* after his three children in ascending age order: Emmanuelle, Jackson and Indigo. It features a 25-metre-long sundeck with a seven-person, 3600-litre jacuzzi and a bar, lounge and outdoor dining area for twelve guests. Meals on *EJI* are usually communal affairs, as they were on the *Arctic P*, where the guests on board are invited to join Packer at the dining setting on the back deck and are waited upon with five-star cuisine and top-shelf wines. Packer's owner's suite features an alfresco balcony that opens out just above the water level. Packer has his favourite living-room couch on board, on which he spends many of his waking hours chain-smoking and reading his iPad or iPhone, or watching business news or live sport on an adjacent wall-sized flat-screen television, which receives the full suite of Foxtel channels from Australia streamed through the internet to wherever he is on the globe.

Despite all its attractions, however, *EJI* is an 'interim boat'. It will be sold over the coming months. A much larger $170-million boat – to be named *IJF* (also named after his children, in descending age order) – is due for delivery mid next year, but construction of this boat is way behind schedule. 'The first boat I bought because the second boat is running so late,' he says.

Asked to explain his penchant for boats, Packer for a moment struggles to find the right words, before offering: 'Boats are very nice. I like being in the sun, I like the water. I don't know why I sold *Arctic* to my sister …'

But, I ask, is it a form of escapism, especially as he battles with his mental health condition? On this point he is far more certain. 'Yes, I think it is,' he replies instantly. 'I can't emphasise it enough: I've put the cue in the rack for the moment.'

*

ONE CONSTANT PRESENCE IN Packer's life in the past two years has been Canadian-born model and businesswoman Kylie Lim, who has been at Packer's side during his trips to Bora Bora, Aspen, Los Angeles, Ellerstina, Cabo, Saint-Tropez, Capri and Ibiza. His friends say Lim, whom Packer first met in Aspen, has been crucial in helping the billionaire get back on his feet. 'Kylie is a good person, a really good partner, and we are taking things slowly, one day at a time,' Packer says, in his first public comments on Lim. 'I'm lucky she's in my life.'

Another renewed presence in his life is the maharishi Thom Knoles, who spent a week with Packer in the Mediterranean in June 2018. Knoles says he has returned to Packer's immediate orbit in recent times as the billionaire has looked to supplement his prescription medication regime with more natural forms of therapy. 'I think the recent well-publicised crash is evidence that it [Packer's prescription drugs formula] wasn't working out. I think it is one of the reasons why I am back on the scene again,' Knoles says of Packer's mental health revelations in March 2018.

Some of Packer's friends are sceptical about Knoles, worried he has done more harm than good. The man who introduced them, UBS Australia CEO Matthew Grounds, also isn't so sure, but hedges his bets. 'In hindsight, this [introduction] probably wasn't one of my better calls,' he says. 'But I guess he seems to make James happy, so maybe it's been worthwhile from his perspective.'

Packer himself says Knoles is 'very generous in providing time for me ... Thom and I obviously have a commercial relationship [that is, Packer pays for his services] that comes with that. But neither of us would do it if we didn't want to do it.' He adds that Knoles 'sees something in me and believes in me. He tries to help me manage my emotions and find more happiness ... And truly holy men aren't bought by money.'

Knoles claims he has only five clients around the world for whom he would consider himself to be on call, and Packer is one of them. 'I know this man. He has a huge amount left in him to give. He is a giver. He is somebody who has amazing stamina and staying power. I think that we are still to see James's best days, to tell the truth,' Knoles says. 'Some research has been done, we have got our outcomes, and James is the kind of person who pays attention to research outcomes,' he adds, seemingly speaking in code about the reworking of Packer's medication regime and his recent realisation that he needed more than simply pills to help his recovery. 'I know he is paying attention, I can see it in his eyes.'

Importantly, in addition to Knoles, Packer has spent much of 2018 reconnecting with others he left behind when he pursued a frantic life in Hollywood and Israel between 2013 and the end of 2016. He has reached out via email and on the phone to friends and enemies alike, including a number in his home town of Sydney, such as Alan Jones, Kerry Stokes, David Gonski, Will Vicars and his sister, Gretel. Jones says, 'He does have a network of people who will give him good advice, not advice which is prejudicial to him nor advice which is beneficial to the adviser. Lloyd Williams is classic, and Kerry Stokes is another – beautiful people who have been really good to him.'

In early July 2018 Packer met up with Matthew Grounds when *EJI* was docked off Italy's Amalfi coast, their first face-to-face meeting since their public falling-out in March. Packer also saw his old friend and Macquarie banker Ben Brazil in the Mediterranean the same month.

In April 2018, soon after he returned to Ellerstina from a treatment facility in Boston, Packer caught up with charismatic Perth businessman and philanthropist Andrew Forrest. Packer even made a rare trip into the Buenos Aires city centre to meet Forrest at his hotel while the latter was in Argentina on business for the iron ore company he founded and still chairs, Fortescue Metals. 'Andrew could not have been more supportive or a better friend. I can't stress how much I enjoyed seeing him,' Packer says.

London financier Arpad 'Arki' Busson – whom Packer describes as a 'good friend, living a big life' – has stuck by

Packer through many ups and downs. Busson says of Packer, 'He had a very difficult relationship with [his father] Kerry over the years. I had a difficult relationship with my father too, so that fosters a bond. Some of our reactions, we kind of know where they come from and we chat about them.

'For me the key to a real and proper friendship is to make a commitment and to be accountable. And to be unconditionally there, for the good and the bad. And much more the bad. I have been through my difficult times as well and [Packer] was always there — physically and on the phone, checking in. He is one of the very few that have been there like that for me, in a not overt but discreet, yet very present way — without judging.'

Busson adds, of his public court battle with Thurman over custody of their daughter, 'It gets very lonely when you are going through these public break-ups. The second one in court for me was one of my most traumatic moments and JP was there being incredibly supportive. I maybe have only a handful of people in the world who I have enjoyed that kind of support from. It is rare.'

*

IN MID JUNE 2018, Packer met with his Crown executive team in Aspen. It was the first time chairman John Alexander, chief financial officer Ken Barton and the Australian Resorts division boss Barry Felstead had set eyes on their boss following his shock resignation from the Crown board in March. They were heartened to find Packer in good spirits and forensic in his study of the numbers in the Crown business plan for the coming years. Also present for the meetings were Mike Johnston and Guy Jalland. The group dined at the upmarket Matsuhisa Japanese restaurant in downtown Aspen one evening, before returning to Packer's lounge room to talk strategy until the early hours of the morning.

Alexander says he was relieved when Packer went public about his mental health battles. 'I have been concerned about his physical health as well as his mental health, and I am glad he is now getting professional help.'

After getting over the initial shock of Packer's decision, his other closest lieutenants are said to be determined to do everything they can to help him one day return to playing a more active role in the management of his public and private companies. As Kerry Stokes and others have commented, the Packer empire is in best shape when James is enthusiastically focused upon his businesses.

But for the moment Packer is stepping back from boards he does not need to be on. During June and July 2018 Mike Johnston removed Packer's name from the boards of twenty-six companies that operate within the CPH group. He still remains a director of the Bahamas-domiciled Consolidated Press International Holdings Limited, the ultimate owner of CPH. Packer, it would seem, hasn't totally stepped back from managing his business interests.

He still worries whether Crown will – as he puts it – emerge as a 'mature business or a sunset business'. CPH owns 47 per cent of the casino company. 'I've said it a couple times but I can't stress how much it devours me on a daily basis,' Packer says. 'I have all my eggs in Crown now,' he says, before adding with a wry smile: 'If I don't finish Sydney, that will be the end of me.' While he may have made the last comment somewhat tongue-in-cheek, Crown Sydney certainly weighs heavily upon him, even after his decision to step back from the Crown board.

It is the biggest thing he has done in Australia, surrounded by controversy and with a queue of detractors waiting to pounce at the first sign of problems with the project. Apartment sales from Crown Sydney have started slowly, but the company's executive vice president of strategy and development, Todd Nisbet, isn't concerned. In fact, Nisbet says he has told his boss that Barangaroo, as a precinct, is going to be better than even he expected. 'We thought it would be good. But now we know it will be really good. Crown Sydney will clearly be the best hotel in Asia. I haven't seen a development site quite like this, and I have seen plenty. We are actually delivering more than what we promised.'

Packer has now entrusted his Crown Sydney dream to both Nisbet and Barry Felstead, to whom he says he already owes a huge debt of gratitude. 'Sydney is my only new business bet. It's three years away. I am not a builder so I am not going to be spending much time in Sydney with a hard hat on, pretending I am adding value to the construction process,' he says.

It will be a special day for Packer when his new boat *IJE* sails through Sydney Heads for the opening of Crown Sydney, scheduled for 2021. Some, however, believe that, at the age of fifty, Packer's ultimate dream in business is still to come.

Peter Barron, who knew Kerry Packer better than most, says, 'I believe that James is yet to find the real business passion in his life, and I continue to think that he will. And when he does, I think he will be very happy and very successful. I still believe James will finish up in a business that marries his numeracy skills with his capacity to understand technology and the business opportunities it throws up. Kerry did not burst out until he was well into his life. In fact, his best efforts were after the Costigan Royal Commission. Something about being through the crisis was good for him.'

*

THE JAMES PACKER STORY is a complex one, but central to it is that his life, in many ways, has been a search for affirmation – of his legitimacy as the custodian of the Packer family fortune and of, at times, his own self-worth.

'I know he has been very conscious that he has been given a legacy that needs to be preserved and he wishes to preserve. He wishes to do better with it and sees himself as the custodian of that money,' David Gonski says. 'For him losing money is failure. I think he does fear failure. I actually think that if James Packer had started with nothing, he would be one of the people who would have made a fortune by taking and embracing new technologies. He has the guts to invest in new things and the capacity to see into the future. Starting with a capital base may actually be more a negative than a positive, because you always feel the need to preserve it.'

Wherever he goes, James Packer has two shadows at his side: his own and his father's.

His father was brutalised during his own childhood and made sure his own son paid for his mistakes, most notably the One.Tel disaster. Phillip Adams, for one, thinks Packer is a victim of his family legacy and his father's tough love. 'I always feel sorry for James. He has been cursed,' he says. 'I feel sorry for people, irrespective of their place on the social ladder, like James. I know kids at the bottom of the social ladder who are as cursed as James. So it has nothing to do with wealth.'

But Packer has no problem with the way he was treated by his father. He has always made it clear – honestly and without the slightest hint of embarrassment – that he will always love, cherish and respect the memory of his father, whatever anyone says about it.

Packer's inherited wealth has certainly made him a target. There is rarely sympathy in Australia for the children of the wealthy. As the son of Kerry Packer – who was loathed by just as many as he was liked – he has had to struggle with public attitudes to the Packer name. Surely there have been times in his life when he must have wished he wasn't the son of Kerry Packer and was relieved of the responsibilities of protecting the family fortune? And had the grounding – seemingly impossible in the world of the super-wealthy - enjoyed by people of the same age living ordinary lives?

Yet his good friend, global private equity doyen Guy Hands, says Packer doesn't have to prove himself to anyone, especially his father. 'He has been an extraordinary businessman and a success. The problem is he always looks at it through the prism of being a Packer,' he says. 'He will succeed as a businessman over the long term. The businesses he was left by his father are ones that have declined in terms of value. If he stayed where he was, he would have one-sixth of what he has today. Relative to where he would have ended up he has made an enormous amount of money.'

Alan Jones puts it more strongly: 'One of the great personal, emotional and psychological weaknesses which I think has dogged him and continues to dog him [is that] he continues to compete with his father and he thinks that he's got to prove to the world that he was better. That he's a legitimate heir. As if there was a contest. I keep saying, "There's none!"' Jones says. 'But nonetheless he's got the figures on the capitalisation of the company, what it was then [when Kerry died] and the capitalisation now. How much debt it had then and now. And all of this consumes him. He is obsessed still by the legacy issue.'

Just to prove Jones's point, when I ask for those figures, Packer reels them off like clockwork. On his father's passing, the Packer empire was worth $5.02 billion and had a net debt of $1.55 billion. CPH today has a net worth of $4.4 billion and a net debt of only $200 million. The net debt of the empire is forecast to fall to zero in four years' time and the net worth is expected to top $5 billion. While Packer won't comment on the terms of their final settlement, it has been reported that Gretel Packer and her children received more than $1.25 billion following her division of the family fortune with her brother.

Many have wondered why, having inherited the amount of money he did, Packer did not park it in safe investments and – in the words of one observer – simply 'put his feet up' while earning hundreds of millions a year, even at bank interest. 'Why would you bother with business at all, least of all gambling?' they ask.

Indeed, his choice to grow the family fortune chiefly through investing in the gambling industry has had its cost. Australians are among the world's most prolific gamblers but, while they love the punt, they loathe the house. The fact that Packer owns the biggest gambling houses in Australia and continues to profit handsomely from them – at the expense of some of the most vulnerable in society – has certainly not endeared him to many.

Yet to Packer the choice of gambling is all about numbers. It is an industry he reckons can deliver solid – if unspectacular – returns for the foreseeable future. Packer has undoubtedly been brilliantly numerate and a risk taker who uses numbers to choose the businesses in which to invest. Unlike many, he recognised the game-changing digital revolution early and restructured the family businesses to escape the threat of being saddled with old-technology businesses.

'James was a visionary across a range of businesses,' his good friend and the best friend of his father, Lloyd Williams, says. 'Going back to the '90s, he understood digital disruption. With Carsales, Seek and media, he understood what was going to happen ... In Macau, James bought the licence from Steve Wynn. It wasn't Lawrence Ho, he was the operator. James was the person that drove the deal.'

Yet Crown's embarrassing exit from Macau in 2017 following the arrests of its staff in China – albeit for a multibillion-dollar profit – was symbolic of a problem that has plagued Packer for the past decade in business: too often he has sold growth assets for the wrong reasons. Assets like Seek and Challenger were jettisoned to fend off a potential corporate raider in Kerry Stokes. His father's pastoral assets were offloaded to de-risk the empire following an ill-timed assault on the US casino market just before the GFC. Zillow was sold to help settle his father's estate with his sister, as was his share in the family's beloved Ellerston pastoral property. After being one of the first to see the disruptive potential of the internet, there is an amazing irony in the fact that Packer now has no investments in internet-related businesses outside his small exposure to venture capital through Square Peg Capital.

Packer acknowledges he has made many mistakes, but he was never going to be content to sit idle. And his compulsive personality would never have allowed him to. 'In a business sense, I've had a go more than anyone else I've known,' he says. He still laments the most recent loss of his reputation for the third time in his life – this time on the global stage – through the horrors of recent years. He's still not sure if he will ever get it back.

Yet Alan Jones believes such an assessment doesn't stand up to objective scrutiny. For Jones, achievement is all about expectations and perspective. 'You were never going to be Bill Gates and you were never going to be Mark Zuckerberg. I mean, the [Packer] fortune is very profound by Australian standards, but at the end of the day you were never going to be an international kingmaker. Therefore, the reputation isn't in any way damaged like you believe it to be. You're obsessing about this. It's not correct. It's not true,' Jones barks at me, as if it were Packer in my seat on the receiving end of his lecture.

'Those obsessions really ignore objective assessment, and by objective assessment he's a very successful person who's put his finger in a lot of waters, and some of them were hot and he got burnt. But he's done pretty well. He's put multiples onto the legacy he inherited. He has honoured the legacy.'

*

JAMES PACKER IS A person of contradictions.

Tall and powerfully built like his father and looking more like him every year, James is often thought by many to have a personality that mirrors his father's. He certainly has his father's explosive temper, when riled. But where his father was notorious for barking expletives down a phone line and dressing down people with his feet on the desk in his Park Street office, his son has preferred to do the same in the hundreds of emails he has sent in anger, far and wide across the globe, in recent years. It is one of the reasons his doctors recommended in March 2018 that his emails be reviewed by his advisers before being sent.

It is also one of the reasons he has made enemies. Some have found his behaviour in recent years – both on email and in person – unacceptable. They refuse to accept the premise that Packer is simply a product of his heritage. They point to other sons and daughters of rich and powerful fathers who have not turned to bullying to get their own way, even if the previous generation used such tactics. Some of these siblings, they argue, have been determined to be different from their parents and chart a different course. Packer, they say, has no excuse for not following their example.

But in reality no one can put themselves in the shoes of James Packer.

Packer, deep down, appears both hard-nosed and soft-hearted. As he says himself, he is more like his mum than his dad. Both traits have helped him make genuine connections with some extraordinary people across the world, highlighted most recently by his Hollywood adventures and the connections he made through that with Israel. The dual aspects of Packer's character, as evidenced in both these arenas, are captivating and perplexing at the same time.

Packer can be both hard-headed and seemingly gullible in the one transaction. In a way it seems that he can be, simultaneously, coolly calculating and recklessly naive. With numbers and investment strategies, he is sometimes brilliant. Yet with relationships he can be fumble-fisted and innocently childlike. Too often Packer throws himself into friendships – personal, professional and political – with almost complete abandon and without sufficient scepticism of the motives of those seeking to gain his trust – and access to his financial power.

He is the first to acknowledge his own fallibility and vulnerabilities, and recognises that not everyone to whom he has shown blind loyalty has had his best interests at heart. 'My actions have been a lot better than my words,' he says, reflecting upon his fifty years on earth. 'There are a bunch of people in my life for whom their words have been far better than their actions.'

On this point Guy Hands describes Packer as having always been 'an incredibly generous person, and people need to be careful not to take advantage of it. He has been let down by a large number of people in his life. Some have done so innocently, some have done so to take advantage of him and some simply have not cared less. The good thing is he hasn't lost his generosity and his sense of humour.'

In some ways, this is endearing. There is certainly a segment of the public that adores James Packer for his flaws.

For his humanity. For his willingness to have a go. Perhaps these people see a part of themselves in him. It partly explains the voluminous media coverage devoted to his life over the decades, especially in his home town of Sydney – not to mention the fact that Packer stories always rate better than most online as so-called click-bait.

Hands' assessment certainly reveals someone who is a giant in some ways, but a very soft giant. Sometimes inside the giant you can see a small boy, still looking for love. And perhaps, deep down, Packer knows it.

*

FOR DECADES, THE PACKER name has been synonymous with wealth, yet for the past two years James Packer has been dogged for the third time in his life by the fear, summed up in the old Chinese adage, that 'Wealth never survives three generations'.

Paul Barry, in the final paragraph of his book on Packer, *Who Wants to Be a Billionaire?* makes a simple and telling observation on this point: 'Perhaps even more than his father, he appears to believe in nothing except making money.' Packer is now prepared to concede on this statement, albeit with some qualification. 'I've always viewed money as the scorecard. To be fair to me, that's how I was brought up. I used to think it was easier than it is to make money,' he says. 'My scorecard is not great. I give myself a four out of ten for running CPH since Dad died. I have made way too many mistakes and trusted the wrong people sometimes. I've sold a lot of assets and businesses we once owned. To pay off debts and obligations and losses and to buy Crown shares. Maybe four out of ten is being too kind to myself.' Such self-analysis reveals how critical he is of his own management of the Packer legacy, and says so much about how heavily the burden of that legacy weighs upon his shoulders.

Packer is also deeply conscious of the extraordinarily privileged life he leads compared with most people and is grateful for it. 'I think I've had an incredibly fortunate life. I've seen and done a lot of things,' he says. 'In business, I love and am so proud of Crown, with my dream of Crown Sydney still to come. Most important to me are my three beautiful kids. And Erica. My family. And my Mum and Gretes. And Joda. And my friends.'

For decades Packer, with his immense wealth, has found it virtually impossible to articulate his own personal problems in a world where the vast majority of people are simply struggling to make ends meet. But six months after his fiftieth birthday, he finally decided to show his truth when he declared to the world his mental health struggles.

'I certainly have regrets,' he says. 'I have depression, which is a manifestation of those regrets. Wealth and fortune don't guarantee happiness.'

The James Packer story seemingly still has many more chapters to be told. He still has his bad days, when he gets down, when he gets angry, when you sense he's on a short fuse. His recovery is certainly a work in progress.

But by exposing his private demons, he has revealed more about himself to the world than ever before, allowing a deeper insight into who he really is. Not just the son of Kerry Packer. Rather, a person who is far from perfect, but who has lived his life, his way. For better or for worse.

It may prove to be a turning point.

ACKNOWLEDGMENTS

WHEN I FIRST SAT down with James Packer in Aspen on a freezing winter's evening in mid January 2018 to talk about this book, he quickly cut to the chase. Seated on his favourite living-room couch – diving into a bowl of Twisties with one hand, clutching a cigarette in the other – he asked: 'Damon, what are you really trying to achieve with this book?'

My answer was simple: to tell the human story of being James Packer, warts and all, good and bad, fairly and accurately. His response was equally succinct: 'Okay then, I am up for that.'

And so we set off on a six-month journey together. Barely a day went by – bar a terrible two-and-a-half-week period in March – when we didn't talk via text message or email. For months on end I would often wake to a dozen or more emails from James overnight, which documented his thoughts on key events of his life.

I am deeply appreciative of the many hours he agreed to be interviewed face to face, of the off-the-record meals and coffees we shared in different parts of the world, and of the countless documents and photographs with which he provided me. I know the process was painful for him, but his word was his bond that he would finish it. And he did.

Most importantly, there were several interviewees who were reluctant to speak to me without James's permission, and I appreciated the encouragement he provided to each of them to tell their truths about him, good and bad. In each of these cases, his message to them was the same: this was not his book, that he would not be reading it before it was published and that there would be many parts of it that would be painful. But that he trusted me to be fair.

I would also like to thank James's closest friends and confidants offshore: Kylie Lim, Guy Jalland, Ben Tilley, Damien Chapman, Ian Morris, Martin Pepa, John Murphy and Joe Aston for their assistance and support. In Australia, I am deeply grateful to Mark Arbib for his assistance and support on what became – for a time – an emotional roller-coaster ride. I'd also like to thank John Alexander, Mike Johnston and Todd Nisbet for their help and comments.

A number of my friends and colleagues in the media provided invaluable reference material for this project, and I hope I have done them justice in referencing their work where I have mentioned it. My friend Pamela Williams, who interviewed James with me back in 2006 when we were both working at *The Australian Financial Review*, encouraged and advised me at the outset. Her wonderful book *Killing Fairfax* became an important reference. My friend Adele Ferguson was also an invaluable confidante and support in my negotiations with various publishers at the start of this process. I also want to acknowledge Packer-family follower and legendary journalist Paul Barry for his book on James, *Who Wants to Be a Billionaire?*, for the number of times I drew upon it.

Newspaper gossip columns have always provided a treasure trove of material on the Packer family, so I am indebted to my friends and colleagues Will Glasgow and Christine Lacy for their 'Margin Call' columns in *The Australian*, Joe Aston for his 'Rear Window' columns in *The Australian Financial Review*, and Andrew Hornery for his 'Private Sydney' column in *The Sydney Morning Herald* and Annette Sharp for her 'Sydney Confidential' musings. At *The Australian* Georgina Windsor was also a great help for her ability to find age-old Packer stories of mine and others in our archives.

There are a host of other friends and contacts in the media, corporate affairs and funds management industries who provided me with valuable insights but who have chosen to remain anonymous. I thank you all for your input.

INTRODUCTION: *I am Icarus*
James introduced me to Warren Beatty to talk about the special relationship they formed when James leased the movie legend's guest house on Mulholland Drive in Beverly Hills during 2015 and 2016. Warren agreed to talk to me – just the two of us – in the library of his private home. We spoke for just over an hour but I wished it was longer. After our interview Warren headed down Mulholland Drive to lunch with James at the Beverly Hills Hotel's famed Polo Lounge. He kindly invited me to join them on an off-the-record basis, which I did for a good ninety minutes, an experience I will never forget. Warren rarely does media interviews, so I would like to thank him for making an exception for me.

For the introductory chapter and throughout the book I am also thankful to Graham Richardson, a long-time adviser to the Packer family, for his insights – especially into the relationship between James and his father, his mental state and his political ambitions.

CHAPTER ONE: *In the Name of the Father*

Broadcaster Phillip Adams, a confidant of Kerry Packer in the 1970s and '80s who once wrote a book on Kerry that he never published, was helpful for his insights into the relationship between Kerry and his son.

I am indebted to the ABC's *Australian Story* episode from April 2014 titled 'Packer's Road' for the quotes I have sourced from Al Dunlap and Richard Walsh on James's early days in the family business.

The deeply private long-serving Packer family adviser Peter Barron – who is rarely quoted on the record – kindly met me for coffee at the Westin Hotel in Sydney, where he gave me his unique perspective on the relationship between James and Kerry, stretching back to when he first started working for the former in 1986. He also generously broke his rule of always talking on background, giving me a number of telling quotes.

CHAPTER TWO: *The One.Tel Curse*

Alan Jones invited me to his Sydney apartment on the sixth floor of the 'Toaster' building at 1 Macquarie Street, with its stunning views of the Harbour Bridge and the Opera House, where over afternoon coffee we discussed the life and trials of his good friend. I am deeply appreciative to Alan for his frankness and honesty. He spoke of subjects few, if any, people have discussed on the record about the Packer family. He did so both with his typical candour and with respect.

Peter Yates, whom I have known for two decades, agreed to meet me over lunch at the Kisume Japanese restaurant in Melbourne's Flinders Lane. Peter has said very little publicly about his time as PBL CEO, so his perspective on the One.Tel collapse, the takeover of Burswood, his own sacking by Kerry Packer and his relationship with James was welcome.

Village Roadshow co-chief executive Graham Burke, a friend I have known for over a decade, met me for lunch at the Thirty Eight Chairs restaurant in South Yarra. He was a good friend of Kerry's and became the same for James, and he was exceptionally helpful in his discussion of James's Hollywood experience. Graham also kindly gave me an introduction to Warner Bros chief executive Kevin Tsujihara, whom I met in Los Angeles.

David Gonski, one of the executors of Kerry's will, a confidant of the Packers for decades and a man I have known and respected for many, many years, has made it his policy to never speak publicly about the Packer family. I am grateful that he made an exception for me in this book, providing me with valuable insights about the complex relationships in the family and his first public comments about the settlement of Kerry's will between James and his sister Gretel.

CHAPTER THREE: *The Pen is Mightier than the Sword*
The deeply private Lachlan Murdoch was open and generous in speaking to me about his history with James as a friend and business partner – for better or for worse in the case of the latter – despite being in the middle of the multibillion-dollar Fox/Disney deal. It was the first time Lachlan had spoken about many of their business deals, including Ten, and for that I am deeply grateful.

Former Foxtel chief executive Kim Williams, a friend I have known for more than two decades, agreed to meet me for dinner at the Felt Restaurant at his favourite Hotel Lindrum in Melbourne's Flinders Street. I am thankful to Kim for his reflections on James's involvement with Foxtel during his time as CEO.

CHAPTER FOUR: *Changing Channels*

I used to have plenty to do with David Leckie when he was running the Nine and Seven Networks and I was writing the media round for *The Australian Financial Review,* so it was a pleasure to renew our acquaintance for this book. As usual, David was frank and colourful with his insights.

Eddie McGuire once helped me get an unusual interview with the then coach of his beloved Collingwood Football Club, Michael Malthouse, for *The Australian Financial Review*'s business magazine, *Boss.* While we don't know each other well, he kindly took almost ninety minutes out from his busy schedule in his South Yarra office to talk about his time as CEO of Channel Nine and his relationship with the Packer family.

I am also appreciative of Gerald Stone for his book *Who Killed Channel 9?* as a reference source for a tumultuous period in James's life.

CHAPTER FIVE: *Wheel of Fortune*

I first met Lloyd Williams with James at a Boxing Day cricket Test match in Melbourne more than a decade ago and I was grateful he agreed to meet me for lunch at one of his favourite Melbourne restaurants, Cecconi's, to talk about his relationship with the man he says he loves like a son. Lloyd was dressed as if he were off to the races, in suit, tie and pocket handkerchief – the only thing missing was a top hat. Few know James better and have stuck with him, through good and bad. As an executor of Kerry's will, Lloyd importantly spoke for the first time about the battle between his children over the Packer family fortune.

I had only briefly met Lawrence Ho once before he agreed to be interviewed about James in the Hong Kong head office of his Asian gaming company Melco Crown Entertainment.

Impeccably dressed in suit and tie, Lawrence was extremely open and frank about the man he still calls a brother. He was especially generous in speaking in detail for the first time about the scandal in China that forced the two men apart in 2016, which he still laments.

CHAPTER SIX: *The Gambler*
As the founder and chairman of Terra Firma Capital Partners, one of the largest private equity firms in Europe, Guy Hands has never courted publicity. Despite being one of Australia's biggest land owners through Terra Firma's ownership of the Consolidated Pastoral Company, he's hardly known here. Yet he was happy to talk to me at length on the phone from his home in Guernsey about his purchase of CPC from James in 2009 and his friendship with him before and since. His comments about James's personality and his private battles in recent years were especially insightful.

CHAPTER SEVEN: *No Sacred Cows*
The Bassat brothers have known James better than most in business, so it was invaluable to have the insights that came over coffee with Andrew at his St Kilda Road office and lunch with Paul at the Thirty Eight Chairs restaurant in South Yarra, which became something of a cafeteria for this project given I also met Graham Burke and had two other off-the-record meetings there. I thank Andrew and Paul for their reflections on their involvement with James at Seek and for their insights into James's personality.

I met Carsales chairman Walter Pisciotta for the first time when he agreed to coffee at his Southgate apartment in Melbourne – with its stunning views over the city – on an overcast autumn morning. I had known his former business partner – Carsales CEO Greg Roebuck, who kindly contributed a comment for this book – for many years, but never met the deeply private Walter. I found him especially engaging and entertaining. His comments on the relationship between James and his father were among the strongest of anyone, and I could see they were genuinely heartfelt.

Brian Benari was also helpful with his reflections on James's involvement with the Challenger financial services business, as was Glenn Poswell for his commentary on the highs and lows of the Ellerston Capital funds management business during his time there as CEO.

CHAPTER EIGHT: *Crowning Glory*
When Barry O'Farrell spoke to me on the phone to recall his experience with the controversial approval process for the Crown Sydney casino project, he was upfront in explaining his new-found preference for not talking to journalists – because he no longer has any reason to. So I was grateful he made an exception for me to again explain his rationale for supporting the project, and his observations of James during what was a difficult period in his life.

CHAPTER NINE: *The Brotherhood*
I have known Matthew Grounds for more than twenty years and during that time some of our most regular topics of discussion have been PBL, Crown and James. Matthew, whom I met in person at his Chifley Tower offices in Sydney and later spoke to on the phone, has shared many ups and downs with his star client. Given James's interest in complex transactions and investment bankers, it was invaluable to have his contribution.

Anthony Pratt, whom I lunched with at Rockpool restaurant at Crown in Melbourne, shares a similar experience with James, given he also had a difficult relationship with his larger-than-life father. But he has always had an admiration and respect for James, which came through in his comments.

CHAPTER TEN: *Dancing with the Stars*

I had never met Brett Ratner when I knocked on the door of his stone-and-redwood mansion in Beverly Hills after he agreed to an interview, his first since the collapse of his partnership with James in Ratpac. But you would not have known it, given his candour and generosity in answering every question I put to him.

Earlier that day I had also met with Warner Bros CEO Kevin Tsujihara at the company's Burbank head office in Los Angeles suburbia. While Kevin and Brett are no longer business partners, together they shared an amazing and wild period of James's life, so their reflections were extremely valued.

CHAPTER ELEVEN: *The Israeli Affair*

Graham Burke's tale of when James first met Arnon Milchan at the Botanical hotel in South Yarra in early December 1993 and their subsequent horror plane ride to Ellerston to meet Kerry Packer provided a wonderful anecdote with which to introduce and analyse the relationship between James and Arnon. In this context, I would like to thank Paul Bassat for his extraordinary recollections of his time with James in Israel, including their dinners with the Netanyahus on two consecutive nights in February 2014.

Arnon, with whom I spoke briefly, off the record on the phone, declined to be interviewed for this book. But I appreciate his providing me with a quote via email from his villa at the luxury resort he recently purchased at Bora Bora in French Polynesia.

I am grateful to Charles Miranda, a former foreign correspondent in Europe and the Middle East for News

Limited for a decade, for reflecting upon the time he spent with James at his Caesarea home in Israel in mid 2015.

I am also grateful to former American ambassador to Australia during the Obama administration, Jeffrey Bleich. While Jeff never travelled with James to Israel, he did speak with him many times while James was there in 2015 and 2016 and became a good friend. His comments on James's Israel experience and on his mental health battles were insightful.

CHAPTER TWELVE: *Blood Battle*

Sydney fund manager Will Vicars, the chief investment officer at boutique investment firm Caledonia Investments, was understandably cautious when I reached out to meet him in person for the first time at the start of this project. But as the months passed Will and I developed a good degree of trust, and I am extremely grateful that he was prepared to comment on the record about his experience in advising Gretel Packer in the difficult negotiations with her brother. Will and I met on two occasions in Sydney.

I also sincerely thank Gretel for being prepared to – for the first time – present her perspective on what transpired on the record. Her comments were heartfelt and frank, which I respect and appreciate.

CHAPTER THIRTEEN: *Rocked to the Core*

I would like to thank Crown directors Geoff Dixon and Harold Mitchell – both of whom I have known for twenty years – for providing the comments they did in the meetings I had with them at Crown Melbourne. Geoff and I met in the executive offices, while I met with Harold over lunch at Rockpool. Their comments are the first from any directors of the Crown board about the China scandal and the governance of Crown at the time.

I would also like to thank Robert Rankin for agreeing to speak to me from his home in London about his time as Crown chairman and CPH CEO.

CHAPTER FOURTEEN: *A Hero No More*
Sydney celebrity photographer Jamie Fawcett provided a unique perspective on James's life, given the number of photos he has taken of his subject and the rapport they have developed over the years in all parts of the world. He was especially helpful with his up-close observations of the relationship between James and Mariah Carey, especially during the weeks he spent trailing them in the Mediterranean in mid 2016.

I would also like to thank Brett Ratner, Guy Hands, Jodhi Meares, Lawrence Ho, Harold Mitchell and James's good friend Arpad 'Arki' Busson for their reflections on their time with James and Mariah.

But my greatest appreciation goes to Kerry Stokes, whom I met at his Sydney office in Pyrmont for more than ninety minutes, for his extraordinary revelations about the role he played in helping James through one of the most difficult times of his life in 2016. It is fair to say that if it were not for Kerry, James and Mariah would have been married in the first week of March that year.

I also want to acknowledge my reliance on a range of sources that documented the whirlwind romance, including *Woman's Day* magazine, *Complex* magazine, *The New York Post*'s celebrity gossip column 'Page Six' and celebrity website TMZ.

CHAPTER FIFTEEN: *Crown of Thorns*
This chapter documenting James's mental health battles was the hardest to write, and I am deeply appreciative to all who expressed their views on the issue, including Paul Bassat, Eddie McGuire,

Jeffrey Bleich, Alan Jones, Guy Hands, Harold Mitchell, Erica Packer, Jodhi Meares, David Gonski and Lachlan Murdoch.

CHAPTER SIXTEEN: *Above and Beyond*

When James returned to Australia in Perth at the end of October 2017, two of the people with whom he first reconnected were Peter Costello and Jeff Kennett. Both agreed to meet me in their respective Melbourne offices – Peter in the glass tower of 120 Collins Street and Jeff in inner-city Cremorne – to speak about that time and their broader relationship with James. Jeff, characteristically, was extraordinarily frank, for which I am grateful.

CHAPTER SEVENTEEN: *Everglow*

Erica Packer initially agreed to talk to me face to face for this book during one of her visits to Sydney, before James went public about his mental health battles. After that she preferred to talk over email, which I understand and respect. Nevertheless, her comments were heartfelt and sincere, and revealed to the world in detail for the first time just why she and her ex-husband remain so close. Most importantly, she provided an insight into the importance of their children as the bedrock of their ongoing friendship.

Jodhi Meares was incredibly generous in opening up about her broken marriage and ongoing friendship with James over morning coffee at her favourite park, the Camp Cove Reserve in Watsons Bay. I found Jodhi extremely open, warm and genuine. She provided a number of reflections on a range of topics that have been helpful throughout this book.

CHAPTER EIGHTEEN: *The Corridors of Power*

For this chapter I want to thank Peter Costello, Graham Richardson, Jeffrey Bleich and Kim Williams for their reflections about James's political ambitions, particularly his consideration of running for the seat of Kooyong, and his record as a lobbyist at both the state and federal level.

Former Qantas chief executive Geoff Dixon also offered some intriguing insights into James's time on the Qantas board, including during the politically charged private-equity takeover offer for the national carrier.

CONCLUSION: *The Pursuit of Happiness*
A couple of months into the book process James offered to introduce me to his spiritual adviser, Thom Knoles, a maharishi of Vedic meditation, who invited James to visit Rishikesh in the foothills of the Himalayas in northern India in 2013. When I interviewed Thom on James's boat on the French Riviera, I found him engaging and perceptive. Thom even kindly led me through a meditation session.

Finally, I would like to thank the team at HarperCollins for all their advice and support, led by CEO James Kellow and head of non-fiction Helen Littleton.

A very special thank you goes to my senior editor Lu Sierra for her insights, passion and composure in helping me through this process, especially when things got difficult. And to my copy editor Nikki Lusk, one of the best editors I have ever worked with. I also want to thank publicist Lara Wallace, picture researcher Linda Brainwood and proofreader Nicola Young.

Thank you also to the editor-in-chief of *The Australian* Paul Whittaker, editor John Lehmann, managing editor Helen Trinca and business editor Eric Johnston for their support and preparedness to give me the time away from the paper to undertake this complex project.

A special thank you to my father and now retired legendary political journalist, Geoff, for his painstaking initial proofreading of every one of my chapters. His ability to help me stand back from my day-to-day immersion in my subject was incredibly valuable. And thanks to my wonderful, gorgeous sister Emma, for her help organising my travel. And to my brother Cietan and his family for looking after my family in Singapore when we needed them.

Finally, a mention to my special mum, Therese – thank you for all your kind words and support – and my beautiful children Johnathon, Alice, Grace and Lucas and my beloved wife Anna.

For many hours during the early part of this project Anna sat glued to the computer till late into the evening as she helped transcribe my many hours of interviews with James and other subjects. She also helped catalogue the photographs and keep track of my expenses. Most importantly, she kept our household running like clockwork during my many interstate and overseas expeditions, which were an essential part of completing a project like this. I could not have done it without her.